Revelations of the Bible

Lifting the Veil on the History and Creation of the Bible

Darryl O. Dickey

Order this book online at www.trafford.com
or email orders@trafford.com

Most Trafford titles are also available at major online book retailers.

Note for Librarians: A cataloguing record for this book is available from Library and Archives Canada at www.collectionscanada.ca/amicus/index-e.html

Printed in Victoria, BC, Canada.

ISBN: 978-1-4251-8863-4

Our mission is to efficiently provide the world's finest, most comprehensive book publishing service, enabling every author to experience success. To find out how to publish your book, your way, and have it available worldwide, visit us online at www.trafford.com

Trafford rev. 10/14/09

www.trafford.com

North America & international
toll-free: 1 888 232 4444 (USA & Canada)
phone: 250 383 6864 • fax: 812 355 4082

Table of Contents

To Carol Jean Radach who helped in so many ways
to
Dana Dickey who laboriously edited the book
and to
Arlene Dickey and Devon Moreland

Introduction

Re ve latio n - disclosure of facts (from Lat. revelationem, translated from Gr. Apokálypsis; "lifting of the veil," "disclosure," or "reveal")

I remember the first time I visited the Huntington Library near Pasadena, California. The library itself is just one building out of many on the grounds of the winter estate of the 19th century railroad baron, Henry Huntington. You enter the library and immediately find yourself in a large two-story open space that is now used for revolving exhibits. A narrow mezzanine around the room is lined with bookcases and is replete with old, leather covered books. The aroma of book oil used to protect the leather book covers drifts down. To a bibliophile like me, it was love at first sight! The library's immense collection of fragile ancient works is archived in the basement, available only to qualified scholars. It is a treasure trove of literature, including the only complete copy of the Dead Sea Scrolls (in photographic form) outside of Israel.

I entered the building and before my eyes had even adjusted to the dimness of the interior, I found, right in front of me, one of the original Gutenberg Bibles, the first book ever printed on a printing press, opened to a page. I stopped and stood there in stunned awe. Never did I expect to see a work of art that had such an effect on me.

The pages were exquisite; it was printed in German in Blackletter type, a form of Gothic type, written in two columns of 42 lines each on hand-made paper. The decorative borders around the type were all hand-painted as were the illuminations of the initial letters of paragraphs. This was a very large book. You would never carry it to church services. With 1,282 pages of very thick paper, it would be easier to carry an unabridged dictionary.

If you ever get to San Marino, California, stop in and see it, or, if you are in Washington D.C., check out our country's own copy at the Library of Congress. There are only 47 copies left in the entire world. I predict that after you read *I Didn't Know That!* you will experience much the same feelings of awe when you see that Gutenberg Bible that I felt, and you will have a whole new appreciation for your own Bible.

That experience started me on the quest that ended with this book. I practiced architecture for many years and then began practicing law which has been my occupation for the last 35 years. You might be asking: what is an architect/lawyer doing writing a book on the Bible? Well, both disciplines require a lot of research and writing, and I enjoy both. Also, I have always been intrigued by history. I enjoy the history of countries and civilizations, but I also enjoy the history of such subjects as architecture, art, music, the etymology of words, and almost every other subject. I discovered that the most compelling subject of all was the history of the Bible. I got hooked and spent the better part of 25 years devouring everything I could read on the subject.

A few years ago a friend, on his way to a Bible study class, dropped me home from work. I asked him what they studied about the Bible. He said that they usually read small portions of the Bible and then discussed what it meant to each of them and to their lives. "But what do you learn *about* the Bible, you know, who wrote it, when was it written, etc.?" I asked. He looked at me like I was a few camels short of a caravan and said that they never talked about that. This was the response I got from everyone. People just do not study about the Bible. It is no wonder that recent studies have shown that Americans are the most religious people in the west but are also the most ignorant about their religion. So I decided to write this book about the Bible's own persona and history.

You might be surprised to learn that Bible history is seldom taught, even in religious universities, except in graduate level classes at a few universities. Few ministers, even though most of them can quote extensively from the Bible, and know all of those great Bible stories, know little of the Bible itself. Unfortunately, most authoritative books on the subject are written by scholars for peer review by other scholars in that pedantic, academic, scholarly writing style that assures that few of the books will ever be read by ordinary people. I wanted to write a book for the rest of us, for the persons in the pews. So I started reading those scholarly texts and put their findings into this book.

When I tell people that the Bible is a really fun book to read, I usually receive a look that says, "Yeah. Right," sometimes delivered with an eye roll. But it can be a fun read and an exciting trip. First, get a good, modern translation. The traditional King James Version (KJV) is a thing of beauty, but it is a very tough read. Face it, if Elizabethan English were easy to understand everyone would be sitting around reading Shakespeare. The KJV is boring. With a good, modern translation, however, the Bible is loads of fun.

There are many English translations of the Bible; about 86 of them currently in print. Get a readable Bible so you can follow along as you read this book. You need a "reader friendly" translation that is faithful to the ancient texts. The number one most important rule is to get one that is not only a faithful translation, but that is fun to read. That is a two step process. First, get one that is written in contemporary words and phrases. Save the old KJV and the Catholic Douay-Rheims version for recording family birth and death records.

The *Revised Standard Version* that came out in 1952 is better, but it does not meet the readability standard either. It also clones many of the same flaws found in the original KJV.

The *Living Bible* has sold over 40 million copies since 1971, but it is not really a translation of the Bible. It is actually a *paraphrase* of Bible stories. It is widely criticized for having serious flaws in the translation, but it is very readable if all you want to do is learn the great Bible stories.

Next to being written in a style and words that are pleasurable to read, it is important to look for honesty in translation that is not corrupted to conform the contents to the beliefs or agenda of a particular group. For example, the Douay-Rheims translation was commissioned by the Catholic Queen Mary to replace the Protestant Bibles in England commissioned by her father, Henry VIII. It's purpose was to make a Bible geared to Roman Catholic beliefs without regard to accuracy in translation.

I prefer those translations that are the product of a group from many different Christian and Jewish denominations. By spirited argument, they are usually able to work out the translation that is most likely what the original authors intended.

There was serious disagreement in the first few centuries C.E.[1] regarding basic aspects of Christianity such as whether or not JESUS was a god or just someone teaching about GOD, or was he the equal of GOD or was he a lesser god, or was he simply another version of GOD? Then they tossed the Holy Spirit into the mix and asked, "Were these three different gods or one god in three forms?" Others disagreed whether JESUS was born a god, or did GOD simply come down to earth in human form, or did GOD occupy the body of a human that was already on earth. These were serious differences in the beliefs of early Christians, some of which persist even today, and some of the scriptures were translated to support one or another of these philosophies.

In the best modern translations the differences between the ancient texts are noted, sometimes by printing both versions side by side, sometimes by footnote, and sometimes, where there is only a word or two in controversy, they show them in brackets like this, ["or . . . ."].

My personal favorite translation of the Bible by far is the *New Revised Standard Version* (NRSV). It is a fun read, it is a faithful translation, very highly regarded by scholars, and it does not espouse the beliefs of any particular group. It was translated by a very broad range of scholars from diverse religions and denominations. Taking this one step further, my favorite version of the NRSV translation, is the *New Oxford Annotated Bible.* The editors include numerous annotations and footnotes which clear up many confusing areas and add color to the stories. Also, it gave

---

[1] Since historians come from many countries and many other faiths, some were offended that dates are referred to according to Christian tradition as BC, "*Before Christ,*" and AD, "*Anno Domini*" which means "in the year of our Lord." Therefore, historians began using the initials C.E. which stand for "Common Era" and B.C.E. for "Before the Common Era." Most of the scholarly books on the Bible use this new tradition as well, so I have followed their lead in this book.

me numerous suggestions of where I could go for additional information.

Something that I did not think possible until I began reading the *New Oxford Annotated Bible* was that many of the writers of the Old Testament had marvelous senses of humor. The authors were not always somber and serious. For example, many names and words, especially in the first five books, had double meanings that must have brought, if not outright belly-laughs, at least a little "show of teeth," out of the crowd when the stories were told.

For example, *Beelzebul,* a frequent villain in many stories, was originally the title of Baal, the powerful storm and fertility God of the hated Canaanites. *Beelzebul* translates as "Baal the exalted" (*Baal-ze-bul*), The Hebrews took pleasure in corrupting the word from *Beelzebul* to *Beelzebub* which sounds about the same, but translates as "Baal, lord of the flies." That had to bring knowing snickers from the Israelite audience. It probably also allowed the Israelites to openly insult the Canaanites without them knowing it. A parallel example from modern times is where some British prisoners who were incarcerated in Communist China during the Korean War got away with calling Mao Tse Tung "Mousey-dung." The murderous prison guards thought it was just an error in pronunciation and never knew that the prisoners were insulting their exalted leader.

There are many plays on words and double entendres like this that must have been very entertaining to the listeners, enjoying a private joke at the expense of their enemies. You will see more examples later on. The double meanings, of course, do not translate into English. However the *New Oxford Annotated Bible* passes them on to us in the footnotes.

The footnotes also give the multiple meanings of words where they are ambiguous or mean something different today. For example, In Isaiah there is a reference to "The wilderness of the sea." What the heck is that? The footnotes tell us that it is merely the name of a geographic area and it refers to the lower part of Mesopotamia, between the Tigris and Euphrates rivers, that is near the Persian Gulf, an area once known in more recent times as "Sealand." There are hundreds of items like this in the footnotes that help you understand the deepest meanings of the text.

I ordered my copy (off the internet) in the paperback version so that I could mark it up with margin notes and highlight passages that I thought to be particularly important. Marking up a hardcover Bible always seemed a little profane to me.

The NIV Bible is by far the biggest seller right now as it is geared toward the fundamentalist Evangelical Protestants, the Pentecostals, and the various charismatics, all of whom are enjoying a huge burst of popularity at present. It is criticized by many as being slanted toward their agenda. However, it is also praised for its scholarship and has one very nice feature—it was written to be understood by the average eighth grade graduate. What a break from the pedantic KJV.

Another translation that I highly recommend that is a little unusual, is a book called *The Five Gospels.* It contains excerpts from a translation called "The Scholars Edition" which is no longer in print. When I am quoting the words of JESUS in this book, I very often quote from this translation. So much of what JESUS said, as I imagine him talking, had a rhythm to it and was rather poetic. His sentences were usually short and memorable. That rhythm, or meter, was often as important as the words spoken, and was probably one reason that people flocked to hear him and remembered his words. I feel that this translation captures that feeling and rhythm of JESUS' speech, as I envision it, more than any other. *The Five Gospels* is a translation only of what JESUS is purported to have *said* and does not include what JESUS did.

The reason that I recommend *The Five Gospels* so highly is because it sets out all the words that JESUS is purported to have uttered in each of the gospels side by side. Many of JESUS' words are included in more than one gospel, called parallel verses. As you will see, of the 666 verses in Mark, Matthew contains about 600 of them in his gospel and Luke used about 300. Many words of JESUS are recorded in two or three of the canonical gospels and a few are found in all four.

When you pick up a Bible it looks much like any other book, except it does not have the author's name on the cover. Did you ever wonder who wrote it? I assumed, without thinking about it, that the Bible was written in one sitting by some unknown person. I never bought in to the concept of God "inspiring" people about what to write. The concept that there was a sort of "Devine steno pool" was a little hard for me to buy. Some of the questions that went through my mind were:

- Just who was it that GOD was supposed to have inspired—the people who wrote the original version, those who edited it, those who made the thousands of hand-written copies, those who translated it, or the people who chose which religious books out of many should be included in the Bible?
- How exactly did this inspiration from GOD occur? Did GOD'S words come in dreams? How many scribes were there all together? Was all of it written at once? Did GOD also write Paul's letters? If the words came to more than one person over the years, how did they all get together to form the Bible?
- In what language were they? Did GOD dictate in Hebrew to Moses and in Greek to Paul? A famous professor of Hebrew used to tell his new students on the first day of class, "Gentlemen, welcome to the language GOD spoke." Hebrew was the predominant language of the Old Testament. JESUS and his disciples spoke Aramaic but the New Testament was originally written in Greek. Were the translators inspired by GOD?

I decided to find the answers to these questions and more. This book is about the Bible, our spiritual "owner's manual." It is not about Bible stories, although there are many of them in it. This is the Bible's own story. It is about the magnificent book itself. It covers such basics as why the Bible is bound into a book rather than rolled up parchment scrolls like the Jewish scriptures. It discusses influences on the people who wrote the Bible—historical, religious, governmental, social, and political. All of these impacted the Biblical authors and the words that they ultimately wrote. Some of these same influences determined what books the church leaders would include or exclude from the official Bible in 397 C.E.

I guarantee that you will enjoy a whole new appreciation for this wonderful book that we call the Bible. The Bible is filled with history, beautiful literature, and music. Over and over again as you read you will find yourself saying, "I didn't know that!"

1

The Setting and the Cast of Characters

The Bible is the inerrant . . . word of the living God. It is absolutely infallible, without error in all matters pertaining to faith and practice, as well as in areas such as geography, science, history, etc.

Jerry Falwell

Nothing happens in a vacuum, and that includes the Bible. Its contents were affected by geography, history, economics, religion, cultural differences, politics, war, and more. A continuing affect, then and now, was the geography of the Holy Land. The land was more lush then, but otherwise much the same as it is today. It is difficult to conceive how so much history could happen in so small a space. Nearly everything that happened in the Bible took place in a land that is only about the size of New Jersey, one of our smallest states in area.

Palestine* sits at the confluence of Europe, Asia, and Africa, making it a melting pot for people from all three continents. Coincidentally, this location is also the source of much of the turmoil throughout history that continues to the present day. With the Mediterranean Sea on the west and some of the most inhospitable deserts and mountains on the east, every conquering army in history had to pass through this land; whether it was

---

* I needed a name for this land that would be instantly recognized by nearly everyone as the geographical area that we are referring to. Realizing that any name that I use would not only be politically sensitive, but also would not be completely accurate, I finally settled on the word "Palestine." The word was created by the Romans in the late first century after the second Jewish War when they either killed or exiled almost all of the Jews living in the land. The name was a Latinization of "Philistines," the Hebrew's ancient enemy. The name was meant to be a slap in the face to the Jews who had the audacity to take up arms against the Roman Empire. But politically incorrect as it may be, when one hears the word, most people know what land we are talking about. This name is undoubtedly repugnant to my Jewish readers, but I hope that they will forgive me.

Egypt attempting to extend its empire to the north, the Assyrians trying to extend their holdings south and west, or the Greeks and Romans extending their empires to the east and south. The armies of these and uncountable more countries and tribes squeezed through the tiny space between the Mediterranean and the Jordan, usually leaving devastation in their wake. Traveling armies, even when they were not seeking to conquer, foraged and denuded the land of livestock and crops just to feed the army. On the positive side, the armies also left behind some of their culture. The land was then, and remains, one of the most culturally diverse areas in the world.

In the south the settlers were particularly vulnerable where, because of the inhospitable mountains and deserts to the east and the Mediterranean to the west, the armies had to squeeze through the Gaza Strip, a area only seven or eight miles wide and about 30 miles long. This was definitely the neck of the bottle and the people living in Gaza really took a beating even when they won the war. The Gaza later became the home of the Philistines.

Conflicts of Culture

As people passed through the land, some of them stayed. The Bible talks about many of them, and they play important roles in the formation of the Bible. Descendants of many of these people, and their cultures, can still be found.

In the Old Testament stories, many of the invaders came from the east. Sumer is considered the earliest civilization in the western world and was located between the Tigris and Euphrates Rivers, in what is now Iraq, toward their junction in the south. This civilization began 5300 B.C.E. and ended in the second millennium B.C.E. when the Babylonian civilization began. Although there were several different ruling dynasties during that period, those who spoke the Sumerian language are usually grouped together. Sumerian, is a language unrelated to any other known language, past or present, and is one of the world's earliest written languages. Before Sumer, there was just a loose assortment of independent city-states. Then came a much more cohesive group, the Akkadians, and about 2350 B.C.E. they spawned one of history's first empire makers, King Sargon. It wasn't long before Sargon ruled all of the Mesopotamian area plus Elam, the country to the east of the Tigris, now known as Iran.

The Akkadians spoke a completely different language from the

Sumerians and it became known as Semitic*. That became the root of many of the Middle Eastern languages still in use today including Arabic, Farsi, Aramaic, and Hebrew. Both the Sumerian and Akkadian languages disappeared. They are known today only from the written languages that they each developed that can still be found on clay tablets. The Sumerian writing is called cuneiform, and there is a wealth of ancient cuneiform tablets that are very valuable to scholars working on the Bible as they often have parallel stories** to those in the Bible. Most people are unaware that the Akkadians also developed a rudimentary written language long before the Sumarians. The cuneiform technique in fact originated with them. Later, the Phoenicians used the Akkadian writings, not the Sumerian, as the foundation for an entirely new idea, an alphabet comprised of symbols that represent sounds. This invention of a written language based upon sounds eventually made the Bible available to everyone, but it was also to become its nemesis.

The descendants of the Akkadians and some of the tribes around them resumed their former nomadic lifestyle when their empire collapsed and became what we might today term "barbarian raiders." Some of these raiders later settled in the eastern part of Turkey and became known as the Hittites. The Hittites retained their inherited reputation as fierce warriors. They were also the first western people to discover how to extract iron from ore by using charcoal for the heat source. This happened about 1200 B.C.E., but the iron by itself was actually less durable than bronze for swords and other weapons. On the other hand it worked great in a new weapon, chariots. About 300 years later, probably by accident, they figured out how to add some of the carbon from the charcoal to the iron to form the alloy that we call steel. After that they became an enormous power in the area. Steel weapons were far superior

---

* Legend has it that the name "Semitic" was derived from the name of one of Noah's sons, Shem, who was given the land in that area after the flood when the ark landed. The term "Semite" was actually first used by a German writer to describe the Hebrew languages in the 18th century and it had nothing to do with Noah's son, Shem.

** Parallel stories are those where the same story is told by two or more people, usually somewhat differently. There are dozens of these in the New Testament. They are very important as scholars use them to verify the truth of an incident, establish dates of the occurrences, and much more.

to bronze weapons. They were stronger and held an edge much longer. They also used steel to make superior improvements to their chariots.

The Phoenician city of Byblos, in modern day Syria, is one of the oldest continually inhabited cities in the world, having first been occupied by early homo sapiens in about 8000 B.C.E. The first evidence of the Phoenicians dates to about 1300 B.C.E. The name *Phoenician* is the Greek name for this group. The Bible does not distinguish between the Phoenicians and the Canaanites and refers to them jointly as the *Canaanites.* The Phoenicians were a diverse group of people that likely came from many different countries, but their origin is in dispute. In any event, they developed a language of their own. Their trade required them to be conversant in three completely dissimilar languages—their own, Babylonian, and Egyptian plus a lesser fluency in the numerous other languages around the Mediterranean. Both the cuneiform of Babylon and the hieroglyphics of Egypt were very difficult written languages with hundreds of symbols. As a result, the written versions of those languages were known to only a few priests and scribes in their own countries. In order to keep track of commerce, the Phoenicians, who had no written language of their own, needed a simpler form of writing that would work everyplace. Therefore, they developed the alphabet.

Another group that later became a real thorn in the side of the Israelite kings Saul, David, and Solomon, was the Philistines. The origins of the Philistines remains a mystery. Both Egyptian and Mesopotamian writings refer to them as the "sea people" from the north. At about 1200 B.C.E. they arrived in Palestine at approximately the same time that the Hebrews crossed the Jordan into Canaan at the end of their long trek from Egypt that we know as the Exodus. The sea people settled in the southern area that we know today as the Gaza Strip. The consensus is that they likely originated in Cypress, but that they were non-natives of that area and were melded from an assortment of cultures.

This was a time of dramatic and often tragic change in the Mediterranean. The enormous volcanic explosion of Thera in 1470 B.C.E. covered the area with ash and blocked out the sun. The resulting tsunami devastated the Cretan civilization and the sea shores of most of the countries bordering the Mediterranean. The centuries following the blast saw the collapse of the Hittite empire (shortly after 1200 B.C.E.), the fall of Troy (1185 B.C.E.), and the invasions by Egypt (c. 1207 and 1175 B.C.E.). These were all part of a major population movement that pushed peoples from the north to the south. Greece was left impoverished when the wealth from the north and west moved to the Middle East. The arrival of the Philistines marked the end of Egypt's domination over the region as the Philistines "corked" up the passage to the north through the Gaza Strip. Try as they may, the Egyptians could not root out the Philistines.

It is believed by many scholars that, upon the fall of the Hittites, the Philistines became heirs to the Hittite iron production secrets. Both tribes had complete monopolies on iron production during their periods of domination; secrets which they guarded fiercely. The Philisines became such a threat to the Israelites in the eleventh century that the Israelites anointed their first king, Saul, to combat them. Goliath was a Philistine.

Each of these disparate groups brought their own gods with them. They were all pagans, but do not equate paganism with idol worship. That mistake was made for many centuries, primarily from passages in Exodus and other books of the Bible. For example, Moses found the Israelites worshiping a golden calf which the Bible described as a Canaanite god. There were other similar references to the creation and worship of idols. Archaeological evidence clearly shows, however, that idols themselves were not being worshiped, but rather the gods that they represented. It is comparable to Christians worshiping before a cross. It is not the cross that they are worshiping, but what the cross represents to them.

There were many other cultures, of course. The Greeks and the Romans will become major players as will such groups as the Samaritans, but we will discuss them later.

What is a "Bible"

Most of us know that the Bible is a book, but when you look at the cover of the Bible, something is missing; it doesn't identify the author. Who did write it? Why is it called the Bible? Latin was the accepted language of the Christian priesthood for centuries, replacing Greek in the third century. The word "Bible" comes from the Latin word *biblia* which means books. The Latin word was taken from the Greek language, and in Greek, the words *ta biblia*, like the Latin *biblia* and the Hebrew name, *has harim*, is not a singular noun; it is a plural noun. They all mean "Books." That is a much closer description of the Bible, a collection of books with a common theme—what we would now call an anthology.

But we're not finished with the origin of the word yet. The Greek words *ta biblia* are derived from yet another language. They come from the Phoenician word, *Byblos*. Remember the name? It was mentioned earlier as one of the oldest continually occupied cities in the world. Byblos was, and still is, the name of an ancient Phoenician city on the Mediterranean. The Phoenicians were traders and they were really good at it. One of the items they traded, and it was primarily manufactured in one city, was papyrus. Papyrus was, and is, a plant with thin, reed-like stems. The reeds were split, dried, stitched together, and burnished and they became the first writing surface that was neither from the hides of animals, stone, nor clay. Our word *paper* is derived from the word "papyrus." *Byblos* is the Greek translation of the word "papyrus," so the town that shipped this material around the world was actually named after the product it produced. Do not underestimate the importance of papyrus. It changed forever the way humans recorded history.

If you can sort through all of those confusing word translations back to the beginning, that is where the word "Bible" came from—the city of Byblos to the Greek *ta biblia* to the Latin word *biblia* that were both derived from the name of the city, and finally, to the English word, Bible.

The modern Bible contains 39 books of ancient Hebrew Scriptures, which Christians call the Old Testament and 27 New Testament books that begin with the birth of JESUS.

JESUS and his early followers were all Jews, and the only "Bible" they had was the "Septuagint," which was a Greek translation of the Hebrew Scriptures, a book we will hear a lot about later. It was supposedly commissioned by Ptolemy II. This was the first translation of the Hebrew Scriptures, and it is a very important book in the history of the Bible. *Septuagint* (sĕp-TŪ-ȧ-jĭnt) is Greek for "seventy," and it is often referred to in literature simply by the Roman numerals for seventy, "LXX." You are likely to encounter this shorthand version in many places, even in the footnotes of your own Bible.

There are several books that no longer appear in most modern Bibles and are now referred to as the "Apocrypha." The word means "hidden things," although nobody has ever been able to discover what they are hidden from. They were mostly Hebrew writings from the first three centuries B.C.E. Many first appeared in the Septuagint. The Jews opposed the inclusion of the Apocrypha in the Septuagint because they were not accepted Hebrew canon. They were on very weak authority and some of the books tended to pit the views of some Jews against those of others.

The Apocrypha were later dropped from Protestant Bibles. Some of the books of the Apocrypha still remain in some translations, notably the Roman Catholic and Greek Orthodox Bibles. The Apocrypha, even though they are no longer part of the Protestant tradition, are often referred to by Protestant ministers, so even some Protestant Bibles now include them once again, but those Bible's clearly state that the Apocrypha are no longer part of the official Canon. The principal value of the

Apocrypha to religious scholars today is to assist in understanding the history of the two or three centuries leading up to the formation of the Christian religion, an age of unparalleled religious and social upheaval.

The Bible is, therefore, a collection of books like a library. Unlike a library, however, the Christian books are all bound into one volume rather than having each book bound separately. The very first known reference to the scriptures by the term "biblia" or books, was by a second century church leader, (St.) Clement. He wrote a letter in which he speaks of "the *books* and the Apostles." The books (bibles) that he probably referred to are the Jewish scriptures and, possibly, the four canonical Gospels plus Acts that were in rather common use at the time. In the Old Testament the only place the word "Bible" appears is in the book of Daniel (9:21) where he states, "I, Daniel, perceived in the *books* . . . ." This reference is, of course, to the Hebrew scriptures.

Did God Write the Bible?

As a child faithfully attending Sunday School, I was told that God wrote the Bible and later heard that Moses wrote the first five books of the Bible. Christians call these five books the *Pentateuch,* which is Greek for "five books," and Jews call them the *Torah* which, loosely translated, means "what people are supposed to do," but is generally referred to as "The Law." So, who actually was the author? Did God write them or did Moses? My old Bible from my Sunday School days starts out, "The First Book of Moses, Called GENESIS." The second book was entitled , "The Second Book of Moses, Called EXODUS." And so on. Newer translations merely refer to them as "GENESIS" and "EXODUS."

I also vaguely remember the uproar when the Revised Standard Bible was first introduced in 1952. I really became aware of it in 1955 when my high school debate teacher, the son of a Methodist minister, raised the issue of the new translation for class discussion and there were impassioned arguments against the new translation. What a scandal! "How dare anyone change our beautiful King James Version!" The new translation was almost universally vilified.

I wondered, why there was more than one Bible? Why did it have to be revised. At the time I thought there were only two versions; there was the King James version and the new Revised Standard version. Was one of them wrong? My high school debate teacher was outspokenly partial to the new Revised Standard version, but in church we always used the King James version.

I did not know then that there were many, many other English translations as well as those two. There were translations of the original Hebrew to Greek, translations of Aramaic to Greek, Greek to Latin, Greek to English, Latin to English, Old English to modern English, and even Hebrew to English. Today, there are over 86 English translations alone that are currently in print.

I was told repeatedly by my evangelist leaders that the Bible was inerrant. It is the "word of GOD." Everything in the Bible is the absolute, God-given truth. Anyone who says otherwise is simply wrong. I believed that. It never entered my mind to question that proposition. It must be true if my minister told me it was true. He was, after all, a "man of GOD." In fact, belief in the inerrancy of the Bible was pretty much the accepted view from the Dark Ages until the 17th Century when the concept went out of style for awhile, only to be revived in more recent times with the Evangelical and Pentecostal explosion. Inerrancy is usually defined today by the statement generally attributed to Jerry Falwell in the epigraph at the beginning of this chapter, although I haven't a clue as to who was the first person to actually came up with the quotation.

The ancient Hebrews believed that Moses wrote the Torah and that it was the absolute word communicated by GOD to Moses. However, most did not feel the same about the balance of the Hebrew Scriptures. The books grouped as "The Prophets," which included the Historical Books and others in addition to the books attributed to the various prophets, were not accepted as Hebrew canon until about 400 B.C.E. As to The Writings, the rest of the current Hebrew Canon, basically the poetic and wisdom literature, little attention was paid to them until the Hebrew priesthood discovered that they were very popular with the laity. While they felt the religious messages in these books was true, the books were rarely historically accurate.

The more I studied the Bible, the more evident it became that the Bible is not inerrant, but full of errors and inconsistencies. If GOD wrote the Bible, and GOD is omnipotent, how could he have made all those mistakes? Genesis says that GOD created all of the wild animals of the earth and He "saw that it was good." If it was so good, why are over 99% of all of the animals that once walked on this earth now extinct? Did GOD make a mistake? Was Woody Allen correct when he commented, "[T]he worst that you can say about [GOD] is that basically he's an underachiever"?

Bible Questions

Most people are familiar with the Bible story of Cain and Able—Cain killed Able and GOD found out and banished Cain, but first GOD branded him so that *anyone he meets* will know that he is favored by GOD and they will not kill him.. The story does not end there, however. After he was banished, Cain *took a wife and founded a city*. Wait, what? He took a wife? Let's see, there was Adam and Eve, the first humans, and they had Cain and Able. Where did Able find a wife? And just who were these people who might want to kill Cain and who were the people that lived in this new city founded by Able and his wife? These are serious questions.

After Adam ate fruit from the tree of knowledge, GOD said, "Behold, the man is become as one of *us, . . ."* Us? Who are these other gods. I thought that there was only supposed to be one god. In fact, in my old Bible the word "us" had the "U" capitalized, "Us." In that King James version, the Hebrew god was always capitalized God. That first person plural pronoun "Us," written in caps, obviously included other gods. GOD then threw Adam and Eve out of the Garden before they could also eat from the Tree of Life because then they would live forever like "Us." So much for monotheism.

In another story, GOD and a couple of angels, all disguised as human beings, sat down and talked with Abraham*. That seemed very peculiar to me. I knew the Greek and Roman gods often came down to earth and took human form or inhabited the body of a human being, but I was not familiar with the Judeo-Christian god doing that. The story continues with GOD indicating to Abraham that He had *heard* that the people of Sodom and Gomorrah were sinners and they were traveling there to check them out *and see if the rumors were true*. He *heard*? Didn't He know? How did these rumors get started? I had been led to believe that GOD was omniscient. How can He not know whether or not the Sodomites are sinners? If He isn't everywhere and doesn't hear and know everything, how could I be sure that He hears my prayers?

I was told that GOD took a rib from Adam and created Eve. That's true . . . in Genesis 2, after He had first created everything else, including the animals. But Genesis 1 says something entirely different. In Genesis 1, GOD created plants, then animals, and then man and woman *at the same time*. Which version is correct, Genesis 1 or 2? There is no possible way

---

*Angels are incorporeal beings; ghost-like, they have no substance. How can they disguise themselves as humans? It seemed that you should be able to see right through them. How could they pick things up? They were even depicted eating food, ingesting it into an incorporeal stomach! None of this made any sense to me then and it still does not today

that they can both be right. If the Bible is inerrant, as Mr. Falwell says in the epigraph, if it is the word of GOD, how could He have made such an obvious blunder?

I used to wonder about GOD bringing all the animals before Adam so that he could name them. What did he call them? What language did he use? Writing had not yet been invented. In fact, all of the ancient patriarchs from Adam to Moses lived before there was a Hebrew language. Adam could not have made a journal to record the names of all these animals for future generations. How did he find out about animals in America? What about the gorilla that was not even known to exist until rumors of a hairy, man-like creature in Africa began to circulate in the late 19th century? What about extinct animals? Were the dinosaurs alive then for GOD to bring them before Adam for naming?

I wondered about these discrepancies but my friends didn't want to discuss them. These thoughts kept gnawing at me and my appetite for Biblical knowledge was whetted.

THE DAYS OF CREATION

The following comparison between the chronology of the creation in Genesis 1 and Genesis 2 shows just how irreconcilable the two verses are:

Genesis 1.0-2.3	*Genesis 2.4-2.24*
Heaven	Earth
Earth	Heaven
Light	Mist
Firmament	Man
Day Land	Trees
Grasses and Trees	Rivers
Luminaries	Beasts and Cattle
Sea-beasts	Birds
Birds	Woman
Cattle, Creeping things, Beasts	
Man and Woman	
The Sabbath	

Basically, nothing matches. The author of Genesis 1, which was actually written long after Genesis 2, has an entirely different concept of the order in which GOD created the universe. The most striking difference is that Genesis 2 has man and woman created at entirely different times while Genesis 1 has man and woman created the same day.

The Beginning of My Quest

About 25 years ago, I found myself again contemplating all of those unanswered questions left over from my youth. I dusted off the cover of the old, tattered Bible I used in Sunday school and began to read it again.

I also began voraciously reading books about the Bible. There is a veritable wealth of material on the subject. The difficulty I had was filtering the books to determine which were the most reliable and best told the story, otherwise I would be reading far into my next life.

I especially wanted to read texts that were scholarly and based upon the "critical thinking" method rather than being based upon a particular religious belief. I found that many people writing about the Bible began with an agenda and preconceived notions. They then "mined" the Bible for verses to back up them up, ignoring anything that might remotely dispute or contradict their preconceptions. These books offered little because the sole purpose of many was to promote the authors' particular beliefs rather than being a search for the truth. Many of the books by popular church leaders fell into this category*.

I discovered I as not alone in my confusion about the Bible. People have been asking the same questions for several thousand years. My research revealed that answers have been found to most of these questions. Once I got started I couldn't stop reading.

You have to be very careful in your choices of what to study. There are some real flights of fiction masquerading as serious Bible scholarship. Just about everything that you can imagine has been written about the Bible at one time or another. I tried to read only truly scientific texts written by real scholars, all of which have withstood energetic peer review.

Most New Testament scholarship appears to have been done since 1950. Since most religious scholars were, historically, either professors in religious universities or monks, prior to 1950 they ran the serious risk of finding themselves out of work if they published any findings that disagreed with church dogma. That began to change in the 1950s when enlightened church leaders began to search for answers and when many scholars gravitated to secular universities where there were no religious preconditions on research.

One day I was reading a marvelous book entitled *The Birth of Christianity* by John Dominic Crossan. Someone walked by and asked, "Who wrote that? Some atheist?" That is a typical reaction I get. Most

---

* One exception was the excellent series of books by John Shelby Spong, an Episcopal bishop who wrote some very incisive books. His strong Anglican beliefs were included in his books, of course, but he never once tried to slant his findings to support the dogma of his church. I read several of his books and they are very informative and entertaining. They are not a bad way to introduce yourself to this subject

people automatically assume that anyone who writes about the Bible is trying to put it down or to attack it. That is simply not true. There are books that do just that, to be sure, but I did not read those except in the very beginning when I was feeling my way along trying to find out how to identify real scholarly texts. Crossan, for example, was a Catholic monk for 20 years and primarily studied only the Gospels during that time. During the '60s when he was a young man, and while other young men were "turning on, tuning in, and dropping out" and attending love-ins, he spent the entire decade comparing the parallel verses of the four Gospels, verse by verse, written side by side. He is now a professor emeritus of Bible studies at a very prestigious Catholic university and was a winner of the American Academy of Religion Award for Excellence. He holds very strong religious convictions and his research has not diminished those beliefs whatsoever. Mr. Crossan is typical of the brilliant authors of the texts that I have relied upon to write this book. They are all internationally renowned scholars, and they justly deserve our highest regard.

2

In the Beginning . . .

Then Moses, the servant of the LORD*, died there in the land of Moab, at the* LORD*'s command.*

Deut. 34:5

Did you ever wonder who actually wrote the Bible? Probably not. The thought rarely enters the minds of most people. Now that you are thinking about it, you are probably coming up with some of the authors—Paul must have written the letters that bear his name; Isaiah and the other prophets probably wrote the books bearing their names. And didn't Moses write the first five books or, as many believe, didn't GOD write everything?

Before we get to the issue of who actually wrote the Bible, let's examine the question of GOD'S contribution very generally. There are basically five possibilities:

1. GOD wrote the Bible and dictated it to human scribes who recorded His words verbatim;
2. GOD inspired human scribes who recorded what they understood GOD was asking them to write, but being human they were not perfect so could, and probably did, make mistakes;
3. Very religious and wise people wrote the Bible as the expression of their belief in GOD'S will and their own origins;
4. Humans wrote the Bible and it contains ancient religious wisdom and history that had been passed down to them by other humans through the ages and includes their own ideas; and
5. Human beings recorded the religious beliefs of their people and cultures at the time they were recorded and are relevant to those people at those times, not to all of the world's people, and also contain their own beliefs, ideas, and interpretations.

In the first view, the Bible is inerrant and there is no room for argument about accuracy and authority. If there appear to be inconsistencies in the Bible it is solely because the person reading the Bible has interpreted it incorrectly. In the last view, the Bible is simply a collection of Middle Eastern myths, legends, and superstitions from their own past or borrowed from other cultures intermixed with their own ideas and interpretations. Everything in between borrows some of these two opposing ends of the spectrum to different degrees. With these five scenarios in mind, let's embark on our journey to find out just who did write the Bible.

Tracking down the authors or scribes is just the beginning of this great adventure, but a very important part. Unfortunately, in most cases we cannot narrow the author down to a single individual with a name, although we can in some instances. However, scholars are usually able to narrow down the authorship to an identifiable group at an approximate time and in an identifiable place. And the key word is "group." It is likely the contribution of several writers in each group.

Let's get started with the first five books of the Bible.

Moses Wrote the First Five Books; or Did He?

According to ancient Hebrew tradition, Moses wrote the first five books of the Bible, the Hebrew "Torah," known to Christians as the "Pentateuch": Genesis, Exodus, Leviticus, Numbers, and Deuteronomy. If this is true, he must have also written the passage in the above epigraph from Deuteronomy as well, where Moses describes his own death. How could Moses possibly have narrated his own death? People have wondered about this for more than 2500 years.

Nor was I the first person to wonder about the discrepancies between Genesis 1 and Genesis 2 that we discussed in Chapter 1. Nearly everyone gets through that much of the Bible before they give up and switch to a good novel or a TV program or grab their baseball glove and head for the park. The differences between the two verses are obvious, even on a casual reading. Then an ancient reader noticed that the Books of Moses refer to the use of camels as beasts of burden. How could that be? Scholars 2500 years ago knew that camels were not domesticated in the Middle East until the sixth century B.C.E. Since the Exodus occurred about the thirteenth Century B.C.E., the skeptic noted, Moses could not have known that some day, 250 years in the future, camels would be used as beasts of burden. Hm-m-m-m. Could someone possibly have added this part of the Exodus story at a later date when camels as beasts of burden were common?

Moses also talked about the Philistines, but they did not show up in the Middle East until a couple of centuries *after* his death, just before the time of King Saul. How could Moses have known about them?

In the twelfth Century C.E., a religious leader, Abraham ibn Ezra, noted that Gen. 12:6 states, in reference to his ancient namesake, the patriarch Abraham, "*At that time* the Canaanites were in the land . . ." The words "at that time" suggested that, for the author of those words, the Canaanites had once been there but no longer were; therefore, Moses could not be the author because during his lifetime, and long after, the Canaanites were still living on the land. Could this also have been a later addition?

Genesis tells us that Abraham came from the town of Ur of the Chaldees. Ur was, in fact, a city in Mesopotamia in the time of Abraham, but the Chaldeans did not occupy Ur until several hundred years *after* the death of Moses. That suggests that the author of that section of Genesis lived much later than Moses and was unaware that the Chaldeans did not occupy the land until the sixth century B.C.E., hundreds of years after the lifetimes of both Abraham and Moses.

Even more to the point, how could Moses have written the first five books of the Bible when Hebrew did not even have a written language at that time with which to do so? We noted that the Phoenicians, who invented the alphabet, first showed up in Palestine about 1300 B.C.E. Sometime thereafter the Canaanites modified it slightly and came up with their own alphabet. It was not until after the Israealites crossed over the Jordan into the Promised Land, about 1200 B.C.E., that the Hebrews even heard of an alphabet. There they intermingled with the Canaanites and the Israelites then adapted their alphabet to the Hebrew language.

A recent archaeological discovery, which has been tentatively dated at 1050 B.C.E., about the time of the reign of King Saul, is a stone tablet which is the earliest known Hebrew writing. It has an abecedary (ā-bē-CĒ-dary) at the top of the tablet which is the Canaanite alphabet and directly below it the new Hebrew alphabet. The object is to show people how to pronounce the Hebrew letters. That indicates that the Hebrew alphabet was very new at that time.

Deuteronomy tells us that Moses died *before* the Israelites crossed the Jordan. Moses was never allowed by GOD to enter the promised land; therefore, it logically follows that Moses could not have written the first five books of the Bible because the Hebrews would not develop a written language for another 150 years.

These were not a bunch of non-believing atheists asking these questions. The only people who had access to the holy scriptures in ancient times were priests and scribes. Nobody else could read and few could have afforded the texts even if they could read. You couldn't just go down to the local Borders bookstore and buy a copy and there were no public libraries. Every book was painstakingly copied by hand, letter by letter. Such facts as the domestication of camels and the arrival of the Philistines were later used by scholars to help date the various writings.

As the quality of Biblical scholarship improved, and as more and more ancient writings were uncovered by archaeologists, the scholars developed a new tool for narrowing down the dates of authorship of the books. One is the recognition of changes in the language itself. Languages evolve. As a grandfather, I can tell you communicating with your grandchildren can be like communicating with someone who is speaking in foreign languages. Every time I turn around there is a new word—faceplant, texting, sliders, etc., not to mention new meanings given to old words. "That girl is hot" does not mean she is running a fever.

Language is dynamic, always changing. The language of Shakespeare differs from this text, for example, even though both are written in English. There are differences in the words used (thee and thou, for instance), in the structure of the language, and the meanings of words. Compare the King James Version (KJV) with a modern translation of the Bible for a better example. The sidebar shows an excerpt from the first Bible translated into English, the Wycliffe. It is incomprehensible today.

Likewise, throughout the history of the Bible, the Hebrew language differed from place to place and time to time. Scholars have learned to tell, simply by the words that were used and the ways that they were used, approximately when something was written. There are entire books written on this fascinating subject. Scholars are even able to tell, in many instances, whether or not a particular individual authored a given portion of a book just by differences in the structure of the writing.

Think about the English language just in your own lifetime. "Cool" used to refer to a temperature; "dude" used to mean an amateur cowboy, and "bad" used to mean "not good," and can now mean "good." Have you ever heard of a "blotter," a "slide rule," a "running board," a "wiffle tree," a "slate," or an "ink well?" These were all common terms when I was younger. It was the same with ancient Greek and Hebrew. When I mentioned in a later chapter that the Egyptians ran into a "buzz saw," my daughter asked what that was, so I used a different word instead. And if you think that slang and colloquial words would never be used in the written record of one's religious history like the Bible, read on.

Word usages changed and the experts use those changes to help date some of the Biblical writings. There are many more tools as well, but they are far beyond the scope of this book. Just keep in mind that the people who work in this field are very good at what they do. When one of them

Portion of John 1:1 from Wyclyffe Bible (17th Century Olde English)

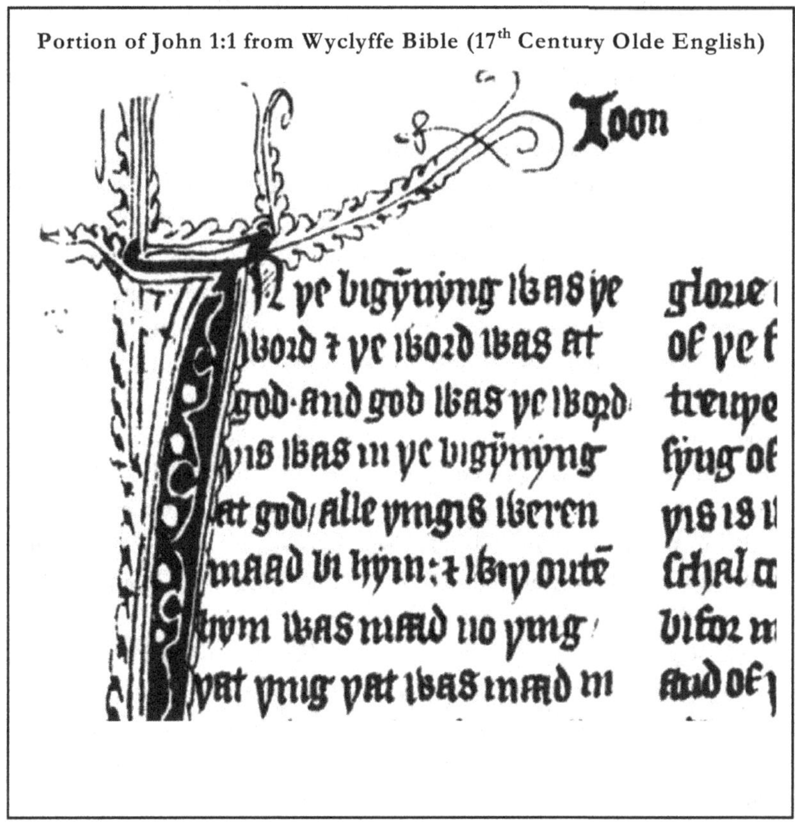

Joon

In ye bigynnyng was ye
word & ye word was at
god. and god was ye word
þis was in ye bigynnyng
at god/ alle yingis weren
maad bi hym: & wiþ oute
him was maad no ying
yat ying yat was maad in

says that a particular writing or portion of a writing was done during a stated time period or written or not written by a particular person, you can take it to the bank. You'll get a taste of this throughout this book.

Who are J, E, D, P, and R?

If Moses did not write the Pentateuch, who did? Nobody knows their real names for sure, but it has been determined that there were at least five authors and by tradition they have been identified with the letters J, E, D, P, and R. This was very heavy stuff when the idea was first suggested out loud (albeit very quietly) that maybe Moses did not write this material. Many people who wondered about this kept quiet in public. The Church had a nasty habit of executing heretics. In fact, it was not until 1943 that the Pope finally acknowledged that there was some substance to this idea and it needed to be resolved. Now this multiple authorship is universally accepted by Biblical scholars of all faiths.

Of parallel interest and importance to identifying the authors was the accurate dating of the various portions of the Bible. The quest to determine the authors and the dates is an absolutely fascinating story. People privately pondered these questions for centuries—who wrote the Bible and when was it written—but it was not until the 18th century that someone stumbled upon the first real clue.

For centuries, Biblical scholars had noted the existence of couplets in the Old Testament. The term "couplets," has many different meanings in both literature and in the Bible, but here it describes two or more stories about the same thing. Earlier, I mentioned the two Creation stories in Genesis 1 and Genesis 2. Together they form a couplet. Many more couplets are found in the Bible. For example, there are two different stories of the covenant between GOD and Abraham and two separate stories of the naming of his son Isaac. There are two versions of Abraham's claiming to a foreign king that his wife Sarah is his sister; two stories of Isaac's son, Jacob, traveling to Mesopotamia; two stories of a revelation to Jacob at Beth-El (Bethel); two stories of GOD changing Jacob's name to Israel; two stories of Moses getting water from a rock at a place called Meribah, and many more.

These couplets appear throughout the "Books of Moses." In many cases, if not most cases, the two versions are so different and contradictory that they are impossible to reconcile with one another. Which versions of the couplets is correct? The answer is, they all are. Whether or not any of them recorded actual historical events is less certain.

In about 1753 a scholar by the name of Jean Astruc very quietly noted that, in many places in Genesis, GOD was referred to as Yahweh. It was spelled YHWH as Hebrew did not have any vowels in those days and usually pronounced YÄH-way today. At one time it was mispro-nounced "Jehovah," although in truth, today nobody knows for sure just how it was pronounced. It was only spoken once a year and that was by the head priest. Since there has not been a Hebrew priesthood for a couple of millennia, and because of the lack of vowel sounds in ancient Hebrew, nobody today knows how is should be pronounced. Astruc also noticed that GOD is often translated in other places as *Elohim*. In fact *Elohim* is the first name for GOD found in the Bible, and it is used throughout the Old Testament over 2,370 times, including the first verse in the Bible, "In the beginning, *Elohim* (EL-o-heem) created the Heaven and the earth." Elohim is a plural word, actually meaning "gods," the singular form being

El. Therefore, properly translated, the sentence should read, "In the beginning, the Gods created the Heaven and the earth." Keep this in mind for later discussions.

This use of two names for GOD caught the attention of some German scholars who expanded the analysis to the other books in the Pentateuch. Finally, in 1878 in a truly brilliant work, Julius Wellhausen synthesized all of the previous works into one composite theory. He identified five different participants in the authorship of the Pentateuch. He referred to the two authors who used different names for GOD as "J" and "E." For the verses that referred to GOD as "Elohim," he called the author "E" (for Elohim). Yahweh is spelled "Jahwe" in German, so he assigned the initial "J" to the author that referred to GOD as Yahweh.

Wellhausen then separated out all of the "J" verses from the "E" verses. He discovered that there were two separate and distinct versions, couplets, of much of Genesis. Someone had, apparently, taken two ancient versions of the same stories, cut them up, and stitched them together to form a continuous story. This brilliant analysis started the

GOD'S NAMES

When GOD spoke to Moses from the burning bush, Moses asked GOD, "If I come to the Israelites and say to them, 'The god of your ancestors has sent me to you,' and they ask me, 'What is his name?' what shall I say to them?" GOD replied, "I am who I am." (Ex. 3:13) That is, of course, the English translation. What he actually said was *Ehyeh* which is a form of the Hebrew verb for the infinitive "to be" and means "I am." But when Moses told the Israelites what GOD'S name was, he said that it was "Yahweh" which is the third person version of *Ehyeh*, or as we would say today, "He is." It is traditionally spelled with the four consonants YHWH as ancient Hebrew did not have vowels. These four consonants are called the "Tetragrammaton." If you do any reading at all about the Bible you will run into this term frequently. Nobody knows how YHWH was pronounced. The name was spoken aloud only once a year, and that was privately by the High Priest.. It was otherwise forbidden to speak the name aloud. Instead, the Hebrews referred to GOD as *Adonai,* which is usually translated in English Bibles as "Lord," or as *Elohim*, translated as "God" in English.

Later he was also called, simply, "El" which was a generic, commonly used word for any deity in the Middle East. *Elohim* is the plural of El as we noted earlier suggesting that god originally meant "gods." In order to make sure that GOD was not confused with any other "El," the name in the Hebrew Bible is often modified by a second word. For example, *El Shaddai* means God Almighty, and *El Elyon* means God Most High. Many place names also contain the word "*El*," such as *Bethel* ("house of God"), *Peniel* ("face of God"), and *Israel* (which means "he will struggle with God").

search for the authorship of the Bible that continues to this day. It started slowly because scholars wanted to keep their jobs and none wanted to be excommunicated and certainly not executed, but eventually, about the middle of the 20th century, it exploded into modern Biblical scholarship.

The stories written by J and E are among the oldest stories in the Bible. We'll get to the other three authors shortly, but let's find out how we ended up with these J and E couplets.

The Division of Judah

How did it happen that there were two versions of the same stories? Why not three, or more? Remember that I mentioned earlier that there were at least six influences on what was written in the Bible? This is an example of how the influences of four—history, politics, economics, and religious differences—affected what was written in the Bible. For centuries the Hebrews* did not have a king. There were priests to handle the spiritual leadership and the twelve tribes were loosely associated, but otherwise autonomous. Each tribe had a titular head called a "judge," but there was no overall Hebrew leader. The twelve tribes banded together for defense when the need arose, but they neither wanted nor needed a king; they enjoyed their tribal autonomy. There was no single Hebrew country. They called the location of each tribe by its tribal name** as though each were a separate country. This all changed in 1020 B.C.E. The threat from the iron age Philistines forced the bronze age Israelites to unite and appoint a leader for protection. Saul became their first king. They called the united kingdom Judah, which was the name of Saul's tribe.

Saul was generally an ineffective king and a bit of a rogue, and was not appreciated by everyone. Many people were having second thoughts about this king business right out of the chute. Saul was followed by David who was a genuine rogue through and through. He could control neither his own basal urges nor his children. In spite of his exalted and

---

* The words *Hebrews, Israelites,* and *Jews* are used pretty much interchangeably in this book and elsewhere. The Romans were the first to use the term "Jews" because those people came from the land known to the Romans at that time as Judea.

** There were actually 13 tribes at the time of the entry into the promised land. The two sons of Joseph each got a tribe and the tribe of Levi became the servants of GOD working as priests and handling other priestly duties for all the tribes. They were provided for by the tithing of the others; so the Levites neither needed nor had a land of their own.

beloved position in religious history, he was a rather unsavory character who at one time even sold out to the Philistines and fought on their side against the Hebrews. He thought nothing of sending Bathsheba's husband, Uriah, off to the front lines to be killed just so that he could marry the widow.

David's was succeeded by his son from the Bathsheba union, Solomon. If Saul and David were bad, Solomon was the last straw. He squandered the kingdom's treasury by building palaces, luxurious stables for his one thousand horses, numerous government buildings, and hiring personnel and facilities to keep his 700 wives and 300 concubines happy. How Solomon gained his reputation for being wise is a mystery to me. He was a horrendous ruler. He was so bad that upon his death in about 950 B.C.E., ten of the twelve tribes of Israel were so fed up that they seceded from the kingdom. Most of the tribes were already living north of Jerusalem and they simply divorced themselves from the south. They formed their own country and called it "Israel." The part of Judah that remained for Solomon's son to rule was still called "Judah," but of the original 12, only the tribes of Judah and Benjamin, David's own tribe, remained. The two kingdoms are very often referred to in Biblical literature, and in this book, as the Northern Kingdom (Israel) and the Southern Kingdom (Judah).

Judah remained a kingdom under the rule of Solomon's son. Israel named a king of its own; in fact, a whole succession of kings. It seems they had an even a worse time selecting decent kings than the Southern Kingdom. Most of them were terrible rulers. However, it is worth noting that the sagas of the kings was written by the Southern Kingdom, and this might explain why the Southern kings were treated in history

WHAT ARE "SCRIPTURES

The words "Scriptures" and "Canon," usually written with the first letters in capitals, have pretty much the same meaning. The word "scripture" comes from the Latin word for writing, and "Scriptures" generally refer to writings considered authoritative by any religious group, such as the Hebrew Scriptures.

The word "Canon" is derived from an ancient Sumerian word meaning "reed," which is written in Greek as *Kanon*. As used by the ancient Greeks, it means a measure or a standard. By about the fourth century Canon came to signify those books considered to be the authority on Christian church belief and practice. The four gospels of Matthew, Mark, Luke, and John, for example, are often referred to as the "canonical gospels" or the "intra canonical gospels" to distinguish them from other gospels not included in the Bible.

more kindly than the Northern kings. The Northern kings were often dismissed with the phrase, "[They] were doing 'evil in the sight of the Lord.'"

Up to this point, there were no written Hebrew scriptures. The entire Hebrew history had been passed down to different generations by way of oral tradition, stories told and retold around the campfires.

According to the Bible, about the time of Saul, 1020 B.C.E. or so, the king's courts began keeping some form of written records of the activities of the kings and the temple priests kept a few records of their own travails with the kings. We'll learn about these records when we get to the chapter on the Historical Books. Then, sometime between 950 and 750 B.C.E., J began to commit the Hebrew's oral history in Judah to writing. Some suggest that J may have been a woman because he or she also was also the likely author of the "Song of Deborah" in the Book of Judges that tells the epic tale of a sort of Hebrew Xena, a woman warrior who was also a prophet and a judge. But man or woman, J was one of the most colorful writers in the Bible.

WHY CAN'T WE JUST BUY THE BOOKS BY J AND E?

Unfortunately the books written by J and E no longer exist. The only way to read these works today is to hunt them down line by line as they are now contained in the Bible, sprinkled around in the Books of Moses, and try to piece them together to sort of recreate the original books. Believe it or not, there are people who have done just that, and their recreations are very interesting to read. Unfortunately, we haven't a clue as to what was left out by the redactor when he assembled these writings into the Books of Moses. Scholars can usually tell when something was added, but whatever was omitted is lost forever.

Traditionally, the author has been referred to as masculine, so I will continue in that trend. His stories were "folksy" and poetic. J's contribution to the creation story, for example, is Genesis 2 where a pensive GOD strolls in his Garden and where he finds Adam and Eve hiding, ashamed of their nakedness. J's writings are very expressive and very visual. They are told the way a really good storyteller relates a tale around a campfire to grab his listeners' attention, and that is probably just what the author did before he began writing the stories down.

Sometime later, probably about 750 or 800 B.C.E., a priest in Israel began writing their version of the scriptures. This is "E". Remember, the only things either of the authors had to refer to was the oral tradition, so there were bound to be differences between the two versions. The years of separation of the Judah and Israel tribes allowed the oral versions to vary somewhat. The E portions are also much drier and more pedantic. Where J wrote in poetry, E wrote in very stilted prose. E also has a Deborah story in Judges. This is one of the couplets that I referred to earlier. Read the two versions one after the other, they are very short, and you will instantly know which version was written by J and which by E (One is in Chapter 4 of Judges and the other in Chapter 5). Don't just take my word for it. Give it a shot and become a Biblical scholar for a few minutes and decide who wrote which chapter.

Paleo-Hebrew Writing

Note how different this looks from the block-script Hebrew writing we see today.

A lot happened in the ancient world before we encounter the next author. Israel's neighbor to the east, Assyria, was expanding its empire at an alarming rate. It had named Israel, Syria, and Judah as its equivalent to the "axis of evil" and prepared to conquer them. Syria realized that their only hope for survival was for all three countries to join forces against Assyria or it would be able to pick them off one at a time. Syria made a believer out of Israel, who appeared to be first on Assyria's wish list, so Hoshea, Israel's king, asked the Southern Kingdom to join with Syria and Israel in resisting this threat. The king of Judah at the time, Ahaz, refused to do so after much soul searching. He asked the prophet, Isaiah, what he should do and Isaiah convinced Ahaz that if he allied with

Israel and Syria, all three countries would probably be captured*. The advice given by that prophet to King Ahaz became one of the most oft repeated prophecies in the entire Bible. Matthew picked it up and used it as a prophecy of his birth story of JESUS. We will come back to it in later chapters, but for now we are mainly interested in it because the prophecy served to convince the king of Judah to refuse military help to Israel which was promptly conquered by Assyria in 722 B.C.E.

Thirty thousand Israelites, basically the entire Hebrew population of the Northern Kingdom**, were then deported to central Asia where they were assimilated into other populations and completely disappeared from history. These are the infamous ten "Lost Tribes of Israel***.

The priests of Israel were not among those deported, however. They fled to Judah and they took their most precious possessions with them, their writings. They set up in small villages with other refugees and began their priesthood anew. They regularly performed their priestly duties as before, including the making of sacrifices at their own "high places," altars for worship. This caused constant friction with the established Judah priesthood. Sacrifices were how the Judean priests got their income because they got 10% of any animal sacrificed. More on this later. This boiled over during the time of our next author.

Hello, D

This leads us to our next author. He was the "Deuteronomist," known as "D." He worked between 700 and 600 B.C.E. As you would guess, he wrote large portions of the Book of Deuteronomy, but he also contributed to other works.

Under King Josiah, the Prophets, including Jeremiah, held unusual power. They were largely responsible for getting Josiah the kingship.

---

* Israel, with its fertile land, was much wealthier than the Southern Kingdom with its swamps and deserts, and was a much bigger prize for an invading army. The Bible suggests that Judah was the bigger prize, but remember, Judah wrote the story.

** Compare this figure of 30,000 with the story of the Exodus which claims six hundred thousand people fled Egypt.

*** The Mormon religion believes that these lost tribes migrated to North America and became the Native Americans. Recent DNA tests, however, have shown that the Native Americans were unrelated to the Israelites.

However, Josiah took over at a very bad time. All was not well in the kingdom. These were very troubled times and there was a serious threat to the country from the Babylonians who had grown very powerful. At the same time, the Hebrews had gotten very sloppy in adhering to GOD's laws. Josiah's predecessor had even practiced idol worship. That was just part of the huge list of forbidden practices commonly ignored by GOD's Chosen People at that time. Josiah was convinced that the country's problems were caused by the people straying so far from GOD's laws that the country was being punished. He began a program of reforms to get the country back in GOD's good graces.

One day in 621 B.C.E., as Josiah contemplated his reform program, a delegation of prophets, one of whom was Huldah, one of the rare women to become a prophet, and including the prophet Jeremiah, came to the king carrying a long "lost" book* that someone had mysteriously discovered. Josiah was under a lot of pressure because the Babylonians (also known as the Chaldeans at this time) were threatening invasion. His reforms had so far not been sufficient to convince GOD to back off on his punishment of Judah. Josiah held very strong religious beliefs and was certain that the impending danger was solely the result of something the people had done to anger GOD. The prophets then read to Josiah from this new book. Upon hearing it, Josiah let out a scream of anguish and "rend his clothing." (People rended a lot of clothing in those days. It was a customary, albeit expensive, way of expressing anguish).

What the prophets had "found" was the book that comprised much of what Christians now call Deuteronomy. In this book, Moses is heard giving a series of speeches that urges Israel to follow the Torah. There would be nothing unusual about the discovery that would justify ripping up one's clothing to shreds, but the laws that Moses presented in this new document varied from the laws he gave in previous books. For one thing, it says that sacrifices can only be done at the Great Temple. That shows some Judean priestly influence because it ended the practice of the old Northern Kingdom priests performing sacrifices in the outlying villages for their own benefit. All of the sacrifices, and all of the 10% portions reserved for the priesthood, were now firmly within the control of Judah's

---

* I think that it is fair to say that no modern scholar believes for a minute that the book was a long lost text that had suddenly been found. It was a contemporary text that appears to be influenced by both the prophets and the priesthood. Josiah bought into the prophets' the deception, though.

Priests.

Since Josiah felt strongly that the reason Judah was being threatened by the Babylonians was because Judah had drifted away from the meticulous adherence to GOD's laws, he immediately revised and accelerated his major reforms in the practice of their religion. He incorporated all of the new versions of the Law found in the newly discovered book. For the first time since the rise of the monarchy, for example, the people would properly celebrate Passover and give it the dignity that GOD demanded, a practice that continues to this date.

There is a discrepancy between this account, which is found in the Book of Kings, and a later account in Chronicles which states that Josiah began his reforms *before* the "Book of the Law" was found. This is typical of numerous contradictions between the versions of the history of Israel and Judah found in Kings and Samuel on the one hand and the Chronicles version of those stories on the other. We will discuss these differences when we get to the Historical Books. There are good reasons for the discrepancies.

THE NAMES OF THE BOOKS

The names of the first five books of the Christian Bible came from the second century C.E. Greek translation, the Septuagint, and they are different from the names in the Hebrew Bibles. The Greek names tend to be descriptions of the contents of the books, while the Jewish names are the opening words or the first significant words in the books and vice versa. For example, Genesis in the Christian Bible is derived from the Greek *kosmou* (Origin of the cosmos), while the name of the book in the Jewish Bible is *Bereshith* (in the beginning). The Christian Bible calls the fourth book, Numbers, referring to the census of the twelve tribes that opens the book while the Hebrew title, *Ba-Midbar*, means "In the Wilderness," which describes the subject matter of the book better as it begins with the Israelites' decision to leave Sinai and cross the desert toward the Promised Land.

But that was not all that D wrote. It is almost certain that he also wrote large portions of the major Historical Books of Joshua, Judges, Ruth, Samuel, and Kings. The scholar Richard Elliott Friedman makes a very compelling argument that the actual author of D is the prophet Jeremiah. Jeremiah was born in Judah about 627 B.C.E. and died in Egypt about 587 B.C.E. There are definite literary "signatures" in the history books that point to D as the author. Some of the same words and phrases used in the Historical Books of the Old Testament were used by the author in Deuteronomy. In fact, there are some actual signatures as well. The signature of Jeremiah's scribe, Baruch, appears in some of the other texts. Baruch was not only Jeremiah's scribe, he was also his very close companion and friend. Where Baruch's name appears, you can be sure that Jeremiah had something to do with it.

The Exile

Not long after the death of Josiah, another tragedy occurred in Judah. As Josiah had feared, the Babylonians under Nebuchadnezzar II, captured Jerusalem in 597 B.C.E. and exiled Judah's king and a large portion of its population. All of Josiah's tough reforms were for naught. Then, ten years later, in 587 B.C.E., the Babylonians destroyed the Great Temple of Solomon. Jeremiah, along with others, ended up in Egypt and was never heard from again. There is no consensus as to whether he was exiled or taken away as a prisoner or whether he died or was executed. He had developed an enormous number of enemies and he no longer had Josiah to protect him. It is hard to believe that he suddenly became contrite when he arrived in Egypt, so execution is definitely a strong possibility. Even some of the Judean kings tried to have him killed before Josiah took a liking to him.

While they were in exile, the priests and other leaders tried to discover the reason they had lost their country. What had they done to displease GOD so much? They were, after all, his chosen people.

In order to grasp what happens next, you need to understand the basic truth that the Hebrew religion did not just suddenly appear one day, complete in all respects the way we know it today. Americans seem to have the impression that the Bible was written like the U.S. Constitution—a group got together and hammered out a Bible all at once. There was some aspect of that much later in history, in the fourth century C.E., but not at this time. The Jewish scriptures were slowly evolving over the centuries. For example, the books of the prophets had to have been written at different times because the prophets lives were often hundreds of years apart. Each prophet advanced new ideas and they were all, purportedly, speaking as a conduit between GOD and the Hebrew people, as GOD no longer spoke directly to the Israelites. The Hebrew religion evolved over the centuries as new ideas from the prophets and others were adopted, and the scriptures reflected this evolution.

Judaism did not even start out with a single god. Monotheism was a later adaptation. Remember those passages in the Creation story that we discussed earlier—Adam "is one of Us" with "Us" referring to other gods that were around in those days. Further, the word that was spoken and written in lieu of Yahweh, *Elohim*, Gods, is the plural form of *El* which means "God." They were including other gods when they used the term. Some of the early gods were borrowed from neighboring cultures such as the goddess Asherah. This only makes sense when you think about it. There were many gods in the Middle East. How was a person to decide which was the real god(s) or the best god(s). They tried many of them and settled on the best. If they adopted more than one early on it could be either because they could not determine which was the true god or they were hedging their bets until they found out. As you read the Old Testament you will see the progression of YHWH from the placid god who walks in the Garden of Eden, poetically enjoying its beauty, to the thunderous god of Moses who strikes people dead and orders the destruction of thousands of people including "women, children, and sucklings," and then on to the god who changed from speaking directly to the people from burning bushes and the like to one who used the prophets as a go-between, and so on. GOD was evolving and so were the methods of worshiping GOD.The Hebrew religion was very different before Moses than it was after. Moses, according to tradition, brought down from the mountain the Laws that changed much of the Hebrew culture and way of life. The Hebrew religion became a religion of laws, an entirely new concept in the world. New laws were added from time to time and others were modified. Starting about 500 B.C.E. the pharisees began studying the scriptures and little by little began to replace the priests as the teachers of the laws. After the fall of the Temple in 70 C.E., the pharisees, or teachers (*rabbis*), completely supplanted the priests. Moses would not even recognize the Jewish religion as it evolved about the time of JESUS. Judaism had become as different from the religion of Moses as Christianity was from JESUS' own Jewish origins at that time.

We will see that the Christian religion had a similar history. The entire religion changed from the days of JESUS' early teachings. In fact, we will see that it often seems like the authors of the various New Testament books are each talking about an entirely different JESUS. There were even disagreements between JESUS' apostles as to what the new religion of Christianity was to be.

Just examine your own experiences. How often do you sacrifice a goat to GOD? Neither the Christian religion nor the Jewish religion still requires the regular sacrifice of small animals. Christians say that this is because JESUS' sacrifice on the cross satisfied the need for "burned sacrifices" and "sin sacrifices" for all time. The Jews, however, hold no such beliefs. Burned sacrifices just faded out of style. That is an example of a gradual change that occurred over time. Under the old Jewish laws, if a man felt that his wife had cheated on him, he could drag her before the priests where she was fed poison. This apparently caused either a miscarriage, a sterilization, death, or all three. I am sure that there are some today who would be angry enough to think that this is a pretty good idea, but mercifully, that is no longer a part of either Judaism or

EARLY MONOTHEISM

What other gods did the early Israelites worship? The Bible is pretty quiet about other gods, but there are several female gods named; the principal being the goddess Asherah who was worshiped in both Israel and Judah as the Queen of Heaven. She was the consort of Yahweh and called God-the-Mother. Her sacred pillars or poles once stood right beside Yahweh's altar. Moses and Aaron both carried one of these Asherah "poles," called Asherim after the goddess, as a sacred staff of power (Ex 34:13). The ancient Israelites were said to be healed simply by gazing at the staff with serpents coiled around it. This symbol, the snakes and the staff later became associated with the Greek god Asclepius, the god of healing, and it has become the modern universal symbol for doctors known as the "caduceus."

YHWH was merely the highest and greatest god of the Hebrew pantheon at that time. The worship of Asherah was among the practices that Josiah tried to eliminate. Jeremiah vehemently opposed this worship:

> *Jewish women traditionally made small cakes to celebrate the festival of Asherah. "Do you not see what they are doing in the towns of Judah and in the streets of Jerusalem? The children gather wood, the fathers kindle fire, and the women knead dough, to make cakes for the Queen of Heaven, and they pour out drink offerings to other gods, to provoke me to anger."*

And later,

> *[The women] make offerings to the Queen of Heaven and pour out libations to her, just as we and our ancestors, our kings and our officials, used to do in the towns of Judah and in the streets of Jerusalem. . . .*

Since these two references are from Jeremiah, it should not come as a surprise that most of the forty references to Asherah in the Hebrew Bible come from sources believed to have been edited by D. Other Hebrew "goddesses" include Anath, Astarte, and Ashima. In the second reference above, Jeremiah says that the people are celebrating the festival as we "used to do." The worship of multiple gods had gone out of style for some time, but in Jeremiah's time the practice had been recently restored because of the doom and gloom from the threat of conquest by neighbors. The people were willing to try anything to prevent the conquest. King Josiah destroyed the "high places" which were altars for the worship of these other gods and any people caught worshiping there were killed.

The Babylonian religion of Mithraism was monotheistic. During the exile, the Hebrews were exposed to that concept and it meshed perfectly with Judaism. All thought of other gods vanished when the Jews returned to Jerusalem.

Christianity. I can't help but wonder how many innocent women met their death in this manner over the centuries. Now you can communicate directly with GOD through prayer without going through the priesthood. The religions all changed with the times and are still changing. If this concept is more than you can buy, that is OK. But just play along with me for awhile anyway.

Back to our story. At the time of the Exile, in the sixth century B.C.E., the idea of individual sin and individual punishment for that sin was a concept that had not yet developed. Sins were always tribal sins and the punishment meted out by GOD was always a tribal punishment. If you did something that displeased GOD, the entire tribe suffered. It was not until the book of Job that we begin to see this change.

At the time of the Exile, the Hebrews felt that the tribe must have done something very serious to displease GOD enough that he would allow his chosen people to be captured. King Josiah had been worried about the same thing when he instituted the strict adherence of the Law according to the newly discovered book of Deuteronomy. He had hoped that by scrupulously adhering to these new rules it would prevent conquest and subjugation by the Babylonian king, Hammurabi. It didn't, so the priests in exile continued the search for clues as to what it was that they had done to so enrage GOD. It is here that we meet our fourth author.

Meet P

Another thing that the priests did while they were in exile in Babylon was to transcribe more of their oral history to writing. There was a huge body of what is now contained in the Hebrew Scriptures that had never been written down. Most of that great body of Jewish writings that are now found in the Old Testament, were first written during the fifty or so years of the exile in Babylon. In addition, the priests and scribes combined, organized, and edited those scriptures that had previously been committed to writing. Unfortunately, those original texts were discarded and the Babylonian copies and new transcriptions no longer exist. We have no way of knowing what they left out or modified. The oldest documents we have today were even later copies of the Hebrew Scriptures made between about 200 to 100 B.C.E. in an entirely different alphabet. Those earlier copies in the old alphabet were also discarded.

This brings us to the fourth Old Testament author, P, the "Priestly" author. His wrote his works between 550 and 500 B.C.E. They are some of the stories most familiar to Christians. P wrote, for example, the

Creation story in Genesis 1 and the first version of the Ten Commandments found in Exodus 20:1-17. P was very concerned about the duties of the priesthood and with the details of the elaborate observances that he felt had fallen into neglect. He wrote nearly all of Leviticus.

The works of P are pedantic and dry. Compare P's words in Genesis 1 with the magnificent poetry of J's Genesis 2, for example*. There is just no way that the same person could have written both versions. The works of P are marked by an obsession with detail. He spends pages justifying the ritual laws of the ancients such as the Passover ritual, ordination ceremonies, the vestments of the high priest (yawn), and the minute details of the construction of the sacred chest that held the Ten Commandments. He is, if truth be told, bor-r-ring.

But just as the works of J and E no longer appear as separate works, with the exception of Leviticus, neither do the works of P. All of the writings of these authors are now found intermixed in other books, a snippet here, a snippet there. Parts of P, as noted, are now the very first words of the Bible, even though they were written much later than the chapters that follow. Since P was a priest, he made sure some of the new rules directly benefitted the priesthood. For example, P codified the concept of tithing, a subject that was near and dear to the hearts of the priesthood. Tithing was now law, no longer merely a custom that could be ignored.

Every Good Book Needs a Good Editor

That brings us to the last author of the ancient works of the Pentateuch. He is called R, the "Redactor." R was perhaps the most important and certainly the most creative author of the Old Testament. He put it all together. Just as any modern book requires a good editor, so did the ancient works. R was the editor of the first five books of the Old Testament. He was the redactor who took the works of the previous four authors, along with all of the previously written works dating from the first Hebrew writings, and wove them into the books we now enjoy as the Pentateuch or Torah.

Sometimes R set out the works of two authors side by side as in Genesis 1 and 2 or the two stories of Deborah, similar to what those who later assembled the New Testament did with the four Gospels—several versions of the same story set out side by side. At other times he wove the

---

* Not all the couplets in the Pentateuch were by J and E. P wrote many of the couplet halves, and Genesis 1 is an example

versions together to form a unified story. The story of Noah's Ark is a good example of the second method. If you read the story of Noah with this in mind, you will see that at times Noah is taking a male and female of each animal onto the ark. In other passages he is taking seven pairs. Still in other places he is taking two of each except for the "clean" animals of which he takes seven. Finally, they all are described walking onto the ark, seven pairs marching on board two by two. The work is so seamlessly done that few people ever notice the discrepancies. In those instances where the stories are melded together, it is very difficult to separate out where J or E ends and P begins. While many of you can become experts at picking out the authors where the stories are set out side by side with what you know right now, it takes a real expert to sort out those portions that are melded together, often within the same sentence.

Who was R? There are some very persuasive arguments that R was none other than the prophet Ezra whom we shall meet later; he has his own book in the Bible. Ezra was one of those whom the Persian king Darius sent back to Jerusalem after the Exile in order to try to put the country back together again, and by all counts Ezra was a brilliant theologian, although a horrendous governor.

The discovery of both the authorship and dating of the Pentateuch launched a Biblical treasure hunt. Entire books have been written about the search for the authors, and they are fascinating reading. It is like reading a mystery novel where you find clue after clue hidden in the text. Here, the words themselves give hints. Then an archaeological excavation in the Middle East fills in a missing piece of the puzzle. A fragment of papyrus is discovered in Egypt that fills in another blank. Historians got into the picture and noted that historical references in various parts of the Bible often correspond to known secular events, and that those portions can not only be accurately dated, but those secular events could determine where portions of the Bible were written. They found parallel versions of some of the Bible stories in other Middle Eastern writings. The scholars pieced all of these clues together until they revealed the identity of the authors. Then the findings and conclusions were published so that other scholars had the opportunity to criticize the ideas or to build on them until there became a consensus. It is that consensus that I have tried to incorporate into this book. This process is known as "critical thinking."

Multiple authorship was a scandalous matter when it was first proposed in the late 19th century, but it is universally accepted by Biblical scholars today. It is a standard part of the curriculum in some secular universities in history classes and other studies. Surprisingly, a review of religious university catalogs indicates that it is a subject that is rarely taught in religious institutions except at the graduate level. There are minor parts of this subject that have never been resolved and a few that are still disputed, but for the most part this has been accepted Biblical history for three quarters of a century.

From the initial suggestion that the couplets represented variations on the same story by two different authors, scholars developed a new way of looking at the Old Testament. After that the mysteries started to fall one after the other in a very short time. One of the most readable of all the books on this subject is *Who Wrote the Bible* by the scholar Richard Elliott Friedman Ph.D. It discusses the authorship of the first 12 books of the Bible and I highly recommend it. After reading the book you will be able to pick up the Bible and read a few passages and say, "Hey. This was written by E!" You will be able to read a verse in Exodus and know which part of the verse was originally part of the writings of P and which were written by J or E before R melded them together.

It is enormous fun to read these old stories in this new light. The study is far beyond the scope of this book, and I do not want to reveal much more of it. It would be like turning to the last page of an Agatha Christie novel and learning "whodunit" before you read the book. It is an exciting journey, and what one finds at each step along the way should come as an original discovery to each reader.

Let me summarize by saying that the "Books of Moses" were not written by Moses. They were written centuries later, and in some cases, more than a millennium later, and they were written by more than one author. The Exodus most likely took place during the reign of Ramses II, known as Ramses The Great, whom most scholars believe was Pharaoh in the Exodus story. That dates the Exodus at about 1240 B.C.E. which was during the reign of Ramses who ruled Egypt from 1279 B.C.E to 1213 B.C.E The Israelites probably crossed the Jordan River about 1200 B.C.E. Parts of the Torah are legends from an ancient oral history of the Hebrews, some of which were committed to writing hundreds of years later; but even more was written in relatively recent times during and after the Exile in the sixth century B.C.E.

The Exile was a momentous time in Jewish history. The Temple had been razed, so they no longer had a focal point for their religion. Remember, some of the laws even stated that the only place one could legally sacrifice animals was at the Temple. The people now had to meet together in small assemblies. The Greek word for "assembly" is *synagogue*. Much later it took on the meaning of the place of assembly, but at the time it was just a meeting. It became the center of prayer, the study of the Torah, and teaching, and also became, centuries later, a place where JESUS' apostles spread the word of "The Way," as his message was called at that time.

Living in a foreign country, the Hebrews rightly feared that their culture would be absorbed into the Babylonians and that, like the lost tribes of Israel, they would cease to be an identifiable culture. To prevent this from happening, the exiles passed many new laws and revitalized other laws that had fallen into disuse to distinguish themselves from all others—they even adopted the shocking, unheard of tradition of taking a day off work every week (the Sabbath). This really got the attention of their captors. They revived the practice of circumcision that had fallen into disuse and adopted dietary laws and other purity rituals. There were prohibitions against Gentiles being invited into the house of an Israelite and prohibitions against marrying out of the faith, and much more to assure that the Hebrew culture remained intact. They were hugely successful and managed to maintain their separate identity and culture while all of the other conquered peoples were assimilated into indigenous populations. They were Hebrews when they became captives and they were Hebrews when they returned to Jerusalem. The only change was that they began speaking Aramaic and Hebrew became a dead language used only by the priesthood.

One of the most important ideas to come from this period is the concept of monotheism. While Yahweh was always the strongest and most important of all gods, the Hebrews came to believe during their exile in Babylon, that he was the only god. This was a rather unique concept in the western world, but in Babylon at this time Mithraism was a popular religion and it was monotheistic, the first in the Middle East. This concept fit in perfectly with the Hebrew ideas of GOD. The Hebrews abandoned all of their lesser gods and demi-gods, although some sneaked back into popularity for a short time later.

This also appears to be the time that the concepts of personal as well as national sin and redemption first began to take root. This concept fills the documents that began to show up after the return from exile and appears in Hebrew poetry and songs as well. Before, GOD not only rewarded his favored people for doing good; he also penalized the entire tribe for the sins of a single member. If GOD was happy, the entire tribe benefitted. GOD was the source of all things, both good and bad. Within two or three centuries, the concept developed that individual sin and individual virtue would reap individual penalty or benefit. The concept began to form that maybe something else besides GOD might be responsible for the bad things. They began toying with the idea that perhaps it was not their benevolent GOD who was bringing bad times to the Hebrews but some malevolent force. This was the beginning of the concept of the Evil One which we know as Satan.

Another major development in that period was the belief by many that GOD was going to send a messiah—a new leader or savior—to restore the Israelites to their previous greatness. Most visualized the new Messiah in the pattern of King David who would again lead the Jews to greatness. The idea of a messiah faded somewhat after the return to Jerusalem, and went in and out of style until the Roman occupation.

Finally, the Exile was the period during which the Hebrew Bible pretty much took its final shape. The Torah was tweaked into final form by "R." The books of The Prophets from Joshua through Kings were finished, although they would not become Hebrew Canon for many years. Most of the Hebrew Scriptures were complete now except for much of the books the Hebrews call The Writings.

3

Understanding the Old Testament

There are no copies of the Hebrew Bible older than the [the Dead Sea Scrolls], now dated to the second century B.C.E. *We cannot change these facts; only new discoveries can alter them. We cannot change the fact that all copies of the Bible were made by hand prior to the invention of the printing press in 1454 or thereabouts and consequently contain mistakes and inaccuracies.*

Robert W. Funk

Before we get into the Old Testament scriptures themselves, let's take a moment to discuss the composition of the Old Testament in general? The Old Testament is comprised solely of ancient Hebrew Scriptures, also known as the Jewish Bible. What do we really know about it? When was it written? Where did it come from? Who decided what ancient Hebrew documents out of hundreds would be part of this text and when was that decided?

These are all fascinating subjects, but let's start with the first question, "when was it written?". The oldest datable sources in the Bible are the books, or at least parts of them, bearing the names of the prophets Hosea, Amos (pronounced Ä´-mōs, not like Famous Amos), and Micah. These were actual, historical people who lived in ancient times and some scholars suggested that those books were written at the time these prophets were living. in the mid to late eighth century B.C.E. It is now pretty well established that, indeed, at least portions of those texts were written at or about the time those people lived. Some of the stories from Genesis were written in this same period, very likely by some of the same authors. Many scholars feel that Genesis 4, written by J, may be the very oldest work, but there are other books that could also qualify as being the oldest including the Song of Deborah.

Genesis, Exodus, and Leviticus, as we know them today, were either written or revised sometime slightly before 400 B.C.E. However, it is generally agreed that they were not written in one sitting. Each was written over many years. They were taken, in part, from old texts dating from about 750 B.C.E. and from other texts written about 550 B.C.E. There are parts of the Old Testament, including portions of Amos and Micah, that probably date back even before the prophets, perhaps as far as 900 or 950 B.C.E., and a few passages, some of the Psalms, for example, may date all the way back to the time of the Exodus. These writings were not taken from books or other writings, but from the Israelite oral tradition. Remember, the Hebrews did not even have an alphabet until about 1050 B.C.E.

The books of Samuel and Kings refer to documents that appear to be court records of the various kings and to some temple records (Eg. 1 Kings 14:19, 14:29). While these do not appear to be narrations that ended up in the Bible, they were probably used as reference materials for names, dates, and events. They are among the earliest Hebrew writings that we know of today and they were written primarily in the late eleventh century, during the reign of King Saul, and into the tenth century as they chronicled some of the kings of Judah and Israel.

In any event, many of the greatest Biblical personalities lived without the benefit of any scriptures at all—Moses, Abraham, Lot, David, Solomon, etc. There is not a single reference to any of these personalities in any surviving written work, either religious or secular, outside of the Bible. The Hebrews were reputedly led out of slavery from Egypt by Moses in about 1240 B.C.E. That is dated by Biblical references to Pharaoh which is generally agreed to be a reference to Ramses II, known as "Ramses the Great." That means that there were over 500 years where the "Books of Moses" were purely an oral history, stories told generation after generation around the tribal campfire. Abraham lived, according to Hebrew tradition, between 1812 B.C.E. to 1637 B.C.E., and according to Christian tradition, from 2000 B.C.E. to 1825 B.C.E., several hundred years before even the most rudimentary Jewish alphabet appeared and 1000 years before any portion of Genesis was even written. That means that there were at least 1000 years in which the stories of Abraham, Lot, and the other patriarchs lived solely as an oral history.

The Oral Tradition

When I was in the Boy Scouts, there was a common game that we played at the nightly campfire assembly, when we had a group of, say, thirty or more scouts. Someone would whisper a couple of sentences in the ear of the scout closest to the front who would then whisper what he heard to the next boy, and each succeeding scout would whisper what he heard to the next. At the end of the campfire, the last person to hear the message was to tell what he heard. The message that was whispered to the last person was never even remotely recognizable as the original phrase whispered to the first scout, and it was always a great laugh when the original message was disclosed. Most people have played this parlor game, sometimes called "telephone" or "gossip," at least one time in their lives and can attest to similar results.

That being said, how can we expect 500 years of story telling around ancient campfires, passed down for over 200 generations, to even remotely resemble the original? What about 1000 years? That is what we are asked to believe of the first 3 books of the Old Testament. Obviously, the ancient Hebrews were going to be more careful about keeping the oral tradition of their religion accurate than a bunch of kids around a campfire passing on a story. In fact, scholars who have studied the oral traditions of modern primitive societies have found that the story tellers, usually priests of some kind, commit all of the stories to memory and then try to pass them down accurately to the next generation. But to expect that somewhere during that 500 years from the time of Moses or 1000 years from the time of Abraham, that there were not some serious deviations from the original version requires true faith indeed. Good story tellers always embellish their stories for entertainment value and to keep their audience interested..I personally believe these ancient Bible stories are likely nothing more than tribal legends passed down over the centuries around the campfire. But not everyone agrees.

Science and the Bible

The religious beliefs of the ancients were also influenced by the degree of their scientific and technological knowledge. It was well into the renaissance before people began to understand the cosmos. The first hint was not until after the death of Copernicus in 1543, when he allowed the publication of his dangerous theory that the earth traveled around the sun instead of the other way around. During the entire time that the books of both the Old and New Testaments were being written, the knowledge of cosmology was that the earth was basically flat like a table top with lumps, was surrounded by water, and that it had a huge, blue dome over the top of it that was held up by the four corners of the earth which acted like table legs. This dome was called the "firmament." Genesis tells us that GOD divided the waters with some of the waters above the dome and some below.

The sun, the moon, and all of the stars were located in the firmament. GOD and his court lived above this dome, and many believed that the stars were openings made in the dome to allow GOD to look down and keep watch on his flock during the nighttime. The dome could easily be breached. When GOD or the angels desired to come down to earth, the Bible describes them simply opening a "seam" in the firmament to gain entry to the earthly atmosphere. During the Great Flood, the Bible describes seams being opened in the firmament so that water above could come pouring down. There was also water under the earth. That is what allowed wells to be dug, according to the ancients, and during the Great Flood seams in the earth as well as the sky were opened to allow the waters to flow and contribute to the big flood.

The ancients had no knowledge whatsoever of the nuclear and chemical composition of matter, let alone any concept of the laws that govern the action of these atoms. The theories of relativity and quantum mechanics were not discovered until the 20th century. It has been empirically proven that Einstein's proposition that nothing can travel faster than the speed of light is correct. That means that for someone coming down to earth from beyond the stars to visit with Abraham about 3900 years ago, as the story in Genesis tells us that GOD and two angels did, it would be millions of years before they got down to earth to visit, even if they were able to break their bodies down to the molecular level so that they could travel at speeds approaching that of light.

Looking at it in a different way, if JESUS departed his tomb 2100 years ago to abide with his Father above the stars he would not even have cleared our own milky way, millions of light years away from the Heaven that was envisioned by the ancients. With modern cosmology and mathematical models of the universe, we know that Heaven is not just above a blue dome. In fact, there is no blue dome. The size of outer space is so immense that it is incomprehensible.

Scientists are not villains out to destroy religion. They are just looking for the truth. Scientific facts exist. They are not invented. The geological record was not invented by some scientist out to prove the Bible wrong. It was formed by nature. This does not mean that there is no Heaven, just that the ancients' concept of its location is incorrect.

There are some cases where science does directly conflict with Bible stories, but until quite recently it was dangerous for a scientist to advance such "heretical" ideas. One good example of science conflicting with the Bible is the story of Joshua stopping the sun and moon in the sky so that the Hebrews would have more light in which to continue their slaughter of the Amorites (Josh 10:12,13). When Galileo suggested that Copernicus was correct and that the earth travels around the sun, not the other way around, the Church was outraged because that meant that Joshua could not stop the sun and the moon from traveling in the sky. We know today that, in order to have given the appearance of stopping the sun in the sky, Joshua would, instead, have to stop the earth from rotating on its axis, a concept that was unknown at the time. The Church treated this blasphemy the same way they treated anything else that dared to conflict with the Bible—they burned Galileo's books and imprisoned him.

When an eleventh century scholar pointed out that a list of the kings discussed in the "The Books of Moses" could not have been written by Moses because those kings had not lived until long after Moses death, he was branded "Isaac the Blunderer" and the Church burned his books and silenced him. In this great tradition of burning books, the Church also arrested a French priest who had questioned something in the Bible, burned his books, and threw him in prison until he recanted. In 1688, an English translator, Tynsdall, while translating the Bible from Hebrew to English, had the audacity to suggest that Moses may not have written the Torah. Tynsdall also recanted that ludicrous suggestion when, after considerable soul-searching, he determined that he must have been wrong. As one writer noted, that decision coincidentally came at about the same time that Tynsdall was released from the Tower of London.

When some branches of Christianity later adopted the position that everything in the Bible is true and correct, they spoke a little hastily. Now, after insisting on this position for so long, they are in so deep that it is tough for some of them to pull back from that position. Their position has been to attack all of science and to ridicule and denigrate it, especially anything proposed by Darwin. Darwin's theory on the origin of species is not only contrary to the creation story in the first two chapters of Genesis, it holds that all animals, including humans, descended and adapted from other species. If Darwin was correct, then the basic premise that man was created in the image of GOD, cannot be correct.

There are many Bible stories that simply cannot be explained away as anything more than ancient tribal stories or legends. There is no rational way to conclude that they are based in actual fact. The story of Noah's Ark is a perfect example. It just could not have happened. Even the ancients had trouble with it. It is really interesting to read Jewish midrash[*] to see how the ancient Hebrews viewed this story of Noah. Much of it was a mystery even to them. As late as the first century B.C.E., the rabbis had trouble figuring out how all that water got off the earth in such a short period of time. One of these brilliant men suggested that what happened was that the winds came up and blew the water off the edge of the earth. Laughable today, this was a perfectly plausible explanation given the known cosmology of the time.

But back to the ark. The story of the ark made perfect sense in the first century. Their knowledge of the universe was almost as primitive as it was in the 8th century B.C.E. when the story was first written down or in the 5th century when it was rewritten in the form that we know it today. But it makes little sense when examined in the light of 21st century knowledge.

HOW BIG WAS IT?

Noah's boat was to be enormous by the standards of that day. In fact, it was to be enormous by the standards of any day, because it was *over twice as large as the largest wooden ship ever built* in the history of the world. Wooden ships just could not be built over about 180 feet in length because wood, and especially wood connections, could not be made strong enough.

In 1837, England's greatest engineer, Isambard Brunel, built a wooden leviathan 236 feet long, and the way he made it work was to design the entire ship as a series of trusses like a bridge.

It was by far the largest wooden ship ever built, and even with the best of 19th century engineering it was beset with problems from the day it was launched and was never very successful, especially as a passenger ship. It's sole claim to fame was laying the first transatlantic cable.

Historically, an ark[**] was a covered, flat-bottomed boat or barge used to carry cargo on the rivers of the Middle East. In Genesis we are told that a simple man with no

---

[*] The beginning of the Rabbinical period of Jewish history began about 500 B.C.E. The Rabbis eventually supplanted the priests as the dominant leaders of the Jewish religion. The Rabbis were intellectuals and, among other things, started evaluating the Scriptures in terms of their application to the current times. Those writings are called "midrash." They are fascinating works to read.

[*] "Ark," the English word for Noah's vessel, is actually and Old English word for box. That is exactly what this was, a box that floated. The ancient ark's that floated on the Tigris and Euphrates were much like a square box.

special training or engineering skills built a wooden boat 450 to 500 feet** long, 75 to 80 feet wide, and 45 to 50 feet high, and that this ship not only floated, it withstood the greatest storm in the history of the world. In his book entitled *Innumeracy: Mathematical Illiteracy and its Consequences,* John Allen Paulos, made a simple calculation and determined that to cover the mountains to a depth of 23 feet with water as we are told GOD did, in a 40 day rainstorm, the storm would have had to average 5 *feet* of rain *per hour.* That would swamp the largest aircraft carrier in the world, let alone this floating barge. We are lucky if we get 5 inches of rain a year in Southern California, and some of those storms are "frog stranglers." And where did the water come from? Rain is merely water that has evaporated from the oceans. The story adds new water on top of the oceans to a depth of thousands of feet. And, of course, the next logical question is, where did it go afterward?

As big as the ark was, however, it could not begin to hold all the animals of the world plus their food. And speaking of food, GOD told Noah to lay in stores of food, but, for most of the animals, their food was . . . well, each other. What did they plan to feed the lions, alfalfa? They were in the ark over a year, and that is a lot of hay. I remember as a child on my grandparents' farm, we had to store hay in the barn just to get a few head of cattle through the month or two that snow covered the pasture. That hay took the whole upper half of the barn, stacked to the rafters just for that short period of time. Some herbivores, such as elephants and hippos, consume hundreds of pounds of plant matter every day.

What did they do about the waste? Who got down in the hold with a shovel? And what about ventilation. The KJV tells us that they built a window one cubit square, and this was apparently all the ventilation that they had! An opening 18 or 20 inches square.

How did the animals get there? Who traveled to North America and picked up bison, cougars, beavers, moose, and all the other animals peculiar to our continent? Back then they did not even know that other continents existed. And how did they get all of those animals across the ocean? Did they build another ark just for that? And when they finally landed one year and 10 days after the rains started, who took the animals back to where they came from? What did they eat when they did land?

** The measure we best know is from the KJV which gives the ark's size in "cubits." A "cubit" is the distance between your elbow and your wrist which is approximately 18" to 20" long. I converted cubits to feet.

There were no crops. After the flood GOD told Noah that he could eat the animals, but there were only 2 of each (or 14 of each depending on which version of the flood you believe), and they would not last very long. They did not have refrigeration, so if they slaughtered a cow, they had to eat all of the meat in a couple of days and throw the rest out.

The tale continues with each of Noah's sons inheriting a portion of the world to rule (with Ham getting Canaan). Who were they supposed to rule? How could they start a new population? Everyone else drowned. The only humans left in the entire world were supposedly Noah, his wife, and his sons.

After the ark landed, Noah and his family spread out and each of Noah's three sons got a portion of the land to rule. However the hapless son Ham walked in on his father when he was sleeping and accidentally saw him naked. For this offense, his father cursed Ham and condemned him *and all his descendants* to be slaves forever. And you thought that "three-strikes" was tough. They didn't fool around in those days.

Unfortunately, a writer of Jewish midrash in the second century B.C.E. interpreted this curse by Noah to mean that all black people (sons of Ham) were ordained by GOD to be slaves and to serve white men. This was a widely circulated text in the middle ages and the early renaissance. The European work force had been decimated by the plague and Europeans used this writing as an excuse to impress Africans into slavery. It was, after all, GOD's will and GOD specifically authorized slavery. Later, Americans used the same document in the U.S. to justify the enslavement of African Americans in the South. Occasionally, even today, African Americans are referred to as "sons of Ham."

What did the Old Testament Look Like?

What did the Jewish scriptures look like? I mean physically. The Old Testament scriptures were not books as we know them today. They were scrolls written on parchment, or leather, and occasionally even scratched in soft copper, and then they were rolled up around a stick of wood. Later some were written on papyrus. These were all rather unwieldy. For example, a scroll of the text of Isaiah that was recently found in a cave near the Dead Sea unrolled to a length of 20 feet. Leather is very heavy, so you can imagine how much that scroll weighs. The entire Old Testament would fill the back of a pickup truck and would look like a load of wallpaper. These books were incredibly heavy and awkward to carry around. But that did not matter much as very few people could read, and those who could were rarely able to afford them, so the demand for "portable" books was low and the concept of circulating libraries was far in the future.

Most of the Old Testament books were originally written in Ancient Hebrew using the old Phoenician alphabet. But this was not Hebrew like we know it today. They badly needed Vanna White so that they could buy some vowels because *Ancient Hebrew had no vowels.* One or two of the very latest Old Testament books were written, at least in part, in Aramaic, an ancient Semitic language originally spoken in the country of Aram in what is now Syria. All of the rest were written in Hebrew.

During the Seleucid period* when the Greeks occupied the Middle East, Greek became the most common language in the Middle East among the aristocracy, especially as to written languages. Following the Seleucid occupation, very few people could even read or understand Hebrew. Even earlier, after the return from their exile in Babylon, the Priests were about the only people among the Hebrews who could still speak that language, let alone read it. So during the Greek rule of the Middle East, legend has it that Ptolemy II, one of the Greek Pharaohs, ordered a Greek translation of the Jewish Scriptures.

Ptolemy purportedly impressed seven translators from each of the twelve tribes of Israel who finished writing the translation in seven months. Therefore, they called the translation the *Septuagint*, the Greek word for "seventy." None of these figures add up to "70, but that is the legend anyway. What is more, ten of the twelve tribes had disappeared by that time, the "lost tribes of Israel," but the person who commissioned the translation, who in all probability was not even Ptolemy, did use numerous translators and the works were translated in an amazingly short period of time. Unfortunately, all of the translators did not possess the same skill and abilities, so some parts of the translation are far more accurate than others. Further, all of the original documents had disappeared long ago. The translators were working from copies of copies that contained many mistakes. In fact, the Hebrew documents that the translators copied were not even in the same alphabet in which the original documents were written, and all were discarded after the new copies were made. . .

---

* Upon the death of Alexander the Great, his empire was divided among his generals. Seleusis became the ruler of the Middle East, founding the Seleucid Dynasty, and Ptolemy became the ruler of Egypt, founding the Ptolemaic Dynasty. Eventually the two factions warred over Palestine and the Seleucids won and ruled the entire area for centuries.

There were other translation problems as well since there was no established Jewish consensus on which versions of the various books were the most authentic. Those less accurate translations and books that were later replaced were to cause a lot of confusion when the Septuagint was used as the basis for yet other translations into other languages, including English. In other words, imperfect copies in Hebrew were translated into Greek by less than stellar translators, and then translated into other languages rather than going back and translating the original Hebrew. Those translators added their own mistakes to the Septuagint mistakes. This caused an additional problem because Greek is very different in structure from Hebrew, and Greek, in turn, is very different in structure from other languages, including English. We will discuss this problem in some detail a little later.

Who Decided What Books Were to be Scripture?

Another three centuries passed before the Jews settled on the books that both Jewish and most Christian leaders sanctioned as scripture*. These selections were widely contested, especially among the Jewish scholars. At the time of the fall of the Temple in 70 C.E., Jewish authority recognized 22 texts as legitimate Jewish scripture. The Christians were adopting many more, including some from the Septuagint, for inclusion in the Bible, and the Jewish scholars protested that the additional books were on very weak authority. In fact some of those, including The Wisdom of Solomon, the three books on the Maccabees, Ecclestiasticus (not to be confused with Ecclesiastes which was, and is, an official Jewish text), and several others are not even included in the Jewish Bible.

These books started out as part of the Christian Bible but were later discarded in Protestant translations. They are now referred to as the "Apocrypha" which means, "hidden." Some of these books remain in the Catholic version of the Bible (the Douay-Rheims translation) and in the translations of other Christian groups.

Other books had troubles as well. The Song of Solomon, also called the Song of Songs or the Canticle of Canticles, which has been described by some twentieth century writers as nothing more than pornography, was, as you may imagine, highly debated, but not because of its content;

---

* Note that at this point we are only talking about which *books*, not which *versions* of those books, were to be sanctioned as scriptural. That is yet another problem which we will discuss later.

the ancient Hebrews did not consider it to be the slightest bit salacious. Many, however, did not consider it to be real scripture because, along with the Book of Esther, GOD is not mentioned anyplace in the book and it does not deal with the Law, prophecy, or religion. Nor does it mention either the Temple or Jerusalem. Ecclesiastes with its dark, brooding feelings about the futility of chasing wealth and wisdom and the inevitability of death, and its deep cynicism led some rabbis to try to suppress the book. But it's great popularity and the mistaken belief that it was written by Solomon saved it.

Who Were the Masoretes?

All of the current versions of the Old Testament in the Christian Bible come from a group of Hebrew scholars called the Masoretes. *Masorah* is the Hebrew word for "tradition." There were so many different versions of the Jewish scriptures floating around that in the second century C.E., the Jewish leaders decided to select from this group an "official" version of the Hebrew Scriptures and preserve them forever. They formed the committee of scholars, which they called Masoretes, to do this. The Masoretes selected one version of each book they considered most likely to be the closest to the original and have preserved them to this day as the official Hebrew Scriptures. All of our modern American Bibles contain the Masoritic version of the Old Testament. The oldest complete copy of the Hebrew Scriptures in existence today is the *Leningrad Manuscript* which was copied in about 1009 C.E. It is Masoritic.

However, there are a number of older translations of portions of the Jewish Scriptures, many in Greek, going back as far as the 3rd century B.C.E. These older texts differ, not only from each other, but from the Masoritic texts as well. The question is, why were there different versions of the same books? One reason was simply because every copy was hand-written, and over hundreds of years and hundreds of drafts there were copying mistakes. Perhaps others were merely earlier versions that were modified as the Hebrew religion evolved. Others may have been intentionally rewritten to conform to the beliefs of a particular sect such as the Samaritans, the Pharisees, or the Essene. Some of the texts are associated with each of these sects and others. The Dead Sea Scrolls, for example, were found in Qumron which was an Essene settlement.

Nobody knows for sure how the variations between the texts occurred. What is certain, however, is that none of the texts the Masoretes certified as the "official" Hebrew Scriptures were anywhere near as old as the Dead Sea Scrolls. These scrolls are still being evaluated and studied, so the "official" versions of the Hebrew Scriptures could change in the future.

Translation Problems

Have you ever noticed that when people ride in an elevator that they always look up, with their eyes focused on an area about where the ceiling joins the front wall above the door? In the 1940's a young man noticed that people riding the busses in Brooklyn did the same thing. He decided that someone could make a lot of money if they sold miniature billboards to fit in those areas near the bus roofs. So he started the business and became enormously wealthy. His name was Walter O'Malley, and he eventually bought the Brooklyn Dodgers and moved them to Los Angeles.

When I was growing up in the 50's, I used to read those advertisements when I rode the bus. One of the ads that was popular for a very long time was an advertisement for a correspondence school that taught speedwriting, a kind of shorthand using ordinary cursive letters, but the words did not have vowels. The sign that everyone memorized over the years said, "F u cn rd ths u cn gt a gd jb." Of course, nearly everyone could translate it into the sentence, "If you can read this you can get a good job."

What has this got to do with the Bible? Hang in with me for awhile and I will tell you. There were many, many errors in translation of the Hebrew texts. Part of this problem was because, just like the bus ad for speedwriting, ancient Hebrew *did not have any vowels.* This made it very difficult to read. The Masoretes later added vowel sounds to the old texts. They considered it almost sacrilegious to invent new letters and change the original Hebrew text, so they added little marks below the letters, called vowel points, instead of changing the existing spelling., Often they guessed wrong when deciding which vowels to use. Consider their difficulty. What if English did not have any vowels? The quote in the bus ad is easy because it was designed so that most riders could easily understand it. But translations without the benefit of vowels are tricky.

In English, the word "LT", for example, could be translated as let, lit, lite, lot, late, lute, elate, or elite, just to mention a few. " RT" could be at least 8 different words, "PT" at least 7, and "PN" could be at least 9, including pan, pen, pin, pun, pane, pine, piny, pony, puny, and open. Is there any wonder that the translations were often wrong and often disagreed with each other? Deciding which vowels to use was often little more than guess work and usually depended upon the translator's ability to determine the context in which they were being used. In the tenth century, after over 100 years of study, the Masoretes issued a version of the Hebrew Scriptures with vowel points. It was far from a unanimous decision, however. As many as 25% of the words in the Hebrew Scriptures are still in dispute solely because of the vowel problem.

There were further errors when that ancient Hebrew was translated into ancient Greek and even more when the Greek translation was further translated into Latin and then into English. The classic example of mistranslation was the old Greek Septuagint (mis)translation of Isaiah in which the Hebrew word *almah*, which means "a young woman," was

Sample Text in Hebrew Without Vowels

c. 200 B.C.E. - c. 800 C.E.

כל בני האדם נולדו בני חורין ושווים בערכם ובזכויותיהם. כולם חוננו בתבונה ובמצפון, לפיכך חובה עליהם לנהוג איש ברעהו ברוח של אחוה.

English Translation:
llhmnbngsrbrnfrandqlndgntndrghtsthrndwdwthrsnndcnscncndshldcttwrdsn nthrnsprtfbrthrhd.

Sample Text in Hebrew with Vowel Points

c. 500 c.e., but used today only in prayer books

כֹּל בְּנֵי הָאָדָם נוֹלְדוּ בְּנֵי חוֹרִין וְשָׁוִים בְּעֶרְכָּם וּבִזְכֻיּוֹתֵיהֶם. כֻּלָּם חוֹנְנוּ בַּתְּבוּנָה וּבְמַצְפּוּן, לְפִיכָךְ חוֹבָה עֲלֵיהֶם לִנְהוֹג אִישׁ בְּרֵעֵהוּ בְּרוּחַ שֶׁל אַחֲוָה.

English Translation:
"All human beings are born free and equal in dignity and rights. They are endowed with reason and conscience and should act towards one another in a spirit of brotherhood."
(Article 1 of the Universal Declaration of Human Rights)

Note the differences between the two translations of the same sentences. The original version not only did not have any vowels, it did not have any punctuation, not even spaces at the end of words or periods at the end of sentences as this copy has. It is almost impossible to comprehend the difficulties the translators had, and still have, trying to decide what words were written in the original documents.

translated incorrectly into Greek as "virgin." The Hebrew word for virgin is *betulah*. The translator was confused because, in slang usage at the time of the Septuagint translation, the word "Almah" was occasionally used as a euphemism for "virgin." However, Almah was never used to refer to virgin in the Bible. Three hundred years later, Matthew based his entire story of JESUS' virgin birth on that incorrect translation. Nearly all of the modern Bible translations correctly change the errant text in both Isaiah and Matthew to "young woman." Isaiah never once mentioned the word "virgin." But the myth of the virgin birth will forever be part of church dogma and nobody seems to be highly offended that the correct terms are used in modern Bibles.

It was important in the first century that JESUS be born to a virgin because most of the major competing religions in the Middle East at the time had gods who were born to virgins. Think back to your grade school studies of the Roman and Greek mythology if you want just a few examples. The biggest competitor to Christianity at the time was Mithraicism, a Persian religion which had an equivalent story to that of JESUS for their savior, Zoroaster (his Greek name, but many know him better by his Persian name, Zarathustra, from the theme music in the movie "2001, a Space Odyssey"). The virgin birth issue is of negligible importance to most twenty-first century Christians, however.

A good example of problems with translation is found in the book of the Prophet Nahum. Here are five versions of a single line from Nahum 2:10 that one scholar unearthed:

The faces of them all gather blackness. (KJV)
The faces of them all are as the blackness of a kettle. (Douay-Rheims)
All faces grow pale. (NRSV)
Every face grows pale. (NIV)
All faces turn ashen. (Jewish Publication Society).

Which translation is correct? There is a site on the internet that has the text of 20 or so Bible translations (http://bible.christianity.com/). If you enter a chapter and verse from the Bible in the search window, they will ask you what translation you want. Sometimes, just for amusement, I select a verse from the Bible and compare six or eight translations. It is amazing how much variation there is between the various Bibles. The question is, which one is the inerrant version?

What about punctuation?

The early Scriptures were also missing punctuation of any kind. They did not even have spaces between words; just a string of letters that continued onto the next line when they ran out of space. When the Hebrews began writing in their new alphabet about 200 B.C.E., they began to write a few letters a little differently (called "sofit" letters) when they came at the end of the word. Later, the Masoretes began leaving a space between words. Western writing took a little longer to put spaces between words, not showing up until the ninth century C.E. when Roman masons began to put a dot or a diamond between words. This first showed up etched in stone on the victory columns that emperors erected to tell all of Rome about their great military victories.

In the early days of the third century B.C.E., Aristophanes, the librarian of the Alexandria Library, invented the terms "comma," "colon," and "period," but the marks that he used bore no relationship or resemblance to the marks that we use today. It took many centuries for this new idea to catch on. In the 11th century C.E. the hyphen as we know it today was invented to show a word that was continued onto the next line, but the word breaks did not coincide with syllables. They were just inserted when the writer ran out of space.

One of the earliest forms of "true" punctuation was introduced by the Greeks. They separated groups of text with a horizontal line called a "paragraphos." These groups of text, separated by the lines, became known as "paragraphs." It was hundreds of years later before the first line of a new paragraph was indented or double spaced. Just before indenting was invented they tried using a punctuation device that is shaped like a small hangman's gibbet like we drew as kids when playing a game of "hangman." This evolved into the ¶ symbol used today.

Moving on to medieval times, the scribes often used daggers (†), double daggers (‡), and similar marks to indicate citations, similar to our footnotes.

Even with these innovations, punctuation was used sporadically, if at all. When used, it was mainly for people who had to read the words aloud or who had to make speeches or, very often, for actors. They needed the marks to tell the reader when to pause or to give emphasis. That is really how punctuation first caught on. Personally, I have always had a problem using the comma. There just does not seem to be a rational rule that governs its use in all cases. But I remember my English teachers telling me to think about how a sentence would be spoken when trying to decide where a comma should be used. "If you feel that a little pause is appropriate, insert a comma." Not very scientific, but it works much of the time. Today commas seem to be losing favor and many of the rules in vogue just a few years ago are being discarded.

It required the invention of printing to demand that forms of punctuation become standardized. Aldus Manutius the Elder (1450 - 1515 C.E.) and his grandson, also called Aldus Manutius,but not surprisingly known as "the Younger," invented the first structural rules for the use of punctuation. It was not until the end of the 18th century C.E. that punctuation became pretty much standardized, although, like the rest of the English language, it still changes from time to time and many of the punctuation rules in the U.K. are not the same as we use in the U.S.

With that background, let's get back to the Bible. When punctuation was first inserted into the Bible, the scribes literally had to mentally "say" the sentence to see what punctuation should be used. The problem was, did the scribe mentally "say" the words in the ancient Hebrew, Greek, or Latin in which they were written, the "source text," or did he say the words in the language into which he was translating, known as the "target or receptor language?" A more significant problem was that by inserting punctuation into the text incorrectly, it often changed the entire meaning of the text. Face it, the translators were not ancient Hebrews. They were not even ancient Greeks. Many were not even native Hebrew or Greek speakers.

You are probably sitting there thinking, "Come on, now, what difference does it really make where the commas and periods are placed?" Well, it can make a huge difference in the meaning of any particular passage. A popular example arose during the feminist movement:

A woman without her man is nothing.

Or, properly punctuated:

A woman: without her, man is nothing.

Oops! Punctuation can make a difference after all. There is no question that the two sentences above, although identical except for the punctuation, have diametrically opposite meanings. Jesus' words are in quotes. What if there is a mistake in quotation marks?

That student complained, "the teacher is lazy."

Or, maybe they quotation marks should be like this:

"That student," complained the teacher, "is lazy."

Quite a difference, isn't it? In case you think that the Bible does not contain passages just like that, here are actual passages from the Bible that scholars have been struggling with. The following is the way it appears in the KJV translation of Isaiah 40:1:

Comfort ye my people.

(Basically GOD is asking someone to comfort his people)

Compared with the following punctuation preferred by scholars:

Comfort ye, my people.

(Here GOD is asking the people to cheer up).

Once again, quoting the modern NRSV:

Comfort, O comfort my people, says your GOD.

Depending upon how the sentences are punctuated, the meaning changes. Let's skip a verse and jump to Isaiah 40:3 for an other example, first in the KJV:

The voice of him that crieth in the wilderness:
Prepare ye the way of the Lord.

(The man crying is in the wilderness)

Today, scholars pretty much agree that the proper punctuation is:

The voice of him that crieth: In the wilderness
prepare ye the way of the Lord.

(The voice is directing people to prepare the way of GOD in the wilderness).

The NRSV translation that I prefer prints it like this:

A voice cries out:
"In the wilderness prepare the way
of the Lord."

Do you see the differences in meaning between the passages? These are just passages where scholars recognize that there is a likelihood that the punctuation is incorrect. Punctuation can make a huge difference, as you can see. Modern translators have tried to clean up these problems through historical research, but some of them undoubtedly remain, sending messages contrary to the intentions of the original author. Nobody knows what they are, so we blissfully assume that all of the punctuation is correct. Incidentally, if the passages you just read in Isaiah 40:1-3 sound familiar, you are probably right. They made such an impression on the English Baroque composer, George Frederic Handel, that he included it in the famous "Handel's Messiah" that we hear every year around Christmas. Next time you hear it you may well be the only person in the theater that recognizes that the oratorio quotes the "crying in the wilderness" phrase incorrectly.

Editing Problems

The differences in the Bibles are not all the result of translation problems. Some are simply changes that people made to the Bible intentionally. For example, consider what, to me, is one of the most beautiful and poignant passages in the Bible: that portion of the Sermon on the Mount about the Lilies of the Field (Matt 6:18). Let me quote the familiar King James Version to show you what I mean.

Consider the lilies of the field, how they grow;
they toil not, neither do they spin.
And yet I say unto you, that even Solomon in all his glory
was not arrayed like one of these.

I can picture JESUS sitting in a field of wild flowers, holding one of them up, and delivering that message to his followers. What a graphic picture he presents! What a powerful statement he makes in so few words! What a beautiful message: even the most inconsequential of GOD's creations, this simple wildflower, has more beauty than man can create with all of his power and riches.

But beautiful as they are, Matthew may not have written those words. They appear in the book of Matthew in all of the surviving Greek texts from which this passage was translated, but they do not correctly translate the original. The two oldest Bibles in existence, which date from the fourth century, are the Codex Vaticanus which is the property of the Vatican and the Codex Siniaiticus. In 1938, the British Museum made the purchase of a lifetime. It bought the Codex Siniaiticus from Russia. Josef Stalin was more than happy to make a tidy profit off what he considered to be trash.

The scholar T. C. Skeat was examining the text of that ancient work under an ultra-violet light when he noticed something remarkable. He discovered that the opening clause of the "Lilies" verse had been erased from the manuscript and replaced with the version of the verse I quoted above. The original version said, "Consider the lilies of the field: they neither card nor spin." The rest was the same. Matthew said nothing about "growing" or "toiling." The verse just does not flow in the original version. (As an aside, the word that was translated as "lilies" actually referred to a flower called *Sternbergia.* It is not a lily at all).

Which version, if either, was written by Matthew? Which version, if either, was actually spoken by JESUS? What we know for sure is that the Codex Siniaiticus was changed at some time after it was written to conform to the surviving Greek texts. The experts may be able to work backward through surviving texts and figure it out. So the text was changed. So what? The edited version really is much better than the part that was erased. Both are consistent with JESUS message; it is something he certainly could have said. The author of Matthew never met JESUS, so even if this was written by Matthew, it is no guarantee that it accurately quotes JESUS.

But it doesn't matter. What is important is that it is a faithful recollection of what His followers believed that he said or that he would have said. Is it any less valid because it might not be his precise words? I think not. It is the recollection of JESUS' message by those very early Christians who lived within one or two generations of JESUS. This was an important part of his philosophy and made such an impression on this listeners that they wrote it down for posterity.

Let me give you another example. At John 8:1-11 someone added another story to the original text. This is the story of JESUS' defense of the adulterous woman who was about to be stoned for her sins. He states the oft quoted lines, "Let anyone among you who is without sin be the first to throw a stone at her." And, "Neither do I condemn you: go your way, and from now on do not sin again."

This entire episode is missing from the Codex Vaticanus and the Codex Siniaticus that I mentioned above. It is not reflected in any early writing, although the general subject matter was often discussed in those writings. Scholars agree that the style of this insertion is different from the rest of John and it interrupts the flow of the text where it is inserted. The first reference to the discrepancy was noted by (St.) Jerome about 400 C.E. when he questioned its credentials. It is now known to be a late second or third century addition to the Gospel.

But once again, what if it is not JESUS' exact words? There is certainly no more Christian message in all of scripture. He very likely said something like that and it so impressed those who heard it that it was remembered and later included in one of the Gospels.

Another example of later editing is the "Secret Gospel of Mark" which we discuss in Chapter 14.

All of this brings us to the question, which of the above versions of the words of the Bible that I have quoted would be the "inerrant . . . word of the living GOD . . . without error in all matters . . . ?" that Mr. Falwell referred to in the epigram at the beginning of Chapter 1?

4

Bible Translations

Bible translation . . . is distinguished . . . [due to] the reverence in which adherents of Judaism and Christianity hold the text, leading to concerns whenever a new translation is published that the text be treated with the respect it deserves; . . .

Editors of The New Oxford Annotated Bible

JESUS only knew the Hebrew Scriptures which Christians call the Old Testament. It was originally written in Hebrew, although a couple of the later books were written, in part, in Aramaic. The Hebrew Scriptures were also translated into Greek in the Septuigint. We will also discover the little-known fact that, after the Hebrew's return from exile in Babylon in the mid sixth century B.C.E., the reading of the Bible in Hebrew for the general public was accompanied by an oral translation into Aramaic because *the Hebrew people no longer spoke Hebrew.* Those Aramaic translations, called *Targums*, were handed down through the generations *only orally*. So, at the time of Jesus, since the peasants to whom Jesus' spoke could not read, Targums were all that they had in the way of translations of the ancient Jewish Scriptures. It is ironic that the Hebrews had no written scriptures until about the ninth century B.C.E., but by the sixth century, with the exception of the priesthood, nobody could understand them unless they were translated.

By the time of JESUS, the peasants had only the oral targums for their knowledge of the Hebrew Scriptures and those of the learned classes had only the Greek translation, the Septuagint. Most early Christian writings were also written in Greek, although it would be centuries before there became an official Christian canon.

The early Christians began to remedy this lack of scriptures. By the beginning of the second century C.E., Christians were making Latin translations of the most popular Christian writings, particularly in North Africa where Latin was by far the most common language. There was no New Testament yet, but the letters of Paul and other Apostles, which were being collected by some of the churches, plus the four Gospels and the Acts of the Apostles were very popular and were the subject of many of the early church meetings. Excerpts were often read and then discussed in detail, much as modern Bible study classes do today. These were the first books known to be translated into Latin out of hundreds that were written. Some early Christians also translated some of the Septuagint into Latin, but the church in Rome continued to use Greek.

Translation Methods

There are basically two approaches to a translation. The first is called *formal equivalence* and it can be described as a "word-for-word" translation. The second approach is the *dynamic equivalence* approach where the translator is more concerned with the substance and final readability of the translation than the actual words.

It would seem at first blush that the formal equivalence would be by far the best method to translate something such as the Bible, especially for religious fundamentalists. However, this method of translation only works where the "source" text and the "receptor" language, the language in which it is to be translated, are similar. It would work well, for example, if one were translating Hebrew to Arabic because the two languages are structurally closely related. The ancient languages of the Bible, however—Ancient Greek, Hebrew, Aramaic, and even Latin—are all very different in structure from modern English. For example, here is a word-for-word translation of Matthew 6:9 -10 from Greek to English:

Father of us who in the Heavens, be holy
the name of you;
come the kingdom of you;
become the will of you as in Heaven and upon earth.

You can probably recognize this as the first few lines of the Lord's Prayer. While it might be possible to "noodle out" the meaning even if you did not know what it said beforehand, other than the words themselves, it is not English, and it is unlikely that anyone would bother to read it. Therefore, most Bible translations to English, which are for the general public, use the dynamic equivalence method. That is one reason they vary so much from each other. You can still find formal equivalence translations, however, which are geared to those who need a text for scholarly study.

Therefore, every translation is also, by necessity, an "interpretation." Sometimes it is even a pure guess. There are words in both the ancient Hebrew and the ancient Greek texts that occur only once in the Bible and cannot be found in any other surviving ancient text, either religious or secular. Therefore, the exact meanings of these words are unknown.

Something as serious as the Bible would never use slang, you say. Not so. Sometimes the translators try to "clean up" the language a little by the use of euphemisms where the words might be deemed inappropriate for the times. Here is an example of how a translator used a euphemism or slang expression that was clearly understood at the time but which has a completely different meaning today; in 1 Sam 24:3, Saul is chasing David and his enemy the Philistines and when he came to a cave he went in:

> "*Saul went in to cover his feet.*" (KJV).

You are probably wondering why in the world Saul would take time out of his search for the Philistines to cover his feet. Didn't he have shoes? This is how the verse reads in modern translations:

> "*Saul went in to relieve himself.*" (NRSV).

The ancient writers were not above using slang terms and euphemisms and this greatly compounded the translator's job.

Sometimes, older translations do not make sense to us today and are intentionally changed to more understandable language such as this statement a couple of verses later in 1 Sam 24:5:

> "*David's heart smote him, because he had cut off Saul's skirt.*" (KJV)
> "*David was conscience-stricken for having cut off a corner of his robe.*" (NIV).

We don't do a lot of "smoting" today and men do not usually wear skirts. The phrase means more to us today with the changes. (Note—cutting off the hem is symbolic of emasculation or usurpation of Sauls's kingdom which is why David was conscience-stricken).

The Vulgate Translation

At about 387 C.E., the Church leaders began to reach a consensus on what religious writings would ultimately be deemed Christian Canon. Although there was disagreement among the bishops, it was finally decided which books from the Jewish Scriptures would become the Old Testament and which of the numerous new writings about JESUS would become the official New Testament Canon. A few years previously, Pope Damasus hired the leading Latin-speaking Christian scholar, Jerome, as his secretary. Many churches had Latin translations of what was rapidly becoming official Canon, and they were all very different and universally lousy translations. The Pope asked Jerome to take the best of those translations and, with the Septuagint, make a new Latin translation to be the official Bible. While the eastern churches still spoke Greek in their services, the western churches, headed by Rome, spoke Latin and needed its own text.

Jerome was, by all accounts, a strange person. He was, basically, a hermit, although that may not have been entirely by choice; he had a rather acerbic personality and was hard to get along with. Nonetheless, he was a tireless scholar. He was fluent in both Greek and Latin, so he dove into the New Testament works. Instead of simply cleaning up the existing Latin translations and choosing the best of each, Jerome started from scratch. He decided to do a brand new translation from the original languages. The New Testament documents were all written in Greek. and, being fluent in Greek, he knocked them out pretty quickly. Unfortunately, as we will see later, he chose some lousy Greek copies to translate, and his translation is now considered to be unreliable.

When he moved on to Psalms he was stumped; he couldn't read Hebrew. All he could do would be to translate the Greek Septuagint into Latin just like all of the other translators before him, and he would probably end up with the same bad results. Everyone knew that the Septuagint was badly flawed even in the fourth century.

What does a dedicated scholar like Jerome do in a situation like this? He decided to translate the Old Testament from the original Hebrew. He checked into a Jewish monastery in Jerusalem and studied Hebrew with the Jewish scholars. By about 391 he deemed himself sufficiently fluent that he began translating the Old Testament from Hebrew and 15 years later he finished the entire Bible, a 24 year long task. That translation is called the Vulgate, which means "common language" and is derived from the word "vulgar" which, like many words, had a different meaning then than it does now. At that time "vulgar" meant common or ordinary*.

Like anything connected with the Bible, when the Vulgate was first introduced it met with a lot of resistance. Everyone liked the translations that they were already using. But it eventually became the dominant translation in the western churches for 1,100 years. In fact, the Gutenberg Bible that awed me so at the Huntington Library was a German translation of the Vulgate Bible.

The years of the Byzantine Empire, beginning roughly 500 C.E. was a rough period in European history. The capitol of what was left of the

---

*This illustrates another problem for translators. Just as the meaning of "vulgar" changed over the centuries, so did the meaning of many of the words in the Bible change from when they were first written. Trying to determine the intended meaning for ordinary words was often very difficult.

old Roman empire was Constantinople, and Rome was a dilapidated shadow of its former glory. The empire was severely divided between the Roman and the Greek factions. The Christian religion was equally divided at the time into the Greek Church and the Latin Church. The Latin branch was headed by the bishop of Rome, who by that time held the title of Pope, and the Greek branch was headed by the Patriarch of Constantinople. The two branches maintained separate armies. There was serious competition between the two branches of the religion, even though they were both part of the empire. When wars were fought with tribes outside of the Byzantine Empire, the terms of the treaties ending those wars usually required the vanquished states to convert to Christianity. Then they had to swear allegiance to either the Latin or the Greek version of Christianity, depending upon which of the Byzantine forces had conquered them. There were major differences between the two versions, some of which remain to this day.

This meant that missionaries had to be sent to these new countries to teach the populace about the new religion they agreed to embrace. Unfortunately, many of these people, such as the Bulgars, the Franks, and the Armenians, to name just a few, spoke neither Latin nor Greek, so the missionaries often made translations into the native languages of at least parts of the Bible for these new converts.

In some cases, the missionaries had even more daunting tasks. When the Greek faction conquered Moravia, the Patriarch sent a priest named Cyril to convert the Moravians. Cyril found that they had no written language at all, so before he could make a Moravian translation of the Bible he first had to invent a written Moravian language. The language that Cyril developed was named, naturally, Cyrillic, and was based upon the Greek alphabet with which he was so familiar*. Cyrillic is the written language of Russia to this day. In the fourth century, another missionary, Ulfilas, did the same thing for the Visigoths. The result was the first Gothic Bible and a new written language for the Goths.

Some of the earliest translations of the books that later became part of the New Testament were also translated into Coptic, a language and writing that was derived from Egyptian hieroglyphics. Some of the Coptic documents we have today are the oldest surviving copies of these books and are as old as the Septuagint. Other very early translations were in the

---

* Since each letter is only a symbol for a sound, the same alphabet can be used for almost any language. The letters you are now reading also work, for example, in French, Italian, German, just to name a few.

language of Syriac which is a dialect of Aramaic. Some of these show the four Canonic Gospels, Matthew, Mark, Luke, and John, woven together into a single work, sort of like "R," did with the two versions of Noah's ark.

There were also translations in the west into Spanish, Swedish, Norwegian, Polish, Italian, Icelandic Dutch, Hungarian, French, Armenian, Arabian, and Ethiopian. All of these were written by hand. By the time of the first printed Bible in 1456, there were already translations into at least 33 different languages. These were for the use of Priests teaching the local populace, not for the people themselves. The official language of the church was Latin which was a dead language, written and spoken only by the Church. The Church wanted to keep it that way so the people would have to get their religious information from the priesthood.

In 1534, Martin Luther outraged the Church by releasing the first translation of the Bible from the original Greek and Hebrew into a modern, western language, High German. This sparked interest in other countries for translations into the language of the local populace. This was a very dangerous venture. The church had a nasty and predictable habit of imprisoning, excommunicating, and even executing anyone who proposed to issue a translation that could be read by the general public. Often the charge was heresy which required death by burning. After all, if the laity could read GOD'S word, why would they need the Church? The priests feared they would all be out of work.

English Translations

In the 14th Century, about 200 years before the KJV, a scholar from Oxford by the name of John Wycliffe entertained the heretical thought that the English people should have their own Bible. He knew that he was going to be in huge trouble, but he plowed ahead anyway, and finished the first English language translation of the complete Bible in 1380. He did not do it alone. He enlisted the help of a couple of fellow scholars who actually did most of the work. The translation was in Middle English, which is almost impossible for people in our century to comprehend (see the sidebar on page 17). This was not a translation from the original Hebrew and Greek—he translated Jerome's Vulgate from Latin to English—a translation of a translation. Many copies of Wycliff's Bible were made, apparently, because over 150 of them, all written by hand, remain to this day. But Wycliffe died shortly thereafter and his helpers were imprisoned for violating the church's ban on translations. Many of Wycliffe's followers, called Lollards, were burned at the stake for heresy.

Since Wycliffe was already dead, they could not execute him, so they did the next best thing. They first excommunicated him and then they dug up his body, burned it, and gave him an ignominious burial. Nice guys!

That definitely put a chill on efforts to translate the Bible. The next translation attempt was not until about 1526, some 200 years later and about 70 years after the invention of the printing press. A highly educated (Cambridge and Oxford) and dedicated cleric by the name of William Tyndalle found that it was difficult to teach his parishioners because they could neither read nor understand Latin. He decided to buck the Church and try a new English translation, and he started a fire storm. The Church drove him from England and he ended up in Germany where he became an associate of Martin Luther at Wittenberg. He was highly influenced by Luther and, in 1525, Tyndale printed his own translation of the New Testament. But his association with Luther left him prey to Luther's enemies who wasted no time coming after him. He managed to ship all of his books and notes to England by hiding them in the boxes of legitimate trade items. When they were distributed, the authorities confiscated and burned all that they could find and sometimes even executed the book sellers.

Undeterred, he kept working on his translations and began work on the Old Testament. He finished the Pentateuch, but in 1535 the authorities found him, threw him in prison for a year, and then strangled him and burned his body for his heresy.

Shortly after Tyndale's death, the King finally relented and allowed Biblical translations. Several translations followed in short order. The first complete Bible to be printed in English was the Coverdale Bible in 1535. It was usually referred to as "The Great Bible," and Henry VIII ordered that a copy of that translation be placed in every church.

In 1553, Henry's oldest daughter, Mary Queen of Scots, became the queen and she was a staunch Catholic. One of the first things she did was order the removal of the Coverdale Bibles from the churches. Her goal was to drive the Protestants out of the country and return to Catholicism. Many did flee and some religious scholars settled in Geneva where they produced their own translation in 1650. It was, not surprisingly, called the Geneva Bible. It immediately became very popular because of its compact size. Another feature that led to its popularity is that it was the first English Bible to incorporate numbered verses. But as popular as it was, it was never approved by the Church of England, even after Elizabeth became queen. But it remained popular and was the Bible that Cromwell carried to battle with him against Bonnie Prince Charlie. It had a very important role in the United States too, because it was the Bible that the Puritans brought to Massachusetts with them in 1620. It soon became the Bible of choice in New England. In all, there were 140 different editions of the Geneva Bible.

Just as Mary chased the protestant scholars out of the country, when Elizabeth deposed Mary and became the Queen of England, Elizabeth forced Catholic scholars to flee across the channel. Many settled in Flanders in a little town called Douay and established an English college there. They began a new English translation of the Vulgate, publishing the New Testament in 1582 and the Old Testament in 1609. The purpose of this translation was to strengthen Catholic doctrine from the heretical Protestant interpretations. The Douay-Rheims Bible, as it is called, has been the predominant Catholic Bible ever since, even though it not only contains the same defects as the Vulgate in has new defects of its own creation..

Elizabeth ordered that the Bible again be placed in every church in England, so the Anglican bishops produced a new translation, known as the Bishop's Bible, a revision of a former translation that was known as the English Bible.

Finally, the King James Version was commissioned in 1611 (some place the date at 1604). Without any doubt, this has been the predominant English translation for the last 400 years. It was the work of 54 university scholars appointed by King James. They were organized into six committees of nine men (no women). Two committees worked at Cambridge, two at Oxford, and two at Westminster. There were no Roman Catholics included. They were all either Anglican Catholics or Puritans.

That a disparate group like this could ever arrive at any kind of agreement is difficult to conceive today. It is even more absurd to imagine that it could occur in the seventeenth century. Somehow it did, but not without major conflicts in the process. It has been reported that some passages were reworked 17 times before they could arrive at a consensus. A version of the KJV, called the Robert Aitken's Bible, was the first *English* Bible printed in America. It was not, however, the first *Bible* printed in America. That honor falls to a Puritan minister who sought to convert the Indians to Christianity. He laboriously learned the Massachusetts language, a language that is now extinct, and translated the New Testament into that language. It was printed in 1663, and there are copies still in existence today, but there is, sadly, nobody left who can read it. We did a pretty good job destroying native American culture.

New Discoveries Required Revisions

Discoveries of ancient Hebrew and Greek manuscripts over the years since the Kings James translation, and even more recent archaeological discoveries, including the Dead Sea Scrolls, revealed serious defects and deficiencies in the old translations. In 1901 there was an American Standard Version of the KJV, and in 1952, the Revised Standard Edition was issued. It was the result of a large group of scholars and was considered accurate by all three of the major denominations, the Roman Catholic, the Protestant, and the Eastern Orthodox churches. Since this was a very British translation, in 1963 a group of American scholars released the New American Standard Bible. This was, as you might suspect, a revision of the American Standard Version.

Is this getting a little complicated? I'll stop here, but there are translations of portions of the Bible into more than 1,900 languages. There are complete Bible translations in 315 languages. There are New Testament translations in 715 languages and translations of at least one book of the Bible in 891 languages. The most widely translated book is Mark which has some 800 translations. The latest translation is a work in progress in the Lakota language of the Nation of Sioux Americans. The first part of the Bible that was translated into that language was the 23rd Psalms, and the translator is now working on the New Testament. There is also a translation in progress into American Sign Language for the deaf. It will be in video format.

There are some unusual problems translating the Bible. For example, it was reported that in a translation to the Eskimo Tlingit language, the phrase, "The Lord is my shepherd . . ." caused major confusion. "You mean that God is a goatherd?" they asked, appalled.

5

The Torah or Pentateuch

And God said, "Let us make man in our image, after our likeness; and let them have dominion over the fish of the sea, and over the fowl of the air, and over the cattle, and over all the earth, and over every creeping thing that creepeth upon the earth

Gen. 1:26

With this background, let's look at the first five books of the Bible, called the *Pentateuch.* in Greek and *Torah* in Hebrew. Some of the stories in the Torah will make a whole lot better sense now that you have a background of Old Testament history. If you spend all your energy worrying about something not being absolutely and literally true and historical, you will miss the beauty of the Bible. Instead of hearing the messages contained in the words, you will be caught up in the words themselves.

Most theologians feel that many, if not all, of the stories in the Bible are "didactic" in nature which means that they are intended to be morally instructive as opposed to being true depictions. I try to avoid words like didactic because I find them stuffy and pretentious. I use that word here, however, because you will run into it many times if you decide to read other books about the Bible and also because there is no other word to describe the history stories in the Bible. In essence, this means that a story is important for the message that the author intended the audience to retain, not the truth or accuracy of the story. They may in fact be accurate statements of what happened, but that is not what was important to the authors. These are stories designed to teach important religious concepts.

The epigraph above from the King James translation has GOD stating, let *us* make man in *our* image . . . ." This implies that there are not only other gods, but that all of the gods looked like man. This could be a very troubling discovery, as it was to me in my youth, but knowing the background of these ancient books and the religion upon which they were based, it makes perfect sense. These words were written hundreds of years after the fact and were based purely upon an oral record. They are basically ancient tribal legends reduced to writing that were part of a large body of stories whose purposes were to tell GOD's stories and inform people of GOD's laws. So let's get started on our whirlwind tour of the Bible.

The original draft of this book covered all of the books and stories in the Bible and the sheer volume of the material became unmanageable. It was over twice as long as this version. Many of the stories had to be included here, however, because they are so important in the historical analysis of both the Bible and the religions that rely on its messages. This is especially true in the New Testament works where we trace the origin and development of a new religion.

Genesis

Most people know that Genesis is the book where you will find the creation story, and that *genesis* is Greek for "Origin" (in the genealogical sense). The Hebrew name for the book is *Bereishith* which means, "In the beginning. . . ." the first words of the book. Many people do not know that it is also the source of many of our favorite Bible personalities and stories. This is where we find the patriarchs Abraham, Lot, and Noah, the Great Flood, the Tower of Babel, Jacob's Ladder, Joseph and his Coat of Many Colors, and many, many more of those great tales that kept us captivated as children.

From the very beginning, GOD had trouble with his human creation and later with his chosen people, the Hebrews. I am sure that there must have been many times when He simply threw his arms into the air in exasperation and cried, "What have I done!" Right out of the chute, beginning with Adam and Eve, humans disobeyed GOD, questioned Him, worshiped other gods behind His back, and, in general, made GOD's life pretty miserable. GOD even flooded the world once to get rid of the lot of them and start over from scratch. But even this did not work. We have already discussed the creation and the problems with Cain and Abel, so let's get on with the story of GOD's trials and tribulations with his *pièce de résistance*, us.

Noah

This is an interesting story for several reasons, one of which is because the portions of this story written by P, the priestly author, and the portions written by J, who wrote the original version of the story, could not merely be set out side by side as were most of the other couplets, such as the stories of the Creation in Gen 1 and 2, because that would make it appear there were two different floods. So R did a very imaginative thing, he wove the two stories together into one. I'll show you in a few places how they are intertwined as we go along.

GOD had lost His patience with his creation and was thoroughly disgusted. He rued the day he had begun this human experiment. The people were corrupt and violent, so he decided to wipe the slate clean and start over. Thus the flood. You will note that there are two versions of Noah and his family and then the animals entering the ark (7:6-16). The P account attributes the flood to GOD opening up a seam in the sky so that the two oceans can meet (7:11), whereas the J version attributes the flood to 40 days and nights of rain (7:4, 12). These two versions coincide with, and closely relate to, the two creation stories in Gen. 1 and 2. The non-priestly text, written in the sixth century C.E., needs seven pairs of the "clean" animals for the sacrifices they would have to make after they safely land. Otherwise, they would be wiping out an entire species every time they made a sacrifice. However, the Priestly version, which was written centuries later, knows that it was not until the time of Moses that there was a distinction between clean and unclean animals and there was no sacrifice upon disembarkation in that version.

It is also interesting to compare the story of Noah with the story of Gilgamesh who was the hero in the Mesopotamian story of the flood which predates the Biblical version by many generations. They are practically identical. One of the few differences is that in Gilgamesh the reason for the flood was because of Devine frustration with human overpopulation and noise rather than on the wickedness of humankind that so disgusted GOD in the Bible version. But both built similar boats, sealing the seams with pitch. Gilgamesh's boat came to rest on a mountain in *Ararat*, part of Armenia.. Gilgamesh sent out three birds, first a dove, then a swallow, each of which came back, and then a raven which did not. And so forth.

In any event, although fundamentally identical to the Gilgamesh story, this was, basically, a brand new creation story. The rains only occurred for 40 days and nights, but the water covered the earth for 150 days. After disembarking from the ark, Noah interrupts his need to repopulate the world (Noah was 500 years old at this time) and decides to sacrifice a few of the animals that he just rescued. This makes GOD happy and He promises never again to curse the ground due to humankind because the human heart is basically evil from birth. He also agrees never again to destroy the living creatures as he did. As a sign of this promise, GOD causes a "bow" in the sky, which was the ancient people's explanation for a rainbow.

GOD, through the Priestly writer, now gives Noah a brand new set of dietary laws. Eating meat is now acceptable. If you recall, GOD originally contemplated a vegetarian diet (1:29-30). GOD now makes it very clear that man shall not commit murder, and if he does he will himself die, because GOD made humankind in His own image.

But the story of Noah does not end quite yet. The J author tells us that Noah had three sons, Shem, Ham, and Hapheth. "[F]rom these three people, the whole world was peopled (9:19)." How that worked remains a mystery, because GOD had just wiped out the entire world's population of women except for Noah's family. There was no one left with which to procreate, but somehow Ham fathered a son whom he named Canaan.

One day Noah, who was a "man of the soil," tested out the new grape crop and got "hammered" on the alcohol. He passed out naked in his tent. Ham accidentally walked in on him and saw that he was naked. He rushed out and told his brothers about it and the brothers took a garment and, backing in so that they could not see him, covered their father with the garment.

Noah woke up later and somehow knew that Ham had seen him naked, so he cursed Ham's son Canaan and ordered that he forever be a slave to his brothers and uncles. There has never been a satisfactory explanation as to how Noah knew Ham saw him naked or why he cursed Ham's son. This seems like a very cruel punishment for someone whose sole transgression was that his father stumbled upon his own father sleeping in his birthday suit. Many scholars feel that there was originally something more to the story that was either lost or edited out of the text. This has been the subject of much speculation dating back at least to Jewish midrash.

The god of Genesis was a very unforgiving god. When Noah's family was sent out to people the earth, Japheth got the northern area in what is now Turkey and the surrounding areas, Shem inherited the area between the Red Sea and Turkey, and Ham got Africa. That is the reason that African Americans are still sometimes called "Sons of Ham," and Noah's curse was why the Europeans after the plague and the United States deep south was able to create a Biblical justification for keeping them as slaves.

Next we come to one of the most important people in the Bible.

Abraham

Abraham, whose name was originally Abram, lived a little before or about the same time as Hammurabi, the great king of Babylon, somewhere about 2000 B.C.E. The traditional dates given for Abraham

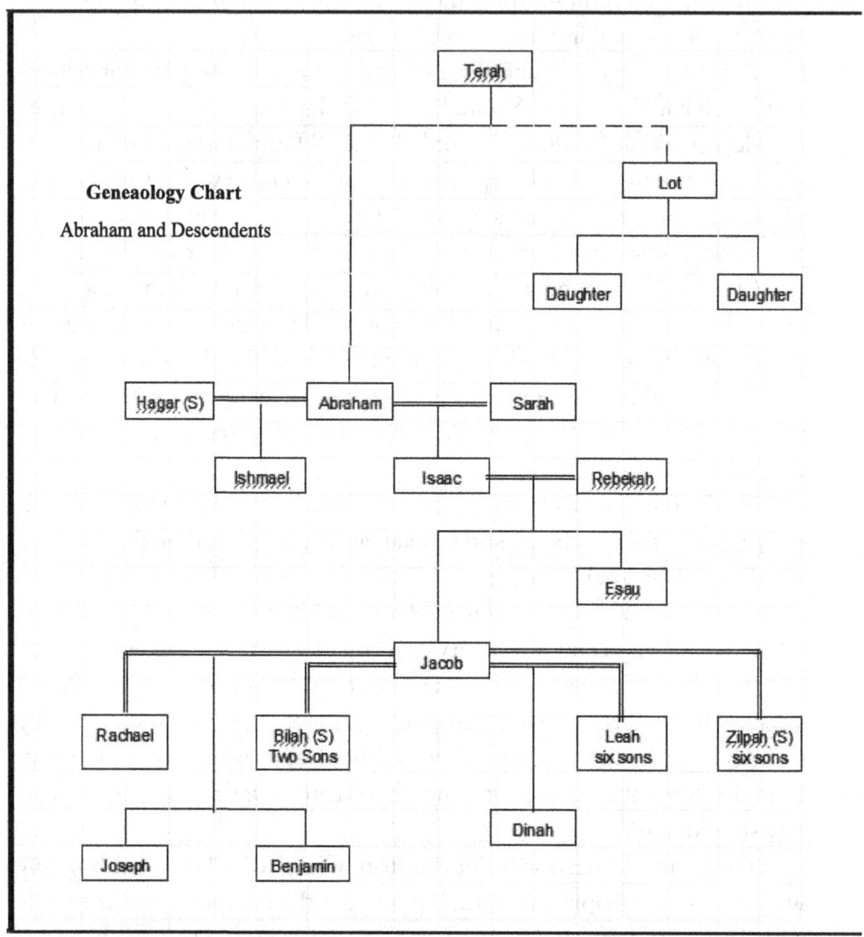

vary. Hebrews date him 1812 B.C.E to 1637 B.C.E. and Christian traditional dates him about 2000 B.C.E. to 1825 B.C.E. Abram was, according to the Bible, a direct descendent of Noah and was born in the city of Ur*. That

* There is some confusion about Abraham's birthplace in the Bible as there are references to him coming from Haran which was in what is now part of Syria and was an important city on the trade route to Ur. Some think that he may have been born in Haran and then moved to Ur, but there is no consensus. Also, (continued...)

is all that we know about his early years as the story quickly jumps to Abram's adulthood. For some reason GOD liked Abram who was, as we shall see, a bit of a reprobate by today's standards. He had a brother named Haran who had a son named Lot (of Sodom and Gomorrah fame). Lot was Abram's nephew. Abram's wife, who was also his half-sister, was named Sarai. Sarai is the first of the three matriarchs who were "barren" in Genesis, the other two being Rebekah and Rachel; in each case GOD's power provided them with heirs.

The Priestly author, P, is evident in many parts of the Abraham story, including the genealogical materials in the beginning (11:27-32) and his first journey to Canaan (12:45) But there is a good bit of J and E intermingled within the stories, particularly in the couplets that we talked about earlier. In fact, many scholars believe that the very first example of couplets is in Gen 15:2-3 where Abraham states objections and the parallel responses by GOD are given in Gen 15:4-5.

But back to the story. At some point, Abram, Sarai, and Lot were in the town of Haran which, to make matters confusing, had the same name as Abram's brother. It is while Abram was in Haran that GOD told Abram to go to Canaan and GOD promised all of the Canaanite land to Abram and his descendants. GOD told Abram that he will found a great nation, but famine struck the area, so Abram traveled to Egypt to seek food. However, when Abram got to Egypt he feared that, because his wife is so beautiful, Pharaoh would kill him in order to get Sarai for himself, so he told her to pretend that she was only his sister, not his wife. Sure enough, she became a concubine of Pharaoh and Abram became very wealthy as a result. When Pharaoh found out about the duplicity, he banned Abram, Sarai, and Lot from the country.

Back in Canaan, Abram was getting a little worried. He was no spring chicken any more, and if he was going to found the great nation that GOD promised, he was going to have to do something quickly. Sarai had not borne any offspring, so Abram was thinking about adopting one of their slave children. In those days, it was always the wife's fault, never the husband's, when there were no children. The very idea that it could be the man's fault was beyond comprehension. A couple was childless because

---

* (...continued)
the Bible refers to Ur of the Chaldeans, but the Chaldeans were not in Mesopotamia until about the seventh century B.C.E., ultimately conquering Jerusalem in 612 B.C.E. and later sending the Hebrews into exile.

the woman was "barren." Sarai suggested that he take the slave that she brought back from Egypt, Hagar, as his concubine. This was a common practice among the more well to do Hebrews at the time. It was very important for a landed man to have heirs in order to pass on his property. Under the Hebraic laws current at the time, since Sarai was barren, a child by Hagar would be considered to be hers and, therefore, Abram's legal heir.

Sure enough, Hagar became pregnant but Sarai was so jealous that she chased Hagar off into the desert. GOD rescued her and told her that she would have many offspring and to return home to deliver Abram's first son. She did, and the child was named Ishmael which means "GOD Hears."

GOD then promised Abram another son. Abram could not believe it because he was now ninety-nine years old and Sarai was ninety. GOD then changed their names. Abram means "exalted ancestor" and GOD changed his name to Abraham which means "ancestor of a multitude." That suggested not merely having a lot of children, but being the patriarch of an entire sovereign unit. GOD also changed Sarai's name to Sarah. Why He did so is a bit of a mystery, because both names mean "princess."

It is at this point, in a segment contributed by P, that GOD and Abraham made their mutual covenant (solemn promise) whereby GOD promised Abraham and his heirs that the land of Canaan would be theirs forever, for which GOD extracted a certain quid pro quo from Abraham, including a request that Abraham circumcise every male in his tribe. Abraham agreed. Among the promises from GOD was that Abraham would have another son through Sarah. This is the first of the Hebrew covenants with GOD that is still referred to today as justification for the Jews to have their own country in the promised land, Israel.

Sure enough, as GOD promised, Sarah got pregnant and delivered a son that they named Isaac. Sarah was determined that Isaac become Abraham's heir*, so again Hagar, along with Ishmael, were banished to the wilderness. GOD met up with Hagar and renewed his promise and assured her that Ishmael would found a nation. She was in the desert without water, and begged GOD not to let her son die, and a spring

---

* There was only one heir in those days, usually the oldest son. This practice is called "primogenitor." The reason for not dividing up the property among all the sons is that there is usually not enough land or other property to go around if more than one son inherits. This practice predominated, even in the west, until very recent times. The practice was prohibited by the U.S. Constitution

miraculously began to flow, saving their lives.

What is important about this little story is that modern day Jews trace their lineage from Abraham through Isaac down to the present, Christians trace their lineage from Abraham through Isaac to Jesus, while the Nations of Islam trace their lineage from Abraham through Ishmael down to Mohammed. That is the common tie between Judaism, Christianity, and Islam. All three religions believe that they descended from Abraham and the other ancient patriarchs in the Scriptures.

There is an interlude here where we hear the story of Sodom and Gomorrah which we will discuss later. Following the Lot story, Abraham's odyssey continued as he went to Egypt for a second time and again passed Sarah off as his sister. This is another example of couplets. The first trip to Egypt was written by J, (12:19) while this trip, which clearly is a parallel to the first trip, was written by E (20:22).

Finally, there is the famous story of GOD telling Abraham to sacrifice his son, Isaac. Abraham was going to do it, and Isaac knew it, but GOD stopped Abraham at the last minute. This brings up the subject of human sacrifice. Nobody talks about it, but human sacrifice was a part of the Hebrew religion until at least the time of the exile in 586 B.C.E. There is no doubt that the Israelites who heard this story told around the campfires would understand what it is all about. The Bible plainly states that the first born of every animal, including human animals, belongs to GOD (Ex 22:29-30).

One other item worth mentioning about the story of the attempted sacrifice of Isaac: GOD was merely testing Abraham because GOD was uncertain about the depth of Abraham's "fear of GOD." At the last instant, GOD said, "Do not lay your hand on the boy or do anything to him; for now I know that you fear GOD. . . ." (22:12). From this passage, Abraham being a "GOD fearing person," the church made "GOD fearing" into a of statement about the strength of one's beliefs. Not everyone interprets it the same.

The word "fear" meant something entirely different when this passage was written than it does today. The Hebrew word for fear occasionally meant being afraid, but its most common use was to mean "deep respect, awe, or reverence." The latter meaning is the most likely under these circumstances and in most places where it is used in the Bible. So a "God fearing man" is one who holds GOD in deep respect, awe, or reverence, not a person who is afraid of GOD.

Back to the story, though, all things considered, I am not sure that I should be all that proud to have my lineage go back to Abraham. I have some real rogues quietly tucked away in my ancestry, but they are saints compared to Abraham. Let's list all of his transgressions that, for some reason, nobody complains about today:

1) He twice gave his wife to another man to use as a sex slave in order to save his own skin (trafficking in slavery; cowardice?);

2) He slept with his wife's maid and got her pregnant (philanderer; adulterer?);

3) He then threw the maid and their son out of the house without support (dead beat dad?);

4) He planed to kill his second son because "GOD told me to do it" (obviously a "head case?" So far, no jury has ever bought into that argument).

When I said earlier that Abraham was a bit of a reprobate, that is what I meant. By modern standards, this would be reprehensible and unthinkable conduct, but all of this made absolute and honorable sense to the ancient Israelites. He would not have been considered the slightest bit immoral at the time.

This is a very important lesson to remember as you delve further into this book. Many things that you read in the Bible had an entirely different meaning at the time they were written than they do today. We will see very graphic evidence of that in our next story. But first, there is a bit more to the Abraham saga.

SACRIFICE OF ISAAC

The English word "sacrifice" is derived from the Latin, *sacrificium*, which literally means "something which has been made sacred." The Bible says that GOD commanded Abraham to sacrifice his son, Isaac, on Mt. Moriah. However, Muslims believe that GOD'S command to Abraham was to sacrifice his oldest son, Ishmael, rather than Isaac.

Today, most people think of Isaac being a child at the time. That is not the traditional interpretation, however. Josephus, the Roman historian who was trained in the Jewish priesthood, wrote in the second century, that Isaac was 25 years old at the time. The Hebrew Talmud, that scholarly study on the Bible, teaches that Isaac was 37, which was computed backward from Sarah's death at the age of 127. In any event, Isaac was fully grown and could have easily prevented his aged father from performing the act had he so desired.

Sarah died at the age of 127, but Abraham wanted more children, so he married the youthful Keturah (the Anna Nicole Smith of her day) who bore him six more children. These became the ancestors of other tribes in what is now the Arabian Peninsula, including the Midianites whom the

Israelites massacred after they left Egypt during the Exodus. Abraham finally died at the ripe old age of 175.

Lot

Lot had gone to Egypt with Abraham on his first trip there. When Abraham and Lot arrived back in Canaan, Abraham, now very wealthy, offered Lot, who was almost as wealthy, the first choice of land. No dummy, Lot chose the rich land in Sodom on the Plain of Jordan and left Abraham with the less desirable property. It seemed like a great selection at the time, but it turned out that he bought into a bad neighborhood. GOD decided to incinerate the place to get rid of the evil that was lurking there. No particular evil is named in the Bible, but readers of the story from early in the first millennium C.E. have decided that the evil was homosexuality. This is one of those examples where Jewish customs at the time were unknown to the early Christians who interpreted and translated the Bible, and they made an incorrect interpretation of the situation that haunts our society to this day. Here is how the story appears in the Bible.

GOD decided that Sodom and Gomorrah had to go because the people were evil. He sent two angels disguised as humans to warn Lot so he and his family could get out of town before the coming conflagration. Lot took the angels into his home and gave them food and sanctuary. The townspeople heard about the visitors and went to Lot's house and demanded that Lot turn over the two strangers so that they could "know" them. That is the word that they used, "know." Although the word can have different meanings, in the Old Testament it usually meant heterosexual relations, not homosexual relations. Most authorities today agree that homosexuality was not the reason that GOD decided to destroy Sodom and Gomorrah. What was it, then?

Travel in those days was hazardous at best. When you decided to stop for the night you could not simply check into the local Hilton. There weren't any. So the Hebrews had a tradition that was inviolate, and still is in many near eastern cultures: if a stranger was found inside the city gates after they were closed for the night, or if a stranger asked a local citizen for food or a place to spend the night, the homeowner was required to extend the utmost hospitality and give sanctuary and food in his own home. It was very dangerous for a stranger to be caught on the streets after the gates were closed. This hospitality was crucial to the civilization, because otherwise it would have been impossible for people to travel from place to place, and commerce would have become nonexistent.

This extension of hospitality was one of the strongest laws the Hebrews had at the time. It was so strong that Lot even offered the crowd his two virgin daughters to do with as they wished if they would just leave his guests alone! Can you imagine how strong that tradition of sanctuary was that a man would offer his own daughters to a mob bent upon rape*? Especially where the two daughters had been promised to two of the men in the mob? That is impossible to conceive in this day and age, but that was how it was in the ancient Middle East, and still is in places there. Scholars agree that the evil in the city of Sodom was not homosexuality; it was the violation of strict hospitality laws. That is the evil that led GOD to destroy the towns. What about the homosexuality aspect of the story? Understand that this was not an act of love between consenting men that was being discussed; it was brutal rape, a universally detested crime.

The stories about Lot and Sodom and Gomorrah that I heard in Sunday school always ended with Lot's wife disobeying GOD by turning back to see the fire and brimstone raining down on Sodom and Gomorrah and GOD turning her into a pillar of salt. The ministers never told us the rest of the story where Lot and his two daughters, fleeing the area, stayed in a cave for several days. The daughters, thinking that the world had been destroyed and fearing that they would never be able to bear children, got Lot drunk and repeatedly had sex with their father until they were both pregnant. By tradition, the descendants of one of the daughters became the Moabites and the descendants of the other became the Ammonites, two tribes that occupied land on the east bank of the Jordan in later years. We will hear more about these tribes later. GOD was apparently OK with the incest as none of them was punished.

Exodus

The Hebrew name for the book of Exodus is *Shemoth* which translates as "the names," from the first words in the book. Exodus, of course, talks about the flight of the Israelites from Egypt. This event comprises only the first fifteen chapters, however. Perhaps the most important parts of this book are those in which the Hebrew laws are first stated because those laws distinguish the Hebrews from any other group in history, even though many of the laws were borrowed from other civilizations. Instead

---

* There is another incident in the Bible that closely parallels the story of Lot in Judg 19:23-25 and Jud 20:6,10. This tradition of hospitality was inviolate.

of laws coming from a king, Judaism was, and still is, a religion of laws from GOD. GOD also wanted to have a home among his people, so there are pages of narration in Exodus giving detailed instructions for the construction of the portable tabernacle (the ark of the covenant), the altar, the vestments of the priests, the ordination of the priests, and the various sacrifices. As you might have guessed, these portions were written by P.

There is doubt as to whether or not the Exodus is history or legend. There are few references to historical events that show up in any secular texts, archaeological excavations, or even religious texts from other religions. There is uncertainty about the identity of Pharaoh, although most agree that it was probably Ramses II, known as Ramses the Great (1279-1213 B.C.E.). Most of the place names, even the location of Mt. Sinai, are uncertain as is the route out of Egypt. Hopefully, archaeology will shed some light on this in the future, although many of the historical sites are in countries that are not likely to allow Jewish or Christian expeditions. There is also a large group of experts who feel that the entire story of the Exodus is metaphorical and that Israelites were never in Egypt. New archaeological finds may have cleared up the uncertainty. We'll discuss this in Chapter 16.

There are definitely problems treating the book as history. Supposedly a million or two people wandered around the Sinai for years but there has not been a single trace of them in all of archaeology. That is by no means proof that they were not there. But common sense would indicate that if there was an exodus, it must have been of a much smaller group. Can you imagine a group larger than the population of Dallas or Philadelphia moving through the desert carrying everything they owned (plus the substantial booty that they purportedly stole from their Egyptian owners), all proceeding at a pace at which all but the very slowest could keep up? It would take weeks just to cross the Red Sea. (Incidentally, that is an incorrect translation. The correct translation is "Sea of Reeds," not Red Sea. Nobody seems to know where that might have been, however. Many think that the place of the crossing was much farther southeast than most reconstructions). By the time everyone finally arrived at the campsite, it would be morning and the earliest arrivals would be ready to leave again.

Most historians now feel that a much smaller contingent left Egypt, if there was, in fact, an Exodus, and that it was not a conquest of city after city, but was an emigration and that most of the tribes and persons who would later call themselves Israelites were already living in Canaan when the new immigrants arrived. This is not just speculation. It is actually the story that the Bible itself tells in the book of Judges. Under this theory, the story was gradually expanded and embellished around the campfire over the years until it took on a typical eastern European epic like the Iliad and the Odyssey which were also legends founded upon underlying fact.

There is no real consensus on the authorship and date of the various parts of Exodus. It is a very complex interweaving of events. Some are obviously written by P (Compare Ex 29:8 with Gen 2:1-3), especially the details of the priestly tabernacle (Ex 25-40). Some appear to be written by the author of Deuteronomy (Compare Deut 7 with Ex 23:23-33) and others appear to be written by J and E and these may be from the oldest written sources in the Bible.

Interspersed are many smaller entries from various times in the history of Israel. These include hymns and parts of hymns, ritual traditions, itineraries, the codification of laws, and various myths and folklore. Some of these are very ancient and are very likely writings based upon authentic historical oral tradition.

Much of Exodus states what GOD expects of his people as his quid pro quo for the covenants between GOD and Abraham. Many very ancient traditions and festivals of the Israelites are reinterpreted, for example: the festivals of Passover, unleavened bread, and sacrifice of firstborn.

Basically, Chapters 1 - 15 tell us about the city in Egypt where the evil Pharaoh has enslaved the Israelites and their eventual escape from that slavery. The first part is a pilgrimage by Moses alone and the last is a pilgrimage of all the Israelites. Chapters 16 - 40 are about the people arriving at the mountain where GOD resides and where He creates the people of Israel. The people build a portable tabernacle (the Ark of the Covenant), to GOD's specifications, so that He can reside among them forever and travel with them*.

It is very difficult to summarize this book. There are so many sub-parts and many portions not only refer to the present but look both forward and backward. The writers of the New Oxford translation set forth the following suggested structure of the book:

- 1.1 - 15.21 GOD liberates Israel from slavery by defeating Pharaoh
- 15.22 - 18.27 GOD journeys with Israel to Mount Sinai
- 19.1 - 31.18 GOD establishes the covenant with Israel

* I always wondered why this omnipotent, omniscient, and omnibenevolent God ("the 3-Os") had to be hauled around in a box to be with his chosen people. Wasn't He simply anywhere and everywhere he wanted to be?

- 32.1 - 34.35 Israel breaks the covenant, but GOD reestablishes it
- 35.1 - 40.38 Israel obeys instructions, and GOD takes up residence with them.

Exodus makes the first known reference to the word "Hebrew*." The word appears about a dozen times in the first 9 chapters of Exodus but only once afterwards. This is also the first place where GOD's name was given, the name "I am who I am" which was discussed earlier (3:14). The name "YHWH," which means *I am the LORD* was first mentioned in Gen. 6:3. This was the name introduced by P and is usually translated simply as "The Lord."

Moses

The main protagonist in this book is Moses. There is an issue as to whether or not Moses was a real person. Scholars point to a similar hero in the Mithrian religion in which their hero, Mises, led their people out of slavery. That story predated the story of Moses by several hundred years and is very similar, not only in the name of the protagonist, but in the overall story and in the details as well. For example, they both carried staffs with which they performed miracles such as getting water out of rocks.

In any event, Moses is a hero in three religions. In the Koran he is known as Musa, and is referred to no less than 502 times, more than any other prophet except Mohammed. The authors of the four Gospels in the New Testament modeled their versions of JESUS on the stories of Moses— where Pharaoh sent out an order to kill all Jewish baby boys and Moses was saved in the Old Testament, Matthew says the provincial governor of Judea sent out an order that all Jewish baby boys be killed and JESUS and his parents escape to Egypt in the New Testament. Moses and JESUS both spent 40 days in the wilderness. Moses went up on a mountain and gives a sermon; JESUS gave the sermon on the mount. And so forth.

Outside of the Bible and the Koran, there is absolutely no evidence that Moses actually existed. If he was an historic person, he would have lived about 3550 years ago. You would suspect that there would be some note of him or the Exodus in the extensive documentation of the rule of

---

* Gen. 1:15. The word Hebrew probably referred in general to displaced persons rather than to a specific ethnic group. It only later took on the latter meaning.

Rameses the Great. The Rameses court kept excellent records that still survive, and it would seem highly unlikely that such events as the deaths of all of the first-born children, the slave rebellion, and the loss of his army by drowning in the Red Sea would somehow not be included in his records. On the other hand, these are not incidents that he would want written down for posterity either. Who wants to be known as the Pharaoh that lost his whole army to unarmed slaves?

There is a common misunderstanding that Moses had a speech impediment or that he was a studder/stammerer. When GOD asks Moses to be his voice to the people, Moses protests that he has never been eloquent, and that, "[I] am slow of speech and slow of tongue (4:10)." It could mean a speech impediment, but more likely it was a metaphorical statement indicating Moses' reluctance to accept the position as GOD's voice to the people.

The ten plagues are interesting in that the number "ten" is never actually stated. It is now known that the ten plagues are the result of the combination of several overlapping plague accounts, none of which narrated all ten plagues. Part of the evidence of this is that many of the plagues cause Pharoah to promise that the Israelites may leave if only Moses intercedes and lifts the plague whereas plagues one, three, five, and six evoke no such response. In some of the plagues, Moses is the sole actor and others it is Aaron and sometimes both. The Aaron passages were the work of P. This is one of the places where R, the Redactor, really showed his abilities at merging the stories of P and J so seamlessly that a casual reader would not have the slightest idea that they were actually two or more stories merged together. Incidentally, Psalm 105 reprises the plagues and it only mentions eight.

No discussion of Exodus would be complete without mentioning the **Ten Commandments** that has been getting so much attention lately. The proper translation is not "commandment," but *Word.* There are actually three versions of the commandments in the Bible, but the version most commonly mentioned can be found at 20:2 - 17. The Bible does not number them. There have been numerous attempts over the centuries to get the number to add up to ten (it was a special number to the Hebrews), and it usually necessitated combining some or separating some.

This version of the Commandments, the version most often seen on public monuments, does not mention stone tablets. It is purely an oral transmission from GOD to Moses and Moses to the people, "Then GOD *spoke all these words*: . . . ." That is, he gave them to Moses orally. To make it easy to discuss these Commandments, let's list them here, numbering by the verse in which they appear in Chapter 20 of Exodus rather than trying to number them as Commandments since the methods of numbering vary:

Commandment	**Discussion**
2 I am the L*ORD your* G*OD, who brought you out of the Land of Egypt, out of the house of slavery;*	Verse 2 is the first "Word" or Commandment in the Jewish tradition because it states the purpose of the Exodus.
3 you shall have no other gods before me.	Verse 3 was traditionally the first Commandment in the Christian tradition. Note that it states, "you shall have no other gods before me." It does not deny the existence of other gods, only that YHWH, who took the Israelites out of slavery, is to be first above all other gods. The Hebrew Bible combines this "Word" with the next to make the second commandment.
4 You shall not make for yourself an idol, whether in the form of anything that is in Heaven above, or that is on the earth beneath, or that is in the water under the earth. *5 You shall not bow down to them or to worship them; for I the* L*ORD your* G*OD am a jealous god, punishing children for the iniquity of parents, to the third and the fourth generation of those who reject me,* *6 but showing steadfast love to the thousandth generation of those who love me and keep my commandments.*	Verses 4 - 6 ban the making or worshiping of idols. This was to set the Hebrews apart from their neighbors whose gods were often depicted as humans or animals. I often wonder how such items as religious icons, statues of the saints, and even Notre Dame University's "Touchdown Jesus," somehow do not count as breaches of this commandment.
7 You shall not make wrongful use of the name of the L*ORD your* G*OD, for the* L*ORD will not acquit anyone who misuses his name.*	Verse 7 is the prohibition against the wrongful use of GOD's name. It is not only a prohibition against swearing, it is also a prohibition against using the Divine name in

magic or divination. The ancient Hebrews so worried about this commandment that they would neither say nor write the name of GOD at all. They used words like "The Lord" when they wanted to refer to GOD.

8 Remember the Sabbath day, and keep it holy.

9 Six days you shall labor and do all your work.

10 but the seventh day is a Sabbath to the LORD *your* GOD*; you shall not do any work—you, your son or your daughter, your male or female slave, your livestock, or the alien resident in your towns.*

11 For in six days the LORD *made Heaven and earth, the sea, and all that is in them, but rested in the seventh day; therefore the* LORD *blessed the Sabbath day and consecrated it.*

Verses 8 - 11 refer to keeping the Sabbath holy. Verse 11 refers to the Priestly version of the creation (Gen 1-2:3). The Ten Commandments are entirely written in the Hebrew second person masculine singular form, meaning that it is addressed to men. Note that the Fourth Commandment says that everyone gets the day off but the wife! Most modern mothers would probably agree that some things never change—the wife cooks, cleans, and takes care of the children while the men celebrate the Sabbath by worshiping at the altar of the NFL or the NBA. America used to have laws prohibiting people from working on Sunday, the so-called "blue laws." Not only were the stores and bars closed, but often checks dated and contracts signed on Sunday were not considered valid. The blue laws have been repealed. It is a bit strange that the U.S. passed the blue laws, because it is basically a Christian society, and Jesus, as you will see later, frequently aroused the ire of the Jewish priesthood by working on the Sabbath. He regularly violated this commandment because healing the sick and other matters were just too important to put off.

12 Honor your father and your mother, so that your days may be long in the land that the L*ORD your* G*OD is giving you.*

Verse 12 says that you shall honor your father and your mother. Mom gets some recognition here, but it is in her capacity as a mother, not as a woman or even as a wife.

13 You shall not murder.

Verse 13 was incorrectly translated in the KJV as, "Thou shalt not kill." The Hebrew word used for "kill" was *rasach*, which more accurately means "murder" You shall not kill what? Animals, murderers, Iraqi soldiers? Dr. Albert Schwitzer, the brilliant physician/ musician/ missionary believed that "thou shalt not kill" meant just that, you shall not kill anything. He taught the natives at his mission that they should not even step on a bug if they could help it. The problem is that "kill" is an incorrect translation. The correct translation is, "You shall not murder." Killing in war and capital punishment were not proscribed by the Commandment. GOD had many crimes that called for the death penalty and He frequently urged His chosen people to kill everyone in a city that they had captured (a concept called "herem" which we will discuss later).

14 You shall not commit adultery.

Verse 14 is the prohibition against adultery. Later laws define just what adultery was to the Israelites.

15 You shall not steal.

Verse 15 says that you shall not

steal. It seems pretty straight forward, but the Hebrew word for "steal" is the same word as the word for "kidnap." It could mean either or both, and we will probably never know the correct translation.

16 You shall not bear false witness against your neighbor.

Verse 16 prohibits bearing false witness against your neighbors. In other words, do not commit perjury. All the commandments were to govern conduct against neighbors. These were meant to be directions for the conduct of one Hebrew toward another Hebrew. They were never intended to be rules to govern the conduct of others. It was perfectly acceptable to murder someone who was not a Hebrew, for instance. Even Moses murdered someone.

17 You shall not covet your neighbor's house; you shall not covet your neighbor's wife, or male or female slave, or ox, or donkey, or anything that belongs to your neighbor.

Verse 17 clearly shows, as if there were any question, that the commandments were directed to males only. Note that the wife is listed between a man's house and his ox and his ass. Again, the wife does not even get the top spot.

Most people think that Moses went up on the mountain and came back with a couple of tablets and that was that. Not true. He made no less than eight trips up the mountain (Eg. Deut 5:6-21 and 10:1-11). Biblical scholarship has clearly shown that the portions of the Bible that contain the Ten Commandments (the verse shown above) were not included in the Bible until about 400 B.C.E. What is more, there are at least three separate versions of the Mt. Sinai stories, one attributed to J, one to E, and one to P, and they all were woven together by R.

In the early 12th century B.C.E. there were many different religions in the Middle East, all of them competing with each other. Nearly all of them had a tradition that their leader went up on a mountain and received "The Law" from their god, and in nearly every case the law was written on two tablets. For example, Mises, the Sumerian version of Moses, received the law from his god on a mountain and wrote them on two stone tablets. The Greek lawgiver, Dionysius, is depicted holding up two tables of stone on which the law was written. The Persian god, Zarathustra, also known by his Greek name, Zoroaster, received the Book of Law from a god on top of a mountain. Minos, the King of the Minoan civilization on Crete, received the law from god on top of a mountain. It is not unreasonable for someone to conclude that the story of Moses receiving the law on a mountain top written on two tablets was a composite of Middle Eastern legends.

If you think that the Ten Commandments were the end of the laws, read on. The next few chapters discuss many other laws, which modern day Jews call *Book of the Covenant,* and interspersed throughout the rest of the Torah are an extensive set of laws that govern both the secular and religious aspects of Hebrew society. Altogether, there are 613 separate laws identified by Jewish tradition, of which the Ten Commandments are only a small part. Judaism is truly a religion of laws which was in stark contrast to the religions of ceremony that flourished in the Middle East at that time, especially by their neighbors in Canaan.

Let's look at some of the laws that follow the Ten Commandments. It should be immediately apparent that these were laws from a different time and a different place. Many Christian groups are working to replace our civil laws with the ancient Biblical laws. The proponents of this idea probably have little familiarity with the Biblical laws as they would not work well in our society. These laws were to govern GOD's Chosen People, and were not intended to be statements of universal rules of conduct. Christian fundamentalists who believe in the literal interpretation of the laws must come to grips with these laws when they try to apply any of the old Biblical laws to the present. Is it acceptable practice, for example, to cherry pick a few laws and apply only those selected laws as being GOD's command and ignore the others? Here are a few and you can decide:

- Slavery was sanctioned. A slave served for six years and then he could go free. However, if he was married and had children, the wife and child still belonged to the master. If the slave could not bear to leave the wife and kids, he said so and the master pierced his ear to show that he was a slave for life (21:2-6). Unfortunately, these laws were used by Americans to justify slavery for years, even though we kind of forgot about the freedom after six years part.

- An impoverished man could sell his daughter as a slave (she was, after all, a mere chattel). There were various rules set forth on how she was to be dealt with and how she could be redeemed (21:7-11).
- A child who struck his father or mother was executed (21:15).
- If you cursed your father or mother you were executed (21:17). The Hebrew verb "curse" could also mean "humiliate" or "treat with contempt." No one knows for sure which meaning was intended.—perhaps all of them.
- When a slave owner struck a slave with a rod and the slave died immediately, the owner was punished. But if the slave survived a day or two there was no punishment "for the slave is the owner's property" (21:20).
- If a thief broke into your house at night you could kill him with impunity, but you could not do so if it was daytime (22:2-3). This was actually the foundation of the English common law crime of burglary which was originally defined as the breaking and entering of a dwelling house *at night* with the intent to commit a felony therein. In English common law it was not considered to be a burglary if it was committed in the daytime or in a place of business or any other place other than the home. The rationale in English law was the same as it was for the Israelites—in the daytime you are awake and have other means to foil the intruder. Also, there was more likely to be physical harm to a person if the act occurred at night.
- When a man seduced a virgin who was not engaged to be married, he had to pay the bride-price for her and make her his wife. But if her father refused to give her to him, he had to pay an amount equal to the bride-price for virgins (22:15-17). Note that this differs from adultery which was a capital crime while this only required monetary compensation. The reason for the difference is that the woman must be married for it to be adultery. Note that the woman had no say in this whatsoever. She was the property of her father and had to live with his decision. The father could care less, but she may have been very happy about the seduction.
- Having sex with an animal was a capital crime (22:19). This was not such a common practice that it needed its own law, but it was

part of the Canaanite religious festivities, along with male and female prostitution and cross-dressing, and GOD specifically prohibited his people from attending such festivals.

- You could not wrong or oppress a resident alien, for you were aliens in the land of Egypt (22:21). How does this comport to the present wrath many hold against aliens in our country when many would deny resident aliens even basic medical care?
- If you lent money to GOD's people you could not charge interest (22:25-27).
- You could not curse a leader of your people (22:28). Wait, what? I'm doomed! Doomed!!
- Every seven years you had to cancel any debts owed to you (Deut 15:1-2). After seven times seven years there was a "Jubilee" year, a year-long celebration and time of forgiveness held every 50 years where *all wealth was redistributed.*
- "If anyone secretly entices you—even if it is your brother . . . your own son or daughter, or the wife you embrace, or your most intimate friend—saying, 'Let us go worship other gods,' . . . you must not yield to or heed any such persons. Show them no pity or compassion and do not shield them. But you shall surely kill them; your own hand shall be first against them to execute them. . . . Stone them to death for trying to turn you away from the Lord your GOD, . . ." (Deut 13:6-10). The next time your daughter comes home from college and tells you that Buddhism sounds pretty interesting, you've got to kill her.

And on and on. I doubt that there are many people in the twenty-first century who would suggest that any of these laws be followed today, if they bothered to read them.

Leviticus

Leviticus is mainly devoted to the matters surrounding the worship of GOD at the Temple. The Hebrew name of the book is *Vayiqra* which means, "And He called." The English name, Leviticus, indicates that it has to do with the priesthood, all of whom come from the tribe of Levi. As you might expect, this book is largely the product of the Priestly author, P, although that is not to suggest that a single person wrote it. On the contrary, there were many pens over many years that were responsible for the content. The P writings are notably in Chapters 17 through 36 which are often referred to as the "Holiness Code" and the "Holiness Collection." This material was undoubtedly written right about the end of the Exile which was in 538 B.C.E.

Before that, interspersed in the first 16 Chapters are works that are collectively referred to as the "Priestly Torah" and the "Holiness School." Although mostly written in earlier times, they were edited into this book early in the years of the Exile. The Holiness Code and the Holiness collection often supplement the two earlier works which are now lost.

This is widely believed to be a sort of training manual for new priests and their assistants. It also initiates the ceremony of Yom Kippur, the Day of Atonement, which was not celebrated until the sixth century, about the time this book was written.

This is a very difficult and technical book for non-Jews who universally lack the background and experience of the traditions depicted. The book presumes that the reader knows all about those traditions and rituals, but most non-Jews haven't a clue what they are. The differences between, and reasons for, some of the sacrificial offerings are detailed, including guilt offerings, burnt offerings, and sin offerings (called "kipper" which today means *atonement."* It is a derivative of the noun "Kippur", as in Yom Kippur which, as noted, means Day of Atonement). It is important to have some understanding of the various sacrificial offerings in order to understand aspects of some of the later books, including New Testament books, but there is a lot of literature that discusses the offerings that is much easier to read than Leviticus. Of particular importance to the New Testament are the burnt offerings and the sin offerings as many believe that JESUS' death was the ultimate sacrifice for all of mankind.

It should be noted that at the time Leviticus was written, the focus of Yom Kippur was the purifying of the sanctuary and the items of furniture in the sanctuary that were polluted both by sin and by other things that were considered impure such as the spilling of blood or placing a human body to lie in state on the premises. The various causes of such pollution are noted in several locations in Exodus and Leviticus as requiring purification. The proper translation for "kipper" at that time was, therefore, *purify,* not the personal atonement for sin as it is referred to today. This is another example of how the meanings of words change over the years.

Leviticus also sets out dietary laws and describes what animals are "clean" and those that are not. The portions of the story of Noah that refer to "clean" animals were written about this same time and inserted into that ancient story.

We also find the tradition of the "scapegoat" in Leviticus. Everyone has heard the term and most people have used the words at one time or another. Few, however, know how it originated. It was a ceremony that took place during the Yom Kippur celebration and the term has a far different meaning today. Very briefly, two goats were sacrificed. One goat was for Azazel*, which means "angry or fierce god,"and one goat was for Yahweh. Yahweh's goat was sacrificed as a sin offering, but first, all the sins and transgressions of the people were ceremoniously transferred to Azazel's goat which was then presented to Yahweh who made atonement over the goat for the "uncleanness" of the people and because of their transgressions and all of their sins. Thus, it became the "scape goat" and was then led into the wilderness and set free, taking with it all of the people's sins to be consumed by the god Azazel.

Chapter 18 refers to various sexual prohibitions. The term, "uncover the nakedness" of someone is a strange saying, but it is used in this chapter as a euphemism for sexual intercourse. The Bible does use euphemisms and slang terms, which puts a real strain on translators. This chapter prohibits incestuous relationships, and describes which familial relationships are taboo, prohibits intercourse with one's wife if she is menstruating, adultery with a kinsman's wife, male homosexuality, and sex with animals. Chapter 20 sets forth the punishments for these transgressions, most of which are death.

At the end of Chapter 22, GOD sets forth the reasons for these proscriptions. He says,

> *You shall not follow the practices of the nation that I am driving out before you. Because they did all these things, I abhorred them [the practices]. But I have said to you: You shall inherit their land, and I will give it to you to possess, a land flowing with milk and honey.*

GOD had real problems keeping his favorite people away from the Canaanite religious ceremonies where they had days and nights of continuous orgies celebrating the coming of spring and other events. We noted above that these orgies included sex with male and female prostitutes and animals and part of the ceremony included the worshipers simulating sex changes by changing into a woman's clothing as part of the season changing fertility rights. Therefore, there is even a prohibition against cross-dressing addressed in Deuteronomy 22. To assure the

---

* Azazel is another of the old Middle Eastern gods worshiped by the Hebrews before they fully adopted monotheism.

fertility of the animals, there were even sexual relations with animals which God prohibits. It was not the acts themselves that God disliked, it was because they were devotions to the Canaanite gods.

Numbers

The narration of the trek of the Israelites from Egypt to the Promised Land continues in Numbers from where it left off in Leviticus. There is a census that occurs at the beginning of the book, and that is where we get the English title. There are actually two different censuses. The Hebrew title is more appropriate, "*Ba-Midbar*" (In the wilderness).

Early on, there is an important change in GOD's demands. In several places in the Torah, the Israelites were told that they must devote the firstborn of both animals and humans to GOD. Animals were sacrificed. First born children could be sacrificed in particular circumstances. There are such sacrifice stories in the Bible, but mostly the firstborn children, rather than being killed, are required to serve in the sanctuary as temple servants of GOD (1 Sam 1:10-11, 24-28). In Leviticus, GOD substitutes the Levites in the place of the firstborn children as temple servants of GOD.

However, the book is really about the travels of the Israelites in the wilderness. It is the sequel to the narration of the travels of the Israelites begun in Exodus and continued in Leviticus. The first census was taken at the beginning of the 40 years in the wilderness and the second census was taken after they left the wilderness.

Scholars are in agreement that this is a combination of Priestly (P), Yahwist (J) and Elohist (E) writings. P includes chapters 1-9, 15, 7-19, 26-31, 34-36, and parts of 10, 13-14, 16, 20, 25, and 32-33. However, these were not written by a single person or all at the same time. So well blended are the contributions of J and E that it is very difficult to determine which parts were contributed by which author. However, there is general agreement that, while it may not always be possible to separate the J and E portions from each other with any expectation of accuracy, they are both far older than the P entries.

There are new laws introduced, including an interesting ruling on female inheritance of land (27:1 - 11). Women generally did not own land anywhere in the Middle East. This has to do with the daughters of a man called Zelophehad who died in the wilderness without a male heir. The daughters plead before Moses, Eleazar the priest, and all of the leaders and the congregation that the name of their father should not be taken away from his clan merely because he had no male heirs.

GOD also tells Moses to pass the word to his subjects that if any man suspects that his wife has been unfaithful, and there are no witnesses, and the husband suffers jealousy, then the husband shall bring his wife to the priest for a gruesome "jealousy offering" wherein the priest gives her a poisonous brew and she apparently either aborts, is sterilized, or both. (5:11-31). I have often wondered how the survivors of the test, if there were any, felt toward their jealous husbands afterward. It hardly seems to fit what people today view as good family values.

GOD told Moses that he can never enter the Promised Land as punishment for all of the rebellions and squabbling among the people under his control, even though he tried very hard to keep his flock in order. As Harry Truman once noted, "The Buck Stops Here." In fact, none of the original group that left Egypt were allowed to enter the Promised Land. Therefore, this book includes the transfer of leadership to Joshua who finally leads the group across the Jordan into Canaan (27:12-23). Numbers is a real "stew" with the acts of the people being the meat and the laws being the vegetables.

GOD then requires the Israelites to wreak His vengeance on the Midianites. An army of 12,000 Israelites, 1000 from each of the 12 tribes, set forth and slaughtered all five kings of Midian and all of the men in the city, including a man by the name of Balaam whom we will meet again later. They took all of the women and children and all of the booty they could find and then torched the cities. When they marched back into camp with their booty and captives, Moses went ballistic because the women had been allowed to live. The women, after all, had seduced the Israelite men (Ch 25). Moses ordered them to put all of the women and male children to death, which they did, but they were allowed to keep the young virgins for themselves. This must come as a blow to those who insist on a strict fundamental reading of the Bible. They also had to get rid of the booty except for the gold and jewels which belonged to GOD*.

This section also covers the distribution of the Transjordan land that they had been occupying (Ch 32). It contains a summary or itinerary of their wilderness travels (Ch 33) supposedly written down by Moses. That was unlikely, because at this point the Hebrew alphabet had not even been invented.

The summary is very detailed, so it was likely well ingrained in the oral

---

* The Hebrews typically were required to keep the precious metals and gems for GOD when they destroyed a town. What GOD would want with gold and jewels is a mystery to me. He could have just taken them or created more and not destroyed all of the lives.

tradition and may have been compiled not long after they settled in Canaan when the Hebrew written language was first used, somewhere between 1050 and 850 B.C.E. Some parts of the summary vary from the previous narrative and other places it summarizes earlier narratives. In still other places, it seems to draw on other, sources that are now lost. A great many of the locations mentioned cannot be located today. Compare this with a similar summary in Deut 1:1-3: 28 where comparison reveals even more differences.

Other parts of this section are the setting of the boundaries of Canaan (Ch 34); homicide laws and the setting aside of places for the Levites to live (Ch 35); the ritual calendar (Ch 28-29); and P's contribution regarding rules about women's vows (Ch 30).

The Israelites began to have sexual relations, and perhaps intermarriage, with the Moabite and Midianite women during the feasts and ceremonies of their god Baal. These are some of the orgy-type ceremonies that so disgusted GOD. Moab, you may remember, was founded by one of Lot's daughters after she became pregnant by him (Gen 19:29-37).

The famous "Aaronic Benediction" appears in this book (6:24-26). This is a very ancient blessing and is still familiar today to Jews and Christians alike. Here it is in its familiar KJV version:

The LORD bless you and keep you;
the LORD make his face to shine
upon you, and be gracious
to you;
the LORD lift up his countenance
upon you, and give you
peace.

This is a good note on which to leave the book of Numbers.

Deuteronomy

Deuteronomy is derived from the Greek *deuteros* ("second") and *nomos* ("law"), and the name is pretty descriptive of the contents of this book in that the voice of Moses reiterates and paraphrases the laws discussed in the first four books. The Hebrew title is *Devarim* ("The words"). The narration about the Israelites in the wilderness picks up where Numbers left off, with the Israelites poised on the plains of Moab where GOD is finally going to lead them into the Promised Land . This is the end of the story that began with GOD's covenant to Abraham clear back in Genesis.

Since Deuteronomy finishes the narration of the exodus of the

Israelites to the Promised Land of Canaan, it has always been a part of the Torah or Pentateuch. However, because it nestles so well with, and is so similar in form to, the books of Joshua, Judges, Samuel, and Kings, it is almost certain the books were all, at the very least, edited together. These books, collectively, are frequently referred to as the Deuteronomist History, meaning that it is history based upon the ideas in Deuteronomy.

The first few versus of Chapter 1 refer to Moses speaking to the Israelites "beyond the Jordan." It is clear from the text that the people are still in the wilderness, which means that "beyond the Jordan" refers to Moses and the people being east of the Jordan and not yet having crossed over into the Promised Land . That is further backed up by the text that follows. In other words, the author of the book was already on the other side, that is on the west side, of the Jordan, already in the Promised Land. This is one of the anomalies that the medieval monks noticed that led them to the determination that the "Books of Moses" could not have been written by Moses as he was never allowed to enter the Promised Land.

The narration of the Israelite exodus is interrupted while Moses gives a series of three speeches which read like high school valedictory speeches. GOD had told Moses that he will never enter the Promised Land , so this is also his farewell to his people. Moses instructs the people about the importance of loyalty to GOD and requires them each to swear an oath to uphold the combination of law and theological instruction that he set out as a covenant with GOD upon the plains of Moab. It was to supplement, not supplant, the prior covenant of Horeb (the name used in Deuteronomy for Sinai). The narrative is then picked up again.

Remember when we first discussed Deuteronomy back in the second chapter? The author was referred to as "D," and he lived about 600 years after the Exodus, hardly an eyewitness. The laws that Deuteronomy has Moses discuss are believed to be those laws that were contained in the "Scroll of the Torah" which the prophets told King Josiah in 622 B.C.E. they had just found (Kings 22-23). That is about the time that the entire book of Deuteronomy was written, but it is believed that the laws themselves were passed down orally from quite ancient times. They vary somewhat from the laws in the previous four books. Josiah then began reforming their conduct to conform to the original Mosaic laws*. The

---

* But see 2 Chron 34:9-14 which indicates Josiah had already begun reforming the practices of Judaism back to the original Mosaic laws, and this (continued...)

country was being threatened and Josiah believed that it was because GOD was displeased that the Israelites had strayed from GOD's teachings. Remember, Josiah's predecessor had erected and worshiped at pagan alters all over the country and basically abandoned the teachings of Moses. Josiah hoped that by instituting these reforms that GOD would again be pleased and that the enemies would go away.

Josiah's reforms restricted all sacrificial worship of GOD to the temple in Jerusalem and removed all foreign elements from the system of worship. He instituted the first centralized Passover at the Temple. Sacrifices were to be made only at the Temple. These were pretty revolutionary at the time. Up until then sacrifices could be made anyplace. In fact the Scriptures stated that GOD would grant blessings "in every place where I cause my name to be remembered (Ex 20:24)." This would have been a tremendous blow to those priests who came to Judah from the Northern Kingdom. They suddenly found themselves without an income as the High Places were the only places they were allowed to perform their sacrifices.

The historical and political influences of Josiah's reforms were due to the increasing threat from other nations. The Assyrians that had destroyed Israel earlier were now threatening Judah. King Hezekiah had previously made a pact with Assyria (2 Kings 18:13) to preserve Judah's autonomy, but Babylon was growing in strength as well. Since Judah had to rely on the good graces of Assyria, Hezekiah had instituted some of the Assyrian religious traditions into Judah's historical traditions. Josiah, feeling he needed to do so to please GOD, banned all of the Assyrian traditions.

Deuteronomy, written during this tension and anxiety, reflects the authors' desire to preserve the Hebrew culture and religious integrity. The authors concluded that the older ways of worship and social organization were no longer realistic. They had Moses address such topics as worship, the festival calendar, justice, kingship, priesthood, prophecy, criminal, family, and civil laws, and ethics. This was the new covenant that Moses extracted from the people in Deuteronomy.

The structure of the covenant was patterned after the Assyrian state treaties of the time such as the *Vassal Treaty of Esarbaddon* (627 B.C.E.), so the authors were very much in tune to international treaty traditions of the period (Deut 15:1-18; 17:8-13; 14:20; 22:13-30). However, the difference is

---

[*] (...continued)
scroll merely convinced him that he was heading in the right direction.

that this covenant switched from being an oath to the Assyrian leaders to being an oath to GOD.

There was another near-eastern convention at the time, and well into the next millennium, in that the authors of works such as Deuteronomy did not attach their name to the work nor did they speak in their own voice. They also employed the very common practice at the time of ascribing the work to an ancient person, in this case, Moses. This is called "pseudepigraphy." You will see examples of this in the New Testament where second century authors often signed letters using Paul's name or the name of one of the people closely identified with JESUS. This tended to grant authenticity to what the document contained.

With that background, let's see how the book was structured and examine the time frame of its composition. The portion of the book that was shown to Josiah was the "Scroll of the Torah" (sometimes called "*The Book of the Law*). It consisted mainly of the laws we now find in Chs 12-26. It probably had a short introduction and closing and it was presented as a treaty between GOD and the Israelites. The people took an oath of loyalty to those laws under penalty of numerous curses (28:15-46).

Later, during the exile in the mid-sixth century B.C.E., the historic introduction was added (Joshua through 2 Kings). At a still later time, perhaps after the Exile, P appended Deuteronomy as the conclusion to the newly formed Pentateuch.

Deuteronomy contains its own version of the Ten Commandments (5:6-21), but there are a number of key differences between the two versions. Next, there is a long sermon (6:1-32) based upon the first requirement of the Decalogue which is restated in 6:4-5, "Hear, O Israel: The Lord is our GOD, the Lord alone*. You shall love the Lord your GOD with all your heart and with all your soul, and with all your might." This is known as the "Great Commandment." In the New Testament this is the verse that JESUS quotes when he is asked which commandment is the first or most important.**

Deuteronomy played a very important role in Mediaeval and Renaissance Europe. Exodus 22:25-27 prohibits lending money for

---

* This is a difficult phrase to translate. It can also mean any of the following, "The LORD our GOD is one LORD," or "The LORD our GOD, the LORD is one," or "the LORD is our GOD, the LORD is one."

** Mark 12:29. Jesus lists the second most important, "to love one's neighbor as oneself. Mark 12:33).

interest "to any of GOD's People." The Christian Church, believing that they also qualified as GOD's People, took this prohibition seriously. The Church would not allow Christians to lend money to other Christians for interest. This put a serious crimp in the burgeoning European trade business; borrowing money was essential to commerce. The Church noticed that Deuteronomy 23:19 said that "You shall not charge interest on loans to another Israelite." Jews could lend money for interest to others as long as the borrowers were not fellow Jews. The Church, therefore, forced the Jews, who were conveniently required to live in ghettos with only one way in and out, to become Europe's moneylenders. That is how the Jews became the major bankers of Europe. It was not their choice, it was by edict of the Christian Church. And, as Shakespeare reminds us in *The Merchant of Venice*, the Jewish moneylender (in that case, Shylock) was reviled, so much so that if a debt became too burdensome to repay, the borrower sometimes simply "whacked" the moneylender.

You will see later in the story of Ruth that she provided for her mother-in-law by collecting the grain that was left in the field. The reason that there was grain left for her to gather was because of the requirement in Deuteronomy that, when you harvest, you leave a sheaf in the field for "the alien, the orphan, and the widow (24:19-20)."

Moses said, "On the day that you cross over the Jordan into the Promised Land that the Lord your GOD is giving you, you shall set up large stones and cover them with plaster. You shall write on them all of the words of this law why you have crossed over, . . .(27:2-3)" In an ancient town called Gilgal, just across the Jordan and less than a mile from Jericho, archaeologists have discovered a plaster covered wall and stele with inscriptions. It is believed by some that this is where the Mosaic order just quoted took place. However, keep in mind that at the time the Israelites crossed over the Jordan, the Hebrews had not yet begun to interact with the Canaanites so as to be exposed to the concept of an alphabet. It would be at least 150 years more before the first Hebrew writings show up. The Deuteronomist, writing five hundred years *after* the Hebrews had a written language, assembled this book from several other ancient texts and from the oral history, and it is quite likely that this tradition of the writing in plaster was from one of those works which came much later.

The book ends with the preparations for, and the death of, Moses. He was buried at a secret location east of the Jordan.

6

Historical Books

And there came out from the camp of the Philistines a champion named Goliath, of Gath, whose height was six cubits and a span. He had a helmet of bronze on his head, and he was armed with a coat of mail.

1 Sam. 17.4,5

The Old Testament is comprised of the ancient Hebrew Scriptures, also known as the Hebrew Bible. For the Jews, there is no New Testament. So far we have examined the first five books in the Old Testament. All of these books are in the same order in the Hebrew Scriptures as they are in the Christian Bible. The rest of the Old Testament is arranged differently in the Hebrew Bible than in the Christian Bibles.

The ancient Hebrews believed that the Torah was true and correct and was written by Moses as dictated by GOD. Those books became Canon very early on. The remaining books in Hebrew scriptures were not generally considered to be so perfect or even necessarily true. Therefore, the Jewish version of the Old Testament is arranged into three sections—The Torah, which we have already discussed, The Prophets, and The Poetical and Wisdom Writings. The Prophets includes what the Christians refer to as the Historical Books— Joshua, Judges, First and Second Samuel (these are written on a single scroll in the Hebrew Scriptures) and First and Second Kings (these are also written on a single scroll)—which are basically books of history, as well as the writings of the various prophets. They also included the books of Ruth and Esther.

These were just some of the many Hebrew writings about their religion, but none were official scripture until the books were accepted as Hebrew Canon in the fourth century B.C.E. For our purposes, we will use the Christian convention and separate the Historical Books from those writings of and about the Prophets. We will also discuss Ruth and Esther in other chapters.

The Christian Bible refers to this group as the Historical Books—

Joshua, Judges, Samuel, Kings, Chronicles, Ezra, Nehemiah, Ruth, and Esther. Do not take the word "history" too seriously, however. In 1959, Werner Keller wrote a book entitled "The Bible as History." He sold millions of copies. When I was in college, nearly every university began offering a class called "The Bible as History" using Keller's book as the text. Many saw it as a way to teach the Bible in a state university without First Amendment conflicts. The only problem was, the entire book was hogwash and nearly all of the classes entitled "The Bible as History" have long been dropped from the curriculum. That does not mean that there is no history in the Bible; there is, lots of it. It just means that the Bible is not, and was never meant to be, a history book like we think of history today.

History was not Really History

In Biblical times, history did not have the same meanings attached to it that it does today. As the editors of the New Oxford Annotated Bible edition of the NRSV noted,

> The idea that historical writings should capture the events "as they really were," that historians should attempt to write an objective account of the events of the past, is a relatively recent notion that developed in the European universities several centuries ago. Before that, history was, rather, to be instructive and, in this case, morally instructive, teaching the readers how to be good citizens or how to lead proper religious lives. . . .

So when you read the "Historical" Books of the Bible, don't get bogged down as to whether or not the stories are accurate documentation of real events, because, for the most part, they aren't. If you do, you will miss the importance of the stories. They are merely stories about the past used by the authors of the Bible to "narrate a past in order to convey lessons relevant to the community" in the present. They are didactic and were never intended to be true history.

There are a great many inconsistencies in these Historical Books, not only *between* the various books but *within* the individual books as well. Much of this inconsistency is the result of interweaving two different versions of the same story. For example, the famous story of David killing Goliath with a sling (1 Sam 17) that many of us learned in our childhood, appears in 1 Samuel, but 2 Samuel 21:19 states that someone named Elihanan killed Goliath with a spear. Even within the same book, 1 Samuel, there are two different stories of David and Goliath, one being the well known story in which Goliath is killed by the stone from the sling (17:50) and a second that states that David merely knocked Goliath out with the stone and then took Goliath's own sword and killed him by cutting off his head (17:51).

Also, the Deuteronomist (D), who wrote huge portions of the historical books, occasionally included some very old works right next to a more current version of the same story. For example, in the story of Deborah which we discussed earlier, there is one version written in prose (1 Jud 4:1) and right behind it is an epic poem telling basically the same story but with some differences (1 Jud 5:1-31). The poem is much older than the rest of Judges, and many scholars believe that this poem about Deborah may well be the oldest part of the entire Bible.

Chronicles is pure revisionist history. It rewrites many of the stories that appear in the other Historical Books to fit a notion of "historical probability." That term refers to a process of describing what really *could have happened* based upon notions of how the world worked. The author twisted the facts at will in order to fit the situation. There was nothing wrong with this. There was no sinister reason for modifying the older versions, it was simply that the author(s) of Chronicles was making a different point than the original authors. Remember, the purpose of these scriptures was to teach the moral behavior that GOD expects.

Again, I don't mean to suggest that there is no history in these books. There is. Some of the incidents are also noted in other Middle Eastern texts. For example, the events surrounding the siege of Jerusalem by the Assyrian King Sennacherib in 701 B.C.E are found in several Assyrian documents and even on the bas reliefs on the Assyrian king's palace. However, while these ancient sources indicate that the parallel account in 2 Kings 18:12-16 are quite accurate, the portion of the story that continues on in chapters 19 and 20 may be less so, particularly verse 19.35 where an angel purportedly killed 185,000 Assyrians soldiers one night. The Assyrian version tells of a much different result. The Bible has other such instances of parallel historical accounts from other countries. Some events and places are also noted in ancient Egyptian texts and stelae. Since we have independent verification of some of the historical stories, at least in part, it is fair to assume that other stories may also be historically based.

The division of the Bible into chapters and verses was relatively recent and was often rather arbitrary. Likewise, the division of Samuel, Kings, and Chronicles into separate Books was also arbitrary and occurred rather late in history. They were first divided in the Septuagint for no other reason than that each book would be of a more manageable size.

Originally, Ezra and Nehemiah were considered to be a single work and it is likely that Joshua and Judges were single works as well. While Joshua and Judges flow very nicely from one to the other, the first two chapters of Kings, which talks about David's life, fit better in the book of Samuel, and many scholars believe that those chapters were originally in that book.

In fact, as I suggested in Chapter 2, it is believed that D, the Deuteronomist, wrote not only Deuteronomy but may have also written much of Joshua, Judges, Samuel, and Kings because they all flow together with a complete chronology and because the writing style of all is the same. The language of the prayer and vision of Solomon in 1 Kings 8:22 - 9:9 are universally recognizable as being written by the Deuteronomist. If the five books were not written by the same author, they were certainly edited by the same person. They narrate a continuous, chronological history from the death of Moses through the Exile and the return to the Promised Land.

At one time, scholars thought that perhaps Ezra and Nehemiah were not only written at the same time by the same person, but possibly Chronicles as well, as there are many similarities. However, continued research indicates that the similarities are almost surely nothing more than they were all written about the same time, some time during the fourth century B.C.E. rather than common authorship.

Ezra/Nehemiah are the closest of all of the historical books to actual history, being written about the time the incidents described actually occurred. Many feel that they are probably more historically accurate than the others historical books which were often written several hundred years after the fact. However, this view is tempered by the fact that the two books definitely have an agenda, and there is little doubt that "history" has been tortured somewhat to satisfy that agenda*.

Ezra quotes extensively from official Persian documents which most historians believe are authentic. Nehemiah skips the documents, but is unique in that it is the only one of the historical books that is narrated in the first person.

The remaining books in this section are Ruth and Esther. Both are short stories, often described as historical fiction. They are interesting to read because they are written in great prose, but the subject matter sometimes suffers in favor of the esthetics of the prose and the

---

*The "agendas" refer to the importance to both Ezra and Nehemiah of the Torah as the central document and the great dangers of intermarriage which those authors felt was what angered GOD and caused the Exile.

ideological purposes. But they are history in that they narrate the past in order to convey lessons relevant to the community. The marvelous story of Ruth is discussed in Chapter 8.

Joshua

Joshua takes over Moses' job after his death and leads the Israelites into the Promised Land. This is the story of the crossing of the Jordan river, the attempted conquest of Canaan, and the distribution of land to the 12 tribes. In Joshua you find the first mention of the concept of the *herem*. The noun form of the word means "devoted thing" and the verb form of the word means "utterly destroy." This is where the Israelites show their devotion and obedience to GOD by the total and absolute destruction of those whom GOD declares to be His enemies. Total destruction means the killing of "every man, woman, child, suckling, and animal" in the town and by burning all of the crops. There must be nothing left as it is GOD's wish that it be so.

Herem is the usual result of an ancient Israelite conquest, and where, on occasion, the Israelites allow someone to survive, or they take some property as booty instead of destroying it, GOD punishes them severely. Gold, silver and vessels of iron and bronze were sacred to the Lord, so those were to be kept and placed in GOD's treasury (6:19).

Herem was a common practice all over the Middle East at that time as a victory was always believed to be a victory of the victor's god over the loser's god.

The book of Joshua simplifies and condenses what was, obviously, a long and difficult occupation. The Canaanites and other peoples the Israelites conquered did not give up their land and their lives freely. Also, the book is designed to illustrate certain messages and does not always follow historical events. The destruction of Jericho is a good example. Joshua marched around the city with all of the warriors, circling the city once each day for six days with seven priests bearing seven trumpets of rams' horns leading the way. Then on the seventh day, they circled the city seven times until the priests sounded a long blast on the trumpets and the entire multitude shouted as loud as they could and the walls of Jericho miraculously came falling down. Following the capture of the town, we see the first exercise of herem; there was a brutal, needless slaughter. The problem is, that Jericho is perhaps the most excavated town in the entire world, as well as being one of the oldest. Archaeologists who originally discovered the walls, which had indeed been destroyed, announced to the world that they had just proven the accuracy of the Bible because the walls had obviously been destroyed in battle. Later archaeology and accurate carbon dating, however, proved that the walls actually had been destroyed long before the arrival of the Israelites.

There is considerable effort in the book to cast Joshua as a new Moses. For example, all of the male Israelites who came out of Egypt had to be circumcised by Moses. Now, before they crossed into Canaan, GOD asked Joshua to "make flint knives" (cringe) and circumcise all of the men (5:2-4). (I think that would be about the time those Canaanite idols would begin looking pretty good to me and perhaps conversion might seem appropriate). All of the men in the twelve tribes submitted.

Then, mirroring the crossing of the Red Sea, when the Israelites crossed the Jordan river, which is usually pretty benign and narrow, it was apparently in flood stage so Joshua ordered the waters of the Jordan "flowing from above to be cut off; they shall stand in a single 'heap'.*

Other examples of the similarity between Joshua and Moses are that Moses led the people out of Egypt and Joshua led them into the Promised Land; Moses sent out spies and Joshua sent out spies; Moses distributed land to the tribes east of the Jordan and Joshua did the same only on the west of the Jordan.

The Israelites failed to fully conquer Canaan. GOD wanted the Canaanites all to be driven out or killed so that their detestable religion would not tempt His chosen people. This failure was attributed to the disobedience of GOD's wishes. The Israelites first attacked the cities and towns in the center of the country near the location where they first crossed into Canaan. Then they turned south and conquered most of that area before finally turning to the north.

The book of Joshua often backtracks and restates itself, overlaps, and uses a technique resembling flashbacks; we'll see these same techniques later in Judges and Samuel. This is generally attributable to the piecing together of the two separate versions of the stories of J and E by the Deuteronomist. Surprisingly, this retracing of steps does not annoy the reader. I guarantee you will enjoy reading these books if you use a good, modern translation.

Joshua refers to *The Book of Jashar* (10:12-13). This is a book that no longer exists. It is just one of several such books referred to in the Bible that apparently contributed heavily to the Bible stories only to disappear.

---

*Josh 3:13. The word "heap" is a very rare word that is used in only one other instance in the Bible, and that is in the splitting of the Red Sea (Ex. 15.8; Ps 78.13)

These books all predate the sixth century B.C.E and it is unlikely that anything so old has survived.

Judges

As one writer noted, this book should be given an "R" rating. There are prostitutes, assassins, rapists, torturers and every description of miscreant you can imagine.

Judges picks up the story from the death of Joshua and ends just before the birth of Samuel, Israel's last judge, about a 200 year period. The beginning of the book acknowledges that the Israelites were not successful in conquering all of Canaan. The religion and moral life of the Israelites sank lower and lower until it reached rock bottom during the time of Samson when the Israelite society finally degenerated into civil war and idol worship.

Judges were not only judicial officers, like judges of today, they were also rulers and military leaders. They were like kings, but only of a single tribe, not over all the Israelites. They were the closest that the Israelites came to having a king until Saul, whom we will hear about in the Book of Samuel. By this time the twelve tribes were scattered all over the country. It is uncertain if all tribes had judges as only a few are discussed.

The Historical Books generally refer to the judges and the people following the judges to war as "the Israelites," but that did not mean all of the twelve tribes. Generally, there were only a few involved in each of the stories, sometimes only one. Some of these stories may have existed in tribal oral tradition and a few may have been in copied from previous writings. However, at the time the incidents occurred, the written Hebrew language was in its very infancy, if it existed at all.

The precise chronology of the events depicted are unknown since they all have to do with local tribal judges and in many cases seem to overlap in time. But once again, this was never intended to be a true history or a true biography of the individuals. The purpose was to teach the Hebrews an important lesson, in this case, the severe consequences of disobeying GOD. This is hammered home again and again. It also sets up the need for a future king. There is a recurring theme of, "In those days there was no king in Israel," often followed by the phrase, "all the people did what was right in their own eyes." In other words, they lacked guidance and continually disobeyed GOD's laws. Note that the phrase, "In those days . . ." implies that the events took place long before the lifetime of the author which strongly suggests that the stories in this book were written long after the events described.

There are six major judge stories and they all follow the same pattern. First, we find the Israelites badly abusing GOD's laws, so much so that GOD allows their oppressor to conquer and rule over them and they become, basically, the slaves of the oppressor for many years. Finally, the people plead for forgiveness and GOD gives them a leader, one of the judges, and the judge receives the spirit of the Lord so that he can lead the people to subdue the oppressor and then the people have peace for many years. Usually upon the death of the judge, they fall back into their old ways and the cycle starts again. The major judges' stories are Othniel, Ehud, Deborah and Barak (together), Gideon and his sons Abimelech, Japhthah, and Samson.

There is barely anyone who is not somewhat familiar with the story of **Samson**, but did you ever read it? The story shows how silly it is to assume that everything in the Bible is true. Most know that Delilah cut off Samson's hair and he lost his strength, but there is a lot more to the story than his hair. All in all, Samson was a strange choice to be a judge. He violated almost every moral code you can think of. He took a "nazirite vow," a lifestyle dedicated to the Lord's service which he frequently profaned. He was a philanderer; instead of chasing enemy soldiers he chased women, even preferring the forbidden non-Israelite women. He never associated with other Israelites in his many conflicts with the Philistines, and he did not deliver GOD's people from oppression like the other Judges. But of all of the judges, people remember him most often.

He reputedly had superhuman strength. In the vineyards around Timnah he was attacked by a young lion. He tore the lion apart bare-handed. Another time three thousand men surrounded him and they asked to bind him and take him to the Philistines. They swore not to kill him. But the Philistines came shouting to meet him, so he broke the ropes, found the fresh jawbone of a donkey, and with it he killed a thousand men. He celebrated by visiting a prostitute. Not exactly the ideal role model for pubescent young Israelites.

Then Samson fell in love with another Philistine by the name of Delilah. She was convinced by Philistine leaders that she should go to Samson and use her feminine wiles to try to find out what made his strength so great. In exchange they promised her eleven hundred pieces of silver. This was just too good a deal to pass up, so Delilah began to work him over.

She cooed to him, "Please tell me what makes your strength so great, and how could you be bound, so that one could subdue you." He told her that if he was bound by seven fresh, undried bowstrings that he would be as weak as the others. So the men lying in wait were summoned after Samson fell asleep (he was apparently a very sound sleeper) and they bound him with the seven fresh bowstrings (which they conveniently had with them). Of course he snapped the bowstrings at will.

Undeterred, Delilah tried again. "You have mocked me and told me lies; please tell me how you could be bound." So he told her that they must use new ropes that have never been used. Again, the Philistines, who just happened to have such ropes with them, entered and bound him with the same result. He slept through the whole process.

Again Delilah tried to collect her pieces of silver. Samson, still not smelling a rat, told her that she should "weave the seven locks of my head with the web and make it tight with the pin, . . ." The web and pin are parts of a loom. While he slept, she did the deed, so when he awoke he had to remove the web and pin from his hair, which he easily did.

She tried yet a fourth time, this time giving him the "guilt trip, " "How can you say, 'I love you,' when your heart is not with me? You have mocked me three times now and have not told me what makes your strength so great." So he told her the truth, that it was his hair. He was a nazirite since birth, and if he shaved his head GOD would leave him. Delilah let him fall asleep with his head on her lap and the Philistines, ever ready with whatever they needed, appeared with a barber who shaved his head. Once again, he apparently felt nothing because he did not wake up.

Well, No Duh! Is it actually possible that any person could be that naive or that dense? Three times Delilah betrayed him and three times he knew that she betrayed him, yet he was still so smitten with her that he decided to tell her the truth? That is a man who did not adequately plan for his mid-life crisis.

We all know the rest of the story. Samson's strength left him so the Philistines scooped out his eyes. They then held a huge party and planned to use Samson like a trained bear to entertain them. For no apparent reason, the party was held in some sort of huge house in which, conveniently, all of the men and women of power were inside and some three thousand of the populace were on the roof watching. By this time Samson had a little fuzz growing back on his head and GOD, along with his strength, came back to him and he pulled the entire house down on everyone, including himself.

This entire story strains credulity. Nobody could be that naive. But remember, this was not intended to be history. It was supposed to be a didactic work to demonstrate the follies of breaking GOD's laws. In that respect, it worked marvelously. It is a very good tale and people remember it when more logical stories are long forgotten.

The stories in Judges are all fun, but there is one very unfunny story that is worth talking about. This is the story of how one man, one of the Levite tribe, managed to start a civil war among the tribes that almost caused the tribe of Benjamin, David's tribe, to be completely wiped out. It is a very strange story, and not one that you will usually hear about from the pulpit. Generally referred to as "**The Rape of the Concubine** (19:1), it bears a startling similarity to the story of Sodom and Gomorrah..

The story of our nameless but shameful Levite begins when he takes a concubine in his town of Ephraim in Judah. She became angry with him and stomped off home to Bethlehem. He followed her, along with a young servant and two donkeys, all the way to Bethlehem, where he spent a couple of nights with his father-in-law in Bethlehem. They apparently worked out their differences, so he and his concubine started back toward Judah. They left late and were only going to make it about half way to their destination, so they decided to spend the night at Gibeah, a Benjaminite town just north of Jerusalem. They sat in the town square, but, contrary to the hospitality laws, nobody offered them a place to stay. Finally, they met an old man who lived in the town and he offered to let them stay in his house as it was not safe to stay in the square after the gates were closed for the night. They accepted his hospitality.

But the men of the city then surrounded the house and demanded that the old man bring out the man that they might "know" him. The man tried to talk them out of it because the Levite was a guest in his house so he offered them his own virgin daughter and the concubine instead to "ravish them and do whatever [they] want to them; but against this man do not do such a vile thing." The men would not listen, so the Levite grabbed his concubine, pushed her outside with the crowd, and he went in and partied with the old man. The Benjaminites then raped the concubine and abused her all night. At dawn they let her go and she collapsed at the door of the man's house.

In the morning our hero found her lying on the threshold. He told her to get up because they were going. There was no answer so he put her on a donkey and went home. When he got home, he took a knife and cut her into twelve pieces, "limb by limb" and sent a piece of her body to each tribe throughout all the territory of Israel. We are not even sure that she was dead when he did this!

This brought an outraged tribal assembly who condemned the crime and set out to punish the guilty parties, the Benjamites. Our Levite hero, being satisfied that his vengeance will be carried out, then sneaked off and disappeared[*].

The tribes attacked the Benjamites three times, losing badly the first two times, but in the final attack, they ambushed and completely destroyed (*herem* again) all of the men, women, children, and animals with the exception of six hundred men.

The book concludes with the gross understatement that the institution of government by judges was unsatisfactory, setting the table for a king.

1 & 2 Samuel

Samuel was a sort of cross between a prophet, a judge, and a ruler. The judges were not working out too well as local rulers and the tribes considered joining forces and anointing a king of all the Israelites. Samuel was one of the few prophets that enjoyed great popularity. He was sort of a de facto king and became the transition leader before the Israelites formed a formal monarchy.

He was originally thought by some to be the author of the original book of Samuel, but that would be pretty tough since he died before the second half of the book began, what is now 2 Samuel. The Philistines were becoming more than a nuisance—they were a threat to the very existence of the Israelites. The time had come to unite all of the twelve tribal states into one country and elect a king. However, in spite of warnings by Samuel, they didn't think this king thing through very well before acting.

First and Second Samuel was originally one book about the beginning of a monarchy and the reigns of the first two kings of Israel, Saul and David. It was divided into two books by the Greek translators of the Septuagint to make it more manageable.

There are three main parts to the book. The first is about Samuel himself (Chs 1-7). Samuel then anointed Saul as the first king of Israel, and the second section is all about Saul (Chs 8-15). Finally, Samuel announced that GOD had rejected Saul in favor of David (Chs 16-31) and this is a preview of the story of David's reign as told in 2 Samuel.

There is an interesting change here in the way GOD passes information to the people. There is no reference to how this was done; not even a hint. Originally, GOD spoke directly to people: there were

---

[*] Note that, as in the story of Lot, the crime was also the denial of hospitality, not the rape.

conversations with Adam and Eve in the Garden; GOD came down to Earth with a couple of angels and spoke to Abraham; and GOD spoke to Moses from a burning bush. Here, GOD communicated directly with his chosen people, but we haven't a clue as to how this was done. How did He warn them not to let the king lead them astray? Beginning with Samuel, GOD communicated to the people through prophets. How did He pass on all of the instructions to Samuel? GOD also told David what to do directly, but there is no hint of how He did it; was it through dreams, personal appearances, or what? Later GOD finally stopped speaking directly to the people and addressed the Israelites solely by using the prophets as intermediaries.

1 & 2 Kings

Kings continues the story of the Israelites that started early in Genesis. This has been a marvelous trek and we are nowhere near the end. The Jews are very fortunate to have such a complete history of their culture, even if it is a bit faulty. First Kings begins with the transition of the reign from David to his son Solomon. Then it turns to the split of Judah into two countries and the parallel reigns of the kings of the divided countries all the way through the reign of the Judean King Jehoshaphat and the start of the reign of King Ahaziah of Israel. Then it abruptly ends right in the middle of Ahaziah's story and 2 Kings begins. This is one of the reasons that scholars are pretty certain that these were originally one long book that was later divided. When one scroll was filled up they just continued on another scroll and it did not matter whether or not they were in the middle of one of the sub-stories.

Both First and Second Kings jump back and forth between the kings of Judah and the kings of Israel. It is very confusing unless you follow along with the chart of Israelite Kings in the sidebar. Kings was not all written from the oral tradition. There are references in the text to other books that have disappeared such as the *Book of the Acts of Solomon* referred to in 11:41, the *Book of the Annals of the Kings of Israel* referred to in 14:19, and the *Book of the Annals of the Kings of Judah* referred to in 14:29. These are likely temple records or court records that read like birth, death, and marriage entries in a family Bible that are "fleshed out" in the book of Kings. There are probably other source books as well. The beginning of the book that continues the story of David may have been taken from a lost book known as *Succession or Court Narrative* which also may have been court records but probably also included battles fought and victories won or lost.

The political and religious divisions of the two countries probably had a lot to do with the general tenor of the book. According to the book, while Judah had some very bad kings, it also had some very good kings, but there seemed to be few redeeming values in any of Israel's kings. The books were written by priests from Judah after the fall of Israel, and that probably explains why they portray all of the Israelite kings as having done "what was evil in the sight of the Lord." The Northern Kingdom is often demeaned and clearly considered to be inferior by the authors of the books. However, archaeological data and the texts of other contemporary countries suggest that Israel was by far the most productive and prosperous of the two nations. That is what made it so attractive to the Assyrians who decided to invade and conquer that country rather than Judah. The conduct of the kings is always measured against the standard of David who "did what is right in the sight of the Lord" and who reformed Judean worship. He removed all of the High Places where the populace (and many kings) tended to go to worship contrary to the will of GOD.

These are interesting and well crafted narrations. The general theme of the books is the attempt by the people to live the way GOD wanted them to live in the Promised Land, but generally the people fouled up due to the failures of their kings. We then see how GOD dealt with their successes and, more often, their failures. The primary characters in the story are the Israelite kings and prophets from the two countries.

The books are formed around a framework known as the "regnal formulae." Basically, each story tells us: 1) when a king begins his reign, always in relation to the reigns of one or more other kings; 2) the length of the king's reign; 3) the name of his capital city; 4) his death, burial, and successor; 5) the narrator's evaluation of the king's religious policies; and, for the Judean kings, the name of the King's mother and his age when he became king.

There is one additional tool that the narrator often uses—he refers the reader to another text if the reader wants additional information. These are the books mentioned above, some of which are very likely to be the actual temple records of the kings such as the *Book of the Annals of the Kings of Judah.* This appears to be a real effort by the author(s) to accurately record history, but the interpretations of these facts may not always be correct interpretations. I think that you can safely assume that the underlying facts are true and correct, but the conclusion, for example, that a particular king did "what was evil in the sight of the Lord" may not

ISRAELITE KINGS

Before the Division of the Kingdom

Saul (1025-1005 b.c.e)
David (1005-965)
Solomon (Yedidiah) (968-928)

After the Divided Monarchy

Judah:	**Israel:**
Rehoboam (928-911)	Jeroboam I (928-907)
Abijam (Abijab) (911-908)	
Asa (908-867)	Nadab (907)-906)
	Baasha (906-883)
	Elah (883-882)
	Zimri (882)
	Omri (882-871)
	Ahab (873-852)
Jehoshaphat (870-846)	Ahaziah (852-851)
	Jehoram (Joram) (851-842)
Jehoram (Joram) (851-843)	
Ahaziah (Jehoahaz) (843-843)	Jehu (842-814)
Athaliah (842-836)	Jehoaz (817-800)
Jehoash (Joash) (836-798)	Jehoash (Joash) (800-784)
Amaziah (798-769)	Jeroboam II (788-747)
Azariah (Uzziah) (785-733)	Zechariah (747)
Jotham (759-743)	Shallum (747)
	Menahem(747-737)
	Pekahiah (737-735)
	Pekah (735-732)
	Hoshea (732-722)
Ahaz (743/735-727/715)	
Hezekiah (727/715-698/687)	

After the Fall of Israel to the Exile

Manasseh (698/687-642)
Amon (641-640)
Josiah (640-609)
Jehoiakim (Eliakim) (608-598)
Jehoiachim (Jeconiah) (597)
Zedekiah (Mattaniah) (597-586)

accurately state the facts. For example, a particular king might have simply gotten sick and died rather than his death being some retribution by God for what the king did.

Also, keep in mind that this is not a complete history of the times. There was a lot going on during this period, which was at the beginning of the Iron Age, that was not included in these books, and there was no attempt to make this a comprehensive history of Israel. The author only included what was needed to get his or her message across. The theme of the book is not what happened in the Middle East, but how the human frailties of the kings and the people did not fulfill the moral and religious expectations of GOD and how this led to the downfall of Israel and the loss of the identity of its people. Israel was conquered by the Assyrians and ceased to exist. Its people were captured and dispersed throughout the Assyrian empire and assimilated into other tribes. These were the ten Lost Tribes of Israel, and they were, indeed, lost forever, although the Church of Jesus Christ of the Latter Day Saints believes that they became the Native Americans*.

These were intended to be didactic stories. The author attempted to "flesh out" our understanding of GOD and to show His position in the world. He is always compared with the other gods in the area which are shown to be merely human creations. GOD is always the moving force in everything that happens, not the kings and the prophets.

There are other teachings that you can follow as you read the books as well. The most important are GOD's demands regarding what is acceptable worship (no idols, for example, and certainly none of the fertility rights of the Canaanites and others who employed fertility rituals such as the use of temple prostitutes, bestiality, and the like) and the places where you worship GOD. Needless to say, GOD was a teensy bit angry with Solomon. However, because of GOD's promises and love for David, he did not strip Solomon of his kingdom, but he did take retribution on Solomon's son and successor. He stripped Rehoboam of all but one tribe from the kingdom. That is the Bible's explanation for the division of the Israelites into two countries, but remember, this was history written by the priests of Judea after the fall of Israel. In any event, it was all downhill for Solomon after he lavished himself with riches and women.

All of the stories of Solomon, including many that are not in the Bible, were apparently contained in the now-lost *Book of the Acts of Solomon*. This is believed to be actual temple records from the time of the events and would be a treasure beyond belief if a copy could be found.

From the death of Solomon, it was all downhill for the Hebrews as well. First, the country split into two separate nations. Next, both

---

* Recent DNA tests have proved that the Native Americans have no Hebrew blood.

kingdoms were cursed with a long series of incompetent kings, all of whom led their countries into sin, including idol worship and the use of both male and female temple prostitutes.

In the fifth year of the reign of King Rehoboam, an incredibly important event took place. Shishak, the king of Egypt, raided Jerusalem and took all of the treasures from Solomon's palace as booty, including all of the gold (1 Kings 14:25-26). What is interesting about this is that the event appears to be pure history. There are two secondary sources that tell the identical story—Egyptian texts and the archaeological record. To date, this is the oldest part of the Bible that has such clear independent verification. This occurred in 923 C.E., so that means that from that date all of the way back to the beginning of time, there is nothing to verify, with any degree of certainty, any of the events in the Bible.

Part of these books are devoted to the ministry of the prophet Elisha, Elijah's successor. The Bible is full of private jokes played by the Hebrews on others, and 2 Kings 1:9-14, contains one of them. Elijah was sitting on top of a hill, and the king sent an officer with 50 men to bring him back. The captain went up and demanded that Elijah come down, but Elijah instead sent down fire from Heaven which consumed the captain and his fifty men. This happened twice, and on the third try the captain gave Elijah the respect to which he was entitled, so Elijah went down.

That is how it translates into English. In Hebrew it is all done with a very clever play on words: *ish 'elohim* means "man of GOD," but *esh 'elohim* means "fire of GOD." In Hebrew the Captains demanded that Elijah *ish 'elohim* (come down) and Elijah, instead, sent down *esh 'elohim.* It is sort of like, "Oh, did you mean *ish*? I would have sworn you said *esh*." That is a story that listeners around a campfire would remember with a smile.

Elijah (literally) passed the prophet's mantle to his son Elisha in a scene reminiscent of Moses crossing the Red Sea. Elijah struck the water of the Jordan with his staff and the Jordan parted so that he and Elisha could cross, replicating the acts of Moses and Joshua (and also the Sumerian Mises).

7

The Prophets

O ye dry bones, hear the word of the Lord

Ezek. 37:4

What exactly was a prophet? They weren't really fortune tellers running around predicting the future as most people assume today, although there was an element of that. They certainly were not priests or persons who assisted the priesthood, although many people think they were. As a group, they were probably the very last people anyone would invite into their home. Being stuck in a room with a prophet would be like being trapped in an elevator with a life insurance salesman. They were aggressive and spoke only of doom and gloom.

The Hebrews were not the only people to have prophets; prophets were common all around the Middle East in many religions, and surviving writings about these other prophets often closely parallel the writings of the Biblical prophets. Prophets were basically unemployed transients who traveled the country, often in groups. Sometimes they lived together in their own communities and held ecstatic forms of religious experience. This was especially true in the early days of Israelite prophets. They were generally looked upon as troublemakers, but a few of them gained an incredible amount of power and influence with the kings.

The Hebrew prophets were the fire and brimstone preachers of their time, denouncing what they perceived to be evil, corrupt, and, especially, immoral, conduct which they managed to find everywhere and in every circumstance. In the very early days, with the earliest prophets, they could be described as "seers," but they evolved into much more than that. Because GOD no longer spoke directly to the people, as He did, for example, when he spoke to Moses from a burning bush or when He told King David to do certain acts. The prophets each decided they were the intermediaries between GOD and man. They claimed that GOD now spoke to the people through them. They became the "messengers of GOD." In fact, if you read any of the books of the prophets, you will see that they very often introduced their speeches with the words, "thus says the Lord," which was the typical language of a messenger ("lord" did not usually mean a god but a person who ruled over an area).

They also acted as intermediaries between the general populace and GOD by passing on to GOD the questions and wishes of the people, and then passing GOD's responses back to the people. This greatly angered the priesthood, as you can well imagine. Prophets were frequently looked upon as being obnoxious nuisances, and sometimes when they became too much of a nuisance they were forced to literally flee the city for their lives. They were able to find something wrong no matter how happy and prosperous everyone was.

The wide range of the acts of the prophets can be seen by the various names that they are called. While we know them only as "prophets" (*nabi* in Hebrew), they are known by many more names in Hebrew, some of which we can mention, including—*'ish'elohim* which means "man of GOD" or, in our modern vernacular, a "Holy man," and *hozeh* which means "visionary." Unlike the priesthood, prophets could also be women. Deborah (Jud 4:4) and Huldah (2 Kings 2) were just two examples; Moses' sister, Miriam, was another.

We have met several prophets already. This chapter is devoted to those prophets that have books written in their names. The prophetic books, with the exception of Jonah which we will discuss in the next chapter, are filled with the endless sayings and speeches of the prophets. However, do not for a minute consider these to be the exact words of the prophets. Remember, these words were spoken long before we had dictating and recording equipment or videos. In many cases, as with the prophets Amos, Hosea, Isaiah, and Micah, the words were spoken by the prophets almost 3000 years ago. Further, at the time the words were spoken, written Hebrew itself was still in its infancy. There were very few people who could either read or write, and it is unlikely that many of the known prophets could either. Those who could write were mostly in the priesthood or were court scribes, and prophets were not popular at either place. So they may be getting a bit of a bad rap. There are some very poetic portions of the early prophetic books and those are some of the oldest known Hebrew writings, but none of the original writings have survived. It is believed that these poetic speeches were delivered by the prophet to public audiences.

The history of the Hebrew prophets began even before the days of the first king, Saul, and continued until well after the return from exile in Babylon. Scholars generally divide the prophets into four different periods. These periods again reflect historical, social, and religious influences that we discussed in the very beginning. Each of these periods is defined by a seminal historical event, and the prophetic writings each carry common themes based upon which of the four periods the prophet lived.

PRE-EXILIC PROPHETS

Prophet	**Date (B.C.E.)**	**Place and King**
Amos	c. 760 - 750	Israel, under Jeroboam II
Hosea	c. 745	Israel under Jeroboam II
Isaiah	742 - 701	Judah, under Uzziah, Jotham, Ahaz, and Hezekiah
Micah	c. 750	Judah under Jotham, Ahaz, and Hezekiah
Nahum	625 - 610	Judah under Josiah
Zephaniah	c. 621	Judah under Josiah
Habakkuk	615 - 598	Judah, probably.
Jeremiah	627 - 587	Judah, Josiah, Jehoiakim, Jehoiachim, and Zedekiah to the fall of Jerusalem

By this time you can probably figure out the periods yourself from what you have read so far. They are defined by the periods of: the Israelite kings: 1) the early days; 2) the Assyrian defeat of the Northern Kingdom of Israel and the capture and assimilation of its people; 3) the Babylonian defeat of Judah and the Exile; 4) and the post-exilic return to Jerusalem and the attempts to restore both the city and the Hebrew culture. The roles of the prophets changed in each period.

In the first period, prophets were often advisors to the kings and were looked to for many strange chores. For example, where the prophet Samuel was sent out to look for some lost livestock and found the boy David. When King Jeroboam's son got sick, the king sent his wife to the prophet Ahijah to find out if his son would live or die. Kings asked prophets for guidance, for example Deborah and Isaiah were consulted in military matters such as whether to go to war or not. Prophets sometimes selected persons to be kings and broke others who tried to become king.

In the second period, the prophets were no longer merely aides to the kings. They took on a very populous role, preaching in the Temple courts and trying to influence public opinion, a change that continued evolving until the end of that period. At that time, the Assyrians were breathing down the necks of Israel and they eventually captured the Northern Kingdom.

The third period was the tragic time leading up to the Exile when the prophets were trying to convince both the kings and the people to straighten out their act and get back to living according to GOD's laws in order to prevent a catastrophe like what had previously happened to Israel. The prophets, Ezra in particular, may even have worked on updating and rewriting the scriptures during the Exile.

Finally, the fourth period prophets, including Ezra as there was an overlap in the periods, were devoted to restoring the Hebrews to their rightful place as GOD's chosen people, including rebuilding the country after their return from exile. The prophets of this period also began to hint about some future cataclysmic event if the people did not toe the line to GOD's commands, and began to lay the groundwork for the apocalyptic movements of the future. These apocalyptic movements culminated in the book of Daniel, which is the only book in the Old Testament that could be categorized as apocalyptic. The Hebrews include Daniel in their catch all books of Writings while the Christian Bible locates Daniel in the prophetic literature category.

POST-EXILIC PROPHETS

Prophet	Date (B.C.E.)	Place
Ezekiel	597 - 563	Babylonian Exile
Haggai	520	Jerusalem
Zechariah	520 - 518	Jerusalem
Malachi	460 - 450	Jerusalem after the Temple was rebuilt
Obadiah	460 - 400	
Ezra	458	Jerusalem,
Nehemiah	455 & 433	Jerusalem,
Joel	350	
Jonah	Lived c. 750, but book of Jonah was written c. 350	

All that being said, most scholars agree that the poetic portions of the books almost certainly originated in the oral sermons or pronouncements that the prophets spoke at public gatherings. Sometime later, one of the listeners, or perhaps even the prophet himself, wrote down what was remembered of the event. The other, non-poetic portions were almost without exception, written much later—perhaps hundreds of years later. These were likely part of the oral tradition that was passed down over the years.

The words of the prophets were not necessarily written just to make a record of what was said. Many of these people so angered the kings and the priests that they never wanted to hear another word uttered by a prophet. A good example is Jeremiah. While Jeremiah was later embraced by King Josiah, who relied heavily on the prophets, he was reviled by Josiah's predecessors. At one time, Jeremiah became such a trouble maker that King Jehoiakim forbade him to ever speak publicly in the Temple. Jeremiah was not one to let a little thing like that stop him, so he dictated his words to his faithful scribe, Baruch, who then took those scrolls into the Temple so that the words could be read by others. The king did not take this subterfuge lightly, and had all of the scrolls confiscated and burned. What did Jeremiah do? He had Baruch recreate copies of the destroyed originals, and to make matters worse, he included new material. The new copy by Baruch probably, but not certainly, formed the foundation for the Book of Jeremiah we now find in our Bibles. This probably gives you a little clue as to why the prophets were so unpopular with kings and priests.

There is a reference in 1 Chr 29:29 where the prophet Nathan was asked, along with others, to record some of the acts of David. There was a similar reference to the recording of the acts of Solomon in 2 Chr 9:29. The only one of the books of the Prophets that was probably a completed work from beginning to end by a single author is the book of Ezekiel. Some books were written over a period of centuries. Isaiah, for example, was started in the eighth century B.C.E., was added to in the sixth century twice, and was finished sometime before the second century. We know that it was complete by that time because one of the scrolls discovered in Qumron included all of the parts of Isaiah known today. Also, the Septuagint, which was a second century translation from Hebrew to Greek, includes all portions.

It was typical that people tinkered with the words of the prophets over the centuries. There is evidence that they were frequently edited. Essentially all of the narrative portions were added at later times by different authors, sometimes by the prophets themselves. For example, Isaiah 6 and 8 were probably autobiographical whereas Ch 7, while also being biographical material, was by someone else.

Why were they edited? The reasons are diverse, and most of them are subject to a bit of speculation. For example, the books of Amos and Hosea were from material originally spoken in the Kingdom of Israel. Later, when they were brought down to Judah after the fall of Israel in 721 B.C.E., they were edited to conform to the views of Judah. Many of the books of the prophets that were written before the Exile to Babylon in 586 B.C.E. show considerable modifications made after the Exile. We will see a dramatic example of this when we examine Isaiah where the foundation of the book was written in the eighth century, and then Ch 40-55 were added during the period of the Exile, then Ch 56-66 were added after the return from Exile, and then other parts were added still later.

These were not random additions. There are recurring themes that run through the entire book.

Another example of tinkering with the books is Zechariah. At one time, the shorter Prophetic Books were copied onto a single scroll. There were twelve of them, and they were often referred to as the "Book of the Twelve." The prophets themselves were often referred to as "The Twelve." As you have probably noticed, the number twelve was a very important number to the Hebrews—there were twelve sons of Jacob who formed the twelve tribes, and this symbolism was continued throughout the history of the Israelites. So the scribes making this scroll needed twelve prophetic books for the scroll. In order to make this work, they took the works of Zechariah (1-8) and added the works of two other prophets, whose names are now lost (9-11 and 12-14), to form a single work. Then, they added another work which was written by an unknown prophet and called it the book of Malachil. *Malachi* means "my messenger," which is a phrase from (3:1) in that book. This, apparently, seemed to be as good a name as any.

None of the changes and additions made to the prophetic books was for a nefarious purpose. The words of the prophets were deemed to be important, not only for the times that they were written, but for different times throughout history. As we have seen in the historical books, it was a common practice to modify the Biblical books to show their relevance to the present day. While the early Hebrews considered the Torah to be the unalterable words of GOD, they did not feel the same way about the words of the prophets or the Historical Books, and certainly not that group called the Writings..

The very first of the prophet/authors, Amos, was typical of most prophetic literature. In a time of tremendous prosperity and happiness he saw nothing but moral decay and ethical corruption. The fact that the Israelites were GOD's chosen people did not mean that they got to enjoy special privileges and happiness. Being "chosen" meant an ever increasing duty to show complete obedience to GOD's laws. In other words, stop enjoying yourselves and start praying more.

Both the Jewish scriptures and the Christian Old Testament contain the stories of the prophets, but there is a difference. The stories of the prophets are listed by the length of the book in the Jewish scriptures where in the Christian Bible they are listed chronologically in the order that they were believed to have lived, except for the books of Isaiah, Jeremiah and Ezekiah, the longest, are placed first. They are called the "Major Prophets" by the Jews. Each of their works was on a separate scroll. The other twelve, those in the "Book of the Twelve." are referred to as the "Minor Prophets." However, that terminology has nothing to do with their relative importance. It is merely a reference to the length of their books. Do not construe it to mean that any of the minor prophets is less important than the major prophets as people are wont to do.

The lists of prophets in the sidebars are chronological. However, use the dates with some caution. In many cases, all or part of the book for a particular prophet was written long, long after that person's death. Jonah is a good example. Jonah lived about 750 B.C.E., but the book of Jonah was written about 400 years later. The book describes events in the time of Jeroboam II who lived between 786-740 B.C.E. That is how they concluded that Jonah lived about the same time. However, the author was obviously familiar with other writings from 320-350 B.C.E. so we know that it was not written at the time Jonah was alive. There is no record that any of the events described in Jonah ever occurred during the time of Jeroboam II.

One further note, the book of Lamentations was originally placed with the Prophetic Books right after Jeremiah because many of the ancient Greek, Latin, and Aramaic translations attributed the authorship of Lamentations to Jeremiah. Scholarly research today has shown that it is highly unlikely that Jeremiah had anything to do with this book even though many of the sentiments are similar to his views.

The stories of the prophets are fascinating, but it is impossible to discuss all of them here. Some of the more significant incidents and ideas fit in well with the theme of this book, and we will talk about them. Some are discussed elsewhere such as the story of Amos noted above. The following are some of the highlights in the stories of the prophets.

Hosea is typical of the first period prophets. As you read Hosea, try to imagine an eighth century Israelite getting an ear full of Hosea's preaching. It is reminiscent of the street preachers in public places today, carrying signs and bellowing out, "Repent Sinners." That is pretty much what all of Hosea is about. You can imagine that people wanted one of these rabble-rousers around about as much as you would want to hang around with someone standing on a soap box in the town square bellowing out, "Praise the Lord." As you read Hosea, it helps if you understand that he very often refers to the Northern Kingdom of Israel by either the name of the most influential tribe in Israel, "Ephraim," or by the capital city of Ephraim, "Samaria." In fact, several of the pre-exilic prophets refered to Israel by those names.

The writing is very clever. In order to understand what he is talking about consider that it is almost all written as a series of metaphors based upon things that the people know from every day life such as agriculture and family relationships. This was a common thread with many of the prophets. For example, in one story Hosea characterized the Northern Kingdom of Israel as a promiscuous wife. The people had, once again, begun to embrace Canaanite religious practices which included sexual intercourse with temple prostitutes. Israel (the wife) was convinced that the fertility of the land that they had been blessed with is a gift from the Canaanite fertility GOD, Baal. For this, GOD divorced Israel but promised to remarry Israel if the people get their act together. If you read this without understanding the metaphor of the promiscuous wife, you will wonder what in the heck the story is all about.

There are some very clever plays on words too, such as the word "knowledge" in Ch 4. Hosea tells the people that GOD *knows* of Ephraim, meaning that GOD is well aware of Israel's prohibited acts, and that they do not *know* the Lord, meaning that they are not loyal to GOD. This is similar to a common religious phrase today, "know the Lord thy GOD."

As I mentioned earlier, GOD told Hosea to marry a prostitute, Gomer, and he did. Although it is a little confusing because she is later referred to merely as an adulteress or a promiscuous woman. In any event, she was repeatedly unfaithful to him. One time he even had to buy her back, although some scholars believe that he actually purchased a second wife rather than ransoming his first wife. The key theme is, that no matter how unfaithful she was, no matter how much she fooled around with other men, and this hurt him deeply, he still loved her and forgave her. Hosea then compares his relationship with Gomer to the relationship between GOD and the Israelites. No matter how many times the people turn away from Him, and no matter how much they hurt Him, He still loves them and will forgive them and bring them back into His house.

This was also a major message that was later taught by JESUS. It is a little difficult to reconcile this incredibly forgiving GOD with the angry GOD who demands that adulterous wives and prostitutes to be stoned to death.

Hosea also has some very strong accusations against the priesthood which must have greatly endeared him to the tribe of Levi. He accused the priests of encouraging the sinful ways of the people because the people then had to make more atonement sacrifices, and the priests got 10% of all the animals sacrificed. In other words, the more the people sin, the greater the profits for the priests.

Isaiah

Isaiah is one of the most interesting books of the Bible. Parts of it are very poetic and some are very familiar. For example, the very famous "Hallelujah Chorus" from Handel's Messiah uses the words of Isaiah as translated in the King James Version. Besides Handel's Messiah, many words and phrases from Isaiah have become staples in the English language:

- Snow-white
- Swords into plowshares
- The people that walked in darkness
- They shall mount up with wings as eagles
- Be of good courage
- They shall see eye to eye
- A lamb to the slaughter

and much more.

The book of Isaiah was written over several centuries and had several different authors. Again, as in most of the Bible, the history of the book of Isaiah is the result of many outside influences, including political, historical, religious, and social influences.

Have you ever heard of the Syro-Ephraimite War? Neither had I. I can't even pronounce it. But this war was the first historical influence on the book of Isaiah. Remember, as in the book of Hosea, the Northern Kingdom of Israel is often referred to by the name of its most influential tribe, Ephraim. From this clue you might suspect, correctly, that Israel had something to do with this war.

Both Israel and Judah had just enjoyed a long period of peace, or as near to peace as that portion of the world had ever seen, and a long period of expansion. Israel had reached the greatest size it would ever attain. Then, Tiglath-pileser III became King of the Assyrian Empire in 745 B.C.E. and he decided that he needed a bigger empire. The land to the west fit in perfectly with his plans. Sitting in his way, however, were the rich and fertile lands of Israel, Syria, and Judah. To remedy this situation, Tiglath-pileser set his sights on all three of them.

Both Israel and Syria knew that if they did not form an alliance with Judah, that Tiglath-pileser could simply pick them off one at a time. Therefore, they tried to get Judah to join with them in a pact to repel the Assyrians. Judah's king Uzziah, who had been king during all of the peaceful years, then died. He was replaced by Jotham, who did not last long, and Jotham was replaced by Ahaz. The kings of Syria and Israel pressured Ahaz to stand with them against the Assyrians. Ahaz wanted nothing to do with the idea and agonized over it. He asked Isaiah what to do. Isaiah said that the LORD would give a sign. In one of the most misquoted phrases in the Bible, Isaiah said, "[T]he LORD will give you a sign. Look, the young woman is with child and shall bear a son, and shall name him Immanuel. . . ."

The original translation of this phrase from Hebrew to Greek was in the Septuagint. It incorrectly translated the Hebrew word for "young woman" as "virgin," and translated the phrase as, "Look, the virgin shall conceive and bear a son, . . ." When Matthew was writing his gospel, he adopted the Septuagint translation (Matt 1:23) and based his entire story of JESUS birth around this phrase. As a result, Mary became a virgin for all time. How the birth of a Jewish baby 700 years later could have been a sign to Ahaz about a military alliance against the Assyrians is hard to conceive.

In any event, Ahaz rejected the proposed alliance. So what did those otherwise reasonable kings of Israel and Syria do in the eighth century B.C.E.? They declared war against Ahaz hoping to force a regime change that would agree to the alliance. That war is what is now known as the Syro-Ephraimite War. Ahaz, however, took the back door route. He went to Assyria and asked for help in his struggles against Syria and Israel. He got the help, but he had to sell out his country to do it. Judah became a vassal state of Assyria. As part of the deal, they had to adopt many of the Assyrian customs which King Josiah would later work so hard to get rid of. As for Syria and Israel, Assyria picked them off one at a time, just as the kings feared.

The second historical event that formed the background of the book of Isaiah occurred when Tiglath-pileser died. Upon his death, the power of Assyria waned. The king of Judah at the time was Hezakiah, the son of Ahaz, and he decided that it was the perfect time to get out from under the yolk of Assyria and he rebelled.. The new king of Assyria, Sennacherib, then attacked all of the cities around Jerusalem and destroyed them. He could not conquer Jerusalem, however. He laid siege to it and eventually Hezakiah ransomed the city with practically all of its assets and the Assyrians left. Evidence of that siege is still visible today.

Sennacherib had a stelae made commemorating his victory and even had the story etched onto a palace wall. It is very interesting to compare the Assyrian version of the siege as written on the stelae with the Biblical version. Both parties claim victory. This well may be the first recorded incidence of political spin.

The above two historical sections of the book are contained in Ch 1-

39 and may have actually been written by Isaiah. But then we move on to a different time and different authors. All parts of the book share common themes, so they meld together quite nicely. The two themes have been identified as the principle that all historical events are orchestrated by GOD, or at least are allowed to occur through GOD's will. This even includes what happens to other empires. GOD is in control of everything. The second theme is that Jerusalem must be the center of both the king's government and of the Hebrew religion. These basic themes are applied to the acts that occur over several hundred years, modified to fit the times. Also, throughout the book, there is also a theme of judgment. The nation is judged by the acts of the people and the nation is punished or rewarded accordingly.

Before we move on to the third historical event, there is one passage in Isaiah that probably has more importance today than it did at the time it was written. It is Ch 34:14 where there is a reference to "**Lilith**." It is the only reference to her in the entire Bible, but the phrase ". . . there *too* Lilith shall repose, . . ." seems to indicate that Lilith was a well known personage, probably part of the Hebrew oral tradition. Who is this mysterious person?

You may recall that in Gen 1:26-27 man and woman were created on the same day. (Actually, some of the oldest copies of Genesis in the original Hebrew strongly suggest that they were the same person, a man/woman). It is only in Gen 2 where man was created first and then the woman last. Many scholars, relying on later Hebrew texts, believe that, in the oldest version of the Creation story, Gen 2, woman was created first, also from dust, just like man. That first woman was named "Lilith." They further argue that the patriarchal society during that time, coupled with the chauvinism of the priesthood, did not want a woman who was strong and dominant, let alone one who insisted on being treated as an equal; one who was actually created before man. The absurdity of it all! So it is believed that they simply wrote Lilith out of the script.

Without a doubt, Lilith was a strong woman. An ancient medieval text relied upon by these revisionist scholars is called *Alphabet of Ben Sira* which records the story of Lilith in which she was described as Adam's first wife. In this version, which is apparently supported by the Talmud, Lilith was created from the earth, just like Adam. She was not the sweet helpmate that Eve was, however. She had the temerity to tell Adam that she did not want to have sex in the male dominant position with the man on top. She demanded to be treated as an equal. When Adam refused, she walked out on him. Then she committed the greatest sin possible at the time, she spoke GOD's name aloud and she was sent to live with the demons, eventually becoming a demon herself. Nearly all of the strong women in the Bible, with the exception of Deborah, are portrayed as evil or somehow tainted. Kings could be as vicious and scandalous as they wanted, but if a woman did the same thing she was demonized. Jezebel and Queen Athaliah are just a couple of these demonized women.

Scholars are unable to determine exactly what or who Lilith was from other Biblical references because the word is only used once so there is nothing to compare it to. The *Talmud* was written by the Rabbis in the first centuries B.C.E. and C.E., so it is also a very late source. Of course, the *Alphabet of Ben Sira* is even more recent, and, therefore, an even less reliable authority. The scholars began to search other contemporary Middle Eastern traditions to see if there was a parallel. They found one—a Canaanite woman called "Lilitu" became a demon who tormented men. This may have been the source of the Lilith story.

Why is Lilith important today? Lilith was discovered by feminists a few years ago and she has since become a very popular subject in feminist literature. In 1997, a band of women rock musicians toured the country as the "Lilith Tour." It was incredibly successful.

But I digress. Back to our story. The third historical event affecting the story of Isaiah occurred some 150 years after Isaiah's death, so, it's just a wild guess, but Isaiah probably did not write this portion of the book. It is found in Chapters 40-55, and is referred to by scholars as "Second Isaiah." The Assyrian Empire continued to crumble and the fortunes of the Babylonian Empire grew in the ensuing years. Babylon conquered Nineveh, the Assyrian capitol, in 612 B.C.E., and the two most powerful countries in the western world were then the Babylonians and Egypt. Each coveted the other's empire. And guess who was right, smack in the middle—little Judah.

When Babylon, under the leadership of King Nebuchadnezzar defeated the Egyptians in 605 B.C.E, he had to occupy Judah in order to do so. Zedekiah, the last king of Judah, made the mistake of rebelling against Babylon, and in 586 B.C.E., Nebuchadnezzar destroyed Jerusalem and sent most of the population of Judah into exile. This event is referred to as, well, the Exile.

Finally, we come to the last historical event that shaped the book of Isaiah, the return of the Hebrews to the Promised Land beginning in 538. The Persians had grown in power under the leadership of King Cyrus, and they defeated the Babylonians. Measured by the other empire builders in the history of the Middle East, not excluding some of the present leaders, Cyrus was a half-way decent guy. He decided to allow the Hebrews to move back into the land of Judah, and even helped them by sending Hebrew "leaders" to Jerusalem to assist in the rebuilding. Many of these "leaders" were prophets and as we will soon discover, some of them were total incompetents at their assigned jobs.

Some of the most oft-quoted lines from Isaiah, and some of the most poignant, come from this period in what is known as Second Isaiah. Also written after the return in 538 and continuing to about 515 B.C.E., there was yet another author which is known as, you guessed it, Third Isaiah and these works are found in chapter 56-66. It is not likely that this was all written by one author nor is it likely that it is a single work.

Much later, the early Christian church, fighting for legitimacy among many long-established religions, tried to connect JESUS to portions of the Jewish scriptures, especially to predictions of the future. That is, if one of the books of Jewish scripture predicted a messiah, the early Christian church did everything that it could do to make Jesus fit into that prediction. This can be seen in the New Testament, particularly in the Gospel of Matthew, but it was even more prevalent in the writings of the "Early Fathers" of the new Christian Church.

This all occurred five or six hundred years after this portion of Isaiah was written. The problem was that the church leaders at that time were all gentiles and knew next to nothing about ancient Jewish history or culture. They often locked onto words that sounded like they described some aspect of JESUS' life and held those words out to be proof that JESUS was the predicted Messiah when the words actually had nothing to do with the prediction of a messiah. Matthew's virgin birth was an example. This is not merely an interesting sidelight, unfortunately. Many modern churches have picked up on these ancient interpretations and still refer to them just as the early church did.

Second Isaiah provided a mother-lode for these misinterpretations. They are all part of the four "Suffering Servant" songs*. If a twenty-first century Christian were to read of any one of them, without knowing the history of Second Isaiah, he or she could easily conclude that Isaiah was talking about JESUS, and that is what the early Christian writers concluded. Here is one example from Ch 53:4-10:

* First Servant, 42:1-9; Second, 49:1-6; Third, 50:4-11; Fourth, 52:13-53:12.

Surely he has borne our infirmities
and carried our diseases;
Yet we accounted him stricken,
struck down by God, and afflicted.
But he was wounded for our transgressions,
crushed for our iniquities;
Upon him was the punishment that made us whole,
and by his bruises we are healed.
All we like sheep have gone astray;
we have all turned to our own way,
and the Lord has laid on him the iniquity of us all.

He was oppressed, and he was afflicted,
yet he did not open his mouth;
like a lamb that is led to the slaughter,
and like a sheep that before its shearers is silent,
so he did not open his mouth.
By a perversion of justice he was taken away.
Who could have imagined his future?
He was cut off from the land of the living,
Stricken for the transgressions of the people.
They made his grave with the wicked
and his tomb with the rich,
although he had done no violence,
and there was no deceit in his mouth.

I think that anyone, just reading this song, would agree that it sounds like they are talking about Jesus. It clearly sounds like Isaiah is saying that Jesus died for our sins. However, going back to the beginning of this song, we see that the author is talking about "my servant." Isaiah stated many times in his poems and songs that when he refers to his "servant" he is referring to Israel (Eg. Isa 41:8-9; 49:3). Old Testament scholars are basically unanimous in their agreement on this.

Remember, this was written at the time the Israelites were coming back from the Exile. Their entire country was in ruins. Their Temple had been razed to the ground. And all of this occurred, according to Isaiah, because the people stopped living by God's laws. Instead, they were embracing Canaanite religious practices; they attributed their bountiful harvests to the Canaanite God Baal; and innumerable other transgressions. Further, according to Isaiah, God has a hand in everything, even the acts of foreign governments. If He had not felt that it was necessary for the Israelites to be captured and sent into exile, He would have prevented it from happening.

Thus, when Isaiah says in the second Suffering Servant song:

Thus says the Lord,
the Redeemer of Israel and his Holy One,
to one deeply despised, abhorred by the nations,
the slave of rulers,
"Kings shall see and stand up,
princes, and they shall prostrate themselves,
because of the Lord, who is faithful,
the Holy One of Israel, who has chosen you

the author of Second Isaiah is not talking about JESUS, he is talking about his beloved country of Judah. Just recently my front doorbell rang and when I answered the door there were three individuals on the porch. One of them handed me a religious tract and pointed to this very phrase from Isaiah and told me that it was proof that the Old Testament predicted JESUS would be the messiah. Sorry, but that is not true. There was a messianic movement at that time, but the book of Isaiah had nothing to do with it.

There is so much in the book of Isaiah that writing about it could fill several books, and it has. There has been considerable scholarly research done on Isaiah. Not only is it filled with history, it is a beautiful book to read.

Jeremiah

From all counts, Jeremiah was a very unpleasant sourpuss with very few friends. He was the king of the doomsayers. He believed that the whole country was immoral and corrupt, even the priests. So as you can imagine, he picked up some very powerful enemies along the way. He was like the guy in the old Li'l Abner comic strips that always walked around with a black cloud over his head with lightening flashing out of the cloud by the name of Joe Btfsplk (the last name is pronounced like a "Bronx Cheer"). He needed a lifetime supply of Prozac Popsicles.

Who could blame Jeremiah for being a little morose. He was told by GOD that he could never marry or have children because they would all die. So he did neither. He was by far the most powerful influence on King Josiah's reform movement. He was protected from harm by the King's court, but when Josiah died in 609 B.C.E. they could no longer protect him. He was arrested, thrown in a dry cistern that was used as a dungeon, and called a traitor and a defeatist because he counseled against war with the Chaldeans (Babylonians). After the defeat of Judah by the Chaldeans, he suffered a further ignominy by being packed off to Egypt where he was supposedly martyred.

Ezra and **Nehemiah**

These are prophets, but their books deal with the history of the Israelites after their return from exile rather than their communications with GOD. Until about 300 B.C.E. the two writings were considered to be a single book and were then separated into two. Their historical accounts, contrary to many of the other historical references in the Bible, match up accurately with Persian and other historic writings of the time. The person who wrote Nehemiah is believed to be the same person who wrote Chronicles.

The return from exile was not like the Exodus from Egypt which was a mass movement of families. The return from exile was a piecemeal process, people trickling in a little at a time. Life was not too bad in Babylon for the Jews. They were generally treated very well and many had great jobs. Some of the exiles never did return.

Not everyone had to leave Judah during the Exile. The Chaldeans left the poorest of the peasantry behind to maintain crop production and herds. Only the better off and all of the elite, the aristocracy, and priesthood were required to leave. So when the exiles came back, they found that those poor peasants had taken over all of the good properties that the families of the returnees had previously owned. You can imagine this caused some very bad blood between those who left and those who stayed. We will discuss this situation in some detail when we get to the stories of Ruth and Jonah.

Ezra is a very important person in Jewish history. He may well have been the most important member of the Hebrews in exile. Scholars think that he was probably "R," the redactor who pieced together the stories of J, E, P, and D. Many consider him to be the second founder of the Jewish nation (after Moses). He was without a doubt responsible for writing the extensive laws codifying what was previously merely custom in the practices of Temple worship and the scriptures. He also began the movement that eventually replaced the priests with rabbis.

The Persian king sent Ezra to Jerusalem to try to get the city back on its feet after the end of the Exile. The sidebar lists him in this position rather than earlier when he was working on the text of the Scriptures, but he could have been listed in several places on the chart. He apparently came to Jerusalem in the third wave of returnees. When he arrived he was shocked to find that those who had remained behind had intermarried with non-jews. While the Jews were in exile, the priests tried to find out what it was that caused GOD to throw them out of the Promised Land. They knew that they must have done something that greatly displeased GOD, so they canonized ancient customs into strict rules governing conduct.

Some of these rules were enacted merely to keep their culture and religion separate and to prevent them from being absorbed into the Chaldean society. They shocked the known world by forbidding anyone to work on the Sabbath (except wives). This definitely set the Jews apart from other groups who had never heard of taking a day off work. They again reintroduced the practice of inflicting grievous harm to mens' body parts. The practice had kind of disappeared over the years. They legislated and enforced strict dietary laws. They were not allowed to have Gentiles in their houses or to eat with Gentiles. And so on.

So when Ezra arrived in Jerusalem and witnessed first hand the shocking intermarriage that had gone on in the absence of the priestly society, his first act was to require all Jewish men to get rid of their foreign wives and the children by those wives. Ezra was sure that GOD was angry at them for diluting the purity of their race. It appears that these women and children were chased out of the city and merely abandoned. The women were not Jews and, since Jewish ancestry is passed down through the mother, the children were not Jewish either.

As much as Ezra did for Judaism, his arrival in Jerusalem was, perhaps, the darkest time in the history of these people. Needless to say, Ezra was not very popular among those who had to dump their families. Also, as it turned out, as brilliant as he was as a scholar, Ezra was an atrocious administrator. So the Persian King Artaxerxes decided that he needed to send someone else out to clean up the mess.

He decided on **Nehemiah** who was actually a Jew that the king had kept around to taste his drinks for poison. That is, he was a taster. But the king was impressed with Nehemiah's abilities and hoped that he might be able to straighten things out in Judah.

After repairing the Jerusalem city walls where they had been breached by the Chaldeans, he established a new political system. He had a bit of a problem. Hebrew society had dual rulers. The king ruled over secular matters and the priests ruled over all things religious. The priests made the laws and the kings enforced them. Since they were still in captivity, although they now had a great deal of freedom, they could not elect a king when the Persian king was the supreme ruler. So they modified the priestly role into being in charge of both religious and secular matters. Gone were the kings and back were the priests. The restored Judah was a theocracy in which the priesthood not only ran the religion, they ran Jewish social life. The political structure and the military remained in the hands of the Persians who did the unclean acts, such as war and executions, so that the priests could maintain their purity.

One very interesting fact emerged from the writings of Nehemiah. This is told in verses 8:1-8, where Ezra brings out the sacred scriptures and reads them to the people assembled in the square, as was the custom in the Middle East since so few people could read, . . . "So they read from the book, from the law of GOD, with interpretation. They gave the sense, so that people understood the reading." What this means is that the people had been living in a foreign country for so long that they no longer spoke their ancient Hebrew, the language of the scriptures. Ezra and his scribes had to read and interpret the scriptures into the language that most of the population used at the time, Aramaic, so they could understand.

From this time forward, until the 20th century, Hebrew was a ceremonial language only, like Latin in the Catholic Church. The priestly class still used it, but not the common people. Aramaic had become their common language. It is a related Semitic language that originated in a country called Aram which is now called Syria. Portions of some of the later books of the Old Testament were originally written in this language including the late additions to Isaiah and parts of Ezra. Within a short 100 or so years, the Hebrews would again be conquered, this time by Alexander and the principal languages would become Greek and Aramaic. The language of JESUS, for example, was Aramaic. Many Hebrews also learned some Greek, a dialect called "koine," which was a form of Greek used by the common working classes and the military.

Ezekiel was apparently the only prophet to accompany the priests and the others into exile in Babylon. He was a little . . . well, weird you might say. Or, of you wanted to be more accurate, he was really, *really* weird. His wife was killed in the siege of Jerusalem and he left as a captive, so that might have had something to do with his mental state. His writings are very rich in prose. Some parts of his book are quite popular because of their magical, mystical qualities with visions of GOD and frightening visions of threats and violence. He speaks out against some practices that were still part of the Jewish tradition such as human sacrifice. It did not happen often any more, but it still raised its ugly head from time to time. He also suggests that during the siege of Jerusalem the people were forced into cannibalism. His writings use very sexual language having GOD treating Israel like a lover but she ignored His entreaties and continued to degenerate, leading GOD to send the Hebrews out of the promised land.

The most famous of Ezekiel's writings, eventually to become the basis of a popular spiritual, is his description of the Valley of the Dry Bones in Chapter 37:1-7 where he was describing the revival of Judah from the desert of destruction. Christians would later incorrectly interpret this to be an image of the Resurrection of the dead.

Another of his visions has led to a great deal of controversy. He warned of a great apocalyptic battle in the future where the "chief prince" Gog invades from a place in the north called Magog to attack Judah. The author of the New Testament book of Revelation seized upon this as evidence of a coming satanic invasion. In the last century, fundamentalist Christians believed that Ezekiel was referring to the Soviet Union and, more recently, to Russia and Iran as this evil empire Magog.

8

A Whale of a Story

And Jonah was in the belly of the fish three days and three nights.

Jonah 1:17

Jesus often spoke in parables and allegories, which is a way of getting a message across by the use of symbolic fictional persons and actions to demonstrate truths about human conduct. It should come as no surprise to you that the Old Testament authors also used allegories to make certain points. But for some reason people do not feel the same way about Old Testament allegories. Nobody believes when Jesus tells the story about the Good Samaritan that he is talking about a real person and describing an incident that actually happened. Everyone understands that Jesus was trying to make a point and was using this fictitious story as an example to get that point across. But many of these same people get very upset if you suggest that some of the stories in the Old Testament did not actually happen but were merely allegories to make a particular point.

We are going to discuss three Old Testament allegories. None of these stories is true. They were never meant to be true just as Jesus did not expect anyone to believe that the Good Samaritan story described an actual event. The three books that we are going to discuss are Jonah, Job, and Ruth. Jonah may have been a real person, but he would have lived several hundred years before this story was written. Job and Ruth may or may not have been real people, but it is certain that the events that are described in all three stories never happened. In fact, the authors of these stories would be upset to think that many people actually believe these to be true events because that would mean that the very important message that they were trying to get across was lost. The Hebrews of the sixth century B.C.E. knew that they were not true, but when the Christian church started referring to these old texts, the church was almost entirely comprised of gentiles. They had no hint about the underlying, hidden concepts that the authors were trying to demonstrate so they assumed they were true stories.

These stories graphically demonstrate how historic, social, and religious matters influenced the content of the Bible.

Ruth

Let's start with the story of Ruth, which we skipped over when discussing the historical books, to illustrate what I mean. All three of these stories were actually early protest literature. They were like articles in the "Berkeley Barb" or the "Los Angeles Free Press" in the 1970s. But unlike the articles in those newspapers, these stories were fiction. They were never intended by their authors to be taken literally. Their purposes were to demonstrate opposition to the insidious practice of ethnic cleansing that occurred when the Hebrews returned from exile.

We introduced Ezra in the last chapter. His ethnic cleansing laws were brutal. If you could not prove that your wife was a Jew for ten generations, she and all of the children of that marriage were thrown out of the country and abandoned. Ezra made a lot of enemies when he enacted these laws; but few people complained. Men found that when they protested they were likely to wake up one morning with the Temple minions pounding on the door ready to escort their own wives and children out of the country. It was a horrible time in Jewish history with people settling old disputes by "ratting out" their neighbors and with knocks on the door in the middle of the night.

The problem was, how could one protest these horrible laws without risking banishment himself and, in some cases, loss of his life? If they stood up in public and complained they could find themselves accused by someone and purged from the country. Their solution was to write a story, anonymously, that pointed out the insidious nature of this religious practice. These stories were read aloud in public meetings in town squares or at the town gates. These meetings were called "synagogues," which we will discuss later. There was no other way for people to find this information because there were no libraries and, even if there were, almost nobody could read. These books only make sense when read with this historical background in mind.

The story of Ruth takes place about 1150 B.C.E. or so, but was written five or six hundred years later after the Exile. Ruth was a Moabite who married a Jewish man named Chilion at a time when he was traveling though Moab with his father and his mother, Naomi. Chilion had a brother who also married a Moabite woman named Orpah. All three men died, and the women became childless widows. The Middle East was a patriarchal society, so it was the Moabite tribe that was responsible for the care of both Ruth and Orpah, not the Jews. Naomi wanted to stay in Judah with her own people but she was finally able to convince Orpah to return to her father where they would take care of her and also protect her. It was extremely dangerous in those times to be an unprotected woman.

Ruth refused to go, however, wanting to stay with her mother-in-law. She said, "[w]hither thou goest, I will go; and where thou lodgest I will lodge; your people shall be my people, and thy GOD my GOD; where thou diest I will die, and there will I be buried." (Ruth 1:16, 17, from the KJV). How many times have you heard these words spoken or sung at a wedding? I wonder what the bride and groom would think if they knew that this very moving, romantic thought was really the words of a woman spoken to her mother-in-law?

But Ruth, despite her vulnerability as an unprotected woman and being of mixed tribal blood, maintained the highest standards of the principles of the Torah. She cared for her widowed mother-in-law as if she were Hebrew. She went into the fields after the harvest to scrape up enough grain to survive*. The owner of the field and all the men who tilled the soil for him greatly admired her. Eventually, Ruth was married to Boaz, a Hebrew who was the wealthy owner of the field who was so impressed with Ruth's labors and principles.

If the story stopped there it would be a great tale of romance with a happy ending, because Boaz had enough wealth to take care of both Ruth and Naomi rather lavishly. Ruth captured your heart because of her dedication, love and devotion to her mother-in-law, and the sacrifices she made. Although Ruth was not a Jew, she did everything that a Jewish wife should do when her husband dies, including taking care of his mother. So this non-Jew was a person who followed GOD'S laws far better than most women of pure Jewish blood. But this was a minor consideration by the author and is certainly not the main point of the story.

The closing lines of Ruth look like more of the "begat" stuff in some of the earlier books where there are pages of "he begat" someone. So most people, including preachers, find these family tree statements boring and skip on to the next part of the story. If they do so with this book, however, they will miss the most important part of the tale. The entire story is told in order to set up those closing lines of the narrative, what I call the "begats."

---

* If you recall, Jewish laws required ten percent of a harvest be left in the fields for the poor

Ruth and Boaz had a son named Obed. He married and had a son named Jesse. Jesse was the father of the greatest king in the history of Israel, David. Whoa! That finally got people's attention at the synagogue. David was not a full-blooded Jew to the tenth generation because his grandmother was a Moabite woman named Ruth! *Under the laws enacted by Ezra, the beloved King David would have to be thrown out of the country.* Further, since Jewish descent is passed on through the mother, David would not even have been Jewish! He would have been a Moabite.

The fact that this book became part of the Jewish scriptures tells us that it worked. The story addressed the conscience of the Jewish people and they listened. This magnificent story loses it beauty and meaning if it is taken literally. One would wonder what in the world it is doing in the Bible in the first place if its real meaning is missed. The Bible is not a collection of Gothic Romances. Each book is there to teach something to the readers.

Jonah

This is a similar story. Jonah (whose name means "dove") may have been a real person and a prophet, but if so he had been dead for at least 400 years before his story was written in the fourth or fifth century. A Hebrew audience at that time would recognize that the story is fiction as Jonah is filled with outrageous suggestions and humor such as commanding animals to fast and to wear sackcloth in mourning. This type of humor is not likely to resonate with people in the twenty-first century, but it worked then.

Jonah hated the people of Nineveh with a passion, not because they were the citizens of the Assyrian capital and the traditional enemies of the Israelites, but because, mainly, they were gentiles and not among GOD's chosen. GOD asked Jonah to preach to the Gentiles in Nineva and he tried everything he could to get out of it. Instead of going east to Nineveh, hoping to fool GOD he got on a boat heading west to a land called *Tarshish* which probably refers to Tartessus in Spain which would be about the farthest possible distance that Jonah could travel from Nineveh. This alone is so audacious that it not only would have brought a little snicker in the fourth century, it was a ludicrous proposition—everyone knew that you can't fool GOD, especially when you get on a boat to head for Nineveh, a town that can only be reached by land.

GOD, of course, was not deceived and sent a great storm that threatened to capsize the boat. The sailors assumed that their peril was the result of someone displeasing GOD. That was always the cause of disasters in those days. Jonah finally "fessed up" to his deception and the sailors cast him into the sea where he spent three days in the belly of a fish (it was never a whale in the old scriptures). Jonah gave a prayer of thanksgiving and GOD had the fish "spew" Jonah onto dry land. Most twenty-first century Christians believe that this really happened, but fourth-century Hebrews knew it was a tall tale. No man could sleep through a raging storm; a fish was not going to pluck a man out of the raging sea, swallow him, and then barf him up on dry land three days later (the literal translation is "spewed" but it means "vomit"); and nobody who had been swallowed by a fish would give a prayer of thanksgiving when a prayer of penitence with a request for forgiveness was appropriate in the Hebrew culture. Again, this would scarcely generate a belly laugh, but the original listeners would at least have had a snicker or two and a little "show of teeth."

Eventually Jonah had to go to Nineveh which is described as a huge town that would take three days to walk across. Nineveh was a large city, but this is a huge exaggeration. Archaeological excavations show that the entire perimeter of the city walls was only eight miles. But the author exaggerated the size to convey Jonah's great success and the enormity of GOD'S forgiveness to the people because he had Jonah tell the people that GOD would overthrow them all in forty days. That is when the king ordered everyone, including the animals, to fast and wear sackcloth and to cry out to GOD. GOD heard them and forgave them.

Jonah was devastated. That is what he feared would happen if he went and was the reason that he fled to Tarshish in the first place. He hated Nineveh and he knew that GOD, being a forgiving god, would do what he just did. Now Jonah would be seen as a false prophet because his prediction of doom did not come to pass. Jonah asked GOD to take his life. The Lord refused, so Jonah left the city and sat under a small booth to await the results. GOD caused a bush grow, believed to be a castor bush, to give Jonah shade. This made Jonah very happy, but the next day GOD created a worm that made the bush die so there was no shelter from the humid wind and the sun that beat down on his head. He became very depressed and morose and mourned the death of the tree.

GOD then pointed out to him that there was something seriously wrong where he had more compassion toward the death of a bush that he did nothing to grow and nurture than he had toward his fellow man, those hated Ninevites whom he could not believe were meant to be the recipients of GOD's concern. Shouldn't GOD be concerned about that great city in which there are more than 120,000 persons living who do not know their right hand from their left?

It is a great story, loaded with meaning, significant even today. These are people that Jonah hated solely because they were not Jewish. He didn't care a whit that they were going to be destroyed in 40 days. They were living, breathing, and feeling people, and Jonah had less feelings for them than he did for a bush on the beach and for his own credibility. It marked a huge turning point in religious history, because it was the first time that GOD was presented as a caring, loving GOD concerned for everything that he had made in the world rather than a GOD of vengeance on Israel's enemies. He was now the GOD of all people.

Why isn't that magnificent message the subject of sermons instead of the ludicrous fiction that Jonah really lived and was swallowed by a whale? The fish became a whale when Christians, certain that this was a true story, tried to reconcile the fact that there was no fish big enough to make the story credible and decided that it must be a whale instead.

The stories of Ruth and Jonah helped arouse the consciousness of the people. They are beautiful and powerful stories and the authors would be astounded if they were to learn that most people today believe that Ruth and Jonah were real people and that all those things actually happened.

Job

Job is also a protest work, apparently written right after the Exile or just after the return to Jerusalem, although its roots were very ancient. You may be familiar with the saying "the patience of Job." This comes from the New Testament letter of James (5:11). The translation of James from the Greek is imprecise. The word "patience" is more precisely translated as "endurance" or "persistence." In fact, in the story Job isn't patient at all but he certainly showed great endurance and persistence. Job refers to a different problem than either Ruth or Jonah, but it is still fiction and the author is unknown. It appears that there were several authors and the beginning and ending are probably from very ancient folk tales. From a historical point of view, Job is extremely interesting. It is a kind of a composite of ancient Middle Eastern literature.

Job was not an Israelite, he was from the land of Uz, wherever that was. It may be as imaginary as the land of Oz. The story of Job was very popular all around the Middle East. Ezekiel mentions Job along with Noah and a man named Daniel as people who "would save only their own lives by their righteousness" (Ezek 14:14, 20). This is not the Daniel from the Old Testament book by that name. This Daniel is actually pronounced "Danel" and was an ancient Canaanite king. His story was found written on stone tablets in the city of Ugarit which predated the Israelites entry into Canaan. There were numerous poems from all over the Near East where a pious and righteous sufferer told of his sufferings and wondered "why me?" and proclaimed his desire for the restoration of his old life. In fact, there is one ancient writing that is remarkably similar to Job, "The Babylonian Theodicy." The major difference is that there is no appearance of a god at the end to make the sufferer whole.

Job is part of the Hebrew wisdom tradition. It draws strongly on Proverbs and ancient hymns from Psalms. There is no mention of the Law or other Hebrew traditions. The question of the good suffering and the wicked having good fortune is discussed in more detail in later wisdom literature, particularly in Ecclesiastes and the apocryphal book of Sirach.

Job also uses ancient Near Eastern legends of the struggles between god and the sea. These are the references to Leviathan, Behemoth, the dragon of chaos, and Rahab. Some of these references are to Egyptian myths.

This brief background on the history of Job is to illustrate that it is a very complex piece of literature and its meaning goes far deeper than one can get in a casual reading. However, sermons about Job rarely discuss its deeper meanings. Scholars do not agree on what all those underlying messages mean. Perhaps it is like some of the parables and aphorisms of JESUS where it is left to the individual to determine the deeper meanings.

On the surface Job tries to explain the mystery of why good people must suffer. This is a question that you hear even today—why do good people suffer while bad people prosper? At this time Jews were asking this very question about the fundamental nature of GOD and his responsibility for the suffering of the Jews. They had been conquered, their capitol city and temple burned, and they were exiled to a foreign country. What went wrong? They were good people. So somebody revived and modernized this ancient tale.

Historically, individual responsibility is a fairly recent idea. It first appeared in the Middle East, except with respect to royalty, about 4000 B.C.E., but it came much later to the Hebrews. It is first suggested in the Bible in Ezekial (597 - 563 B.C.E.). Prior to the rise of individualism, the tribe was thought of as the basic unit of life. You stood before GOD as a tribe, not as individuals. If the people worked well together and pleased GOD everyone flourished. If there was evil in their midst, the tribe suffered. Sin called for group punishment. The sins of the fathers "shall be visited upon the children to the third and fourth generations" we are told in Exodus. When Achen sinned at Ai, for example, his whole family was destroyed.

Then came Ezekial and when he wrote "the soul that sins shall die," individualism was born to the Israelites. If you sin, you, the sinner, will die rather than the whole tribe being punished. The concept grew very slowly until the great "wisdom literature" appeared. The central idea of Wisdom, which we will get to in the next chapter, was set out in Proverbs— hard work, high morals, kindness, forgiveness, etc. The idea was that wisdom brings happiness and the lack of wisdom brings misery. That was the whole idea of Job. It was a way to convey the idea of Wisdom to the masses.

Job was a saintly man, but he was never described as a Jew. This good man had the world at his door step. He was very wealthy and had a loving wife, ten great children that he adored, and many friends. But along came a character called Satan. In Hebrew, *Satan* merely means "the accuser" or "adversary." This Satan was, in fact, a member of GOD's court, not an evil fallen angel residing in the bowels of hell.. A satan's basic duty, as in the Book of Zechariah, was to accuse human beings before GOD. It was not until Christian times when New Testament authors identified the word "satan" with the fallen angel we know as the devil. The dualism between two powerful supernatural entities, an all-good GOD and an all-evil Satan, were unknown in Jewish scriptures until they began to show up in Jewish non-canonical writings about 200 B.C.E. and evolved thereafter. This entire concept was contrary to the monotheistic foundation of Judaism in that there is only one GOD, so there was no place in Jewish beliefs for a good GOD and an almost equal bad GOD. We'll talk about Satan in more detail later.

At the beginning of the tale*, GOD is seen boasting about how faithful a servant Job is when Satan comes along and chides GOD. "Sure he is faithful and a nice guy. He has everything that a man could want. But take away all of those things and then see how faithful he is." So GOD accepts this dare or bet and allows Satan to do just that.

Now that should be a tip off that this is not a true story. Why in the world would GOD be making such a bet with anyone? The GOD I know does not have to answer to anyone. But in this story GOD allows Satan to do all sorts of bad things to Job. His beautiful house is blown down in a

---

* Told here in the "historical present" manner, that is, telling historical events as if they were just now happening, a technique often used by Mark.

windstorm and all ten children die. GOD then allows Satan to cover Job's body with painful, putrefying sores. Job's wife encourages him to end it all and stop this suffering, suggesting that he just curse GOD and die. But Job is still faithful, saying that he must take the bad with all of the good. Again, does this sound like the GOD you have learned to love and respect? He allowed ten innocent children to die to prove that a man loves him? Does GOD 's ego require that degree of reassurance?

Most sermons that I have heard about this story end right there. But the main part of the story is still to come. Next, three of Job's close friends arrive at his bedside to console him but end up accusing him of doing something horribly wrong to have incurred GOD's wrath. He angrily protests his innocence. Then a man called Elihu appears and tries to describe his own view of GOD's mysterious ways. Job counters his arguments with further protestations of innocence pointing out how wicked people appear to prosper.

Finally, GOD himself arrives speaking from a whirlwind. GOD had not appeared in person like that for centuries. He communicated through the prophets, so this should also be a tip off that the story is only allegorical. GOD tells Job that it was presumptuous of humans to discuss how GOD functions because His ways are beyond mortal comprehension. GOD is showing how much he likes Job by appearing in person, but he dresses him down a little anyway. He reminds Job of the great life he had up to the present. He tells Job that he has no idea what a tough job it is being GOD; all of the things that He has to do. Job is repentant for questioning GOD and recognizes GOD's awesome power.

Then GOD orders Job's three "friends" to make special sacrifices and He restores Job's prosperity. He even gives Job ten new children and Job has more happiness than he had before.

Sermons rarely questions GOD's acts. Would GOD really stand by and let someone destroy that good man and his family for no reason other than that GOD made a bet with Satan? And what was Satan doing in Heaven anyway? Wasn't he thrown banned from Heaven centuries before? Would Lot really be happier then ever before if GOD gave him ten new children to replace those that he allowed to be killed? Lot loved those kids. The story, if taken as an actual event, does not make a lot of sense. That would certainly not be a god that I could respect.

Ok, so what is the point then? The fact is that this was not a true story at all. The Book of Job is allegorical. There is one concept on the surface and others buried deeply. Up until the return of the Israelites from Exile, there was no formulated concept of individual punishment for sin and individual reward for good. It was always a tribal sin and it was the tribe that was either punished or thrived, not individuals. GOD was the source of everything, both good and bad. If some individuals worshiped an idol, the entire tribe suffered the wrath of GOD. Job is an example of the Hebrew religion evolving. After the disgraceful conduct of the Hebrews following their return from exile when the suffering of the Jewish people was blamed on intermarriage, some religious thinkers began to rethink the concept of sin. They finally discovered that there could be individual reward and punishment for obeying or disobeying GOD's will. The concepts of reward in Heaven or punishment in Hell as we know them today were still a long way off, however. But this was a start in that direction.

The concept was, if you live a virtuous life and follow the Law you will ultimately be rewarded. The reward should come within your lifetime. "But," some people complained, "I know lots of virtuous people and they are suffering just like the rest of us, and I know some despicable people who are wealthy and living wonderful lives." Someone wrote the book of Job to express this feeling. Job is generally considered to be a protest of the concept of an ultimate reward for being good.

That is the obvious meaning. What about the deeper concepts? The main issue in the book is stated in the question posed by Satan, "Does Job fear GOD for nothing?" (1:9). That is, will human beings demonstrate the same love and respect for GOD if there are not rewards for doing so and punishment for not doing so? Job's friends tell him that it is all his fault because he has not shown fear of GOD. Job, in some beautiful poetry, seeks a way to prove his righteousness to GOD. When GOD finally deigns to answer, He disavows the arguments of Job's friends but doesn't satisfy Job's pleas either. There is nothing in the book itself to tell us one way or another. Some scholars believe that GOD is rebuking man for having the audacity to question Him or His acts. Others suggest that it is humans that are wrong to try to suggest that it is more complex than merely being good or evil. Some hold that it points out the uselessness of trying to guess GOD's intentions.

Job doesn't really get a reward. He isn't even made whole. I don't think anyone thinks that getting ten new children can make up for the loss of the first ten. This is a very complex story, and individual listeners will probably reach different conclusions based upon their own lives.

9

The Writings

A fool takes no pleasure in understanding, but only in expressing personal opinion.

Prov. 18:12

The final section of the Hebrew Bible, The Writings, is comprised of Hebrew books that defy categorization. This section includes the following books, listed here in the order in which they appear in the Hebrew Bible:

Psalms
Proverbs
Job
The Song of Songs
Ruth (discussed in Chapter 8)
Lamentations
Ecclesiastes
Esther
Ezra (Discussed in Chapter 7)
Nehemiah (Discussed in Chapter 7)
First Chronicles
Second Chronicles
Daniel

Of course we have discussed Ruth, Job, Ezra, and Nehemiah earlier, but this is where their stories appear in the Bible. In general, these are books that could be categorized as "miscellaneous." For example, Ezra and Nehemiah were prophets, but their books are also history. They could be placed in more than one category.

Proverbs, Job, Lamentations, Ecclesiastes, and others in this chapter originated with the Wisdom movement. As we noted, the movement started with Ezekiel in the late sixth century B.C.E. When he wrote, "the soul that sins shall die" he advanced a truly revolutionary idea—that a person is destined to thrive or perish based upon his own conduct. You stand before GOD as an individual, not simply as one member of a tribe.

Today, that statement draws a yawn from the listener. But in Ezekiel's day it would have drawn gasps. It took awhile before "individualism," as it was called, was fully accepted.

Once the seed of individualism was planted, it grew quickly. It is the dominant theme in the books of Proverbs, Ecclesiastes, the Song of Songs, and in the apocryphal books of Ecclesiasticus, Sirach, and the Wisdom of Solomon (See Chapter 10). The wisdom movement also had a huge influence on one group of early Christians, the Gnostic movement; at one time was almost as large and powerful as the Catholic (Universal) movement before it was banned as being heretical.

What was "Wisdom" as the Hebrews understood it? It is another of those words that mean something completely different today. Then, it was the ability to determine the pattern of GOD and the ability to conform one's individual self to that pattern. The first step was to acknowledge that GOD was the primary force in the universe. "The fear (deep respect) of the Lord is the beginning of wisdom" (Prov 9:10). The rabbis taught that if you seek wisdom and then conform your conduct to that wisdom, you will be rewarded by GOD. This was without qualification—wisdom (righteousness) brings success; wickedness leads to destruction. Some of the later psalms touch on this philosophy (Ps 37 and 110, for example).

Psalms

This is a collection of 150 poetic prayers that were sung or recited in religious services. It is sometimes called the "Psalter." The Hebrew title is *Tehillim, which* means "praises." The word "Psalms" used in the English translation of the Bible comes from the Greek *Psallein* or "play on a stringed instrument" such as a harp, which is a Greek translation of the Hebrew *mizmore.* Most people know that it is also the longest book in the Bible. Other facts about Psalms are battered around, especially over the internet: the middle chapter of the Bible is Psalm 118; the longest Chapter of the Bible is Psalm 119; the shortest chapter of the bible is Psalm 117; the exact center of the Bible is Psalm 118:8. Of course, all this depends on which translation of the Bible you use. The Hebrew Bible does not have a New Testament, so the statistics do not work there at all. Nor does it work on the Douay-Rheims (Catholic) or the Eastern translations which include portions of the Apocrypha in their Bibles and this also changes the calculations. Many calculate Psalm 117 as the center of the KJV, including a recent computer calculation by Snopes.com, but that's not true in other translations.

Whether sung or recited, the psalms are poetry; but unlike the poetry familiar to most of us, ancient Hebrews made no attempt to rhyme the verses. Instead they were rhythmical thought patterns. They often employ a form called "parallelism" where two lines relate to each other in a repeated rhythm. Unfortunately, the rhythms do not translate into other languages, so we are left with some very beautiful prose that most would not recognize as poetry. Many scholars have written that they had no idea how beautiful the Bible was until they were able to read it in its native Hebrew and Greek.

Many of the parallel verses are arranged with a statement followed by another way of saying the same thing, always in the same rhythm (called "synonymous parallelism"), for example:

> O *Lord my God, in you I take refuge;*
> *Save me from all my pursuers, and deliver me (7:1).*

In others, the second statement contrasts with the first (antithetic parallelism);

> *[F]or the Lord watches over the way of the righteous,*
> *But the way of the wicked will perish.*

Some verses are arranged in what is known as "acrostics." That is, the first letter of each stanza is a different letter of the Hebrew alphabet and continuing in sequence. In English, it would be like beginning the first stanza with "A," the second with "B," and so forth. It is believed that this was done to simplify memorization of the psalm. (Eg. Ps 9, 10, 25, 34, 111, 112, 119, and 145). Acrostics were also used in Lamentations 1-4 and Proverbs 31:10-31. This process is, of course, completely lost in translations.

Most translations of Psalms include headings or "superscriptions" for 116 of the chapters. These headings did not appear in any of the original manuscripts. They first show up in the Septuagint, where many titles were added. They were first added in the third century B.C.E. but we no longer have any of these documents. The titles often include the name of the purported author and/or the historical circumstance which occasioned the narrative, and other information such as how the psalm should be performed, for example, whether it is to be sung or recited. Scholars do not consider any of the superscription information authoritative.

At one time each chapter of Psalms was written as a separate book. Children were told to, "Study your chapters," and that referred to those books of psalms. At some unknown time, Psalms was divided into five sections which are still reflected in our modern Bibles. These are: Book 1 (Psalms 1-41); Book 2 (42-72); Book 3 (73-89); Book 4 (90-106); and Book 5 (107-150). Each of the "books" ends with a doxology, which is a praise of GOD. Psalm 41, for example, is a classic doxology:

Blessed be the Lord, the GOD of Israel,
from everlasting to everlasting. Amen and Amen.

Doxologies are common in Christian writing as well. They are from the Greek *doxa*, which means "glory" and *logos*, "word," and are short hymns of praise to GOD. The most well known doxology is the last phrase of Matthew's version of the Lord's Prayer, "For Thine is the kingdom, and the power, and the glory, forever." The last doxology in Psalms is variously referred to as verses 145-150 or simply as verse 150.

I doubt that any other portion of the Bible is as frequently read as the book of Psalms. Psalm 23 is almost always recited during funerals and is one of the most recognized verses in the Bible. Throughout history, when the Bible was first translated into new languages, including modern translations, often the very first portion of the Bible to be translated was the twenty-third Psalm. Psalms is by far the most commonly quoted Hebrew Scripture in the New Testament. According to the gospels, JESUS often quoted from Psalms, which suggests that the Psalms were well established in the oral tradition in the first century.

Psalms became the songbook of the Jews and later popularly used by Christians. An enormous number of psalms have been set to music over the centuries, some being very familiar even though people might not recognize that they came from Psalms. Nearly all of the great classical music composers set at least one psalm to music such as Psalm 121 by Johann Sebastian Bach, 112 by Antonio Vivaldi, 13 by Franz Liszt and Johannes Brahms to 40 and even modern works such as 116 by the rock band U2.

The great majority of the Psalms were composed just before the exile, during the exile, and just after the exile. Some of them, however, go way back in history. Contrary to legend, David did not write the psalms. The tradition that David wrote the psalms stems from the fact that many begin with the phrase "of David," which the ancients assumed meant that David wrote them. In all, 73 psalms bear his name. This was supported by the traditions that David was a poet and musician (1 Sam 16:16-17; 2 Sam 1:17-27). The authors of the superscriptions that were added in about the third and second centuries B.C.E. linked some of the psalms to parts of David's life.

Scholars no longer attribute the authorship of any of the Psalms to David as he was not even alive when most of them were written. That being said, however, some of them may actually date to the time of his reign (Ps 2, 16, 18, 29, 68, 82, 108, and 110). Some go back even farther than that and likely have roots back to the time in Egypt, as early as the thirteenth century B.C.E. The oldest psalm is believed to be Ps 29 which was a Hebrew adaptation of a poem used by the ancient Canaanites.

Numerous writers contributed to the psalms, and the subject matter varied greatly. Some psalms were recitations of the history of the Israelites, some were praises of the king, and some related to the cycle of planting and harvest. Nearly all of them came from the Southern Kingdom of Judah and the majority were from the time of the kings (after Rehoboam) to the Exile. A few originated in the Northern Kingdom of Israel, however, such as Ps 80 and 81.

Between 1928 and 1933, the great German biblical scholar, Hermann Gunkel, used a "form-critical" method of examining Psalms. He had previously performed such an analysis of Genesis where he categorized the verses as being either a saga, legend, taunt, curse, hymn, etiology, or a proverb. The idea was to evaluate Bible verses as to their form or genre in order to identify their *Sitz im Leben* ("setting in life"). The formats he used were found in other literature and were not specific to the Bible. He classified some verses in Psalms as *hymns,* which spoke of GOD generally as the creator or redeemer. These are personal appeals to GOD. Gunkel found both individual and communal *laments* which, together, constitute about one-third of the psalms. The laments basically have three parts, an invocation to GOD, a description of a particular problem that requires GOD'S help, and an appeal to GOD for Devine intervention. Sometimes they remind GOD of past entreaties where He had given assistance. There are individual and communal *thanksgivings* and *royal psalms* which focus on the king. Some of the psalms are called *wisdom psalms* because they use the same language as the wisdom books of Job, Proverbs, and Ecclesiastes, and, as mentioned, they focus on the same issues that are paramount in those books. There are still other categories.

This idea of form-critical evaluation soon dominated much of the early 20th century biblical scholarship. Other scholars continued this process into the New Testament, categorizing JESUS' sayings into groups such as parables and aphorisms, and each of these is subdivided into other categories such as aphorisms that are beatitudes, paradoxes, admonitions, prayers, etc. This methodology proved very important in understanding JESUS' message.

Today, nobody knows for sure how the Psalms were used in religious services. Many of the words describing their use are uncertain or ambiguous today. Some psalms appear to have been sung at sacrifices, such as 118:27. Others seem to have been used in other ceremonies such as the burning of incense. A few even refer to musical instruments which may have been used in the ceremonies.

Proverbs

The book of Proverbs spelled out exactly what you were supposed to do to obtain wisdom and to conform your conduct to that wisdom. And it was not easy. According to the authors of Proverbs, GOD required "hard work, high morals, moderation, kindness to the less fortunate, loving one's family and home, sincerity, modesty, self-control, chastity, a willingness to live and learn, an attitude of forgiveness, and even being kind to animals." It is kind of hard to disagree with any of that today. You will note as you read the book that Proverbs never discusses right from wrong. That is supposed to be self-evident. The message it was sending was simple and clear; wisdom brings happiness and the lack of wisdom brings misery and doom. You reap what you sow. They had a name for this concept. You may have heard it; it is battered around quite a bit these days. It was called "moral retribution."

The authors of Proverbs were numerous and mostly anonymous. Some of the proverbs are quite ancient, but the great majority of them were written shortly after the Exile. Much of Proverbs was influenced by ancient Egyptian writings, especially by Amen-em-ope who lived about 1100 B.C.E. Much of the book was the work of the Israelite temple scribes, so many tend to be on the snooty side, but the message is soundly based in ancient Hebrew folk wisdom.

The book was probably written as a primer for older boys to prepare them for the responsibilities of adulthood, including how to be the head of the family, so it is very male oriented. Much is devoted to finding a good wife (12:4) and ruling over the household. In some of the verses there is a shadowy woman that is never identified and she seems to take several personalities. Sometimes she is the "strange woman" (5:1-23), the "foreign woman," sometimes a prostitute, and other times an adulteress (7:1-27). The young men are told to be wary of this woman, but the way she is described the warnings probably had the opposite effect on young pubescent males. The writers spend quite a bit of time on adultery. In fact,

Proverbs suggests pretty strongly that prostitutes provide a very necessary service which, for the cost of "a loaf of bread," may reduce the attractiveness of an adulterous relationship (6:26). In other words, if you must stray, employ the services of a prostitute rather than looking to someone else's wife.

But keep in mind that, at this time, reward and punishment for dallying with a married woman were still dealt within the present life. As noted, when we discussed the story of Job, the concept of transferring the rewards for this conduct to a life beyond this one on earth had not yet been formulated. Job may have helped advance this concept, as it clearly asked the question, why do good people suffer and bad people prosper if this wisdom idea is correct? Look around. Good people suffer every day, and some of the most obnoxious reprobates live the good life. If the wisdom theory is correct, then the rewards and punishments must be in an afterlife of some kind. Proverbs did much to advance this concept.

The book begins by inviting the reader to try Wisdom as a way of life. It is described in very practical terms, almost a recipe for living in accord with righteousness, justice, and equity. "Fear of the Lord" is the beginning of knowledge, and only fools despise wisdom and instruction. The book points out that the proverbs are not to be relied upon individually—they are to be used in conjunction with each other. There should be no attempt to "cherry pick" certain proverbs over others. They are not there to tell the reader a story. They are to demand thought and consideration and deep understanding of what each saying means with respect to the rest of the proverbs. Many people today like to quote individual proverbs. That is not the way the book works. The proverbs work in conjunction with each other. Together they form the concept of Wisdom.

Song of Songs

The Song of Songs is a strange book to appear in the Bible. It is one of only two books that do not mention GOD. Not only that, it is definitely "R" rated for sex. The Song of Songs is, quite simply, a love poem. It is a dialogue between a woman and her lover (male). It celebrates the act of physical love.

The age of this work is a little difficult to establish, as the source of the poetry could go back even before the time of David. The work may have roots in Egyptian love poetry and the poetry also bears a strong resemblance to Arabic wedding songs. But whatever the origin, the version that we have was almost certainly composed after the return from exile. It mentions the name of Solomon several times, and because of

Solomon's reputation with the hundreds of exotic women in his court, it was at one time attributed to him.

Why was it included in the Hebrew Bible? Nobody knows for sure. The rabbis decided that it must refer to GOD's love for Israel. Christian priests decided that it must refer to GOD's love for the Christian church. But if you read any of it at all, you will be hard pressed to accept either of these views. This is quite simply, very erotic literature.

I think that the real reason for the book is that the passionate love for a man and a woman was a very important part of the Jewish religion. Remember, GOD and his priests had to do something to keep the flock away from those salacious Canaanite religious festivals. I can only imagine that when the priests read from the book of the Song of Songs that the attendance at synagogue was a little higher than usual.

Ecclesiastes

For those of us who reached adulthood in the 60s, the words of the preacher Ecclesiastes, especially beginning with chapter 3, are very familiar. One of the smash record hits by the Byrds, written by Pete Seeger, used the words of Ecclesiastes, "Turn, Turn,Turn." These words so moved President Kennedy that they were read at his funeral:

> *For everything there is a season, and a time for every matter under Heaven:*
> *a time to be born, and a time to die;*
> *a time to plant, and a time to pluck up what is planted;*
> *a time to kill, and a time to heal; . . .*

As beautiful as this poem is, Ecclesiastes is a very difficult book to understand. It asks questions about GOD and His plans that are almost impossible to answer. It is a book searching for answers. Unlike many ministers today, the preacher Ecclesiastes* not only does not condemn people for questioning GOD and faith, he encourages such questions.

This is a dark, somber, depressing book. If you are amused by the bumper sticker that says, "Life sucks, then you die," you are going to love Ecclesiastes. The author sets the tone of his writings right off the bat,

---

* The title of the book comes from the Greek and Latin versions of a Hebrew word that meant "leader of an assembly or congregation." The word was loosely translated as "preacher." The Hebrew bible translates it more accurately as *Qoheloeth* which means "teacher."

"Vanity of vanities, saith the Preacher, vanity of vanities; all *is* vanity." (The Hebrew Bible uses the word "futility" which is, apparently, a more accurate translation than vanity). He talks about the futility of seeking riches and the inevitability of death. Some of his thoughts are so cynical that many rabbis tried to keep the book out of the Hebrew Scriptures.

This book was also originally attributed to Solomon (how anyone thought that he might have had time to write all of these books and still keep his harem happy is beyond me). That would have been impossible in any event because the original text uses many Persian words that were not even known at the time of Solomon. Most scholars set the date at around 300 B.C.E.

The book is almost a "stream of consciousness" record. It is very philosophical, and it all stemmed from the question, "What does one gain by all of one's toil." As one author summarized the book:

> *[H]e looks for meaning in the typical answers: work, pleasure, riches, but finds none. He even questions the basic issue of right versus wrong, but decides that good is not invariably rewarded and the same end comes for all. All lies end in death and fate has already been decreed by GOD. That is a pretty stark departure from other wisdom, contrasting most sharply with Proverbs, which celebrates the modest life of hard work and the continual search for wisdom.*

Esther

This book had even more trouble getting into the Bible than the Song of Songs. It was well into the fourth century before the rabbis caved. Not only does it not mention GOD, there are no laws, miracles, prayers, or mention of Jerusalem. It is not even slightly historical. It tells a story like a fairy tale about its heroine, Esther (*Hadassah* in Hebrew). It is included in the Christian grouping of wisdom books, but it has even less relevance to wisdom than the Song of Songs.

Briefly, the plot is this. A fictitious Persian king gave an elaborate banquet and he had a bit too much of "the grape." When he decided to show off his trophy wife queen, she refused to be displayed like a prize ox. He then deposed her as queen and ordered all women to obey their husbands. The king then held a beauty contest to select a new queen. Esther, hiding the fact that she was Jewish, won the contest. Then, she and her cousin Mordecai foiled a plot against the king's life. He was very grateful. When Mordecai refused to bow in obeisance to the king's chancellor, Haman, he became enraged. He persuaded the king to decree death to those "certain people" who keep their own laws, meaning the Jews. The king issued the decree as requested.

Esther and Mordecai learned of this plot and at another banquet she told the king that she and Mordecai, the two who saved the king from death, were under death sentence from the decree and that it is all a vicious plot by Haman. So the king rescinded his decree and instead ordered Haman and his ten sons to die on the very gallows that had been built for the Jews. Esther's triumph is celebrated in the Jewish festival called Purim, a very ancient festival celebrating the arrival of spring. Why is this in the Bible? Your guess is as good as mine. I'll bet that Haman's ten innocent sons were not too thrilled with the story either.

Lamentations

Lamentations is a short book of very sorrowful poems about the tragic destruction of Jerusalem by the Babylonians in 587 and 586 B.C.E. It was almost certainly written by someone who had remained in Jerusalem during the Exile. The origin of the title is interesting. The Hebrews often called it *Ekhah* ("Oh How!"), in the tradition of naming the books by the book's first words, but sometimes it was called *Kinoth* which means "dirges' or "laments." When the Old Testament was translated into Greek in the Septuagint, the word used was the Greek word for "Dirges," *Threnoi.* The Vulgate Bible called it *Threni Id Est Lamentationes Jeromiae Prophetae,* which means, "Lamentations of the Prophet Jeremiah." This was an incorrect attribution—Jeremiah was already dead when it was written—but that is how the book got its name.

The poems are real downers. It is like studying your checkbook balance or reading a collection of grave side eulogies. You want to call your doctor to "see if Prozac might be right for you." But they are very well written and very interesting. I also think they are a bit of an exaggeration. They make the Jews' time in exile sound just horrible, but from everything I have read, most Jews did pretty well during the exile; at least those who were sent to Babylon. Some of them even rose to high offices in the king's court. In fact, when Cyrus the Great told them that they could return to Judah, only a small portion went back home. They had been in Babylon for two generations and had homes and families there, and many had intermarried. They had a place to worship and Babylon was a great and exciting city. It was like the song that was popular when the G.I.'s returned from Europe at the end of the Great War, "How're ya gonna keep 'em down on the farm after they've seen Paris (sung, 'Paree')." They had been living in one of the greatest cities in the world at the time, and Jerusalem was practically a ghost town.

In fact, what was truly lamentable was the sight that awaited those who did return to Judah. They were greeted by a devastation; their city was in ruins, their Temple was destroyed, and other people were now living on their property. Those lamentations, however, were recorded in other books such as Second Isaiah.

Chronicles

The two books of Chronicles, which the Christian Bible locates with the Historical Books, have been described as "the earliest example of 'revisionist history,'" that is, changing history to suit a specific purpose. They are loaded with contradictions of some of the other books in the Historical Books section. It has been suggested that the two books of Chronicles may have once been combined with Ezra and Nehemiah into one long book. Many Biblical scholars felt that, at the very least, they were all written by a single author. The consensus now is that the close similarities between them are more likely simply because they were written about the same time. The author was likely from the priestly clan or a Levite because of the way that the facts in the other books were also modified, and they were probably composed between 350 and 300 B.C.E.

Basically, it is an abridged "Readers Digest" and "cleaned up," apologetic version of history from Genesis on. Sort of an early Cliff's Notes. A lot of the objectionable parts of the original stories, like the blood and gore, were left out. The omitted parts were not insignificant, though. For example, he "forgot" to mention the David and Bathsheba affair, but he greatly enhanced David's part in planning the Temple. Solomon's avarice and spending excesses were ignored. The books of Samuel, Kings, Genesis, Exodus, Numbers, Joshua, and Ruth are all quoted verbatim in places, although they are never mentioned.

The main revisions are due to the then-growing acceptance of the "retribution theory;" the concept that we have been discussing about individual reward for good deeds and punishment for sins. This concept had not yet developed at the time of the other historical books. The author rewrote portions of the other history books to add punishment or reward for the acts of some of the characters.

The first nine chapters of 1 Chronicles are the "begats," the author's attempt at the genealogy of the descendants of the Israelite tribes from Adam to David. The author was from Judah, so there is very little of the rich history of Israel or its leaders in these books. The writer pushed for a very strict religious observance and tried to set out a model for how everyone should act. His depictions of David and Solomon are idealized. They are as he would like them to be, not as they were. He skips the defeat of the Hebrews by the armies of Babylon and the ensuing Exile and moves directly to the return to Jerusalem.

Daniel

The final book in The Writings is Daniel which was written partially in Aramaic and partially in Hebrew. This is really a "guy thing" for young boys; kind of a Biblical Hardy Boys. It is basically two stories of four young Hebrew boys, featuring a lad by the name of Daniel. The boys are raised in the Persian royal court by a court eunuch who gives them Persian names. In the first story, three of the boys, who were given the names of Shadrach, Mesach, and Abed-nego, are saved from death in a furnace by their faith. Their names are familiar to most of us from popular spirituals.

In the second story the fourth boy, Daniel, impresses the king by interpreting his dreams. Later, Daniel becomes more of a prophet than an interpreter of dreams. At one time he is thrown into a lions den and escapes unharmed. These escapes from death by fire and lions were quite elaborate stories when told by my Sunday school teachers. However, they skipped the rest of the stories. After Daniel emerged from the Lions den, the men who threw Daniel into the den were themselves then thrown in along with their wives and children who were immediately devoured by the lions. Talk about a story that should be "R" rated for violence. The men who threw the three boys in the furnace and their families received a similar fate in the furnace.

The story of Daniel took place during the exile into Babylon about 586 B.C.E., but the book was actually written in the year 165-164 B.C.E. and finally came into acceptance as Hebrew canon in 90 C.E. It was the very last of the Jewish Scriptures to be so accepted, but it was not without huge controversy. It should in no way be considered history, because the names and dates of the Babylonians and the later Persians are badly confused. But this is, after all, an allegory, so all of that is irrelevant.

The author pretended to be writing from the sixth century so that everything that he wrote was to appear as a prediction of the future. Of course, he already knew what had happened up to the end of the story. The purpose was, apparently, to lend credence to his final predictions of an apocalypse. A first or second century reader, after seeing four or five hundred years of predictions that came true (because they had, unknown to the reader, already happened before the book was written), certainly would take the real predictions of the future seriously. And they did. You will see later that Mark, writing in the New Testament, absolutely believed in Daniel's predictions and that Mark calculated that the apocalypse was going to occur in 74 C.E from the information in Daniel. . We'll see just how Mark did that when we get to Chapter 16.

Although Mark did not know this, modern scholars with the benefit of over 2000 years of study, have shown that the author of Daniel was badly confused over the historical facts in the earlier centuries. For example, right out of the chute, in Dan 1:1-2, he says:

> *[I]n the third year of the reign of King Jehoiakim of Judah, King Nebuchadnezzar of Babylon came to Jerusalem and besieged it.*

The problem is that Jehoiakim was never conquered. He reigned for eleven years. It was his son, Jehoiachin that was king when Nebuchadnezzar captured Jerusalem in 605 B.C.E. While the names are similar, someone writing at that time would know precisely who the ruler was. Then Daniel writes about the fall of Babylon to Persia in the year 539 B.C.E.,

> *[T]hat very night Belshazzar, the Chaldean king, was killed. And Darius the Mede received the kingdom, being about sixty-two years old.* (5:30)

The only thing wrong with this is that it was Cyrus the Persian, not Darius the Mede, who conquered Babylon. In fact, there never was a King Darius the Mede. Daniel evidently confused him with Darius the Persian who succeeded Cyrus' son in 521 B.C.E. Daniel also says that Cyrus succeeded Darius when in fact Darius succeeded Cyrus' son, and he says that Belshazzar was the son of Nebuchadnezzar (5:11), but he was actually the son of Nabonidus. There are many more problems like this in Daniel. Those who say that the Bible is inerrant in all things, including history, apparently never read Daniel. But Daniel was very accurate about historical matters in the second century B.C.E. which started scholars on their quest to accurately date the text.

You need a little history to fully understand Daniel. After the death of Alexander the Great in 323 B.C.E., his empire was divided among five of his generals. The two most important portions of the empire went to Ptolemy (Egypt) and Seleucus who took over the old Babylonian Empire. Originally, Judah was between the two empires, and even though both coveted it, neither Ptolemy nor Seleucus would claim it. They had been comrades at arms for years and had too much respect for each other. After their death, however, their descendants had no such respect, and Ptolemy's successor made it part of the Ptolemaic empire. Eventually the Selucids managed to wrest it away from the Ptolemeys for themselves. At the time Daniel was written, the Jews were suffering under the dreadful rule of King Antiochus IV, one of the truly horrible Selucid kings who ruled the Middle East in those post Alexander years.

Of course, it was not long before these two powers again began to lust for each others land, and Judah was, once again, as throughout history, caught in the middle. The Jews were very weak at this time. They were ruled by a high priest and a council of aristocrats and priestly families called the *Sanhedrin.* This is another period where the Jews do not spend a lot of time reminiscing, because there was intense infighting for the position of the high priesthood with palace intrigue that rivals that of the rivals for the throne in medieval England.

Also, the Greek way of life greatly appealed to the young Hebrews. They soon began adopting Greek customs, Greek names, Greek ideas, and philosophies. They began to abandon circumcision and other indicia of Jewish identity. To illustrate how Hellenistic the Hebrews had become, two of the people competing for high priest were named Jason and Menelaus, both Greek names. The infighting got so bad that the Seleucid king sent in an army. They slaughtered 80,000 Hebrews and sacked and desecrated the Temple.

As in other times in the past, this spawned a group of very orthodox and very nationalistic Jews who wanted to counter this loss of Jewishness. They called themselves the *hasidim,* which means the "pious." The author of Daniel was believed to be from this group. Certainly the message of Daniel, with the three boys refusing to eat unclean foods or to bow down to idols, was one with which this group would sympathize and promote. Those who were oppressed and persecuted as religious and ethnic minorities would find hope and salvation in this book.

In the concluding chapters, Daniel is no longer interpreting dreams. In fact, he needs the help of angels in order to interpret his own prophetic dreams that he is suddenly experiencing. These apocalyptic "visions" have been the source of much controversy over the years. It is believed that they would have been easily understood by those in the author's own circle, but they have provided 2000 years of controversy and speculation to everyone else. They appear to have been written just prior to the Maccabean revolt against the assimilationist policies of Antiochus. Those apocalyptic visions are favorites of the modern Christian fundamentalists who put great emphasis on the apocalyptic portions of the Bible.

This book is unique in that it was written in two different languages. Daniel 2.4b - 7.28 was written in Aramaic whereas 1.1 - 2.4a and chapters 8 - 12 were in Hebrew. By this time almost nobody spoke Hebrew and it was basically a language of worship much like Latin is today. There were several later additions to the book that are often found in the older translations—Susanna, the Prayer of Azaria, the Song of the Three, and Bel and the Snake. Most modern translations of the Bible include these in the Apocrypha, our next subject.

10

Transition Between the Testaments

Several centuries ago, the Pope decreed that all the Jews had to convert to Christianity or leave Italy. There was a huge outcry from the Jewish community, so the Pope offered a deal. He would have a religious debate with the leader of the Jewish community. If the Jews won, they could stay in Italy, if the Pope won, they would have to leave.

The Jewish people met and picked an aged but wise Rabbi, Moishe, to represent them in the debate. However, as Moishe spoke no Italian and the Pope spoke no Yiddish, they all agreed that it would be a "silent" debate.

On the chosen day, the Pope and Rabbi Moishe sat opposite each other for a full minute before the Pope raised his hand and showed three fingers. Rabbi Moishe looked back and raised one finger. Next the Pope waved his finger around the room. Rabbi Moishe pointed to the ground where he sat.

The Pope then brought out a communion wafer and a chalice of wine. Rabbi Moishe pulled out an apple. With that, the Pope stood up and declared that he was beaten, Rabbi Moishe was too clever and the Jews could stay.

Later, the Cardinals met with the Pope, asking what had happened. The Pope said, "First I held up three fingers to represent the Trinity. He responded by holding up one finger to remind me that there is still only one God common to both our beliefs. Then, I waved my finger to show him that God was all around us. He responded by pointing to the ground to show that God was also right here with us.

I pulled out the wine and wafer to show that God absolves us of all our sins. He pulled out an apple to remind me of the original sin. He had me beaten and I could not continue."

Meanwhile the Jewish community were gathered around Rabbi Moishe. "What happened?" they asked. "Well," said Moishe, "First he said to me that we had three days to get out of Italy, so I said to him, Up yours! Then he tells me that the whole country would be cleared of Jews and I said to him, Mr Pope, we're staying right here." "And then what," asked a woman.

"Who knows?" said Moishe, "he took out his lunch, so I took out mine."

Author Unknown

The Apocrypha

The Apocrypha (from the Greek *apokryphos* for "hidden things"), also referred to as the Deuterocanonical books, are books by Hebrew authors that are not part of the Hebrew canon but at one time were included in the Christian canon. Most are no longer included in Protestant Bibles and some are omitted in others. When the Hebrew Scriptures were first translated into Greek in the "Septuagint," the translation included several books of Hebrew writings that the Jews did not consider to be part of their scriptures. They claimed that the books were on very weak authority and that they too often tended to place one Jewish sect against another. When Jerome translated the original Hebrew into the Vulgate Bible, he also included these books, but he included a note at the beginning that stated these were not part of the Hebrew Canon. That note became lost in later copies, and many subsequent translations retained the books as if they were part of both the Hebrew and Christian canon.

The early Christian Church used Greek translations of the Hebrew religious writings and read them all as if they were official Canon. It was not until Jerome wrote his Vulgate in the late fourth century that this began to change. Finally, in 1566 Pope Sixtus of Sienna made it official that the books we now call the Apocrypha were not canonical. This was a bit of a problem, because some of the books were sequels or additions to Christian Canonical books and were often read together—some were additions to Psalms, Esther, and Daniel. Eventually, these were removed and included in a separate section of the Bible and it all got sorted out.

All of these books are Hebrew in origin, although it is very difficult to determine where most of them originated. Some were frequently quoted and referred to by Rabbis but no written documents have been found. They were widely quoted verbatim in later Rabbinical literature, however.

Although the books were eventually dropped from the Protestant translations, some continued to be found in the Roman Catholic, Greek Orthodox, and Slavonic Bibles and are still there today where they are perceived as Canonical. Most of these books are also still used by many Protestant ministers and priests in their sermons and teachings because of their relevant content in many circumstances. Most scholars, while they recognize that they are no longer canonical, consider the books to be of immense value in understanding the Greek and Roman periods of Hebrew life and the early New Testament times as well. They are remarkably historical in many respects, in particular 1 Esdras, and 1 and 2 Maccabees. Others have portions that are considered to be historically accurate. Some Christian churches, especially the Catholic church, still include a few of the apocrypha in their Canon.

It is worth taking another moment to add a little more history to our discussion about the Seleucid rule. That history was extremely important in forming all of these books as well as the entire New Testament. Remember when we discussed the return of the Jews from Exile? Ezra and Nehemiah were very concerned about intermarriage of the Jews with outsiders. There was a similar problem at this time. There were many very devout and observant Jews living among non-Jewish groups and many

Jews fully embraced the Greek lifestyle and culture. The Middle East had become thoroughly Hellenistic. There were also large groups of Jews outside of Palestine, known today as "diaspora Jews," living as abused minorities among the larger populations. Some of these books were directed to the problems of this intermingling such as Tobit, 3 Maccabees, Greek Esther, the Prayer of Azariah, and the Song of the Three Jews in Chapter 3 of Daniel.

The Seleucid kings eventually pressured everyone in their kingdom to adopt the Greek gods, and a few did. Most refused, however, so the King Antiochus invaded Jerusalem in 169 B.C.E. He outlawed the Hebrew religion and made teaching of the Torah a crime. He even desecrated the Temple, using it for worship of the Greek Gods.

This was the final insult. The Jewish Hasmonean family headed by Mattathias and his five sons, caused the first Jewish Revolt, and it was successful, although it took twenty years from the start before they finally installed a Hebrew government. One of the sons was named Judas. He had the nickname of *Maccabeus* which means "the hammer," and the Hasmonean government became known as the Maccabees. This government lasted from 164 B.C.E. to 63 B.C.E.

If you think that finally installing a Hebrew government after centuries under foreign rule would be just what the Jews wanted, you would be wrong. Most people felt that the Maccabeans were just as bad as the Greeks. At first it was just the fundamentalist Hebrew sects, mainly the Essene and the

The Apocrypha

Books and Additions to Esther and Daniel (Roman Catholic, Greek, and Slavonic Bibles)

- Tobit
- Judith
- Additions to Esther
- Wisdom of Solomon
- Ecclesiasticus (Wisdom of Jesus, Son of Sirach)
- Baruch
- Letter of Jeremiah
- Additions to the Greek Book of Daniel
  - The Prayer of Azariah and the Song of the Three Jews
  - Susanna
  - Bel and the Dragon
- 1 Maccabees
- 2 Maccabees

Books in the Greek and Slavonic Bibles but not the Roman Catholic

- 1 Esdras
- Prayer of Manasseh
- Psalm 151
- 3 Maccabees

Slavonic Bible and the Latin Vulgate

- 2 Esdras
- 4 Maccabees

Sadducees, protesting, but it grew into a general revolt of the populace, and this became a huge problem for the Maccabees. One of the Maccabee officials at the time, without adequately thinking through the consequences, came up with the brilliant idea of asking Rome to help them put down the insurrection. Rome was only too happy to oblige. It sent them Pompey who conquered the Macabees and the land, and Rome held power for several hundred years. I don't think this was quite what that desperate Maccabee had in mind when he petitioned Rome for help.

Above is a list of the apocryphal books categorized into the Christian groups that still consider them Canon. They will not be discussed in detail here. However, many of these books have an apocalyptic theme that was developing in some Hebrew circles and some also predicted a new messiah that would lead the Jews back to power, and this will be discussed later. Many, building on the visions of Daniel, contained visions and revelations of the future, some of which also included a messiah. These concepts became major themes in early Christian writings. These books definitely laid the groundwork for the coming of JESUS. The books also developed the concept of the resurrection of the body after death, a concept that was previously foreign to both Jewish and Greek beliefs. Both had toyed with the idea of the *spirit* of the deceased rising, but not the body itself. The books further developed the idea of future retribution for sinful conduct, including retribution for the oppression by the present ruling party. Together these new concepts set the table for JESUS and his followers. Many of the books exhibit a strong Wisdom slant.

The books also resurrected an early Old Testament phenomenon, angels, that was further developed in the book of Hebrews and by the writings of early Christian leaders such as Augustine and Pope Gregory. Up to this point angels were basically messengers of GOD. Now they assumed many new roles, even that of warriors.

These books were transitional between the Old and New Testaments. Many historical Hebrew traditions were being modified or questioned. The concept of a Messiah to lead the Jews back to greatness was being advanced more often than in the past as was the idea of an apocalypse where GOD would destroy their enemies, These concepts laid the groundwork for early Christian beliefs.

Intertestimental Period

Traditionally, the Hebrew Scriptures and all Christian Old Testaments end with the book of Malachi which was written about 397 B.C.E. The New Testament begins with the gospel of Matthew which was written about 80 C.E. That four century gap is called the "intertestamental period." In most early Bibles, this period is merely a single blank page, and people tend to think that the New Testament picks up immediately after the end of the Old Testament. It doesn't, of course. Lots of Hebrew and early Christian history happened in that period including the occupation of the Middle East by Greece, the Hasmonian (Maccabean) period and the conquest by the Roman Empire.

Actually, the intertestamental period is not four centuries long. The ancients did not have the tools to accurately date documents that we have today. The book of Daniel, which is included in the Prophets section of the Hebrew Scriptures, was written about 165 B.C.E., long after Malachi. Since Daniel talks about events four centuries earlier and appears to predict future events that will occur late in the millennium, the document was originally dated much earlier. Esther was written in the first or second century B.C.E. In the New Testament, before Matthew or any of the other Gospels were written, Paul began writing his letters, the earliest being about 45 C.E.. But that still left a time differential of over 200 years between the Old and New Testament writings, no matter what books you consider being the last in the Old Testament and the first in the New Testament. That is not to say that there were no Hebrew writings during that period—we have just read about many of them in the Apocrypha. That time differential was even greater when you consider the enormous changes in Palestine that took place during that period.

The silly story in the epigram, which I found in my email one day, illustrates an important point in understanding early Christian literature. JESUS was a devout Jew. His original disciples and apostles were Jews. The people who wrote all of the Old Testament and most of the New Testament were Jews. The problem was that in 70 C.E. the Romans had destroyed the Temple and, before the end of the first century, the Romans, after fighting two bloody wars with the Jews, had banished all of them from Judea, and proclaimed the death penalty on any who returned. They even renamed the country Palestine after the traditional Jewish enemy, the Philistines, as a sort of permanent slap in the face.

The only people remaining in the country to run the new church were the gentile Christians. Today we think of the word "gentile" as being a Hebrew word for Christian, but it isn't. It is actually from the Latin *gentilis*, meaning of or belonging to a non-Hebrew clan or tribe. The Hebrew word is *goy*. Both are plural words which refer to a community or country of non-jews, not an individual, although the common meaning today is, simply, "non-Jew."

In the first century the gentiles were pagans. They knew little of the current Jewish history, culture, or society, let alone the ancient society that is described in the Hebrew Scriptures. With the exception of Paul, none had been trained in the Hebrew Laws or in the Talmud. Until the death of JESUS, while Jewish priests were instructing people about GOD's laws, gentile priests were reading the entrails of sacrificed animals. But these gentiles suddenly found themselves in the position of having to interpret all of the Old Testament books that were written by Jews, sometimes several hundred years previously, in a language that they could neither read nor understand. Many times their interpretations were incorrect. Sometimes, as in the epigraph at the beginning of this chapter, they were incredibly wrong, and they are still wrong today. Let's look at a couple of examples.

Gentile Misunderstandings

The concept of adultery is a very good example of the lack of understanding of old Hebrew customs by the new church leaders. We all know what adultery means today—a married person having sexual relations with someone other than one's spouse. The question is, what did it mean to the people to whom it was directed, 1200 years before the birth of JESUS? What did GOD expect his people to understand by His proclamation that they should not commit adultery?

The Commandments were not laws intended to govern the world; they were intra-tribal laws. The first four commandments made it clear that GOD was talking only about his chosen people. Hebrews could not trespass against other Hebrews. All such societies had laws, but they usually came from the ruler. The Israelites did not have a king at that time, however, so the laws originated from their GOD and were passed down by the priesthood.

The Laws were not absolute. For example, one Commandment says, "You shall not murder." Yet Moses himself was a murderer, without remorse, except that he was afraid that he might be caught (Ex 2:11 ff). The lovable and venerated King David and his band of bullies and toughs once killed 200 innocent men so that they could mutilate their corpses and take their foreskins (still attached) to King Saul to impress him and win the hand of his daughter. Why were these not sins? Why were Moses and David not condemned as immoral sinners destined for Hell? One simple reason: because the people that they killed were not part of the tribe. The laws only applied to killing other Israelites. Yahweh was not yet the god of all people.

A typical example of this dichotomy is GOD's anger at the Hebrews for not killing all of the Midianites. Having just captured the city, He commanded Moses and his followers to kill all the men, women, and all the male children, but the Hebrews could keep the young virgins for themselves (Num 31:15 ff) until they were finished with them. On its face, this demand by GOD blows several of the Commandments right out of the water, except for the fact that the Commandments were strictly intra-tribal laws. It was OK to kill Midianites. Adultery was the same. This proscription did not pertain to the world at large, only to the Tribes of Israel. It was perfectly acceptable to rape the women that the tribes of Israel conquered.

What then did adultery mean to Hebrews in the 13th Century B.C.E? Beginning with Lamech and then Abraham, nearly every man of wealth had more than one wife and usually several mistresses. The beloved King David had numerous wives and concubines. King Solomon, his son, had an incredible 700 wives and 300 mistresses, all living happily(?) together in his palace (1 Kings 11:3). So much for the Commandment against adultery. King David even had the notorious liaison with Bathsheba. They had an affair and David sent her husband, Uriah, off to war with instructions that he be killed so that David could marry Uriah's wife. Why was this OK? Because Uriah was a Hittite, not of one of the Twelve Tribes of Israel. And David is one of the most beloved people in the Bible. GOD is even reputed to have said that the Messiah will be from the House of David. And, in fact, Luke's version of the birth of JESUS lists him as a descendent of David. Matthew's version says that he is a descendent of Abraham, but has him born in Bethlehem, the city of David. Paul repeatedly speaks of Jesus as being from the house of David.

Adultery was a capital crime in those days, however, and a transgression against GOD. But it was basically a female crime. Men could commit adultery only if they had relations with *married Hebrew* women*. Men could have all the affairs they wanted with impunity *as long as the woman was not married.*

Why is it a female crime? Partly because of the low standing of women in Jewish society. A woman was a mere chattel and brood mare. But the main reason why adultery was a crime for a woman had nothing at all to do with morality. It was simple economics. One of a man's sons inherited everything upon the man's death. It was very important for a man to know that the person inheriting his land and his fortune was, indeed, his own son. The only way he could be sure of that was if his wife remained chaste. That is all that adultery meant in the ancient Middle East. An adulteress was not considered immoral for her transgression, she was condemned because she sullied the line of inheritance, and for this she was guilty of a capital crime. For that reason the man who soiled her and her husband's line of inheritance had to be likewise punished. If she was not married, she might be punished, but the man was not punished at all. The worst thing that could happen to the man was, if she was a virgin, he had damaged her marketability and he could be ordered to pay her father the "bride's price." In other words, reimburse him for the potential loss of the income he would realize when he sold her into marriage.

---

* At Lev. 20:10 it does state that if a man commits adultery with the wife of his neighbor both shall be put to death. This appears to be the only condition upon which a man commits a wrong for sleeping with a woman other than his wife; that is, when the woman I both Hebrew and is married. Otherwise, a man, even a married man, could have as many sexual liaisons as he wanted

As you will see later, the word "adultery" changed in meaning from the Old Testament to the New Testament. Neither is consistent with the meaning today. Not only have the meanings of words changed over the centuries, so have the very concepts expressed by those words changed.

Consider changes in English over the years. In 18th century English common law, from which nearly all of the early laws of the United States were derived, *burglary* was defined as, "the breaking and entering a dwelling-house by night with the intent to commit a felony therein." Modern day definitions of burglary are much different. California's law is pretty typical and it defines burglary as follows,

> *Every person who enters any house, room, apartment, tenement, shop, warehouse, store, mill, barn, stable, outhouse or other building, tent, vessel, . . . floating home, . . . railroad car, locked or sealed cargo container, whether or not mounted on a vehicle, trailer coach, . . . any house car, . . . inhabited camper, . . . vehicle, when the doors are locked, aircraft . . . or mine or any underground portion thereof, with intent to commit grand or petit larceny or any felony is guilty of burglary.*

Quite a difference isn't there? There no longer has to be a "breaking," just an entering. It is no longer limited to nighttime activity. It is no longer even limited to a dwelling-house— almost any structure counts including motor vehicles, mine shafts, and cargo containers. The word is the same but its definition is far different from the Bible definition.

The meaning of a huge proportion of terms in the Bible have changed over the centuries as well. That is one reason you cannot expect a modern day literal interpretation of the Bible to be correct.

Other Translation Problems

Translating JESUS' words was even harder. JESUS and his followers spoke Aramaic, a Semitic language in popular use in the Middle East at the time and still spoken in places today, but the official written language was Greek. Structurally, these two languages are very different. Also, there was not the same degree of scholarship in the first century that exists today. For example, JESUS reputedly said, "It is easier for a camel to go through the eye of a needle than for a rich man to enter the Kingdom of Heaven." Isn't this a strange analogy? Camels do not go through needles or anything that looks like the eye of a needle. What the original translators did not know is that the Aramaic word for camel is almost identical to the word for a large rope or cable (ropes used to be made from camel hair). Isn't it much more likely that JESUS said, "It is easier for a rope to go through the eye of a needle . . ."? This makes sense. It is an appropriate metaphor where the camel is not.

There were other translation problems. These are covered in a later chapter.

11

What Are the Scriptures

All scripture is inspired by God and is useful for teaching, for reproof, for correction, and for training in righteousness, . . .

2 Tim 3.16

I am often referred to that quote from Second Timothy as proof that the Bible is "the inerrant word of GOD." The words "inspired by GOD" have morphed into "dictated by GOD" or even "written by GOD." First of all, the quote is not proof of the matter stated by any logical standard. Secondly, the two letters to Timothy are second century forgeries and were not even written by Paul as you will see later. While that does not mean that the statement is not correct, it does cast some suspicions.

Scriptural forgeries was huge problem for the early Church. Even Paul himself was concerned about it and warned his readers about it in some of his letters. Well-meaning church leaders were severely punished when it was discovered that they had created a fraudulent document even though most did it out of love and a misguided devotion to GOD and/or to Paul. Also, it was customary in the Middle East at that time to write documents in the name of someone of authority in order for some of that authority to rub off on the fake document. Until we get to those discussions, you will just have to trust me. Paul did not write the pastoral epistles of either 1 & 2 Timothy or Titus. This has been known since the second century from the writings of (St.)Ignatius and Polycarp. They were among the earliest forgeries that the Church uncovered, but they were already part of the church dogma and the fact that they were forgeries was generally withheld from the parishioners, and still is. They were important to the Catholic church to counter the arguments and beliefs of the Marcionites and the Gnostics. The three letters do accurately reflect certain early church dogma where church leaders wanted the priesthood to be "men's club."

For the sake of argument, assume that Second Timothy was written by Paul. Precisely what were the scriptures that he says were "inspired by GOD." Certainly Paul did not mean to include his own letters that comprise much of what is now called the New Testament as being part of the "scriptures." The church in Ephesus was starting to collect his letters by the end of the first century C.E., but Paul was a very controversial figure in his lifetime. His own letters are replete with efforts to exhort his churches to ignore the "false prophets," the name he used for those who disagreed with his opinions on JESUS' message. He was often at odds with the Christian movement's leaders, whom he called "The Pillars." Further, the letters of Peter, John, and others in the New Testament and the four canonical Gospels and Acts had not even been written in Paul's lifetime, so he could not have been referring to them, had he actually made that famous statement. You will see that it was not until 395 C.E. that the Christian Church finally (sort of) agreed upon what documents were going to comprise the Christian Scriptures.

Next, any beginning student of Logic 101 knows that you cannot use the words of a writing to prove its own authenticity. It is not proof of inerrancy to say, "I am Holy, because I say that I am Holy." That is circular reasoning, not proof.

Finally, what did church leaders actually consider to be "Scriptures" in Paul's time? At the time of the destruction of the Temple in 70 C.E. (Paul began writing in about 35 C.E. until his death about 65 C.E.), the Jewish Priests recognized 22 scrolls as scripture. The only Old Testament that was available in the Middle East in the first century C.E. that could be read by other than the Hebrew Temple Priests was the Septuagint, the Greek translation of the Old Testament. Scholars are almost universal in agreement that the author of Second Timothy must have been referring to the Septuagint when he referred to "scriptures" and we already know that translation is deficient in many respects. It could hardly be called "inerrant."

There are approximately 50 references to "the scriptures" in the New Testament and *almost without exception they refer to the Hebrew Scriptures.* In 2 Peter 3:16, the author compares Paul's letters with "the other scriptures," and that is the only reference to any New Testament writing. By the Bible's own words, there is no way that the quote from Second Timothy, could have referred to the New Testament scriptures.

What is a "Codex?"

The early Christians started writing their documents in a new format, which we now call "books," but were then called "codex." These were much handier. Scrolls were bulky, heavy, and very hard to manage.

However, do not get caught up in the modern thinking that the codex form was just technological progress. It was, but to the ancients, the codex was considered to be second rate. All of the truly important writings were still done on parchment scrolls. The Holy "scriptures" continued to be thought of as those documents preserved on scrolls. It would be many years before ideas committed to writing on a codex would achieve equal status.

When Did Writings Become Scriptures?

Perhaps the more interesting question is when were the Scriptures as we know them today assembled into one book called the Bible? There were a lot of people writing religious tracts and books over the first few centuries C.E. Who decided which of this enormous wealth of religious literature were Scriptural or Canonical and which were not? We have discussed the Masoretic texts of the Old Testament which are what we see in all modern Christian Bibles. But what about the New Testament scriptures?

Believe it or not, most of the decisions about what books should make up the New Testament did not happen until the end of the Fourth Century C.E. By the beginning of the second century a huge volume of Christian literature had been written, far more than we know about today. In addition to the four canonical gospels there were the Gospels of Peter, James, Thomas, Infancy, Pseudo Mark, Sayings Gospel Q, Secret James, Ebonites, Egyptians, Nazoreans, and the Hebrews that we have at least fragments of today. All together, we know of about 40 gospels. In addition to Paul's letters and the other letters in the New Testament, there were hundreds of letters written by apostles other than Paul.

At some time, church leaders began to think about putting together a book of sacred scriptures similar to the Hebrew Scriptures. By the middle of the second century an early church leader, Marcion, began pressuring his peers to stop talking about it and do it. Finally some got together and began compiling a list, but not all lists included the same books. Most included Matthew, Mark, Luke, and John as the acceptable gospels out of the entire list. Each of these gospels were written for a different audience of readers and together they appealed to a wide audience. Out of the huge number of books on the early history of the Christian church and the early apostles, they chose only the book of Acts. They then selected all of Paul's letters that were still in existence, not knowing that many were actually written by others, and they included letters claimed to be written by Peter, James, John, and Jude, also unaware that these were not written by the early church leaders by those names.

Other books were being written, but most had only local distribution. The Gnostic movement, among others, maintained their own collections. There was still no universally accepted collection of Christian Canon, but it was a start.

The Roman Empire

Nowhere else were the influences of history, politics, and religion more important than in the selection of the writings that were finally decided to be included in a single document to be known as the Holy Scriptures—the Christian Canon.

Two huge influences were the historical and political facts that

Constantine became the emperor of Rome and ultimately decided to make Christianity the official religion of the Roman Empire. The story that circulated was that the night before the major battle against Maxentius who was trying to usurp the throne, Constantine dreamed of a Cross. So powerful was this vision that the next morning, before the battle, he had a cross sewn onto all of the soldiers' tunics, even though most of the soldiers embraced the Mithraic religion. In any event, the opposing forces met near the bridge over the Tiber River called the Milvian Bridge, and there Constantine devastated the other army and Maxentius lost his life in the process. Constantine converted to Christianity and prohibited the further persecution of Christians. He later named Christianity as the official religion of the empire. It was not until 600 C.E. that Charlemagne officially changed the Roman Empire to the "Holy Roman Empire," but for all practical purposes that is what it was after Constantine's conversion.

A third influence was the internal religious and political struggles of the Christian religion itself. Think about Christianity today. There are the Roman Catholics, Anglican Catholics, Greek Orthodox, Lutherans, the Presbyterians, Seventh Day Adventists, Methodists, Unitarians, Jehovah Witnesses, Mormons, Pentacostals, Evangelicals, and many other Christian denominations. What if you called a conference of all of the leaders of these various churches and this group had to decide what was going to be the unanimous position on all issues of the united Christian Church for all time. Do you think that you could get position on all issues that everyone of the participants could agree upon? Not even in your dreams.

That was the problem that the early church had in the fourth century. In fact, that was the major problem from the time of JESUS' death until Constantine and, to a lesser extent, even today. In the following chapters you will see that there was not a single written word in the Bible, or elsewhere, for that matter, from JESUS himself. Other than the reference in John 8.6 that says JESUS marked in the dirt in the story of the attempted stoning of the adulterous woman, and a reference to him being asked to read a passage from the scriptures when he was a child, there is not even the slightest suggestion that JESUS was literate. In fact, it was highly unlikely that he was.

You will also see in the succeeding chapters that there were definitely different interpretations of JESUS' message among the early Christians. Paul went before the recognized church leaders, James, Peter, and John, those who had known JESUS in his lifetime, on at least one occasion, possibly more, to see if what he was preaching was acceptable to those de facto leaders. Many of Paul's letters were written to rebut the contrary teachings of other apostles who spoke to the churches that he established on his missionary travels. Each of the followers of these various beliefs wanted a say in what was to be included in the Bible.

Two of the most important factions were the Gnostic Christians who embraced JESUS' sapiential message of wisdom and that of the Catholic Christians who embraced the more apocalyptic messages of Paul and John the Baptist.

JESUS, as you will see, was not an apocalyptic preacher like John the Baptist, contrary to what present fundamentalists denominations teach. This is something else where you will just have to trust me until we get to those chapters where this is discussed and you can make your own evaluation. John the Baptist was an apocalyptic messenger. John spiritually cleansed his followers by a symbolic Jewish baptism in the Jordan River and then sent them home to await the coming end of the world. After John's death, many of his followers turned to the JESUS movement so there was a large group of these new followers of JESUS who believed in the coming apocalypse, and they demanded representation in the Church and in any Bible. We will get into these internal struggles of the new religion in a later chapter. It was far more divisive than it is today.

Counsel at Nicea

Emperor Constantine, for one, was fed up with the constant bickering between the different Bishoprics. There were endless debates, in the manner of the ancient Greeks, on such things as whether Jesus was *homoousios*, that is, was he made of the same substance as the Father, or was he *homoiousios*, similar but not the same substance. This was just one example of numerous differences, some of which were fundamental to Christian beliefs. These seem like trivial arguments today, but they led to insurrection and bloodshed in those days. Constantine was not going to tolerate the bickering any longer. He decided to get all the Bishops together at once and force them to "duke it out" for all time. He called the first ecumenical counsel in 325 C.E. at the city of Nicea in what is now Turkey. The Bishops thought they were going to another intellectual discussion, but when they arrived, they found the entrance to the palace surrounded by the emperor's soldiers with their swords drawn. After this friendly greeting, the meeting started. The ground rules were set, anyone who did not agree on a point was "invited" to leave. In that manner, Constantine was able to get a sort of consensus.

An official document was drafted that said, essentially, that both JESUS and GOD were made of the same stuff. That may not sound like much, but it was a pretty big deal at the time. It was in very vague language, however, and all sides to the argument felt that they could conform their own theories to fall within the wording of the document.

Later modified slightly, the document became known as the **Nicene Creed**, and that modified version is still recited in many churches every Sunday. It is important to the theme of this book to note, however, that nothing decided in the conference at Nicea, including the later agreed upon wording of the Nicene Creed, is found anyplace in the Bible. It is a later addition to the Christian tradition added by the church.

On the other hand, the wording of the document was so wishy washy that the various factions were able to go on believing as they always did, so very little was solved. Although there were discussions about assembling an official Christian Canon, there was no universal agreement on what books should be included. Constantine wanted an official Canon so all of his churches would be teaching the same thing. He asked Bishop Eusebius, a leader of the Council, to prepare a list of books that he felt should be the Canon of the Christian scriptures and to make copies for 50 of his churches. (We'll return to this episode later). The books he selected were principally based upon the Marcion collection we discussed

The Search for Relics

The word "relic" comes from the Latin *reliquiae* which means "remains." It refers to objects, often human body parts such as bones or objects that have some religious meaning. It is believed by some that a person's holiness, or healing powers, do not die with him or her but continue to reside in his body and are available to any believer who in some way makes contact with the remains of objects associated with that person.

After Constantine declared Christianity to be the official religion of the Roman Empire, his mother, Helene, became a true believer and set off for Palestine with her entire entourage and began a search for all of the places that JESUS visited and started buying relics. Boy did they see her coming! Collecting relics predated Christianity by a long time, but she gave it a whole new meaning

This was 350 years after JESUS death, but they sold her such things as the crown of thorns allegedly worn by Christ, the nails that pierced Jesus hands and feet on the cross, and the sign in the crowd calling Jesus "King of the Jews. She acquired the clothing supposedly worn by Christ, an entire marble staircase said to be from the palace of Pontius Pilate, and several other items. They even sold her the "True Cross." How did she know that it was really the True Cross? They laid it across a seriously ill woman and she was miraculously "cured." She sent parts of that cross to churches everywhere.

They convinced Helene that a particular spot was the location of Golgotha and of JESUS' sepulcher. So she bought the property and had a church erected on it that Constantine named Saint Macarius. It was destroyed and replaced with the Church of the Holy Sepulcher. That church was destroyed as well as other replacement churches, but there is still an old Romanesque church by that name on the same spot today. She bought a lot of other property as well along with bones of various saints.

People took those relics very seriously. Crusades were fought when some of them fell into the hands of the "infidel." Before her death, Helene spent a fortune in the Middle East, but Constantine apparently felt that it was cheap enough just to keep her out of his hair.

earlier. Athanasius, bishop of Alexandria, called an ecumenical counsel of his own in 367 C.E. and his list of Christian books was discussed in detail, along with the Hebrew scriptures. This was a pretty active discussion, as there were a lot of books to consider. There was still no consensus reached.

From the middle of the first century the church at Antioch had collected many of Paul's letters, and by this time the letters of many other early church leaders had also been collected by other churches. They all wanted their collections included as part of the Bible. There were also many apocalyptic books written. They ultimately settled on a single book from this group, Revelation. Why that particular book was chosen we do not have a clue, but it was a very controversial decision. They also included some Old Testament books that the Jews felt were on very flimsy authority. These were the "apocrypha" that we talked about earlier

They were getting closer to agreeing on a set of books to include in the Christian Bible, but so far no cigar. It was to be many years before they were all finally selected. The leader of the Latin speaking churches of the west, Augustine, sent out a similar but slightly different list from that of Athanasias. Augustine then called another ecumenical council that was held in North Africa in 393 C.E. to vote on his selections. It obtained great support but was still far from unanimous, so Augustine called another council in 397 C.E. and the leaders finally endorsed the books of the Bible that are basically as we know them today, with the exception of the Apocrypha. All of the other books were considered heretical and had to be destroyed. Most were, but a few have been discovered in secret hiding places.

Ancient Bibles

You would think that would settle it once and for all. However, remember, all Bibles were painstakingly hand copied in those days, and errors were made. We have discussed problems in the translations of the Old Testament. The New Testament had problems of its own, but very different problems. The copies, and the original Old Testament books, were made by professional scribes who were not only literate, they were quite faithful in their copy work. However, as we have seen, there were still so many different versions of the Scriptures that it required a committee be set up to determine which was closest to the originals. That committee was, of course, the Mazoretes. The differences in the copies were often intentional to conform scriptures to the beliefs of a particular Hebrew sect or translation errors when the old alphabet was changed to block script. New Testament scribes, unfortunately, were not nearly so qualified or as scrupulous in their accuracy.

How extensive are New Testament errors? In 1701, John Mill, a British scholar, examined about 100 ancient Greek New Testament texts.

He identified over 30,000 errors in those 100 documents, and that was only counting the major errors—he did not count those that were just minor errors like misspellings, changes in word order, and similar errors. He published this in a book that marked all of the variations in all 100 documents for readers to identify omitting the minor errors assuming most readers would recognize on their own We now have hundreds more of the ancient Greek copies than Mill had. The estimates of the number of errors now run into the hundreds of thousands. The great majority of these errors are of no consequence. Many, however, change the very meaning of the words and concepts. Many add information that the original authors did not include and deleted information that was in the originals.

Most of JESUS' audiences were comprised of Jewish peasants. They were nearly all illiterate. The few who could read and write did not seem to put pen to paper. After JESUS' death, a few began to write down the recollections of those who had actually heard JESUS speak. Many of these were several people removed from those who actually heard Jesus. They would be called double or triple hearsay in an American law court. So far as we know, nobody who actually heard JESUS speak wrote down any of his words with the possible exception of the author of the Gospel of Thomas. The scribes got the words second hand at best.

Most of the copies were made when someone merely borrowed a manuscript of one of the books from a friend to make copies for his or her own use, but many times others would ask them to make an extra copy for them. These people were not professional scribes and the work was all done in their spare time. They were merely individuals who were considered to be literate, and that was a very low bar in those days. The ancient Romans claim that 10-15% of the populace at that time was literate.

Further, the Roman description of who is literate would not pass muster today. Many were considered literate if they could merely sign their name and copy, letter by letter, another document without knowing what the document said. This was even true of many paid government scribes. People would bring them documents to certify and they would merely copy word-for-word the text of the official certification statement, without being able to read what it says, and then sign their names. There are examples of such documents were the statement was initially copied correctly but one time the scribe made a mistake and omitted a letter. All subsequent certification statements had the same missing letter. The scribe "clones" his mistake each time he recopied the certification.

If you have ever tried to copy text written in a language foreign to you, you will understand just how difficult this is. It is very easy to miss words or write the same line of letters over again. A very common error was where there were couplets that ended with the same words. Often the scribe saw the second set of words and thought he was about to duplicate the same line so he skipped it. Another common mistake when translating was to mistake similar words. Remember when we discussed the camel through the eye of a needle problem? I noted that the word camel was very similar to rope. It is very likely that a scribe, not recognizing the difference, merely copied the wrong word.

That was the way documents were copied in the first 400 or so years after JESUS' death. Someone of very modest literacy would ask for permission to copy, say, a letter by Paul, and the copy would be made by that person in his spare time. These early copies are loaded with mistakes. After the Council at Nicea, Christianity became a mainline religion, and when Constantine converted, it became "The" religion. The Christians no longer had to copy documents secretly. As we have seen, church leaders decided to agree on what writings would be church Canon and then to copy and disburse them. They then began to employ professional scribes to copy important Christian documents. When Constantine ordered the 50 copies of the Canon from Eusebius to send around to the various bishoprics, the Church had to set up an actual scriptorium and to hire and train numerous scribes. This the church did willingly, not only because the king ordered the copies, but because he said the empire would pay for them. Now that the church had credibility, they also needed the money.

The advent of professional scribes was not the end of the copying problems, however. The scribes still made accidental errors and often purposely made changes in the documents. A famous pagan writer by the name of Celsus complained that Christians changed the writings like they were intoxicated. There is a very famous margin note in the Codex Vaticanus. our oldest surviving Bible, where the scribe accused a predecessor scribe of altering the text. Subsequent documents show the complained of changes restored to the original.

What usually happened, though, was that a mistake was made and the document was recopied with the same mistakes. These mistakes eventually ended up in numerous copies. These new copies then picked up even more errors along the way and those errors were also cloned. All of these early books were written in Greek. In some of the western churches, where both the church leaders and the congregations spoke Latin, they began making Latin translations of these Greek documents. The errors in the Greek document were then cloned into Latin, plus new errors were made just due to translation difficulties. Again, those copies made after Constantine were much more accurate than those before because of the use of professional scribes, but the accuracy depended hugely on the accuracy of the particular Greek copy used as the source. Later, the church had monks who did nothing but copy documents in many more locations than the original scriptorium in Caesarea. Their copies were quite good, but many of the source documents were far removed from the originals and were loaded with inherited errors.

Remember, none of the original documents still existed, even at that time. All of the earliest documents we have are copies many generations removed from the originals. The oldest copy of any New Testament document is a fragment of the Gospel of John which was dated at about 125 C.E. However, professional scribes or not, it would seem, intuitively, that the very oldest copies were probably the most accurate because there would be fewer chances for error. Unfortunately, while that is true for the Hebrew Scriptures, it is not always the case with Christian writings. How, then, were the 5th century professional copyists to determine which of the copies was the most accurate?

Fortunately, there were other documents available that could help. Many of the early Christian leaders were also prodigious writer s—mainly 2nd century writers such as Polycarp, a bishop of Smyrna; Justin Martyr; Origin, Marcion; (St.) Clement; (St.) Augustine; and others—had access to very early copies which were no longer available in the 5th century. In many of their writings they quoted extensively, word-for-word, from these early documents. In Chapter 13 we will see a good example of this when we discuss a letter where Clement quoted The Secret Gospel of Mark word for word. This had been removed from all of the existing copies of Mark sometime in the 2nd century. If it hadn't been for Augustine's letter, it would have been lost forever. It is still not included in any Mark translation of which I am aware.

Some of the very earliest examples of true Biblical scholarship were medieval scholars trying to devise a method to determine which of the numerous copies of documents were most like the originals. There was little progress made until the end of the 18th century when two scholars, Brooke Wescott and Fenton Hort, came up with a method of analysis that worked, and Hort wrote a step by step description of the process they used. They devised a method for making sort of a "family tree" of the various documents based upon rules of reconstruction that they invented. Basically, they began cataloging the variations in 100 documents. If two documents had the same variation, they probably came from the same source, although the original variation may be many generations older. Then they compared other documents to trace back the same variations until they found a document that does not have the error. That would be the matrix. If there was more than one variation in a document, and there were usually hundreds, they traced those variations as well. Gradually they built up a family tree of the documents based upon their variations. Of course the process was much more complex in practice. It took Wescott and Hort 28 years to catalog all 100 documents and thousands of such documents have been discovered since their groundbreaking work. The concept was brilliant, however, and their procedure is still used today.

They determined that each of the surviving documents can be traced back to, basically, one of four "families," listed here in the order of their overall quality of documents:

- The *Syrian* text, also known as the Byzantine text or the Eastern text, are mostly documents from the late middle ages. There are a great many of them, but they are relatively recent and are not considered particularly authoritative.
- The *Western* text was comprised of very early documents, mostly from the second century. You would think that these would be very close to the originals, but remember, at this time all New Testament copying was being done by amateurs, many of whom were barely literate. The reliability of the documents suffer badly from this. While it is called "Western" text, the problem of incompetent early scribes was endemic in all parts of the Christian world and contemporary, non-canonical documents from the same period are in this category as well, no matter where they originated,
- The *Alexandrian* text. The Alexandria scribes were highly trained and scrupulous in the accuracy of their copying, but they were not above making intentional changes. Anything from Alexandria is generally considered, initially, to be better than the others. Scholars tend to consider them the most reliable until something comes along to change their minds. However, remember that Alexandria was the home of some of those powerful, competitive Christian sects that were pressing the Catholic church for dominance, such as the Gnostics, and many scribes felt compelled to make changes in the texts that the Gnostics could use to support their position.
- Finally, there are the *Neutral* texts. These are manuscripts that scholars determined do not have serious errors or revisions from the original; these were the closest to the originals that the scholarship at the time could determine. The list is, of course, constantly being examined and updated.

Unfortunately, when Jerome made his Latin translation, he took what he judged as one of the better examples of Latin translation to use as the "background" of his book and picked some of the Greek Eastern texts to "clean up" the Latin for his famous Vulgate. Thinking that the oldest texts would be the most accurate, Jerome made bad choices. The Eastern texts he used are now considered to be the least accurate of the four families. There are many major errors in the Vulgate as a result.

After the invention of the printing press, there became a race to publish the first Greek New Testament. A scholar named Erasmus became the first, but he had to hurry and take a lot of shortcuts to get there. There was already another Greek document printed, but it had not yet been published, so he cut a lot of corners. In his rush, Erasmus could not find many texts to work from, but he found one that was relatively complete and used it for the "background." To fill it in, he relied on numerous Eastern texts including 12th century copies of the Epistles, the four Gospels and Acts. The only copy of Revelation he could get was a copy owned by a friend that was almost unreadable in spots and overall very difficult. Worst, the last page was missing entirely. He hurried around for a copy and found an old Latin translation and retranslated the last six verses back into Greek and used them as the ending for his translation of Revelation. Those final six verses cannot be found in any other Greek text. It was published in 1515, but it is considered to be very unreliable.

You'll never guess what happened next. The Erasmus copy was the version that the King James translators used for the KJV New Testament. They used one of the worst Greek manuscripts as their model and all of the mistakes in that version were translated into English. It amazes me that so many ministers today still use that book and often recite from it in the old Elizabethan English. In fact, many church leaders refer to the KJV as THE inerrant version when it is one of the most inaccurate.

What do we have, then? The official translation used by Protestants for centuries was based upon a lousy Greek manuscript and the official translation endorsed by the Catholic church (still) is the Douay-Rheims which is an English translation of the faulty Vulgate. Very few modern scholars rely upon either the KJV or the Douay-Rheims translations, but church tradition dies hard.

Many modern Bibles, such as the New Revised Standard Version, quietly and without fanfare, print the most competent known translations but they also footnote many of the variations between the four families. There are still passages in even the most modern Bibles that many scholars consider to be later modifications of the original. Many remain in most English translations because they are so ingrained by tradition that people are reluctant to correct them. You'll see some of them later.

On numerous occasions I have heard televangelists quote a statement from the KJV that I know was never part of the original New Testament. Either they are blissfully unaware of their error or they are being untruthful. Some of these are among the most well-known and often quoted portions of the Bible. I am sure many will be familiar to you. Sometimes they are quoted and other times paraphrased. Here are some of them that we will discuss later (shown in the KJV):

- 1 John 5:7—*For there are three that bear record in Heaven, the Father, the Word, and the Holy Ghost: and these three are one.* (This is the only statement in the Bible that suggests the Trinity concept. Without it there is no Biblical support whatsoever for the belief that there is but one God in three forms, the Father, the Son, and the Holy Sprit, a concept that is fundamental to Christianity).
- Mark 16:17—*And these signs shall follow them that believe; In my name*

shall they cast out devils; they shall speak with new tongues; (Relied upon by the Evangelical, Pentecostal, and charismatics to support the idea of speaking in tongues).

- Mark 16:18—*They shall take up serpents; and if they drink any deadly thing, it shall not hurt them; they shall lay hands on the sick, and they shall recover.* (This is the key language relied upon by the Snake Handling sects).
- Luke 24:12—*Peter, however, got up and ran to the tomb. Bending over, he saw the strips of linen lying by themselves, and he went away, wondering to himself what had happened.*
- Luke 24:51—*While he was blessing them, he left them and was taken up into Heaven.*
- John 5:4—*For an angel went down at a certain season into the pool, and troubled the water: whosoever then first after the troubling of the water stepped in was made whole of whatsoever disease he had.*
- John 8:7-11—*He that is without sin among you, let him first cast a stone at her. . . hath no man condemned thee? She said, No man, Lord. And Jesus said unto her, Neither do I condemn thee: go, and sin no more.*

When I examine a Bible translation that I have not seen before, I usually check to see how the translation handles these verses. Do they print them but footnote that some texts omit them; do they omit them altogether; or do they print them and not inform the reader that they are in dispute. There is little dispute among scholars about the inauthenticity of these seven verses.

Now we turn to the question of who wrote all of the original Greek texts that became the New Testament.

12

Who Wrote the New Testament

Have I not seen Jesus our Lord?

Paul, 1 Cor 9:1

While the Old Testament was written over many centuries and spanned many more centuries in content, the New Testament was completely written in about a single century and its content covers about the same amount of time. Its protagonist is arguably the most influential person in the history of the world, a young Jewish man who died a horrible death before his time. The New Testament covers JESUS' birth, life, teachings, tragic death, and his resurrection. It also records the beginnings of the new religion that was named after him, first as a sect of Judaism and later as a new religion that reached out to all people.

The New Testament has two other heros: JESUS' disciple, Simon, called Peter, and a Jew named Saul, who later Romanized his name to Paul. Paul came from the town of Tarsus in what was then Syria but is now part of southern Turkey. Paul is clearly, hand's down, the star of the New Testament—after JESUS, of course.

Most of the books of the New Testament are credited to Paul's authorship, although sometimes incorrectly. Peter only makes a cameo appearance in the Bible, but Peter is hugely influential in the formation of the new religion of Christianity. He is widely thought of as the first Pope, and his influence on the formation of the fledgling church should not be underestimated. Most have heard the story where JESUS said to Peter, "*Tu es petra*" ("you are the rock"), upon which our church will be founded. That phrase became a mantra that the Bishops of Rome repeated over and over until the College of Bishops finally acknowledged that the Bishop of Rome, whoever it was, would be the leader of the church—the Pope. However, you won't see much of Peter in this text. As I noted in the introduction, this is a book about the Bible, not a book about the church, and most of the stories about Peter, including his death, are not contained in the Bible.

Paul's comment in the epigraph was contained in one of the letters he wrote to the church that he founded in the Greek city of Corinth. The statement that he had seen JESUS is the only comment of its type in the entire Bible. But we know from Paul's own writings that Paul never saw the historical, living, breathing JESUS, the JESUS that walked among us. Paul tells us that he only saw JESUS in a vision.

I have mentioned it before, but it is very important to keep in mind as you read this book, that nobody who wrote a single word in the Bible ever saw the historical JESUS or even claims to have seen him. In fact, with the possible exception of the Gospel of Thomas, there is not even a surviving secular writing where the author actually saw JESUS. All we have to go by is second, third, and fourth hand statements about JESUS.

The Words of JESUS

If any of the statements recorded in the Bible and attributed to JESUS were to be offered into evidence in any court of law in the United States, they would be deemed inadmissible because they are all hearsay. Luke frankly admits in the very first verse of his Gospel that his work is pure hearsay and suggests that the other Gospels were written the same way; statements that would not be contested by New Testament scholars. There is other evidence as well that the Gospels were not based upon first-hand knowledge. See for example Matthew's story of the empty tomb (Mt 28:11-15) where some of the tomb guards went to the priests and told them that JESUS had disappeared. The priests then bribed the soldiers to say that the disciples had stolen the body while the guards had fallen asleep. Certainly neither the guards nor the priests wrote this in Matthew's book and they were all long dead by the time it was written, so it could be nothing else but hearsay. Matthew even goes on to say, "And this story is still told among the Jews to this day." In other words, it circulated as a rumor.

We know within a few years the date when each of the four intra canonical Gospels, Matthew, Mark, Luke, and John, were written, and they were all written long after the deaths of the original disciples by those names. More on this later, but it does make one wonder how the authors of the Gospels could have known that those words attributed to JESUS and printed in red in my old Bible were really uttered by him. These are purportedly word for word quotes translated into Greek from words spoken in Aramaic 40 to 90 years previously, transcribed by someone who was not there to hear them. It takes a real stretch of faith to believe that these are stenographically accurate quotes.

Even the very earliest gospel was written between 35 to 45 years after JESUS' death by a person who had never seen JESUS. How could those word for word quotes survive intact over three decades of oral tradition? They did not have tape recorders and camcorders in the first century. There were no daily YouTube postings of cell phone videos in those days. We will discuss some of the reasons why people remembered JESUS' words in the next chapter, but there are many quotations that do not fall into such categories. Some people did write down recollections of excerpts from JESUS' sermons that were told to them by people who actually saw Jesus, but there do not appear to be any from people who actually heard the words, with the possible exception of the Gospel of Thomas.

The Gospels of Thomas and "Q" appear to be collections of such quotes and it appears that at one time there were hundreds of these collections. These are referred to today as "sayings gospels" to differentiate them from the gospels of Matthew, Mark, Luke, and John which are called "narrative gospels" because they not only quote what JESUS said, but also narrate what he did. While we know of many sayings gospels, the four intra-canonical gospels are the only known narrative gospels. But people rarely remember what someone else said word for word. They usually recall the substance of what was said, not the words themselves, so even those very early writings are unlikely to be true and correct quotes.

A primary source for the intra-canonical Gospels was an oral history passed on through generations of recollections. While the Aramaic language spoken by JESUS and his followers did, and still does, have a written form, Greek was the official written language of the day. The New Testament was written almost entirely in Greek. Therefore, the authors had to transcribe JESUS' words into Greek, and some of the authors had a pretty shaky grasp of Greek. I would be amazed if even a very small portion of the sayings attributed to JESUS were actually recorded in the way he spoke them. I do believe, however, that many of those words attributed to him in the Gospels accurately express his philosophy and accurately represent the message that He was trying to communicate to his followers. I also believe that they were the best recollections of those who tried to record JESUS' words. I also believe that there are words in the Bible attributed to JESUS that are wholly the invention of the author, and we will discuss some of these. We will also see how the recollections of JESUS' words varied when written in two or more of the gospels. We will see quite a bit of this when we discuss those parallel verses. It is beyond dispute that people did not remember the words precisely as they were spoken.

The Gospels describe how the early Christians *understood* JESUS' message. The authors all understood the message somewhat differently. We will examine some of those differences as well. Undoubtedly many of the words attributed to JESUS are very close to what he said. The question is, which words were most likely spoken and which acts most likely performed by JESUS and which were probably words that were put into JESUS' mouth from the imaginations of the evangelists who were writing the books. Many of those parallel verses in two or more of the Gospels occur where the authors are copying from the same source, but they are rarely the same. The authors each modified the source material. In other words, the authors of the Gospels often had JESUS saying basically the same things but saying them differently. Sometimes, however, the differences in the wording of what JESUS said changes the meaning. The question then becomes, which if any of these sayings are correct?

The suggestion that every word attributed to JESUS is not correct is far from a new concept. Marcion, an early second century Church leader that was a tremendous influence on the formation of Christianity, omitted from his version of the scriptures all references that he did not think were authoritative. (St.) Augustine, the most respected Christian author after Paul, once left the church for several years because he did not believe all of the words attributed to JESUS were really his own words. Thomas Jefferson carried his own version of the New Testament in which he had redacted all the words he did not think that JESUS actually spoke plus all of the miracles which he thought were all nonsense.

A few years ago the Jesus Seminar worked on this subject. This was a group of over 75 Biblical scholars from around the world representing most mainline Christian faiths. They published their findings in a book called *The Five Gospels*, in which they divided the words of JESUS into four categories: 1) Jesus undoubtedly said this or something very like it; 2) Jesus probably said something like this but it has suffered in the passage of time; 3) Jesus did not say this, but the ideas contained in it are close to his own; 4) Jesus did not say this—it represents the perspective or content of a later or different tradition. They printed each category in a different color* and gave detailed explanations of how they arrived at each decision. Their arguments are very persuasive and are a classic example of "critical thinking."

Let me give you just one example to show you what I mean. We are told that JESUS and his disciples went to the garden at Gethsemane** after the Last Supper. The disciples all fell asleep, and JESUS went into the garden to pray. His prayers are described in detail and printed in red ink in many Bibles. But immediately thereafter, he was arrested, tried, and executed. His disciples were asleep and then fled when the minions arrived to arrest JESUS (Mt 26:39-45). How can anyone suggest that what

* Red ink was used for the first category, pink for the second, gray for the third, and black ink for the fourth in keeping with the tradition of red ink for the words spoken by JESUS.

** The garden at Gethsemane sounds delightful, conjuring up images of a beautiful garden; but *gethsemane* means "olive press," and Jesus and his disciples were actually in an olive orchard.

JESUS did or said between the slumber of the disciples and the arrival of the arresting party is true and correct? There were no witnesses and no hidden cameras. All you can do is create the fiction that the writer of the story, whoever it was, was somehow divinely inspired. The Fellows of the Jesus Seminar determined that this did not justify a red letter position in the Bible.

There are also portions of the gospels that are not historical and the authors never intended they be considered historical. Many modern Christians assume they are true facts and miss out on the important message the author tried to convey. Here is one example. The Middle Eastern cultures at some time in their history began using patronymic names like most of Europe. These are names derived from one's father or from a male family patriarch. For example, in Scotland the term "Mac" before a last name means "son of." MacDonald, therefore, means son of Donald. In Ireland the O' before a name means "son of" as in O'Reilly. In the Middle East they did the same thing. For example, Osama bin-Laden means "Osama son of Laden." Hebrews used the word "ben" and in Aramaic the term "bar" meant son of.

Keeping this in mind, consider the story of JESUS' trial where Pontius Pilate offers to commute the sentence of either JESUS or another prisoner named Barabbas and the crowd is forced to choose who should be spared. The crowd overwhelmingly chose Barabbas, leaving JESUS to die on the cross. Ministers universally consider this an historical event. It has also been used to blame the Jews for JESUS' death. However, the story of Barabbas was not historical at all but was allegorical. The authors of the Gospels intended the story to mean something very special to the readers that the early Christians knew but modern readers do not.

JESUS always addressed GOD as "Father." In the language of his time, Aramaic, the word for "father" was *abba*. In the Lord's Prayer in Matthew, for instance, the phrase, "Our Father . . ." was written in Aramaic as "*Abba*" even though the rest of Matthew was written in Greek. JESUS always addressed GOD as *Abba*, and all first century Christians knew it. Two of the Gospels tell us that JESUS' last words were, "*Abba*, why have you forsaken me!" As noted above, the word *bar* meant, and still means, "son of" in Aramaic. Barabbas, therefore, means "sons of the father," more properly *bar-Abbas*. The symbolism then is that Barabbas, a criminal, a man full of sin, represented GOD'S sons, that is, all mankind, that are also full of sin. By his death, JESUS was granting life to all the sons of GOD; that is, to all of the Barabbas's in the world, even those who were sinners.

Now doesn't that explanation make more sense than just inserting a story so we can blame the Jews for JESUS' death? There never was a custom of allowing one condemned prisoner to go free in Roman history. That was an invention purely for this story. The very name Barabbas seems contrived to convey a powerful meaning. Doesn't this explanation make a whole lot more sense. That is powerful symbolism that is lost to most because church leaders today do not speak Aramaic and do not understand what the writers of the gospels were trying to communicate. The Christians in the first century knew, though. JESUS became their "burnt offering" or "sin offering" to GOD, replicating the scape goat story in the Hebrew Scriptures. Because of JESUS dying for the sins of mankind, people never again had to make sacrifices to GOD.

It is also very important to distinguish between what was written about JESUS in the Bible and what has become church dogma over the years. This is not a book about Christianity or Judaism. The *religion* of Christianity was formed primarily in the second, third, and fourth centuries. We are only interested in what the Bible itself says about the early formation of Christianity, all of which was written in the first and very early second centuries. JESUS lived in the first third of the first century. In order to tell the Bible's story, it is necessary to separate the writings found in the Bible from later church dogma which is found in other documents. For example, there is not a single word in the Bible about the immaculate conception. That was the creation of (St.) Augustine in the second century as was the concept of original sin. The Bible makes no mention of Mary Magdalene being a prostitute. That was the invention of Pope Gregory I. Another example is the Trinity (the Father, the Son, and the Holy Spirit which are three versions of the same god according to Christian tradition) was not accepted dogma until the end of the fourth century and is not mentioned in the original versions of the Bible. The rapture that is so important to the Evangelical church was not invented until the late 18th century. These are important aspects of many people's Christian faith, but they are not mentioned in the Bible and are not, therefore, covered in this book except where they relate to the story of the Bible.

There is no single instance in the Bible where JESUS claims to be a god. Therefore, there were huge differences of opinion among the early Christians about whether JESUS was the human son of GOD; whether GOD himself came down to earth and took a human form (as many of the Pagan Gods did); whether GOD came down and simply occupied the body of an existing human (as did some of the Pagan gods); whether JESUS was a god when he was born or was he only a god after his resurrection; is he now equal to GOD or is he a lesser god; is the Holy Spirit part of GOD or something else entirely? These questions still divide some branches of the Christian Church, although blood is no longer shed over who is correct. These were bitterly contested issues in the first few centuries of the common era.

If you read something here that does not agree with what your minister told you, it is most likely because this book is not about the various ideas and beliefs that were later adopted by the Church. This is only about what the Bible itself says.

Categories of New Testament Writings

There are mainly two broad categories of writings in the New Testament; the more or less historical books and the more or less letters or epistles. There are a couple of exceptions, and we will talk about them as well.

The historical books are the four gospels; Matthew, Mark, Luke, and John, plus the book written about JESUS' apostles and the beginnings of Christianity, the book of Acts of the Apostles, more commonly called, simply, Acts. These are the first books in the New Testament, but they were not the first New Testament documents written. Paul's letters all predate the Gospels. We are going to examine the New Testament books in a slightly modified chronological order, not in the order in which they appear in the Bible. First, we will discuss Paul's letters (Epistles) in the order in which they were written, which differs from the order in which they appear in the Bible. Then we'll take on the four Gospels and Acts, which were all written after Paul's letters. Are you now thoroughly confused? It will all sort out as we go.

Before we get to the gospels themselves, however, I need to throw some other ingredients into the stew. Matthew and Luke both contain material from a previous gospel that has disappeared except for those portions contained within the text of Matthew and Luke. This gospel is called the Gospel of Q, and it was written very shortly after Paul's letters. We will discuss Q before the gospels as it picks up the story of the early church where Paul left off. It is sort of a transitional book.

By studying the books in the order in which they were written, you can see the dramatic progression of the birth and growth of Christianity. This is a very interesting exercise. This order of study allows us to follow the creation of Christianity, from the early words JESUS delivered to a few peasants, to how Jesus and his words became a major world religion. Christianity did not become a religion in an instant. It grew out of JESUS's words, the interpretations of those words by Paul and others, and the understandings of the words by the new converts which were mostly Greco-Roman pagans.

We will study and analyze the letters of Paul and then briefly discuss the other epistles. In Paul's time there were no written documents in existence that he could give to the new churches he founded. Paul's teachings were oral, the same way everyone taught in the first century. After Paul moved on to found new churches, other itinerant preachers like Paul came behind him and spoke at his existing churches, and these evangelists did not always agree with Paul's positions. Therefore, Paul began a tradition of writing letters to his churches to clarify and update his teachings and to rebut the teachings of others whom he called by many names, the least offensive being "false apostles." Copies of these letters were used as guides for the church leaders and often ended up in many churches, not merely those to whom the letters were addressed. The churches began saving Paul's letters and some of them eventually became part of the New Testament. Many other letters written by Paul were lost over time. The only written material Paul himself had to refer to was the Septuagint.

While Paul was pretty much "winging it" on his own, the authors of the four gospels and Acts all had other written works in front of them as they wrote. Mark was the first to write, and both Matthew and Luke used huge portions of Mark's work in their own gospels. In fact, one goal of both Matthew and Luke was, apparently, that their own works would update and replace Mark, and that almost happened. The earliest copy of Mark that has been discovered was written almost 200 years after Mark first penned it. The Gospel of Mark, along with many other gospels, was almost lost to history. The Gospel of Q was lost and can now be found only inside the gospels of Matthew and Luke, just as the writings of J and E can only be found now in the Old Testament. The Gospel of Thomas was also lost until a copy was found in Egypt in the twentieth century. Recently, a copy of the long lost Gospel of Judas was found amid much publicity. Today we have all or portions of about 20 gospels and we know of about 40 total, but there were apparently many more circulating at the time.

Matthew used 600 of the 666 verses of Mark in his gospel and Luke used about 300 of Mark's verses. These are all parallel verses in the Bible and can be laid out side-by-side and compared. Someone very recently discovered that if you remove from Matthew and Luke all of those verses that came from Mark, there were still a lot of parallel verses remaining. Someone then put all of these non-Mark parallel verses together and discovered that both Matthew and Luke had almost certainly been working from another text in addition to Mark. These verses were ultimately separated into a separate book. The person who discovered this was German and he named the book *Quelle* which means "source" in German. To most, it is now almost universally known simply as the Gospel of Q. There were a lot of doubters in the beginning, but there are few New Testament scholars today that do not subscribe to the concept that Matthew and Luke used that now lost book, written by an unknown author, for large portions of their gospels.

Then we will study the intra canonical gospels in the order in which they were written; Mark, Matthew, Luke, and John*, plus the book of Acts. We will also touch on another gospel that is not included in the Bible, the Gospel of Thomas. We will not go into much detail about this very important book simply because it is not part of the Bible, but it does help us explain portions of the other gospels, and we will use it for that purpose. There are parallel verses to many of the canonical gospels in Thomas and it enhances the likelihood that the words were actually spoken by JESUS. In the language of the scholars, it is an "additional attestation" that helps verify the authenticity of the canonical gospels.

The following time line shows some important dates in the New Testament including the approximate dates each book was written. There is no unanimity on exact dates, but most of the calculations by the scholars are fairly close to each other. Some date Mark's gospel as early as 65 C.E., for example, but Mark clearly discusses the destruction of the Temple of Solomon that occurred in 70 C.E.; therefore, I have used the following timeline that reflects this view. Some scholars might want to tweak these dates a little but they are not likely to be vigorously disputed by anyone. Additionally, as you will see, many of the documents were edited over the years, often by the authors themselves but sometimes by others, so the dates shown could vary depending upon whether the date used is the date it was originally issued or after one of the modifications. For example, you will later see that the authors of Matthew, Luke, and John probably added the birth and death stories of Jesus at a later time.

Timeline of New Testament Works

37-4 B.C.E	King Herod, also known as Herod the Great, was King of Judea when Jesus was born.
4 B.C.E -39 C.E.	Herod Antipas who ruled the Galilee area during JESUS' life. It was this Herod who beheaded John the Baptist.
6 B.C.E.	JESUS is born.
26-36 C.E.	Pontius Pilate was the Roman procurator, sort of like a governor, and who ordered Jesus' execution.
30 C.E.	JESUS is crucified..
50 C.E.	**1 Thessalonians**, Paul's letter to the Thessalonians

* Some scholars argue with pretty convincing authority that Luke was written after John. The consensus is, however, that Luke was written before John and that only the book of Acts, also written by the author of Luke, was written after John

	written from Corinth.
52-53 C.E.	**Galatians**, Paul's letter to the people of Galatia in the winter of 52-53 from Ephesus.
53-54 C.E.	**1 Corinthians** and **2 Corinthians**, Letters from Paul to his church in Corinth from Ephesus in the winter of 53-54.
Probably 54-55 C.E.	**Philemon**, Letter from Paul to his friend, Philemon, the leader of a small house church in Colossae, written from prison, probably in Ephesus. The date is uncertain, however.
Probably 54-55 C.E.	**Philippians**, Letter from Paul to the church at Philippi; three letters combined, apparently by accident, the first two of which was written from prison, probably in Ephesus.
55-56 C.E.	**Romans**, Paul's letter to the church in Rome, written from Corinth in the winter of 55-56 C.E.
Mid 50's -late 60's - early 70's C.E.	**Gospel of Thomas**. This is not in the Bible, but it is a very early source of the sayings of JESUS written by someone who may have met him.
Mid 50's C.E.	**Hebrews**, is a collection of preexistent sayings and narrations without a known author. It may have been a sermon or a collection of sermons.
Mid to late 50's-86 C.E.	**Sayings Gospel Q**. This is a collection of the sayings of JESUS used by both Matthew and Luke in composing their Gospels. There are apparently three different groupings of the sayings (called layers), a sapiential layer which is referred to as 1Q (or as Q^1), an apocalyptic group referred to as 2Q (Q^2), and an introductory layer which is, of course, 3Q (Q^3). Each of these layers, it is believed, was from a different period of time; 1Q was from about 50 C.E., 2Q about 65 C.E., and 3Q about 86 C.E. after the fall of the Temple.
65 C.E.	Paul's death or execution in a Roman prison.
70-75 C.E.	**Gospel of Mark 1**. This was the original version of Mark before a section of the gospel called "the hidden gospel of Mark" was redacted because the church felt it was repugnant to Christianity. It was probably written in or near Antioch, Syria.

75-80 C.E. **Gospel of Mark 2**. This is the version of Mark that appears in the Bible with the exception of verses 16:9 - 20 which were added in the second century.

75-80 C.E. **Colossians**. Originally attributed to Paul, it was actually written after his death, possibly by one of his students.

90 C.E. **Gospel of Matthew**. It was probably written in Antioch in ancient Syria.

Late 90's C.E. **Gospel of Luke**. The date is uncertain, but it was after Matthew and before the Gospel of John, written someplace in Greece. Some argue that the date should be in the early second century C.E.

Late 90's C.E. **Letter to the Ephesians.** Probably written by a Jewish Christian who was either an admirer or follower of Paul. It draws heavily upon the ideas established in Colossians.

Late 90's C.E. **Revelation to John**. This was written from the Roman penal island of Patmos off the coast of Turkey close to the end of the century. It was probably written during the time that Domitian was the Roman emperor.

100 C.E. **Letter of James**, written in Syria.

110 C.E. **Gospel of John I.** The first version of this Gospel was written about this time and was later modified. Some scholars switch this date with that of Luke.

112 C.E. **1 Peter**. Written in Rome in Peter's name to encourage Christians that were being persecuted.

118 C.E. **1 John**. The first letter of John was written by an unknown author in John's name. When the Gospel of John first came out, it caused a dispute between those who were devoted to John's teachings. This letter supported the Catholic position.

120-125 C.E. **Gospel of John II**. This is the version that appears in the Bible.

125 C.E. **Acts of the Apostles**. This is the sequel to the Gospel of Luke and written by the same author; the stories of the Apostles and the new church after

	the death of JESUS, and was probably conceived of at the same time as the gospel, although written much later.
125 C.E. and later	**1 Timothy**. The two letters to Timothy and the letter to Titus, referred to as the "pastoral" letters because they have to do with the matters of the church leaders, the pastors. None of them were written by Paul who was long dead by the time they were written.
125 C.E. and later	**2 Timothy**. (See 1 Timothy).
125 C.E. and later	**Titus**. (See 1 Timothy).
130 C.E.	**2 Peter**. Not written by the apostle Peter.

Parallel Verses

Parallel verses are those in which the same words spoken by JESUS or the same events are described in two or more different writings. JESUS' words were originally recorded orally and only later written down. This leads to people remembering things differently. For example, most people recall the phrase, ". . . a date that will live in infamy." Did Roosevelt say "date" or "day?" Did he say "which" or "that?" Few can tell which is correct because people remember things differently; also, sometimes changes are made intentionally as in Matthew and Luke.

As we have seen, both Matthew and Luke copied much of Mark. In a few cases, even John has a parallel writing, but that is probably because John heard the same story elsewhere; there is no evidence that he had read any of the other gospels. Here are just a couple of examples of parallel verses in which Matthew and Luke copied Mark differently (See Chapter 17 for other examples):

Those Ashamed of Me

Mark 8:38 - 9:1	*Matthew 16:27 - 28*	*Luke 9:26-27*
Those who are ashamed of me and of my words in this adulterous and sinful generation,		*Those who are ashamed of me and of my words,*
of them the Son of Man will also be ashamed when he comes in the glory of his Father with the holy angels.	*For the Son of Man is to come with his angels in the glory of his Father, and then he will repay everyone for what has been done.*	*of them the Son of Man will be ashamed when he comes in his glory and the glory of the Father and of the holy angels.*

And he said to them, "Truly I tell you, there are some standing here who will not taste death until they see that the kingdom of GOD *has come with power.*	*Truly I tell you, there are some standing here who will not taste death before they see the Son of Man coming in his kingdom.*	*But truly I tell you, there are some standing here who will not taste death before they see the kingdom of* GOD

Parable of the Sower

Mark 4:3-9	*Matthew 13:3-9*	*Luke 8:5-8*
"Listen! A sower went out to sow. And as he sowed, some seed fell on the path, and the birds came and ate it up.	*"Listen! A sower went out to sow. And as he sowed, some seeds fell on the path, and the birds came and ate them up.*	*"A sower went out to sow his seed; and as he sowed, some fell on the path and was trampled on, and the birds of the air ate it up.*
Other seed fell on rocky ground, where it did not have much soil, and it sprang up quickly, since it had no depth of soil. And when the sun rose, it was scorched; and since it had no root, it withered away.	*Other seeds fell on rocky ground, where they did not have much soil, and they sprang up quickly, since they had no depth of soil. But when the sun rose, they were scorched; and since they had no root, they withered away.*	*Some fell on the rock; and as it grew up, it withered for lack of moisture.*
Other seed fell among the thorns, and the thorns grew up and choked it, and it yielded no grain.	*Other seeds fell among thorns, and the thorns grew up and choked them.*	*Some fell among thorns, and the thorns grew with it and choked it.*
Other seed fell into good soil and brought forth grain, growing up and increasing and yielding thirty and sixty and a hundredfold."	*Other seeds fell on good soil and brought forth grain, some a hundredfold, some sixty, some thirty.*	*Some fell on good soil, and when it grew, it produced a hundredfold."*
And he said, "let anyone with ears to hear listen!"	*Let anyone with ears listen!"*	*As he said this, he called out, "Let anyone with ears to hear listen!"*

What is important to note is that these differences were not accidental. Both Matthew and Luke had Mark's version before them and they made conscious decisions to modify it.

From Whence Came the Words

As you can probably guess from our discussions of the books in the Old Testament, the New Testament did not come down as a single work put together by a committee either. Christianity grew cautiously from the early teachings of JESUS into a religion, step by step.

Since none of the authors of the Bible were around to hear or see JESUS, the best chance we have of really knowing him, "up close and personal," is to find the earliest writings we can find that talk about him. Some of the writings in the Bible were written within 20 years of JESUS' death while other writings were written more than 100 years after his death. The general feeling among scholars is that the writings that are the closest to the time JESUS lived are probably more reliable evidence of what JESUS actually did and said; and in fact, that seems to be the case when all of the evidence is assembled and studied.

Please recall what I said earlier about the Jewish historical books. Written history as we know it in the twenty-first century is not the same as written history in the first century. Historical writings in the Mediterranean area in that period were never intended to be faithful records of what actually happened or accurate biographies. They were didactic and were usually intended to serve as a teaching tool, and they were loaded with religious, political, and philosophical viewpoints. The same is true of the Gospels; therefore, when we discuss the gospels, we will consider the author's intended audience and the intended message and how different persons might interpret the words differently. Remember, JESUS' audiences were Jews, Roman pagans, Greek pagans, pagans from other Middle Eastern countries, Samaritans, and many other cultures. They all heard JESUS' words differently or understood them differently.

Let me give you an example. Most of what we know about the birth of JESUS comes from the Gospel of Luke. Matthew's version is much shorter. For a few minutes set aside all the things you have been told over all the Christmas seasons and look at Luke's birth story of JESUS as though you were hearing it for the first time.

Luke actually has two birth stories—the birth of JESUS and the birth of John who was later called "the Baptist." The two birth stories sort of blend in together. The story begins with two elderly people, Elizabeth and Zechariah, who wished for a family but had long given up hope of ever having children. GOD gave them their wish and Elizabeth became pregnant with the child whom they name John.

Mary then became pregnant with JESUS. According to Luke, Mary was a cousin of Elizabeth and went to visit her. Mary informed Elizabeth that she was also pregnant and that Elizabeth's son was destined to serve Mary's son. And Elizabeth agreed! Have you ever in your entire life known any woman willing to admit that someone else's unborn child is going to be better than her own child and that her own unborn child is destined to serve the other? It is a bit of a stretch. And Elizabeth does not even know about JESUS' devine conception.

In any event, everyone seems very happy. Mary is so happy that she spontaneously bursts into a song that she composes on the spot (the *Magnificat*, which is still sung in church). After a little more conversation, Zechariah, who had been stricken mute for years, is so overwhelmed that he suddenly regains his speech and also instantly composes and sings an original song (the *Benedictus*, still sung in church). Later, after JESUS' birth and ritual circumcision, he is taken to the temple for presentation and Simeon is so overcome with happiness that he also bursts into song (the *Nunc Dimittis*, composed on the spot and still sung in church).

This isn't history; it's a Broadway show! Have you ever in your entire life heard of someone spontaneously bursting into song when they are happy—a song that they composed on the spot? A song in which, even though nobody was there to write it down, was somehow preserved in written form 120 years later?

These canticles are still sung in church services to this day, but how did Luke know about them? Luke wasn't even born at the time Mary purportedly visited Elizabeth. Yet Luke is credited with translating into Greek, word for word, original songs composed on the spot in Aramaic by uneducated peasants110 years earlier.

There is no possible way Luke's narrative can be historically correct. This can only be classified as legend like our own legends of George Washington and the cherry tree and throwing the dollar across the Potomac. Luke used the story to continue the tale of JESUS devine birth and to introduce John the Baptist. There isn't the slightest bit if evidence that John and JESUS were related other than this story. It is pretty well settled, however, that John baptized JESUS and that he was, for a time, one of John's disciples. Later JESUS left and began his own ministry. After John's execution, many of his followers moved into JESUS' camp. The messages of John and JESUS differed in very significant ways, however, so it was important to lay a foundation to demonstrate that JESUS was destined to be greater than John; that way, where there was conflict between the messages of JESUS and John, JESUS' position would always win.

Nearly all of us who were raised in the Christian faith have appeared at one time or another in a Christmas pageant. If you read Luke's nativity story closely, it reads like a pageant. The canticles fit in very well. But in addition, as noted by at least one scholar, every scene in Luke's nativity story has a distinct ending and a beginning. It is as if someone had written "curtain up" and "curtain down" in a script.

> "*In those days Mary set out and went with haste to a Judean town in the hill country* . . . ."
>
> [Curtain up].

"And Mary remained with her about three months, and returned to her home. . . ."

[Curtain down].

"Now came the time for Elizabeth to give birth, and she bore a son. . . ."

[Curtain up].

"And the child grew and became strong in spirit, and he was in the wilderness until the day of his manifestation into Israel. . . ."

[Curtain down].

And so forth.

Many Biblical scholars believe that Luke's nativity story actually may be an early Christmas pageant. Whether Luke was writing the pageant or quoting a pageant that he had seen, no one knows. But it is very theater-like with its songs and its beginnings and endings.

The Epistles

There are basically four categories of epistles or letters—there are letters written by Paul, letters purportedly written by Paul but which were actually written by others, letters by other authors, and documents that are not actually letters at all. There is a large cross-over in these categories.

The arrangement of the Epistles in the Bible is a little strange, but there is some method behind it. First, they lump together all of the letters that were originally attributed to Paul. However, there is no attempt to put them in chronological order as most of us would do today. Instead they are inserted into the Bible in the order of their length. Romans, being the longest, is the first in order down to Philemon with Hebrews being the last because it is the shortest. The letters attributed to other authors followed. These other letters are usually called the "universal letters" or the "general letters." Note that the letters written by Paul and those purportedly written by him but actually written by others all bear the title of the intended recipient, while the general letters all bear the title of the of the person who purportedly wrote the letters. The uncategorized book of Revelation is placed last.

Letters Purportedly Written by Paul

Paul's writings are the earliest New Testament writings, however, he did not write all the epistles credited to him. Very early in the history of Christianity, church leaders noted some strange discrepancies in the pastoral letters of 1 and 2 Timothy and Titus. The first discovery was that they refer to "bishops" and "deacons" and those were terms that had not even been used in the lifetime of Paul. Regardless of what you may have seen on recent television documentaries, Paul and the early apostles did not speak before large crowds in the amphitheater at Ephesus or any other place. Paul's churches were small groups of just a handful of people, a half dozen or so, and the concept of a Bishop did not even make sense.

There were also other events discussed in the pastoral letters that did not occur until after Paul's death. Some statements even conflict with other texts. For example, in 1 Timothy Paul laments the fact that Timothy was not with him when he was in Macedonia. But Acts states that he did, in fact, accompany Paul in Macedonia. Today Acts is considered to be a very flimsy authority on Paul and his activities, but at the time this discrepancy was noticed, people believed that the author of Acts was an intimate friend of Paul, so that raised doubts about the authenticity of the three pastoral gospels.

By the same detection methods early church leaders discovered that Paul did not write Hebrews, which is now believed to have been a sermon, and most scholars do not believe that he wrote Ephesians. Many of the terms used in Ephesians, for example, "Heavenly places," "dividing wall," and "fellow citizen," were never used by Paul any place else. Also, some of the terms and phrases in the letters that are confidently attributed to Paul are given new meanings or are completely absent. Finally, the writing style is in very long sentences which is uncharacteristic of Paul. For a long time many felt that Colossians was written by Paul, but this is now a distinct minority. However, he did write many of the letters bearing his name: Romans, 1 & 2 Corinthians, Galatians, Philippians, Philemon, and 1 Thessalonians.

Some of the letters that are considered genuine letters from Paul have been edited and rearranged. For example, early copies of Romans show that the 16th chapter was not part of the original letter and the two letters to the church in Corinth were actually a compilation of four letters that were rearranged by some unknown later editor.

The General Letters

In addition to the disputes as to Paul's genuine writings, there were other letters purporting to be by Peter, John, James and Jude, that were not written by those persons, although there is a small minority who feel that Peter was actually written, at least in part, by Simon called Peter. These were early church writings that were attributed to those persons but were written long after their deaths.

The books are generally referred to as the "Universal Letters" or the "General Letters," however, most of them are not letters at all. They are more like religious tracts that were distributed to several churches. Some may have been copies of sermons.

Unlike Paul's letters, the universal letters are not named after the addressees or recipients; they are named after the supposed authors. James, for example, attacks some of Paul's ideas, and the author might have wanted to use the name of JESUS' brother, James, who was a leader which is quite poetic. But it is absolutely certain that the disciple of JESUS known as John, son of Zebedee, was not the author of any of them.

I hate to introduce uncertainty here, but some of the non-Paul letters could have been actual letters rather than religious tracts or sermons as most believe. There is a cross-over between the categories of letters and the unclassified books that are wrongfully ascribed to apostles. But it is safe to say that none of the books were written by the names on the book titles, unless they were written by persons who coincidentally had the same names as those who were disciples of JESUS.

The Gospels

Nobody knows who wrote the Gospels because none of them were signed. That was the custom for such writings in the Middle East at that time. The Gospels were some of the first books of what became the New Testament that people began collecting. There were many gospels written at the time, but the four intra-canonical gospels appear to have been the most widely circulated. Most of the others were sayings gospels. The church tried to find out who wrote the four gospels, but their ancient forensic tools were woefully inadequate for the job. Where did the names come from? We don't know for sure, but we have a lot of clues. What we do know, within a very few years, is when they were written. We also know that none of the four was written by the person to whom the work is attributed.

Each of the gospels was written for a different audience. It is important to keep that in mind as you read them. Matthew, for instance, wrote for an audience of Jews that either had, or were candidates to, convert to Christianity. You can see from the very beginning that most gentiles would not have a clue about what Matthew's message was. The first thing they come across is a genealogy of JESUS and they would not have any idea who any of those people were. Jews, on the other hand, would not only know who they were, they would expect to see a genealogy. Matthew calls JESUS the "Messiah," a distinctly Hebrew term that has no counterpart for the gentiles. Matthew goes to great pains to show how JESUS fulfills ancient Hebrew prophecies that would mean nothing to the pagans.

Mark, on the other hand, wrote for an audience of Roman pagans. He had to take pains to explain Jewish laws, customs, and practices. In one instance, JESUS was criticized by the scribes and Pharisees because JESUS' disciples did not wash their hands when they ate bread. Matthew said very little by means of explanation because his audience of Jews already knew GOD's laws. Mark, however, had to explain in detail to his audience of pagans that the washing of the hands was not to get the dirt off but was a ceremonial cleansing in the tradition of the Hebrew elders because Jews did not eat unless they washed their hands in a special way.

Luke was probably Greek; at least Greek was his first language, and he was the only person writing in the entire Bible that was not Jewish by birth. His audience was, apparently, Greek gentiles. His gospel was addressed to "the most excellent Theophilus" which is a Greek name, but it means "friends of GOD," so it could mean any group of Greek Christians. In any event, it appears to be addressed to Hellenic gentiles. Whereas Matthew tried to show how JESUS fulfilled all of the Hebrew prophecies, Luke tried to build JESUS credibility by referring his ministry to historical events.

John also had a gentile audience. He had a different message, though. For John, JESUS was a god from the very beginning, then he came down and lived among us, and then went back to sit by GOD ("In the beginning was the Word (JESUS), and the Word was with GOD, and the Word was GOD"). John's intent was to destroy any remaining need or respect for the priesthood and their assistants who were in positions of power solely by inheritance and coddling to the Romans. He was very hard on Jewish religious leaders. He shows that JESUS was always a god, but also emphasizes that he was purely human until his resurrection.

Mark

Scholars agree that, although it comes second in the New Testament, the first of the four intra canonical gospels to be written was Mark. The early church leaders recognized the writings of this book as being very close to the philosophies of Peter. They concluded that the book must have been written by Peter's friend and translator, John Mark. They speculated that after Peter's martyrdom, Mark took the notes of his conversations with Peter to Alexandria and expanded them into the book of Mark. Scholars no longer believe any of this, but they have been unable to discover the correct name of the real author, so Mark it will be forever.

One thing is pretty apparent, though. Whoever wrote Mark was not Greek. It was obviously the author's second language. His Greek is atrocious. It is written in *koine*, which means "common" or "rustic," and is the form of Greek spoken by the peasantry as opposed to the high Greek of the upper classes in which books were normally written. It would be like writing a Shakespearian play in Cockney. Most scholars agree that the author probably originally wrote the book in Aramaic and then later translated it into Greek. Both Matthew and Luke tried to "clean up" Mark's dreadful Greek when they incorporated verses from Mark into their own gospels. Mark was probably written in southern Syria, not Alexandria as originally believed. The church in Alexandria did possess an early copy of Mark, however.

Later writers, including Matthew and Luke, wrongfully thought that Mark was a percipient witness to what JESUS said and did. They copied extensively from Mark thinking that they were getting first-hand knowledge. Luke indicates in his first verse that he was writing the accounts ". . . just as they were handed on to us by those who from the beginning were eyewitnesses. . . ." But they were mistaken about Mark having been an eye witnesses. He was not.

Mark appears to be drawn primarily from the oral tradition. When Mark quotes from the Old Testament, he mixes up the quotes, gets them wrong, and intermingles them. This is a sure tip-off that he was writing from the oral tradition and did not have written texts of the Hebrew Scriptures in front of him as he was writing. Because so much of Mark was used in the other two gospels, it is thought that one purpose of both Matthew and Luke was to replace Mark with their own gospels. In fact, Mark was a lost gospel, like Q, for over 200 years. We do not have a single fragment of any copy of Mark from either the first or second centuries and only one from the third. On the other hand, there are eight of Matthew and four of Luke dating from the second and third centuries.

The Secret Gospel of Mark

In 1958 Professor Morton Smith of Columbia University made a truly remarkable discovery. In a monastery near Jerusalem he found a letter written by Bishop Clement of Alexandria, one of the most highly respected of the early church leaders. He is known as First Clement and was sanctified and even has a holiday named after him.

One of the Bishop's very promising young students, Theodore, wrote him a letter. Theodore was confused about some church doctrine. One of the Gnostic sects, the Carpocratians, had apparently been interpreting one of the passages from Mark in a manner inconsistent with the official (catholic) church position. (Actually, the church was having the same problem with another sect in Corinth that Paul referred to in one of his letters, but that encounter was not mentioned in the Clement letter. We will examine Paul's problems when we discuss his letters). Theodore attacked the Carpocratians for this heresy and wrote Clement about what he had done. Clement wrote back to him and that letter to Theodore is what Professor Smith found.

This is a very good example of how people tinkered with the New Testament scriptures. Also, Clement quotes a portion of the Gospel of Mark word for word—*a portion of Mark that had been redacted and lost for centuries,* and is now called the Secret Gospel of Mark. Fortunately, many early Christian writers quoted portions of the Scriptures word for word in their letters and that has provided a fertile source for modern scholars to mine when trying to discover which of the ancient copies of the Scriptures is closest to the originals. Here is the part of Mark under discussion in the letter, first a paragraph by Clement that tells where the words occur in the text of Mark and then the word for word quotation:

> [T]o you, therefore, I shall not hesitate to answer the [questions] you have asked, refuting the falsifications by the very

words of the Gospel. For example, after 'And they were in the road going up to Jerusalem,' and what follows, until 'After three days he shall arise,' [the secret Gospel he refers to] brings the following word for word:

> *"[A]nd they come into Bethany, and a certain woman, whose brother had died, was there. And, coming, she prostrated herself before JESUS and says to him, 'Son of David, have mercy on me.' But the disciples rebuked her. And JESUS, being angered, went off with her into the garden where the tomb was, and straightway a great cry was heard from the tomb. And going near, JESUS rolled away the stone from the door of the tomb. And straightway, going in where the youth was, he stretched forth his hand and raised him, seizing his hand. But the youth, looking upon him, loved him and began to beseech him that he might be with him. And going out of the tomb they came into the house of the youth, for he was rich. And after six days, JESUS told him what to do and in the evening the youth come to him, wearing a linen cloth over [his] naked [body]. And he remained with him that night, for JESUS taught him the mystery of the kingdom of God. And thence arising, he returned to the other side of the Jordan."*

This remarkable passage appears in no existing version of the Gospel according to Mark. The story is familiar in its basic outline, however. We know it as a version of the Raising of Lazarus reported in the Fourth Gospel. There are many differences, but they are not important here.

There is probably a great deal more of Mark that was either lost or edited. Clement's letter refers to a whole section of Mark that was kept secret from all but those selected few that were in the inner circle. Scholars feel that it was likely that Matthew and Luke also had secret sections for the inner circle only and that they were all excised from the copies of the books that were available to the general public. So far none of these secret sections have been found other than the excerpt related by Clement.

That is not the only part of Mark changed by succeeding generations. In all of the oldest Bibles, Mark ends at 16:8. It is a strange place to end the story. The other three Gospels go on to tell about the resurrection and appearance of JESUS, but Mark ended abruptly. In fact, the last word in his gospel in the original Greek is the Greek word for the preposition "for." Verses 16:9-20 were added by someone else at a much later time. These verses are often referred to as "Pseudo Mark." There was probably nothing nefarious about this. The later gospels all had resurrection and appearance stories and someone thought that Mark's should too, so he added Pseudo Mark. This is a good example of how the Bible was edited many times throughout history.

What I find particularly interesting is that this addition after 16:8 contains the reference to JESUS telling the Apostles that believers "*will pick up snakes in their hands, and if they drink any deadly thing it will not hurt them. . . .*" In about 1909 this so impressed an American Baptist, George Hensley, that he started a whole sect of snake-handling Churches of God in parts of the South. He eventually died of snakebite in 1955, but the interesting part is that his entire church doctrine rested on a forgery of part of Mark's gospel. At least 78 people have died from snake-bites because they believe in this passage that was added to Mark by an unknown editor a couple of hundred years after Mark wrote it.

Matthew

Matthew was the second of the canonical gospels to be written and it was probably also written in the southern part of Syria. The early church leaders for some reason decided that the tax collector who was a disciple of JESUS, Matthew, was a likely candidate to be the author. The problem is that both Mark and Luke refer to the tax collector disciple as "Levi." Scholars no longer believe that a disciple named Matthew wrote this book. One reason is that they have now determined that Matthew was written about 50 years after JESUS' death, so it is unlikely that the author was even alive when JESUS walked on the earth. It is equally unlikely that any other disciple of JESUS was alive at that time. It is also certain that Matthew never saw either JESUS or Paul.

Matthew apparently had at least three reference sources in front of him when he wrote his gospel; a copy of Mark, a copy of Q, a copy of the Septuagint, and, possibly, another reference that is usually referred to by the initial M. M could even be material that Matthew himself invented. In any event, there is no other source of this material in existence today. Most of the M material is in the resurrection appearances of JESUS.

Luke

The search for the author of Luke is more interesting; It is like solving a whodunit. First of all, it is clear that the author of Luke is also the author of Acts. The first verse of each book removes any doubt. It is almost certain that Luke was Greek because of the extraordinary beauty in his prose which, of course, was written in Greek. The two books were written in the classic Hellenistic style which, while known to the Hebrew writers at the time, was not their forte. The first line of Acts states that this is merely another chapter in the story. So who did write the books of Luke and Acts?

An early church scholar was reading the books and comparing them to some of Paul's letters when he noticed that there were several places in the Book of Acts where the author referred to himself and Paul in the first person plural. That is, "we went," and "we saw." That scholar assumed, therefore, that the author of both Luke and Acts was a close associate of Paul's and was with him on some of his trips. He then set about scouring all of the letters attributed to Paul to match up any reference to Paul and his traveling companions that correspond with the instances where the first person plural was used in Acts. He then cross-checked to see who actually accompanied Paul on those occasions. He found one name that stood out, a confident of Paul's named Lucas (Phil 1:24; Col 4:14) who was purportedly a physician.

This was clever and inventive scholarship and the Church bought it and assigned the authorship of both the Gospel of Luke and Acts to this physician named Luke. Unfortunately later discoveries have pretty much blown that great bit of detective work away. Today, while nobody knows who did write the book, it is pretty certain it was not the Lucas referred to as Paul's traveling companion and that, whoever it was, he was not a physician. The book was written someplace in Greece, though.

In fact, as we shall see in Chapter 16, it is highly unlikely that the author of Luke ever met Paul, let alone traveled with him. In Acts, the author attributes many things to Paul that disagree with what Paul wrote in his own letters. Many of these disagreements go to the very foundation of Paul's message. There are so many conflicts between what Luke describes that Paul did or said and what Paul himself wrote, that Acts is considered to be very thin authority on what actually happened historically regarding Paul.

At least one author makes a very convincing argument that Luke was a woman. I do not make that assertion here, but after I read the arguments, I reread portions of Luke and Acts with the mind-set that Luke was a woman, and I must admit, it really did make a lot of sense. Women play a much greater part in Luke's gospel than in all of the others put together. In Luke women accompanied JESUS on his travels and even sponsored him and helped pay his keep. There are suggestions that women later traveled as apostles as well. It is also interesting to note that Luke and Acts always have the men asking JESUS to clarify his statements which have them totally befuddled and confused. JESUS, as was the style in the Middle East ever since Socrates, instead of answering directly, asked the men what they thought the answers were and they fumbled around and could not come up with a plausible response. The women in the group, on the other hand, always come up with brilliant responses, making the men look like bumbling fools. The women always outshine the men in Luke's books.

Like Matthew, Luke obviously had copies of Mark, Q, and LXX in front of him while he wrote. Like Matthew's M, Luke also had some information in his gospel that has no parallel in any other gospel, and his was also primarily in the resurrection appearances. Luke's special source is called L, and it could be from another text or it could be Luke's own invention. However, most of the L entries seem to replace verses of Mark that Luke chose not to use where Matthew's M entries merely supplement Mark. The consensus is that Luke was probably referring to a now-lost writing that he felt better told the story of the resurrection appearances than the verses of Mark that they replaced. Scholars are quite certain that neither Matthew nor Luke saw the other's gospel before writing their own.

"Q" as Used by Matthew and Luke

Matthew and Luke did copy Q, but they did not merely copy word for word. They adapted Q into their own philosophy. A good example of this is how they treated the Lord's Prayer. There are three versions of the Lord's Prayer, two of which are in the Bible, the most familiar of which appears in Matthew 6:9-13, and a shorter version in Luke 11:1-4. There is also a version in the *Didache* (Did-ar-kay), an early church guidebook of Christian instruction often considered to be the first catechism, which was written at about the same time as Matthew and Luke. Matthew's and Luke's version was taken from the Gospel of Q, and Luke's shorter

THE LORD'S PRAYER COMPARED

Matthew 6:9-13 (KJV)	Luke 11:2-4 (KJV)
After this manner therefore pray ye:	And he said unto them, When ye pray, say,
Our Father which art in Heaven, Hallowed be thy name. Thy kingdom come,	Our Father which art in Heaven, Hallowed be thy name. Thy kingdom come,
Thy will be done in earth, as it is in Heaven.	Thy will be done, as in Heaven, so in earth.
Give us this day our daily bread.	Give us day by day our daily bread.
And forgive us our debts, as we forgive our debtors.	And forgive us our sins, for we also forgive everyone that is indebted to us.
And lead us not into temptation, but deliver us from evil.	And lead us not into temptation; but deliver us from evil.
For thine is the kingdom, and the power, and the glory, for ever.	

version is thought to be the closest to the original in Q. The version in the Didache is closer to Luke's version than Matthew's. The prayer consists of an introductory address to God followed by five petitions to God in Luke and the Didache and seven petitions in Matthew's version. Differences in the three versions are attributed to variations in the ways the Christian groups to which the authors of the gospels belonged recited the prayer. Most doubt that Jesus gave his followers such a structured prayer as this. It is more likely a composite made up of parts of several prayers that were combined over the years. The gospel of Q is the only known source of the Lord's Prayer, and if Jesus really had taught his followers such a prayer it is hard to imagine that there would not be more than one source of attribution. Hundreds of people would have been reciting the prayer, just as they do today.

John

The fourth canonical gospel is John which was written about 80 or 90 years after Jesus' death. About ten years later it was revised into the book that we now recognize as the Gospel of John. The oldest fragment of any New Testament document in existence today is a small portion of the revised Gospel of John. It has been carbon dated to 125 C.E. John did live a long life in Ephesus, but he did not live long enough to have written this book. The author was not the "disciple whom Jesus loved" that is referred to in the book. Many feel this gospel was written by a disciple of John's who was a leader in the Christian movement that was founded on John's beliefs. It is now believed that the book was actually written in Alexandria, not Ephesus as long assumed. book. The author was not the "disciple whom Jesus loved" that is referred to in the book. Many feel this gospel was written by a disciple of John's who was a leader in the Christian movement that was founded on John's beliefs. It is now believed that the book was actually written in Alexandria, not Ephesus as long assumed.

Like Matthew and Luke, John also had a special reference book in front of him when he wrote; however, it was not Mark's gospel. It was also a lost gospel like Q., although it was much more difficult to reconstruct. The hidden text in John was more problematic because there are no parallel sources to compare. We have no idea what John left out of this hidden book, only what he included.

Such is the advanced development of New Testament scholarship, however, that scholars have been able to do a great job at recreating this text. It is generally referred to as "The Signs Gospel" because it calls Jesus' miracles "signs." These verses are found in John 2 - 14 and are distinguishable because the stories of Jesus' miracles are combined with the sayings of Jesus so that the miracles Jesus performs become signs pointing to some spiritual event. For example, when Jesus turned water into wine at the wedding in Cana, it was a sign of his glory. His miracles were not to impress people, they were "signs" of his glory.

It is pretty certain that John was written by two different people. The portions of John that included the Signs Gospel were written by one person and then, later, the book was edited and redacted. There are quite different viewpoints between the works of the first author and the second. Some call this second author the "redactor, but because of possible confusion with the Old Testament redactor, which we know as R, the second author of John is usually referred to as "John 2."

John is very different from the first three gospels. There are very few parallel verses.

Acts of the Apostles

The last of the New Testament history books is the book of Acts. It is the continuation of the Gospel of Luke by the same author, probably conceived at the same time but written years later. It is the story of the birth of the new religion, Christianity. You will probably be surprised to discover that JESUS did not found the religion of Christianity; his apostles did. Acts is the story of those apostles and how they created this new religion based upon the words and acts of JESUS. The entire book covers about 30 years, beginning with JESUS' return to Earth to speak with his followers.

There are many discrepancies between the book of Acts and the letters of Paul, so that very few scholars rely upon Acts for historical data. If Paul wrote that he did something it is, naturally, considered far more reliable than what someone else, who never met Paul and writing years after Paul's death, said that Paul did or said. Acts is also considered to be very shaky in the factual history department. Luke had an agenda and both his Gospel of Luke and the Acts of the Apostles were written to further that agenda. Since it was written about 75 years after Paul's letters, the letters are considered much more reliable from an historical perspective. That is not to suggest that there is not a huge amount of reliable data in Acts. There is and we will cover it. Luke was very familiar with portions of Paul's gospel, just not about what Paul did.

Revelation to John

Revelation to John has its own special section because it has a huge influence on the movement of the Evangelical, charismatic, and Pentecostal groups that have grown so rapidly in the United States in the last few years. Whoever this particular John was, he was not the disciple of JESUS, the son of Zebedee who formed half of the "thunder brothers," and who was one of the Pillars that we meet in Paul's letters. This new John refers to the original twelve apostles in Revelation, but he does not include himself in the group; he of all people should know if he was one of the twelve. So, in addition to the fact that John, the son of Zebedee, would have long been dead by the time this book was written, this author himself is not suggesting that he is the disciple John; nor was he either the person(s) who wrote the Gospel of John or the person(s) who wrote the three letters under that name, although they were contemporaries. He is generally referred to as "John the Devine" or "John of Patmos" to distinguish him from any of the other Johns.

The author was a believer in one of the Christian movements who preached the message of JESUS. John belonged to one of the many divrse groups of early Christians. Whatever group it was, he was apparently very devout, so much so that he made the mistake of upsetting the Roman authorities, and he got himself arrested. He was such a pest that they sent him to the island of Patmos (now called Patino) off the coast of what is now Turkey, east of old Ephesus, and in the very south of the Aegean Sea. It was being used as a Roman penal colony at the time. There he lived as a hermit in a cave. When he emerged, he reported that he had received visions that he describes as being a revelation from GOD.

There were many apocalyptic books like this in the Near East, beginning about 250 B.C.E. The one thing that makes this particular book different is that all of the other apocalyptic books we know about were pseudonymous. That is, the writers authored the books in the names of some beloved and respected religious figure instead of their own name. In Revelation, John used his own name, probably because he was well known at the time by the intended recipients of his writings; unfortunately, he appears in no other known document, so nobody today has any idea who he was.

What we do know about the author is that he had an encyclopedic knowledge of the Hebrew Bible. Of the 404 verses in Revelation, 275 include at least one allusion to passages in the Septuagint, the Greek version of the Hebrew Bible. Very few people had access to these works. Also, his literary style was typical of that used in Palestinian Judaism. All of this convinces the experts that John was probably a Palestinian Jewish Christian who fled Judea as a result of the First Jewish Revolt against the Romans. He identifies himself closely with "the seven churches," writing to individuals in those churches and calling them by name and deed, strongly suggesting that they probably knew him as well. This is a reference to the seven churches that were located in the area above Judea that is now western Turkey in the towns of Pergaumu, Smyrna, Thyatira, Sardis, Philadelphia, Ephesus, and Laodicea. It seems he was so well known among these churches that he was likely one of those wandering apostles that flitted from church to church—the kind that gave Paul so much trouble when they showed up at one of his churches and preached a different version of The Way*. He lived much later than Paul, however.

The Sapiential Message of JESUS v. the Apocalyptic Messages of His Followers

You will see that JESUS' apostles—Paul, the authors of the gospels and Acts, and John of Patmos—all have an apocalyptic message, in varying degrees, woven into their works. When you read the chapters on the Epistles and the Gospels, look for the apocalyptic message and compare it with JESUS' own words. I'll point much of this out as we go.

Biblical scholars commonly refer to the terms "eschatological" or "apocalyptic" works. I find the terms a little pompous, but as much as I have tried to avoid using them, sometimes it is impossible. If you do any further reading on your own, you will run into these words frequently. Here is a brief description of what the terms mean and how they differ.

"Eschatological" is a word that refers to the end of time. The word comes from the Greek *Eschaton* which means "last or utmost." It usually refers to a time when the world will end, and it is a common theme among apocalyptic writers and preachers. The belief in such matters is frequently referred to as "millennialism." It can be either a cataclysmic or peaceful ending. An "apocalypse" is a specific kind of eschatology; it has a violent ending, in which GOD plays a major role, coming down to earth and destroying everything that is bad and taking the good back to His holy domain with Him. An apocalypse is always an eschatological event, but the contrary is not true. The term "eschatological" does not necessarily mean that this will be an apocalyptic event as we know it today. The end of all time could be a very peaceable event. Eschatology was always a popular belief during times of extreme oppression among the Jews such as what they endured under Greek, Hasmonean, and Imperial Roman rule. That was several hundred years of oppression. Eschatology was a very Jewish concept long before the days of JESUS. It was also a belief among some Jewish sects that the spirits of the dead (as opposed to the bodies) would rise to the Heavens at the end of time. These were not new ideas raised during and after the time of JESUS. It was commonly believed by many Jews in the 200 years before JESUS' death that this entire process was prophesied in the scriptures. Early Christians, especially those who originally aligned themselves with apocalyptic preachers such as John the Baptist before turning to JESUS, believed in this also.

Apocalyptic books proliferated after JESUS' death. The only book in the Old Testament with an apocalyptic message is a portion of Daniel; but there are some references in the inter-testamentary literature and many

---

*Before anyone conceived of the word "Christian," JESUS' message was referred to as "The Way."

references to an apocalypse in the New Testament. Revelation, of course, is entirely devoted to the subject, but it also shows up in some of Paul's writings and in Mark as well. As we noted, some feel that Matthew's version of the Lord's Prayer (Matt 6:9-13) has an apocalyptic message and even Luke's shorter version maintains much of the language that some feel is an apocalyptic message (Luke 11:2-4).

John the Baptist was a Jewish apocalyptic prophet. His message was that you have a ritual Jewish baptism, both physically and symbolically, by spiritually and actually crossing over the river Jordan from the wilderness beyond into the Promised Land, just as the ancient Israelites did. You immerse yourself in the waters of the Jordan in a ritual cleansing away of sin. John's followers were then told, basically, to go home and wait for the coming apocalypse. It was expected to happen that soon. (It is interesting to note that the gospel writers hedged on the concept of John baptizing JESUS because it was inconceivable to them that JESUS had any sins to cleanse).

JESUS appears to make many statements that suggest there is an apocalypse on its way. But a funny thing happened. When the Fellows of the JESUS Seminar spent several years trying to determine which words in the Bible that were attributed to JESUS were absolutely, without any reasonable doubt, spoken by JESUS, and they set all of those sayings aside, they were stunned to discover that there was not a single apocalyptic message in the entire group. They went back through all of their research and found the same result. How could this be? JESUS' apocalyptic message was a huge part of the ministry of the religious right that has dominated Christianity in the United States in recent years. Billy Graham began preaching it in the '50s.

The discovery that perhaps JESUS did not have an apocalyptical message jump-started a whole new study of JESUS and his beliefs. In the last 20 years there has been enormous burst of scholarship looking into the 'historical JESUS," the JESUS that walked among us as opposed to the JESUS of legend. Some of these works are nothing short of brilliant, and they are enormous fun to read. They have found many discrepancies in the older writings on JESUS, including the gospels. We have already briefly seen how the various gospel writers "tweaked" JESUS' life and his sayings to fit into their beliefs. This is still being done today. You can walk into any book store and pick up five books on JESUS and you will read five versions of what JESUS said and did. What is amazing is that people seem to think that the same thing did not happen in the century immediately after JESUS' death. Just because the words were written 2000 years ago does not mean the writers of those words did not take liberties with them.

The majority of scholars now believe that those apocalyptic statements supposedly uttered by JESUS, were placed on JESUS' lips by the authors of the New Testament books. JESUS' message was substantially different from what people thought for 2000 years. Jewish tradition did not have an afterlife concept, and JESUS did not say otherwise. He spoke of the Kingdom of GOD as something that was already present on earth and all you had to do was to learn how to find it. It was not something that would come in the future. You did not have to die and go to Heaven or to anyplace else to find it. It was here and has been here all the time. All you had to do was to open your eyes and find it.

JESUS told his disciples bits and pieces of what they had to do to get there. He told them you cannot find the kingdom if your life is consumed with attaining wealth because you cannot serve both the god of money and Yahweh. You must first get rid of your money and then look deep inside of yourself and into the world; only then will you find the Kingdom of GOD and true eternal happiness. This was an exciting concept to his audience, but JESUS never told them precisely what they had to do; he gave them tantalizing hints and parables and aphorisms. Each person was different and each person had to find his own way in.

We will examine the words of JESUS in the next chapters; both as they were interpreted over the early centuries after his death, and how they are now interpreted by the scholars who have studied the ancient works and who have also done the modern research. Remember, at the time of JESUS, even the most brilliant people in the world believed that the world was flat. We now know that they were wrong about that and it is pretty certain that they were also wrong about JESUS' message. We think we know now, but there are new scholars being born as you read this who may find something else that nobody before had ever considered. This is a dynamic new field. The great majority of our knowledge is from the middle of the 20th century on. It is a very slow process. Scholars develop a hypothesis about some aspect of the story based upon their observations. They test it and .if it works, they publish their findings and submit them to other scholars for peer review. It takes many years before the issue will be settled as other scholars either build on the hypothesis or attack it. Eventually there is a consensus. I, in turn, am giving you their findings as of this date.

When I was in college I read an article written about 1950 by the head librarian at a large university. He stated, as I recall, that 90 percent of all human knowledge had been discovered since the beginning of the twentieth century and that 75 percent of all knowledge had been discovered in the last 20 years. That was an incredible statement, but the discoveries in the 50 years since then have dwarfed even that statement. Knowledge increases at an even faster rate and the technology age has made that learning available to everyone in their own homes. It is fair to say that knowledge of the Bible and its history has had a parallel growth. Most of the research on the Bible has been done in the last 50 years, and the coming years promise to bring exciting new discoveries.

12

What Was JESUS Really like

The first century of the common era is obscured from our contemporary view by three giant filters. The past is recorded almost exclusively in the voices of elites and males, in the viewpoints of the wealthy and the powerful, and in the visions of the literate and the educated.

John Dominic Crossan, *The Historical JESUS*

There were no cameras in the first century. And JESUS' ministry was so short that there was no time for anyone to paint his portrait. Actually, portraits and statues in that period were not realistic representations of what a person actually looked like anyway. They were idealized versions—sort of how the subject wished he or she looked. The only portraits and statues from the first century were of people of huge wealth and social stature. There are no known depictions of Jewish peasants, so we cannot guess what JESUS looked like from art.

Further, people were far more interested in JESUS' message than they were in his appearance and background. People took notes of what he said, but if anyone ever bothered to make notes of what JESUS looked like, none have survived. We actually know a lot more about him than most people think we do, but we must be very careful about relying upon contemporary writings. JESUS was a peasant. His disciples were mostly peasants. Few, if any, of these people could read or write, probably including JESUS.

For the most part, everything that we know about JESUS today was committed to written history by people very unlike JESUS. They were all educated and literate and likely at least moderately wealthy. JESUS and his disciples were mostly very poor and illiterate. It is unlikely that JESUS was well educated in spite of his obvious brilliance, although the Jews always provided schooling for bright students and he probably had some form of formal education. He certainly had a working knowledge of the scriptures. Although he never quotes from them he does use examples from the Hebrew Scriptures in his stories. The children of Jewish peasants had to work to help support the family, so it was likely that JESUS had a rather sparse and intermittent education at best. A typical work day usually lasted from sun up to sun down.

Let me give you an example of how we are often misled about JESUS.

I recently read an article written by a Christian minister who was trying to prove that men wearing long hair and beards were un-Christian. He pointed out that all of the sculptures and paintings that have survived from the time of the Roman occupation of Judea in the first century show the men as being clean shaven and with short hair. Some of you may remember the Caesar hair style from the ´50s. Therefore, he concluded, JESUS must have had short hair and been clean shaven.

The fact is that the sculptors and painters of the first century, and later, were not painting and sculpting Jewish peasants, they were recording the appearances of the landed aristocracy. It is fair to say JESUS did not have a Caesar haircut. Let's look at the more likely appearance of JESUS.

JESUS was a Jew

JESUS was born and raised a Jew and, according to the gospels, he often preached at synagogues. When His followers asked Him to teach them how to pray, the words he gave them (The Lord's Prayer) could not have been more Jewish. As Joseph Fitzmyer wrote, the prayer "is a thoroughly Jewish prayer, for almost every word of it could be uttered by a devout Jew. . . ."

A Jewish peasant who survived long enough to have a sixth birthday had an average life expectancy of just 22 more years. That is all, only 28 years to live. It is even worse if you beak it down: one-third were dead by the age of six, two-thirds by sixteen, and only one in four survived until twenty-six. Life was very rough for them and they tended to die young. They also married young; women got married as soon as they could bear children. They were always living on the edge of bare subsistence, so they knew well the delicate line between poverty and destitution.

They were unimaginably poor. In the Roman agrarian economy, the aristocracy took nearly all of the agricultural products that were grown, leaving only a bare subsistence for the peasants who grew them. That was the standard of practice in the history of the Roman empire and in most other agrarian societies for that matter. In the first century C.E. it was even worse. They were in the midst of a long, protracted drought and the Romans took even more crops than normal. The peasants worked from dawn until dusk. Since their only light at night was a little sheep's tallow in a shallow dish with a wool wick, they generally went to bed at dusk. They had no books, no radio, no TV, hence, no real reason to stay up late. If they had any spare time for entertainment, perhaps after synagogue on the Sabbath, they might listen to one of the itinerant speakers like JESUS who wandered from town to town.

They had neither the money nor the time to get a haircut and a shave. They could not even afford to purchase the implements that would allow them to shave or trim their hair or beards. So the first thing that history tells us about JESUS is that he probably had the typical unkempt look of all peasants at the time. He undoubtedly had long, untrimmed hair and a beard; not a nicely trimmed beard like we see in the renaissance paintings of JESUS, or modern television and movie renditions, but a full, scraggly beard. As we will see, he tended to emulate the cynic philosophers whom he admired in many ways, so he probably wore his hair in the wildly flying style of that group.

JESUS was reputedly from a little village in the Galilee called Nazareth and there is no compelling reason to believe otherwise. The Bible and secular works by contemporary historians such as Josephus all refer to him as being from Nazareth. If he was from that small, extremely poor village, he grew up next door to another town that had recently been rebuilt by the ruling Tetrarch, Herod Antipas. The town was called Sepphoris and was only four miles from Nazareth, close enough to be seen. Sepphoris was everything that Nazareth was not. It was solely inhabited by the aristocracy and was filled with riches and wealthy people and characterized by indulgence and debauchery. Nazareth, on the other hand, was a village in the depths of poverty where people labored from dawn to dusk. To graphically illustrate the difference, the life expectancy of the aristocracy living in towns like Sepphoris was almost twice that of the 28 years the peasants of Nazareth could expect.

Sepphoris, was on the main road between Nazareth and almost any place in the northern Galilee, so JESUS must have passed through the city many times. He could not help but note the difference between the lives of the people in his own little village and those in the openly hedonistic

Josephus

Josephus is a perfect example of what Crossan was referring to in the epigraph about the historians being members of the aristocracy. He was born Joseph ben Matthias, the son of a wealthy and influential Jewish family. He was trained in the Jewish priesthood, but in the First Jewish War, while still in his twenties, he was made a general and was in charge of the defense of a city/fortress. When the Romans were about to overrun the town he escaped and placed himself at their mercy. The town was destroyed and the people in it were put to death.

He was also to be put to death, but when he prophesied that the Roman leader, Vespasian, would someday become emperor of Rome, he was granted a stay of execution. The Romans put much stock in prophets of any type, even Hebrew prophets. He then Romanized his name to Flavius Josephus. Vespasian then removed Josephus' death sentence and he did in fact become the emperor we know as Tiberius as prophesied.

Josephus, who was literate, was kept around as a court historian and eventually became the governor of Palestine. His two books on the Jewish Wars are some of the most authoritative surviving history of the Middle East in the first century C.E.

city of Sepphoris. They were living in luxury and he was living in abject poverty. This constant reminder of the difference between the "haves" and the "have nots" must have played an important role in his later ministry where he says, "The poor shall inherit the earth" and "it is easier for a camel to go through the eye of a needle than for a rich man to reach Heaven."

JESUS was a Lower-class Jewish Peasant

Besides being Jewish, we can also be pretty certain that JESUS was trained as a carpenter. The Bible refers to his father, Joseph, as being a carpenter's son (Mt 13:55), and it was common for a son to follow in his father's footsteps and learn the same trade. Another gospel refers to JESUS as "the carpenter (Mk 5:2-3)." But do not confuse the esteemed modern trade of carpentry with that trade in the first century Roman Empire. Carpenters were not upper middle class craftsmen, they were lower class peasants. Social status was a lot different in the ancient agrarian societies than in the modern industrial societies. In the first century C.E. in Judea there were two major societal classes, the ruling class and the peasantry. Most New Testament scholars refer to the works of Gerhard Lenski, probably the greatest scholar on the subject of agrarian societies, for information about first century Judea, and I see no reason to do otherwise. According to Lenski, an agrarian society, including the first century Roman Judean society, broke down like this:

Social Strata in an Agrarian Society

Ruling Classes	Peasant Classes
Ruler	Peasant Farmers
Governing Class	Artisan Class
Retainer Class	Unclean and Degraded Classes
Merchant Class	Expendable Class
Priestly Class	

Briefly, the **Ruler** was at the top of all society. At the time that was the Emperor of Rome. The **governing class**, senators and the like, comprised about one percent of the population and they received at least a quarter of the national income. Combined with the Ruler, the two classes claimed at least 50% of the total empire net income. The **Retainer Class** was next and comprised about five percent of the population. It was made up of the scribes, bureaucrats, generals, and top soldiers in service of the Ruler and the Ruling Class. The **Merchant Class** generally ranked in the upper classes because of their ability to market products. They had little authority, but were valuable because of their marketing abilities. Many of them came up from the Peasant Classes. Finally, there was the **Priestly Class**. They were, from time to time, huge property owners, as in mediaeval Europe.

On the other side of the equation were the **peasants**. They represented the vast majority of the population. Upon them fell the burden of supporting the state and the privileged classes. This was especially true of those peasants who owned arable property, the **Peasant Farmers**. The problem was, that there were simply too many children in line to inherit the property. If a property owner, by his will, divided the property among all of his sons, none would have enough land to support a family. So, like most agrarian societies, they usually practiced primogenitor; that is, the oldest son gets the farm. What could they do, then, with the sons who did not inherit?

Consider, for example, nineteenth century Ireland. They also had the rule of primogenitor. Daughters were simply married off, but what happened to the sons who did not inherit? The usual rule of thumb was that the first son inherited the family manse, the second son went into the military, the third son became a priest, and the other sons emigrated. The United States and Australia received the benefit of many of the young sons from this hard-working stock.

There was a similar order for those sons unlucky enough to be born second or third in Roman times, but they had fewer options. If you were the second son of a peasant, you tried to learn a trade—tinker, baker, carpenter, butcher, etc. These people formed the **Artisan Class**. A first century carpenter was a very poor person indeed. He had no land and depended upon finding itinerant work. He did not build houses or temples or make fine cabinetry. He made stools and chests, yokes for oxen, wood plows, and other implements that the farming peasants used. Usually, a carpenter worked out of his house, often with a first-floor workshop open to the street. This was a tenuous existence, and sons were usually brought up in the same trade so that if there was a premature death of the man of the house, which was likely, the sons could continue to support the family. That is one reason to believe that JESUS did not have an extensive education other than, perhaps, Jewish instruction on the targums or oral scriptures.

That is where JESUS fit into the society in which he was born. He was in the Artisan Class. Artisans earned much less, on the average, than the landed peasants who had marginal subsistence levels themselves. So when you read in the Bible that when JESUS went back home after he enjoyed such success in his ministry the local population said, JESUS? "'Is not this the Carpenter, the son of Mary and brother of James and Joses and Judas and Simon, and are not his sisters here with us?'And they took offense at him (Mk 6:3)" you can understand why they had a hard time believing that it could be the same person. They had a hard time grasping that this uneducated, itinerant carpenter could be the source of the wisdom that everyone was talking about. Matthew had a similar account (Mt 13:55), but in his account the townspeople ask, "Is not this the carpenter's son?."

The two social classes that were even lower than the artisan class were the **unclean and degraded class**, which included prostitutes, miners, common soldiers and the like, and the lowest class, the **expendables**, which included criminals, outlaws, beggars, and the chronic unemployed. So you can see that there were not many social groups lower than JESUS.

What about His education? JESUS obviously had some education in the scriptures. The Hebrews always had a program of education. Students learned the scriptures, and a few even learned to read. These were usually sons of the priestly class (the Sadducees), or the relatively new group who studied the law (the Pharisees). JESUS had nothing but contempt for these people and frequently ridiculed them. So it was unlikely that JESUS ever spent enough time in school to learn to read and write*. After all, he had a trade to learn. But according to the Bible he demonstrated knowledge of the Law, so he likely had some education in the Torah. The fact that he is not known to have quoted the scriptures suggests that he learned them from oral transmission.

What was JESUS' real name?

The Bible calls him JESUS Christ, but that was not his real name. JESUS is the Greek translation of his Aramaic name. His name would have been something like *Joshua ben-Joseph* in Hebrew or, as he would be called by his followers, *Yehoshua bar-Yosef* in Aramaic. Translated into English, *Yehoshua* means "savior" (thus our reference to JESUS as The Savior), and *bar Yosef* means "son of Joseph."

Where did the word "Christ" come from? Christ is the English translation of the Greek word *christos,* which means "messiah," "savior," or "redeemer." But Christos is a not an entirely successful attempt to convert into Greek the Hebrew word it translates, *mashiach.* Mashiach originally simply meant GOD's anointed one. In Israel's early history only the king was anointed with oils and only the king was called GOD's anointed one, or GOD's Christ. Later, other high officials such as priests were anointed as well.

This practice was carried down in western history until very recent times. Anointing the King of England, for example, made him GOD's chosen one. A King's throne was not safe until he was anointed, and that very act often prevented all but the most impious from trying to overthrow the King. There are numerous stories of the successor to a

---

* There is one reference in the Bible to JESUS writing, and that is when he wrote in the dirt in the story of the woman caught in adultery who was to be stoned [Jn 8:6] and another reference to him reading from the scroll of Isaiah [Lk 4:16-30]. Scholars are pretty unanimous in proclaiming that neither of these events actually took place.

dead king rushing to get anointed before someone tries to get the crown ahead of him.

In the first century the word *messiah* meant more than merely a new Jewish king. They expected the messiah to lead them out of Roman subjugation and to restore Israel to its former greatness. They started calling JESUS their *mashiach*. It became *Yehoshua the Mashiach*. This was translated into Greek as "JESUS the Christos." Later the article "the" was dropped and Christ became a proper name. He is now known for all time as JESUS CHRIST, often simply as "Christ," omitting his real name completely.

What do we know for sure about JESUS?

By that, I mean, what do most Biblical scholars agree upon? There are many things written about JESUS that are very controversial where there is simply no universal agreement among scholars. But there is a lot where all, or at least nearly all, agree:

- JESUS was a Jew and was very pious and passionate about his religion.
- His original disciples were all Jews.
- He was born about 6 B.C.E., because it is pretty much agreed that he was born during the reign of Herod the Great who died in 4 B.C.E. (There is a usual range given for JESUS' birth of between 4 and 7 B.C.E., but 6 is most commonly used).
- He died about 30 - 33 C.E., measured by the fact that Pontius Pilate's tenure ended in 36 C.E. (Also, Tacitus wrote that JESUS was crucified during the reign of Tiberius who died in 36 C.E.) Again, there is some flexibility in the actual date, but 30 is the most commonly accepted date. Luke says that JESUS was "about 30" when he began his ministry (3:23) and that is probably pretty close.
- His Parents were Joseph (probably) and Mary, and he had brothers, James, Joses, Judas (later called Jude for obvious reasons), and Simon. It is uncertain about his sisters. Matthew and Mark say that he had sisters, but they are not identified and the number is not given.
- His native tongue was Aramaic, but there is evidence that he also had some familiarity with the common Greek used by the lower classes (*koine*). The Bible carries it a step further and the older versions of the Gospels quote him speaking in Aramaic on a few occasions. There appears to be a universal belief that JESUS was significantly more educated than the typical Judean peasant. However, most doubt that he was literate.
- John the Baptist was probably an historical person, and most scholars agree that JESUS was likely baptized by John and became

one of John's disciples for a time; but JESUS later abandoned John's apocalyptic message for his own very different ministry. Contrary to Luke's birth story, it is unlikely that JESUS was related to John.

- There is less certainty about his disciples. Simon (called Peter or Cephas) was almost certainly a real person, as were James and John, the sons of Zebedee who were known as the "Thunder Brothers." Mary of Magdala is very likely an historical person as well. There is little known about any of these people and almost nothing about his other followers. Several other disciples have been named, but there is doubt and uncertainty about them. For instance, Matthew was supposedly a tax collector, but the disciple who was a tax collector in both Mark and Luke was named "Levi." Thomas (the doubter) is mentioned and few others such as Philip, Bartholomew, Thaddaeus, Judas the son of James, Simon the Canaanean who was also called the "Zealot." Over the centuries these names have been confused with other persons by the same name. For example, Thomas has been attributed to the authorship of the Gospel of Thomas. The name means "twin" in Aramaic, so some have advanced the idea that the gospel was written by JESUS' twin, a person who does not exist in the Bible. Even the name "Judas Iscariot" raises some issues. It is unlikely that JESUS had twelve primary disciples; he probably had many more and sometimes less as they came and went with his travels. Twelve is an important number in Jewish numerology and is associated with the original twelve tribes of Israel, and the writers of the Gospels tried to associated JESUS with anything they could find in the Hebrew Scriptures. One thing for certain, the followers that we do know about were socially undesirable by any first century measure: the poor and hungry, publicans, the hated tax collectors, the sick, and the grieving.
- JESUS was a healer and an exorcist and probably successfully healed many people which undoubtedly got the attention of his followers. But the healing stories are not all true and many are certainly exaggerated. Think for a second about the religious healing centers in the modern world, such as Lourdes, where the crippled and infirm go to get healed. Many of these places have a trash pile where people who arrived on crutches were able to throw their crutches into the trash pile and miraculously walk away unassisted. There are thousands of crutches, walkers, canes, wheelchairs and the like in those trash piles, but, as Crossan, pointed out, there is not a single one of these places where you will find a prosthetic limb or a coffin. See what I mean? Healing is one thing, raising the dead is another. Also, leprosy in the first

century referred to any skin disorder such as rashes and eczema. It definitely was *not* Hansen's Disease which we call leprosy today. So when JESUS healed a "leper," he was not curing that person of Hansen's Disease. It is also important to understand that religious healers were all that the peasants had aside from simple folk remedies. There were many "healers" walking the countryside and all of them cured what we would call today "psychosomatic" illnesses. They did not dispense herbs or other medications; they were basically "faith healers," and what they treated successfully were what we call today psychosomatic illnesses. So, while it is true that JESUS was a healer, and apparently a very good one, that does not necessarily imply Divine assistance.

- JESUS did not offer to cure people; people asked him to do so and he often was reluctant to accommodate them. He also never initiated a debate with others. He merely responded to their questions or accusations. He was not like those people we see today in front of the courthouse yelling, "Repent! The end is coming." He was more like the Greco-Roman philosophers.
- JESUS was considered to be an exorcist in that he exorcized demons. Knowing nothing of modern medicine, people of the time believed that illnesses were caused by bad demons that had taken over a persons's body, and to cure that person the demons had to be driven out. Consistent with those beliefs, people of the day assumed that exorcists were also demons themselves or were otherwise insane. JESUS was often accused of both, even by his own family. He was said to be under the control of Beelzebul by some. These were common accusations that he and other healers had to endure.
- What did JESUS wear? Men universally wore two items of clothing in the first century. The inner garment was a belted tunic that came down just above the knees. Over that they wore a long robe-like item that served a great many uses, including service as a blanket at night. Their entire wardrobe consisted of just those two items. They did not wear "skivvies." He wore no sandals, he did not carry a bag or a purse on the road, and he did not take a change of clothing.
- What did he eat? Since JESUS was a devout Jew you would naturally expect that he ate Kosher, right? Not so. A very important part of his ministry was to eat at the table of those he taught and to share their food, often referred to as his "table ministry." Since his students were not all Jewish, he often ate food that was prohibited by the Jewish dietary laws. When some pharisees complained that he was not following the Laws, he told

them, as only he could, "*What goes into your mouth will not defile you, but what comes out of your mouth, that will defile you.*" In other words, worry about what you say, not what you eat.

What did JESUS Take With Him?

As Jesus told his original 12 disciples, "Carry no purse, no bag, no sandals" (Luke 10:4 - 7). This is discussed in further detail later as the list differs in the various gospels. However, Jesus was very much into the counterculture life style of the Greco-Roman cynics, who were radical, itinerant preachers of the time. Their lifestyle was a protest statement. In fact, many of the things Jesus said and did have strong parallels to the cynic philosophers.

This Greco-Roman Cynicism was studied by Leif Vaage, and this is what he said about the dress of the Cynics, "The standard uniform of the Cynics was a cloak, a wallet, a staff. Typically their life included barefooted itinerancy viz. indigence, sleeping on the ground or in the baths and other public buildings, a diet of water and vegetables." They also had shaggy "wildly" unkempt hair and beards. I think that it is fair to say that Jesus had shaggy unkempt hair.

- Contrary to popular belief, and some entries in the gospels, JESUS never spoke about himself in the first person, nor did he ever claim to be the messiah. He never gave practical advice like Dr. Phil or Dr. Ruth. When asked he usually refused to respond or turned the question back on the questioner. For example, when asked about paying taxes he said, "*Give . . . to the emperor the things that are the emperor's , and to GOD the things that are GOD 's.*" In other words, make your own decision. You know the penalty for evading taxes with the government and you also know the penalty for ignoring GOD's needs.
- JESUS preached in the synagogues in the Galilee region, but please note the discussion of synagogues in the cameo; they are not what you might think. He did not pray in synagogues, however, or anyplace public; he prayed in private seclusion.
- Where did his travels take him? He most likely had a regular circuit in the Galilee that he traveled several times. He preached in his home area in the Galilee in the north and spent some time around the Sea of Galilee. The town of Nazareth was in the south central part of the Galilee, just south of Sepphoris by about four miles. It is unlikely that he preached there, but he very probably plied his carpentry trade there. The Bible tells us that he also went to Jerusalem in Judea and he also preached in Judea in the south. In between these two parts of the Tetrarchy of Herod

Antipas which was later called "Palestine," was the huge central area known as Samaria, the home of the dreaded and hated Samaritans. This was not a safe place for Jews to travel, even though JESUS was usually in the company of several others. Most feel that to get from the Galilee to Judea he probably did as most Jewish travelers did, crossed east over the Jordan River and followed it south until he passed Samaria and then crossed back over the river near the Dead Sea.

- Some things that he did not do were: change water to wine; walk on water; feed the multitudes with fish and bread; calm the storm; cause the miraculous catch of fish, and raise the dead. Sorry. In addition, he was born in Nazareth, not Bethlehem, and Mary was not a virgin who was divinely conceived.
- How long was his ministry? John the Baptist began preaching in 27 C.E. and preached for about a year before his death in 28 C.E. So JESUS' baptism took place in one of those two years. He then went into self-imposed exile in the desert and developed his future ministry. As noted above, the most likely date given for JESUS' death was 30 C.E., although it could have been as late as 36 C.E. So his ministry was, by any calculation, very short. References in the New Testament indicate that it was likely to have been, tragically, for as little as one, according to Matthew, Mark, and Luke, to as much as three years, according to John. Considering the effect his ministry had on the world, it is hard to believe that it was so short. How much have we lost because of this abbreviated ministry?
- JESUS was somehow involved in a Temple incident; he was arrested, the priesthood probably had something to do with the arrest, and he was scourged and executed. He unlikely had any trial but was probably summarily convicted. The Temple incident, however, whatever it was, was unlikely to have been anything mentioned in the Bible. The Temple area was 35 acres, the size of over twenty-six football fields, and on the holy days it was filled with hundreds of merchant's stalls and thousands of people. There were itinerant speakers drawing small crowds everywhere. It would be like one of our county fairs on steroids. Can you imagine a garage sale the size of 26 Rose Bowls? It is unlikely that JESUS could have stirred up much of a ruckus no matter how many tables he overturned, although it would not take much to get the attention of the Roman guards. He very likely would be arrested, but it is unlikely it would have caused much of a stir or serious concern.

You can see from this list that, while we do have some knowledge of what the man JESUS was like, it is a pretty short list. There is an ancient writing that contains a physical description of Paul, but there is nothing known today that describes JESUS in any way. Of course, as I noted above there is not even a word written by anyone who actually saw JESUS, either in the Bible or elsewhere, that we know of. Nevertheless, you would think that someone would have described him someplace in some writing. If it happened, no such writing has survived to date.

From what the outline above shows that we do know about JESUS, he was probably a pretty ordinary looking person, dressed like everyone else, with a long wild beard and hair to match. Not to be disrespectful, but if a twenty-first century person, living in America, were to see JESUS walking down a dusty Judean road, hunched over a walking stick, with a long scraggly beard and untamed hair, one might well think that he was looking at the fourth person from the left on the evolution chart. He was unlikely to physically resemble any of those who have played him in the movies.

On the other hand, there is Luke. He tells us that a lot of women played very important role in JESUS' life. He seems to have had an unusually strong following of women: they were among his disciples, they invited him to speak at symposia in their homes, they even helped finance his mission. Maybe he was a real "chick magnet." He certainly seems to have entranced Mary of Magdala. We have no way of knowing.

The point is, that whether or not JESUS was physically a commanding figure, it was his message that reached the people and changed mankind, not his physical appearance. and he was pure genius when it came to the spoken word.

What Did JESUS Say

While he may have been ordinary in appearance, JESUS was anything but ordinary in his oration. There were hundreds of sages and teachers wandering the Levant during JESUS' time, and thousands both before and after. But today we remember only the words of JESUS. He made words so memorable that they stuck in people's minds like a familiar melody that keeps repeating itself in your consciousness. People remembered those words for years and passed them on to others, some of whom later wrote them down.

JESUS did not cite the Hebrew Scriptures to back up his message except in crude paraphrases, although he often referred to Old Testament stories and prophecies for contrast. He did not try to give himself authority by quoting Moses or the prophets. JESUS was his own man through and through. He did not mind in the least that he frequently stepped on historical toes or violated Judaic laws. He had a brand new message—the Kingdom of GOD. It is not a reference to Heaven—it is where GOD lives and rules; it is already here and he tries to tell his listeners what they have to do to gain admittance and reside with GOD. He also taught that all people are equal in the eyes of GOD and that the

Golden Rule was the most important law after honoring GOD.

Capture the Feeling as Well as the Words

Most of the quotations below are from the translation by the scholars of the JESUS Seminar and used for writing *The Five Gospels*. Much of what JESUS said seems to me to be very poetic. I imagine many of his sayings spoken in very rhythmic and very poetic language. His words must have had a meter and a rhythm that probably does not always translate well into English. However, the Scholar's Version that was used in *The Five Gospels* seemed to communicate this poetry and feeling far better than any other translation. For that reason, I have generally used it for the words spoken by JESUS.

JESUS very often did not explain precisely the point that he was trying to get across but instead challenged the listener to figure it out in the classic Socratic method. If someone asked Jesus a question, rather than answering the questions he would say something like, "What do you think the answer is?" He forced his audience to think about what he said and apply it to their own lives. The words were not allowed to go in one ear and out the other. That is one of the reasons that people remembered his words long after they were spoken. They had to think about those words and analyze them in order to decipher JESUS' message. For the reader of today, it is not always obvious what message JESUS was trying to communicate because he used very homely concepts. He spoke of things that were part of the daily lives of his listeners, things like crops in the field, lamps and their fuel, foxes and their dens, and lost sheep. We live in a different age and a different culture. We do not always recognize the significance of his references, but his listeners most certainly did..

My choice of Bible to use in quoting JESUS was also the translation that seemed to best replicate the *feeling* of what JESUS said. I have no way of judging whether or not it is the most accurate translation, but it seems to best explain in modern English what his message was. Let me give you an example. JESUS was reprimanded by the temple officials for not eating according to the strict dietary laws. His response, according to Mark 7:14 was, as translated in *The Five Gospels,*

> *What goes into you can't defile you;*
> *What comes out of you can.*

This little couplet is short and punchy and causes the listener to think. "What did he mean? JESUS did not mention which orifice he was referring to." Obviously, fecal matter can defile you. Nor does JESUS mention how "what goes into you" gets there. That is, was it by mouth as in food, or by vision or ear as in thoughts. It would be more typical of JESUS to be referring to what goes into and comes out of your mouth but meaning food going in and thoughts coming out. What you say can certainly defile you as well. So this snappy little saying was short, punchy, amusing with the double entendre, and easy to remember. Only pure genius could come up with such a retort off the cuff.

Many of his sayings, in fact most of them, have a surprise ending as we will see. Let's compare the NRSV translation of the same phrase:

> *There is nothing outside a person that by going in can defile, but the things that come out are what defile.*

This is possibly a more literally accurate translation, but it lacks the punch and rhythm of the other translation. Few listeners are likely to remember it phrased in this manner. If you were a listener, which version would you more likely remember weeks or months later? Personally, I would be more likely to remember the short, rhythmic, punchy version.

Why we Remember JESUS' Sayings

Think of the things that you remember clearly from many years ago. Many of them are proverbs such as, "a penny saved is a penny earned." Or, "an apple a day keeps the doctor away." "He who hesitates is lost." "Better safe than sorry." "The Lord helps he who helps himself." They are short and catchy little sayings. Other memorable sayings are momentous in their message such as, "Yesterday is a date that will live in infamy." Some are clever little stories with surprise endings. You hear them once or twice and they become cemented into your memory banks.

Then there are some that grab you by their internal conflict or tension: "The only thing that we have to fear is fear itself." You hear it and your first reaction is, "Hey, wait a minute." But upon a moment's reflection it makes perfect sense and you remember it forever. These are also called "couplets" because there are two parts to the saying:

> Part One: "The only thing that we have to fear"
> Part Two: "Is fear itself."

There is a tension between the two, almost a contradiction. JESUS was a genius at coming up with couplets off the top of his head. We still recite them today. "The Sabbath day was created for Adam and Eve, not Adam and Eve for the Sabbath day (Mk 2:27)." Foxes have holes, and the birds of the air have nests, but the human being has nowhere to lay his head (Lk 11:58)." These also have a rhythm and meter, so there are two more techniques used by JESUS that help us remember them.

Short and colorful bits of poetry also seem to linger in your memory. "Roses are red, violets are blue, . . ."

JESUS employed all of these techniques and more, and he seemed to do it "on the fly." He was Mark Twain and Will Rogers in a robe. He used parables, aphorisms, paradoxes, double entendres, parodies, and humor. Throughout ancient history, even long after the time of JESUS, people primarily learned orally. There were books during some periods, but they were inaccessible to most people. The most common way of teaching was for a sage/master/scholar to sit on a bench and have his pupils gather around him. Sometimes the teacher began by giving a short lesson, but then it became a question and answer period as the students tried to figure out precisely what the teacher was trying to say. Plato's famous *Dialogues* with *Socrates* is a perfect example. The students did not take notes—they remembered. Later, many did write down their recollections, but it was not a word-for-word restatement. They remembered the gist of what Socrates said, not, likely, his actual words.

That is one of the reasons why most of the sayings of JESUS that have survived are short and peppy. Long dissertations are not going to be remembered, but certain passages from the longer works may be. JESUS' rather long Sermon on the Mount might seem to be a contradiction to that idea, but the "sermon" is almost certainly the separate recollections of many of his sayings, likely from several people, assembled together in one speech. The fact that portions of the "sermon" show up in other places in other gospels bear this out.

That is the way JESUS taught. Many of his sayings are his responses to questions from his followers, and his responses are brilliant. They are short, catchy, and all demand that the listener do the work and ponder what was said. There are a few longer recollections, but they have other memorable structures that make them easy to recall. Here is an example of a longer passage that has survived (note the emphasis):

> *As k, and it will be given to you*
> *s e arc h , and you will find*
> *kn o c k, and the door will be opened for you;*
> *For everyone who as ks , receives;*
> *and everyone who s e arc h e s finds; and*
> *for everyone who kn o c ks , the door will be opened*.*

There are three simple, short statements, with three key verbs (ask, search, knock). The symmetry is amazing. The same key verbs are then repeated in the responses. Very clever poetry and very easy to recall as a result. But a word of caution, every listener does not always hear the same thing or, if the same thing was heard, it might not be recalled the same

* Lk 11:9 - 10, from a portion of Luke attributable to "Q

way by other listeners. Here is another version of that same poem from the Gospel of Thomas that was written at about the same time but by a different listener:

One who seeks will find;
for one who knocks it will be opened.

Thomas only recalled part of the poem. He got the general idea, but he missed the beauty of JESUS' rhetoric.

Parables

That being said, JESUS also told longer stories, and people remembered at least a few of them as well. The parables are good examples. There are more than 20 in the Bible that scholars believe to be authentic JESUS sayings. They were generally filled with homely images that the listeners could relate to and they almost always had unexpected endings. There were the stories of the Good Samaritan, the Prodigal Son, unleavened bread, and mustard seed just to name a few. Let's look at the story of the Good Samaritan the way that JESUS' first century followers would have understood it.

First, let's refresh our memories with the story itself. This was JESUS' response to a question about his statement that you should love your neighbor as yourself. A listener asked who his neighbor was. That was a great question. In the Old Testament Laws, "neighbor" meant another Israelite, but they were a close-knit group at the time with few outside friends. This new message from JESUS seemed to include others. JESUS responded with the parable:

A man was going down from Jerusalem to Jericho and fell into the hands of robbers, who stripped him, beat him, and went away, leaving him half dead. Now by chance a priest was going down that road; and when he saw him, he passed on the other side. So likewise a Levite, when he came to the place and saw him, passed by on the other side. But a Samaritan while traveling came near him; and when he saw him, he was moved with pity. He went to him and bandaged his wounds, having poured oil and wine on them. Then he put him on his own animal, brought him to an inn, and took care of him. The next day he took out two dinarii, gave them to the innkeeper, and said, 'Take care of him; and when I come back, I will repay you whatever more you spend. (Lk 10:30-41)

We know this story only from Luke who was, as we will see later, a Greek pagan who became a Christian but had neither met nor heard the living JESUS. Luke wrote this gospel at least 60 years after JESUS' death. He interpreted the story of the good Samaritan to be a lesson about JESUS' moral standards regarding conduct toward others. Indeed, loving others and treating others as you would like to be treated was one of his main teachings. However, that may or may not be the way that JESUS' audience would have interpreted it. Let's look at that for a minute.

Assume that you are a member of the audience and JESUS has just told all of you this story. If you were, say, an unschooled Jewish peasant, how would you understand the message? While the story doesn't tell us the nationality of the victim, since he was on that old Roman road between Jerusalem and Jericho in the country of Judea, he is most likely Jewish. In fact, since Samaria was located between Judea in the south and the Galilee in the north, Jewish travelers going from one place to the other usually walked east along this road and crossed over the Jordan River to safe country and did not cross back over the river until they had reached Galilee, bypassing Samaria. It was extremely dangerous for a Jew to travel in Samaria, especially if he was alone.

The first thought of everyone that listened to JESUS tell the story probably was, "What the heck was he doing on that road by himself anyway." The ancient road to Jericho was a dangerous road through the wilderness (and still is to this day). Aside from condemning his bad judgment, most people probably felt sorry for the poor man and sympathized with his plight.

As the victim is lying on the ground near death, a priest and Levite pass by and ignore him. At this time the priests and their assistants, the Levites, were selected by the Romans and were nothing more than tools of the Roman aristocracy. Most Jews considered them to be traitors and loathed them. They lived in relative splendor and catered to themselves and the Romans, not the Jewish people. The reaction of the common Jewish peasant in the audience was probably something like, "What else would you expect from the priesthood? All they care about is themselves and their callous indifference to that poor man's plight is absolutely predictable."

On the other hand, there were still Jews at the time who were deeply pious and still clung desperately to their traditional values. That was the only way many of them could cope with the brutal Roman occupation. They would say, "What do you expect? They had to avoid him. Touching blood, or even worse, a dead body, would defile them and require lengthy purification rituals and they would not be able to tend to our needs. They were just doing their job."

We hardly need to mention the reaction of any priests, Levites, or pharisees who may have been in the audience. They would be outraged at the way they were portrayed. JESUS undoubtedly had pagans in his audience, Greeks and Romans who were interested in JESUS' message. They would probably have compassion for the poor victim and would not likely see anything wrong with the clergy passing by without helping. The clergy then, unlike the clergy today, was not involved in ministering to the needs of society. Their job was purely the performance of religious ritual.

Then along came a Samaritan who did the unthinkable—he helped the robbery victim. In modern society it is almost impossible to conceive the mutual hatred between the Jews and the Samaritans in the first century. The Samaritans, if you recall, were those lower class Hebrews who were left behind in the Exile to Babylon and intermarried with other races and cultures. When the Hebrews returned from exile, all of their prize land had been taken over by the Samaritans. Since the Temple had been destroyed and the priests exiled to Babylon, the Samaritans had made their own temples for worship (the "high places") and continued worshiping Yahweh. When the Hebrews returned from exile, they made the Samaritans banish from the country all of their wives and children who were not Hebrews to the tenth generation. They then destroyed all of their high places and generally persecuted them. That brutality was neither forgotten nor forgiven.

Both the common man and the pious Jew would be appalled that JESUS would make such a despicable person as a Samaritan the hero of this story. The priesthood would be furious that a Samaritan would be displayed in a better light than the priest and Levite. The pagans would not likely recognize the tension and interplay between the Jews, the Samaritans and the clergy. They would probably interpret the story the way Luke did, and the way most twenty-first Century Christians would, a story about loving your enemies and being kind to those in need; being a good neighbor to anyone who needs help.

In telling this story JESUS divided his listeners into separate camps, each getting a different message. Each would think about the story, ruminate on it, and begin to draw conclusions about what it meant to them and not have a clue that the others might not see it the same way. Each would come to a different conclusion about who JESUS included as one's "neighbor." That is pure genius.

JESUS often built up internal tensions like this in his stories. Like the ancient Greek philosophers he forced the students to analyze the problem and come to their own conclusion rather than merely telling the students the answer which they would promptly forget. What, then, is the correct meaning of the parable? I suspect that there is no single correct answer; it is what each listener took away from this story. It seems certain that your "neighbor" does not merely refer to a close friend living near you. It means everyone in need, even if they are your enemy. But that is only my take.

That is the genius of JESUS. Even today people interpret this story differently—the Roman Catholics have one interpretation and Evangelical Christians another, and that is precisely what JESUS intended.

One further note about this story. It is in the classic form of folk tales everywhere in that it follows the "rule of three." There are three action settings: the beating and robbery; the responses of the people; and the aftermath at the inn. There are three main players: the priest; the Levite; and the Samaritan. The rule of three is almost universal in folklore, except in Germany where, for some reason, they use four. The three bears; the butcher, baker, and candlestick maker; etc. It is even prevalent in modern folk tales and jokes—"a rabbi, a minister, and a priest went into a bar . . ." for example, or "A plane caught on fire and there were three people on board but only two parachutes . . ."

JESUS spoke in words and told stories to the Jewish and gentile peasants who were his primary audience. He always spoke about everyday, common subjects and events to which they could relate. He spoke of ordinary people doing ordinary things—farmers planting, people getting married, the poor begging, dinner parties, lost coins, lazy workers. He talked about everyday concerns like food, clothing, beggars, dangerous roads, corrupt temple officials and toll collectors, and the like. The members of JESUS' audience all had experience with these subjects.

What is surprising is that he rarely spoke of the Hebrew scriptures. He seldom mentioned the Law or the sacred ceremonies except when someone else brought up the subject. In fact, he often flaunted the dietary laws, prohibitions about defiling yourself when you touch people with skin diseases, and healing people on the Sabbath just to give a few examples.

At all times, even though he always spoke of things familiar to his audience, judging by their reactions, everyone understood that he was actually communicating a deeper meaning. He never attacked a subject directly—he used metaphors, parables, proverbs, and aphorisms and challenged the listener to connect the dots. He often led his listeners down the garden path, letting them silently agree with what he was saying, and then, like the Galilean fishermen in his audience, after he feels the fish nibbling at the bait, setting the hook with an unexpected ending. Just when the listener is anticipating the answer, the story makes a U-turn. He was a master story teller. He always said the unexpected. He also had a great sense of humor, some of which, unfortunately, does not translate well either. Also, the modern clergy usually seeks the moral message and often completely misses the humor. I'll point out some of these instances in later chapters.

Another technique JESUS used was to talk about things that his listeners all knew but with an unusual spin. Here are three aphorisms that are mentioned together in both Matthew and Luke:

When someone slaps you on the right cheek,
turn the other as well.
If someone sues you for your coat,

give him the shirt off your back to go with it.
When anyone conscripts you for one mile,
go along for two
(Mt 5:39-41; Lk 6:29).

All three of these expressions are commonly used today but few people understand the true meaning of the phrases. The first is the famous "turn the other cheek" saying. What did it mean to JESUS' listeners? There are two ways that someone can slap you on the right cheek; he can give you a back-handed slap with his right hand or an open palm slap with his left hand. The second option was quite simply never done. Nobody in the Middle East ever touched anyone with their left hand in the first century. That is true to this day. The origin of the prohibition is that the left had was used for unclean acts such as the removal of fecal matter.

In addition to all of the ancient Hebrew Scriptures found among the Dead Sea Scrolls, there were also a number of secular documents and some of them have been of immense importance in learning about Near Eastern society at the turn of the millennium. One of the laws found in those documents was that if someone even *gestured* with his left hand he had to perform ten days of punishment. The left hand was unclean. Second, most people were right handed then as now. It would be awkward for most to slap someone with their left hand. Third, you could hurt someone badly with an open-handed slap, even causing deafness in an ear. The slap was to send a message, not harm them.

However, it was very common at that time to give someone a back-handed slap to the face. This was generally done by a superior to an inferior to remind that person of his or her place. Examples are Roman slapping Jew, master to slave, and, sadly, husband to wife and parent to child, among others. This is almost certainly what JESUS was referring to and what the audience understood, even though most of us today would not.

JESUS says that after getting hit we should offer the left cheek as well. Most people interpret this to be a demonstration of pacificism. But is it really? The options for the slapper when you turn the other cheek are limited. He cannot backhand you because that would mean hitting with his left hand which would be prohibited. Using the right hand could cause harm when all that he intended in the first place was to "put you in your place." Instead of turning the other cheek being a pacifist act and the "slappee" all the while appearing to be the supplicant, it is really a clever act of defiance. It puts the slapper in the position of appearing to be a bully if he strikes again, this time using an open hand. JESUS is showing his disciples how to put a superior in his place without being accused of insurrection which carried a death penalty.

The second aphorism is the "give them the shirt off your back" saying and refers to a common practice among the first century Jewish peasantry: pawning their robe. Their robe was often their sole possession and if they needed to eat or obtain something, they could usually get a small loan against the coat. Jewish laws in Deuteronomy require that the coat be returned each night but if the debt is unpaid the robe must be delivered up again the next day and so forth until the debt is retired. If the debt is not paid there are procedures to sue and keep the robe. This aphorism says that if someone sues to get the robe, give them your tunic as well. That would certainly get a little chuckle from the audience because Jewish peasants only had two items of clothing; a belted tunic and the long robe. They wore no "skivvies," so if they gave their shirt as well they would be naked, something that was not only socially crude, it was also unlawful. If we look to the civil laws at Qumran again, to expose yourself to a companion, even accidentally when you remove your hand from your robe, required 30 days of penance. As with turning the other cheek, this was another way to protest with dignity. They knew that you would not remove your tunic and would not dare demand that you do so, but your *offer* of the tunic got the message across.

The third is the "go the extra mile statement." Under Roman law, a military commander could conscript any peasant in an occupied country to help his troops move or to carry gear at any time, but he could only conscript them for a distance of one mile from their home. After that they were free to go back. To refuse the order was considered rebellion and subjected the peasant to severe penalties, sometimes death. To stop what you are doing and carry the gear was an act of subservience. JESUS' solution was simple—go the extra mile without comment. That was a statement that you were doing this of your own free will and not because you were a servant of the Romans. Its purpose was not, as is often stated, to save some other Jewish peasant from being conscripted to replace you, although that was a side benefit.

All three of the acts JESUS proposed were forms of protest that were designed to get the message across but were unlikely to draw an undesirable response from the authorities. This was very typical of JESUS' teachings. Many Jews at this time were rebelling against the severity of the Roman rule, and the Romans treated the rebels summarily, usually with death. JESUS had other ideas—let them know how you feel with an act of silent and non-threatening protest—a first century Ghandi or MLK. No centurion would dare arrest and execute anyone for doing one of these three acts.

The mustard seed parable is also an example of how much of JESUS' messages get lost today because our religious leaders are unfamiliar with the ancient ways. This parable actually refers to a statement the prophet Ezekiel where he speaks of the famous Cedars of Lebanon as the symbol of Hebrew hopes for a messiah in the mold of David. Here is Ezekiel and Matthew side by side:

Ezekiel 17:22-24
I myself will take a sprig from the lofty top of a cedar;
I will set it out.
I will break off a tender one
from the topmost of its young twigs;
I myself will plant it,
on a high and lofty mountain.
On the mountain height of Israel
I will plant it,
in order that it may produce boughs and bear fruit,
and become a noble cedar.
Under it every kind of bird will live;
in the shade of its branches will nest
winged creatures of every kind.
All the trees of the field shall know
that I am the Lord.
I bring low the high tree,
I make high the low tree;
I dry up the green tree
and make the dry tree flourish.
I the Lord will have spoken;

Matt 13:31-32
The kingdom of Heaven is like a mustard seed
that someone took and sowed in his field;
It is the smallest of all the seeds,
but when it has grown it is the greatest of shrubs
and becomes a tree,
so that the birds of the air come
and make nests in its branches.

The lofty cedar in Isaiah became a symbol to Matthew that there will be an apocalypse and God will send a new David (plant a twig) who will restore Israel. This symbolism was well known at the time and can also be found in other books (Isa 11:1; Jer 23:5-6 and 33:15; and Zech 3.8 and 6.12). The new messiah will bring in people (birds) from all races and from all places into the fold. Note that messiah here merely means an anointed one or king and that this person will be in the pattern of David. This does not refer to a messiah as in the New Testament which equates that word with Jesus.

Jesus contrasts this example with his own, albeit non-apocalyptic, version of the restoration of Israel with the mustard seed. The mustard seed, which is a pesky weed, is planted and matures into a mighty tree, replacing the Old Testament cedar as a symbol of a new David. Again birds from all over come to roost in its branches and seek food and shade on the ground around the tree. Jesus promises the restoration of Israel but on a more modest scale than that of a mighty cedar, and most importantly, without an apocalypse. Note that Jesus is not claiming to be that messiah.

When the parable is told without the background of the Ezekiel prophecy much of the meaning of the parable is lost. It is much more powerful when we understand the contrast with the Old Testament which JESUS' mostly Jewish audience surely knew but which few recognize today.

There is much more. Studying the language techniques JESUS used is enormous fun and gives one a whole new appreciation of his brilliance. One thing that he did not do, however, is give practical advice. He was neither Dr. Phil nor Dr. Ruth. If he did give such advice, it was not something that his listeners remembered and later wrote down. He taught his audience guidelines on how to live and each person had to decide how those guidelines applied to their own lives.

JESUS' Basic Messages

JESUS' responses to his disciples' questions can usually be related back to the fundamental principals that were most important to JESUS. There were two basic concepts that seemed to permeate all of JESUS' teaching. The first is the Kingdom of GOD. That is the traditional English translation. This is another one of those problems where there are multiple meanings for a phrase in one of the languages. Many modern translations modernize the saying eliminating the archaic term "kingdom" which has a dual meaning of being either GOD's home or an activity, namely GOD's rule. Some modern translations distinguish between these two meanings; some use something like "GOD'S domain" when the reference is to a place and "GOD's imperial rule" when it refers to some act of GOD. When we say it refers to a place, we do not mean a piece of ground or territory. It refers to GOD'S domain.

The Hebrew word for "kingdom" is *maljuth* (*maljutha* in Aramaic). The Greek word for kingdom that was in all of the original scriptures was *basileia.* Mark and Luke used the phrase *Basileia tou Theou*, which is generally translated into English as "Kingdom of GOD." Matthew, on the other hand, was writing for Jewish Christians, and since Jews could never speak GOD'S name, he substituted the phrase *Basileia ton Ouranon*, which translates into English as "Kingdom of Heaven."

Whatever words were used by JESUS, they had a particular Hebrew reference. The Kingdom of GOD referred to an event; the time when GOD'S covenants with Abraham and David would be realized. At this time, they will have their promised land and they could worship and serve their GOD forever through the restoration of David's lineage. They all refer to JESUS' belief that the Kingdom of GOD is already here; all you have to do is look for it and JESUS will show you the Way and how to enter. JESUS' Kingdom of GOD was not something that would appear after the apocalypse when GOD came down and threw out the bad guys. On the contrary, the Kingdom of GOD was already here, and JESUS would show you how to find it. Here is how he described it:

> *Once* JESUS *was asked by the Pharisees when the Kingdom of* GOD *was coming, and he answered, "The Kingdom of* GOD *is not coming with things that can be observed; nor will they say, 'Lo, here it is!' or 'There it is!' For, in fact, the Kingdom of* GOD *is among you* (Lk 17:20-21).

There was no need to "level the playing field," because nobody had an advantage to entering the Kingdom of GOD. Wealth and status meant nothing. "*GOD causes the sun to rise on both the bad and the good, and sends rain on both the just and the unjust* (Matt 5:45)." The only advantage, if any, goes to the poor. "*It is easier for a camel to go through the eye of a needle than for someone who is rich to get into the kingdom of* GOD (Mk 12:17; Matt 19:24; Lk 18:25)." You cannot serve both GOD in Heaven and the god of accumulation of wealth. The Kingdom of GOD is open to everyone, including society's outcasts such as beggars, the diseased and infirm, even lepers, enemies such as the hated Samaritans, and to those who are undeserving such as tax collectors and prostitutes. In fact, the gates of the Kingdom are wide open to those outcasts. It is the wealthy and privileged who have problems opening the gates.

The second basic concept is loving others, including your enemies: He refused to allow spite and retaliation. "*Do onto others what you would like them to do onto you* (Lk 6:31)," "*Love your enemies* (Mt 5.44; Lk 6:27; 6:32; 6:35)," and "*Forgive and you'll be forgiven* (Lk 6:37)." This includes those whom most people consider to be the dregs of society.

JESUS was not a moralist. He did not demand moral conduct or try to impose his own views and morals on others. He did not advise people how to behave or live. He never gave practical advice and did not tell people how to conduct their lives. When he was asked whether or not someone should pay a tax, he said, "*Pay the emperor what is due the emperor and pay* GOD *what is due* GOD (Mk 12:17; Matt 22;21; Lk 20:25)." He simply side-stepped the question and forced his listeners to set their own priorities. He was not going to get involved in running their lives. The listener knew how the Romans treated those who did not pay their taxes and it was his decision to make. This is typical of how JESUS treated requests for practical advice.

This second principle seems to say that if you want GOD to forgive you, you have to be full of forgiveness yourself. Where John the Baptist preached fire and brimstone and the eminent coming of the end of the earth, JESUS preached doing good and advocated doing good things for everyone, even to your enemies.

This is called a "sapiential" message and is the direct opposite of the apocalyptic or eschatological messages of John the Baptist and John of Potmos who wrote the book of Revelation. In the apocalypse, GOD will come roaring down to restore justice by wreaking death and destroying the oppressors. There was a strong apocalyptic movement in Palestine in the first century. John the Baptist was one of the chief proponents and he had a huge following. Most scholars believe that JESUS was baptized by John and that he briefly toyed with John's message.

However, JESUS is believed to have abandoned apocalyptic notions before he began his own ministry. Whether or not that took place while he was in the wilderness fighting demons for 40 days is beside the point. His philosophy was just the opposite of John's. He preached a sapiential message where one looks to the present rather than the future. The Kingdom is here already. We do not have to wait for the fire and brimstone. You can enter the Kingdom by changing your lifestyle to one of virtue, forgiveness, and goodness. You enter the Kingdom with "wisdom" as that term is understood in the Old Testament wisdom writings.

Although the fundamentalist churches today emphasize the fire and brimstone portions of the Bible, it is very difficult to reconcile the few apocalyptic references in JESUS' words with his repeated theme about the Kingdom of GOD.

13

The Epistles

Every kingdom divided against itself is laid waste, and no city or house divided against itself will stand.

Matthew 12:25

The early Christians during the time of Paul's ministry were operating under a huge handicap. They had no written scriptures other than the old Septuagint. The Gospels of Matthew, Mark, Luke, and John were not written until much later. In fact, of the forty or so gospels that we know of today, none were written before Paul's death. There were no universally accepted written works that described JESUS' message. Remember, many of the apostles were just like Paul. They had neither seen nor heard JESUS, so it is not surprising that they often had very different ideas about JESUS' message. Also, even people who heard JESUS speak did not all get the same message as that was often JESUS' purpose.

As Paul and the other apostles went from city to city founding churches, or speaking to churches founded by others, they had no written guidelines to leave behind. Their messages were delivered orally, much in the same way that JESUS himself delivered messages to his listeners, and the listeners then passed the messages around to others orally. It was not until the end of the first century in Syria that the first church order was written, the *Didache*. It explains rituals and prayers, describes the church officials and their functions, and even sets out "rights and wrongs."

But, as the epigraph notes, a house divided against itself will not stand. With no written guidelines for JESUS' message, churches in the same area often had different ideas and interpretations of The Way. Roaming apostles often passed through cities and spoke to the churches with viewpoints that were very different from that of the church's founder. The church members would be in a quandary. Which of the versions of "The Way," as JESUS' message was called in those days as the term "Christian" had yet to be invented, were correct? The churches often asked their founding apostles for help, and there became a tradition of letter writing. The purpose of many of Paul's letters was to try to "straighten up" the churches so that they did not stray from Paul's position and were not being "misled by others."

The churches saved these letters as their guidelines for teaching and conducting church business. Copies of the letters were often passed on to other churches as well. In fact, sometimes the letter writer sent the same letter to more than one church. These letters were called "epistles" from the Greek *epistello*, which meant "to send to." It was sort of an early version of "reach out and touch someone," and it was originally not a writing at all, but a message sent verbally by a messenger. But the word "epistle" has now become synonymous with "letter." Even then, epistles were not letters like we know them today. They were usually written on papyrus, rolled up, and tied. They were given to someone trustworthy to deliver, and very often that person read the letter to the recipient who, as often as not, was illiterate. The messenger often went to several different churches reading the message, although it might be addressed to a single church. Some of these epistles were saved in the New Testament.

What was a Church or a Synagogue?

When people in the 21st Century think of a "synagogue" or a "church," they generally think of a structure built for worship. That was not the meanings of those terms in the early first century. We've touched on this before, but the distinction becomes more important now that we are in the first century.

A synagogue traditionally was an assembly of persons and it did not necessarily mean an assembly for religious purposes. In fact, nearly all of the religious meetings were held in the Temple in Jerusalem. The synagogues were assemblies for teaching, judging civil and criminal matters, hearing news, town meetings, reading stories to the assembly, such as those we studied in Ruth and Jonah, and other matters. The leader of a synagogue could be anyone from a priest to a civic leader. A synagogue was most often conducted in the open air, either in a town square or at the gates to the town, but sometimes there were also multipurpose assembly buildings for these meetings.

When you read of JESUS teaching in a synagogue it is highly unlikely that it was in a structure. It was almost certainly in a town square or at the city gates if it was in town or it could be on a pleasant place in the countryside outside the town walls. The same was true of Paul. His preaching in the synagogues was almost certainly outdoors. Jesus and Paul did, however, speak at *symposia* which were meetings in people's homes, often over a meal.

After 70 C.E. everything changed. The Romans destroyed the Temple and religious leaders had to find a new place to meet and the open air where anyone, including Roman soldiers, could eavesdrop was not a highly recommended choice. That is when the small structures that came to be known as synagogues were first built and were used for reading the scriptures, religious ceremony, and education. These small meeting places fit in well with the move toward rabbinical Judaism and away from the priesthood where religious matters took place at the Temple. The story in Luke 4:16-30 that suggests JESUS was teaching in a building could be factual, although unlikely, and the depiction of him reading from a scroll is considered to be quite unlikely.

Paul never mentions the word "synagogue." The first time that word is used is in the gospels which were all written after the destruction of the Temple and buildings for religious meetings were becoming commonplace (See Mk 1:21, Mt 4:23, Lk 4:16-20, Acts 18:7). The authors of the gospels were likely referring to the familiar structures by that description that they saw around them at the time they were writing, unaware that they did not exist at the time of JESUS and Paul.

In the first century C.E., "Church" also had a different meaning. Just as the Hebrew word synagogue originally meant an assembly so did the Greek word church also mean an assembly. As Paul, or one of the other apostles, went into a town, he tried to get together a group of people who might be interested in his message about JESUS. These groups of people getting together to discuss the subject were called "churches." Sometimes they met at open air synagogues, but they more commonly met in people's homes. These came to be known as "home churches" and the entire church might be comprised of no more than five or six individuals.

Churches were loose and informal groups, originally without much structure. There was usually someone chosen to lead the group, often the homeowner, but not always. The apostles instructed the church leaders on how to preach The Way. The church leaders were charged by the apostles with spreading JESUS' message and increasing the church membership after the apostles moved on to another city.

Sometimes an apostle would establish more than one of these home churches in a city and from time to time they all met together. Paul describes such joint meetings. Toward the end of the first century C.E., the churches began to consolidate and they grew larger and became more formal. They had regular leaders, established regular services, and they developed rules and regulations for guiding the leaders. The rules were ad hoc in nature and varied from church to church. By the end of the first century, books were written setting up universal rules for all to follow.

Paul and His Letters

About 100 C.E., about 35 years after Paul's death, the church at Ephesus began collecting Paul's letters to his churches and even to one that he hadn't founded, the church in Rome. The letters of other apostles were collected by other churches, but Paul's was the version that eventually prevailed, and it is the collection of his writings that comprise much of the New Testament. Those letters by the other evangelists have all been lost, mostly destroyed after Paul's letters were canonized, and that is a tragedy.

Paul's letters are far and away the most important documents in existence today in explaining the birth of Christianity. Although Paul never actually met JESUS, he began writing his letters about 50 B.C.E., a mere 20 years after JESUS' death. These letters are authentic in that they were actually written and/or signed by the author whose name was attached to them. There are no other first century texts that meet that description. We also know a lot about Paul himself from his own autobiographical statements in his letters. Paul is the first real, live Christian that we know anything about. He even tells us about his conversion. The following is what Paul tells us about himself.

As we know, Paul was a Jew. He was not a Jewish peasant like JESUS, though, by any stretch of the imagination. He may also have been a Roman citizen, a fact that is attributed to saving his life a couple of times. We get some real clues about Paul from his letter, written in his later years, to the church in Philippi:

> *[He was] circumcised on the eighth day, a member of the people of Israel, of the tribe of Benjamin, a Hebrew born of Hebrews; as to the law, a Pharisee; as to zeal, a persecutor of the church; as to righteousness under the law, blameless* (Phil 3:5-6).

He was clearly proud of his Hebrew heritage and was from the tribe of Benjamin, the same as King David. A Pharisee was a very devout Hebrew who studied The Law, including the dietary and purity laws. The Pharisees reasoned out ways that the ancient Biblical laws should be applied to the Jews at the present time, as opposed to the time the laws were first stated by Yahweh. Hebrew life as a Roman subject was far different from the life of the traveling nomads of Moses' time. The purity codes became of prime importance during the Exile in order for the Hebrews to maintain their culture and not be swept out of existence like their brothers in the Lost Tribes of Israel. The rationale for the modern applications of those ancient laws was carefully preserved in what is known as the Talmud, and only the best and the brightest students of the law could become Pharisees. So Paul was special and highly respected in the Jewish community. Being a Pharisee meant that he was especially conservative when it came to observance of the purity codes, the laws regarding one's cleanness or righteousness.

Paul's letters are filled with the complex reasoning process that was typical of the Pharisees. He claimed to be schooled in "the traditions of my fathers (Gal 1:14)" which suggests that he was a student in the classes that the Jews have always had for their children. He had an obvious facility with the Hebrew Scriptures and was able to quote them freely. We will see many examples of that in his letters where he searches the ancient scriptures to find a rationale to support a particular proposition. This was all done in the very recognizable style of the rabbis. He was obviously highly educated in the Greek language and literature and in the Greek method of argument.

Paul was very well acquainted with the Jewish diaspora synagogues in what is now southern Turkey. He claimed that he once "preached circumcision (Gal 5:11)." That referred to an old problem that was quite pronounced at the time of Paul: what to do with gentiles who wanted to convert to Judaism. The old Greek and Roman religions were losing out with the general populace. Those gods were capricious, treacherous, conniving, and untrustworthy. The eastern gods, including the Hebrew god, were beginning to look more and more attractive. The concept of a loving god was enticing. The problem was, in order to convert, a gentile not only had to honor the god of Israel, he also had to be (gasp) circumcised. Many rebelled at the idea of circumcision but still wanted to become Hebrews. There was a large liberal Jewish faction that wanted to waive the requirement rather than lose those potential converts who wanted to devote their faith to Yahweh. The conservatives, like Paul, strongly objected to waiving this requirement. In fact, some of the followers of JESUS were allowing gentiles to join some of the JESUS sects without the requirement of circumcision. The same loving god idea of the traditional Hebrew religion of the Jews attracted gentiles to the various JESUS cults. This so inflamed Paul that he "was violently persecuting the church of GOD and was trying to destroy it (Gal 1:13)."

Paul was also very well acquainted with the Christ Cult, one of the groups of early Christians in that southern Turkey area. In particular, one concept from that group seemed to mesmerize him, "There is no longer Jew or Greek, there is no longer slave or free, there is no longer male and female; for all of you are one in [or because of] Christ JESUS." This solved some major problems for Paul. Paul attacked the problem in the tradition of Pharisitic study of how the ancient laws should be applied to modern society.

What if someone did convert to Judaism and did suffer a painful adult circumcision? He would be accepted into the faith, but *he still would not be Jewish.* He would still not have the equally important genealogy, history, and culture of Judaism. If these important attributes that makes one truly a Hebrew can be waived, why shouldn't the requirement for circumcision also be waived? Maybe there was something in this JESUS idea of equality after all. He then had a revelation from GOD that JESUS was GOD's son* and that tied everything together for Paul. It was this revelation from GOD that Paul credits for his conversion from one who persecuted the Christians to one who is buying into their ideas. These two things, Paul's analysis of equality in the eyes of GOD and the revelation that JESUS was the son of GOD were to change, not only Paul, but the history of the world.

Some eighty years later, there would be another story about this revelation to Paul, this time written by Luke in the book of Acts. This is the most famous version, the story about JESUS encountering Paul on the road to Damascus and striking him blind. Acts, considered to be very slim authority for the conduct of Paul, most scholars ignore that story in favor of Paul's own version of his revelation from GOD in Galatians which is a simple appearance after His ascension. After all, Paul should know.

Paul's letters tell us a lot about Paul as a person, his mission, and his gospel. However, the letters only tell us a small portion of Paul's story. He never specifically tells us his missionary strategy, his primary audiences, or what he talked about when he spoke to the small churches. We have no sermons or anything else to tell us what his primary teachings were.

His letters were almost all written in response to problems in his congregations, apparently about subjects that were not part of his original mission. Paul was trying to straighten out problems or to respond to questions from the congregations. Many of his stops, such as Athens, are not the subject of any of his surviving letters. It is very important to understand that we have nothing that discusses Paul's actual gospel in any detail with the possible exception of his letter to the Romans. Since the first century, people have been trying to determine Paul's message and what was of particular importance solely from his letters, but most of the letters were devoted to things that his churches did not clearly understand. For all we know, these were very minor considerations to Paul's message and have received undue emphasis merely because we have nothing else.

Some of the churches Paul refers to were not founded by Paul but later came to be identified with him; Corinth and Rome for sure, and probably Ephesus and Athens as well. JESUS message had a life of its own. His concept of the Kingdom of GOD was exciting, and people were getting together all over talking about it. They met in small groups to

---

* Gal. 1:15 -16. This is a bit confusing. According to Paul, GOD "was pleased to reveal his Son to me." Modern translators believe that the word "to" is an incorrect translation of the Greek word *en* which means "in" or "by means of," but never "to." The correct translation is probably "was pleased to make his Son known by means of me." In other words, GOD did not introduce Paul to his Son but, rather, was authorizing Paul to introduce JESUS to others. The incorrect translation of the Greek *en* has been a problem elsewhere in the Bible.

discuss what JESUS said, and Paul came upon these groups and gave them his interpretations of JESUS' message. These small cells were like clubs (*koinonia)* in the model of the Hellenistic fellowship, and they argued avant-garde concepts, some of which were the teachings of JESUS. They often invited speakers such as Paul.

These spontaneous groups, and others that Paul met, were very likely either Jews who liked JESUS' message or gentiles who had already been leaning toward Judaism but were not yet converts, often because of the circumcision issue. Luke says that Paul's audience was primarily among "godfearers." This is one of the few places where scholars believe that Luke was right on when he talks about Paul because it meshes with other evidence. "Godfearers" was a term that referred to gentiles who were already loosely associated with a Jewish synagogue. They believed in the Jewish god but were not considered to be true members of the religion, again, usually because of the requirement of circumcision.

You can imagine that Paul's gospel, which allowed non-Jews to become full members—able to worship and enjoy the benefits of the Jewish god they already adored, and yet avoid "the knife"—sounded pretty good to them. Paul was, basically, poaching on potential Jewish converts, and this probably explains much of the enmity between Paul and the Jewish establishment. To make matters worse, JESUS' message was already luring away some of those who were Jewish by birth. JESUS was a fun-loving guy who was not afraid to hang out with publicans and to break bread with gentiles, and he traveled with women in his entourage. That wasn't quite as exciting as a Canaanite orgy, but it beat the heck out of the strict Hebrew laws governing conduct and cleanliness.

Imagine yourself in Palestine at the time of JESUS to fully understand how enticing his message was. If it can entice Paul—an adherent to the conservative fundamental Jewish traditions, a highly intelligent and educated Jew, a man who was deeply trained in the ancient traditions and was a pharisee, the group that later became known as rabbis—to change his mind and embrace the teachings of the Christ Cult, then almost anyone could be enticed away.

Paul had one last step before he could be certain of his evangelism. He had to put two ticklish concepts before the group that was the de facto last word on JESUS, those who were among JESUS' own disciples and who actually knew him, the "Pillars*" in Jerusalem. He met with James, Peter, and John and asked two questions: first, for gentile converts to the branch of Judaism known as the JESUS cult, is circumcision a requirement

---

* This was Paul's name for the group. They did not seem to have an actual church group, but, because they all knew JESUS, everyone wanted their counsel and their approval carried a lot of weight.

for one to be welcomed into JESUS' house; and secondly, would it be acceptable for the converts to share table fellowship with gentiles. If he got a "No" response, it would severely cripple Paul's message. His gospel was already being challenged by other apostles who came after him, and he needed to assure his converts that he had the blessing of the "Pillars" of Jerusalem on these issues to counter the charges of the other apostles.

This meeting occurred about 14 years after Paul's conversion, or about 48 C.E., before any of his letters, the earliest of which is 1 Cor which was written about 50 C.E. Basically, Paul was enchanted with this new concept that everyone, including gentiles, were now welcome in the house of Israel. The concept was "freedom from the law," which meant that it was no longer necessary to be slavish to the racial purity laws that Paul had spent most of his life studying and analyzing. If the purity laws could be waived, it would seem that circumcision and the prohibition against breaking bread with gentiles would also be waived. Everyone was welcome in GOD's kingdom, and Paul felt compelled to spread the message. This basic concept, so simple in its terms, turned out to be extremely complex in application as Paul discovered.

It appears from Paul's letters that the Pillars had not given much thought to those issues. They were, after all, not active in the JESUS cults. They were leaders solely because they actually knew JESUS and had heard his message first hand, so others looked up to them. Peter was outraged at Paul's suggestion. If you were going to be a Jew you had to abide by the Law. John didn't see a problem, however. It remained for James, JESUS' (half?) brother to find a compromise. He decided that Peter would be in charge of the conversion of Jews to the new cult and that Paul would be in charge of converting the gentiles. Paul could do as he wished regarding circumcision and table fellowship. It was not all clear that the Pillars actually reached a consensus, but that is the way Paul interpreted the meeting and he had no qualms about telling people who objected to his mission that he had permission from the Pillars. So Paul was on his way. He possessed what he believed to be permission to convert gentiles without requiring either circumcision or adherence to table fellowship laws.

Now let's examine Paul's letters in the order in which they were written to see how his gospel changed over the years. You will see that he advances new concepts about Christianity and sometimes his ideas work and sometimes they do not. Remember, these letters primarily address problems that he did not discuss in his ministry and most seem to be problems he did not anticipate. His letters continuously build on previous letters or quietly discard previous ideas that did not pass the test of time. He introduces language that tempers the harshness or rashness of some of his earlier ideas. We will see how, in the twilight of his career, and of his life, he wrote a long, heart-felt letter to the church in Rome. This letter is a summary of Paul's final thoughts. He polished all of his concepts that worked and jettisoned those that did not. Romans is the final sum of all of Paul's long and hard labors.

I find it hard to imagine someone being as dedicated to his beliefs as Paul. He walked thousands of miles to spread his message to others. He suffered multiple imprisonment, physical and mental abuse, and exile. He was in shipwrecks and almost lost his life several times. He did this for almost 30 years, longer than the entire average life-span of most Jewish peasants at the time. Some form of JESUS' message might have survived if Paul had not existed, but it would be a far, far different religion. I think it is fair to say that, without any doubt, Paul was the father of Christianity.

Letters Actually Written by Paul

The letters that the scholars comfortably agree were actually written by Paul, in chronological order, include 1 Thessalonians, Galatians, 1 & 2 Corinthians, Romans, Philemon, and Philippians. We will study them in that order. All of the others are no longer believed by most scholars to have been genuine letters from Paul.

Before we get to the letters themselves, there is an issue that must be discussed. Paul was incredibly brutal in his verbal attacks on the apostles that came after him and criticized his message. Even by the standards of the modern political campaigns these seem harsh. He treated those apostles as human piñatas. Paul first trashed the others' reputation and then trashed their message. There is no attempt at being fair. This was very typical of the Greco-Roman debates at that time. It was unheard of to present both sides of an issue. A good example is Galatians 5:10-12, where Paul writes:

> *[W]hoever it is that is confusing you will pay the penalty. . . I wish those who unsettle you would castrate themselves!*

Wow! Pretty tough language. Castrate themselves? That is the way people argued at the time. So don't be hard on Paul for such conduct. All was fair in Greco-Roman polemics.

Paul's Letter to the Thessalonians

Thessalonica was a large and wealthy port on a finger of the Adriatic Sea, straddling the main trade route from the Adriatic Sea to the Bosporus. It was founded after the death of Alexander by one of his generals, Cassander, and it was, even after over two centuries of Roman rule, a Hellenistic city through and through. In Paul's time, it was the capital city of the Roman province of Macedonia. Because of its location on the main trade route, it was a very cosmopolitan city with diverse cultures and contact with many of the eastern religions. Thessalonica was ripe for a new idea that was soundly based on a highly respected and ancient religion.

Paul's letter to the church in Thessalonica was the first letter that we have from Paul, but Thessalonica was not his first stop when he began his mission. From this letter we learn that Paul had spent some time in Philippi before going to Thessalonica. We have no idea if he made previous stops in other places, but after he left Thessalonica he went to Athens. His mission in Thessalonica had been successful beyond his imagination. From comments in 1 Thessalonians, we can determine that Paul was almost certainly the founder of this church; they became members of the JESUS cult as a result of his gospel (1:5-6), he refers to himself as an apostle of Christ among them (2:7), and he was "like a father with his children" (2:11).

While he was in Athens, Paul decided to send his friend and assistant, Timothy, back to Thessalonica to encourage the church to maintain the faith that it had shown during Paul's visit there. Timothy returned with the good news that the Thessalonians were keeping the faith. Paul and Timothy then moved on to Corinth. This letter was probably written from Corinth about 50 C.E. The letter was congratulatory and expressed Paul's joy on their faithful keeping of the faith. Paul had proven himself capable of forming a congregation around his gospel. However, there was an undercurrent in the letter that suggested that both Paul and this new congregation suffered from mistreatment and persecution from others and, apparently, suggestions for change from other evangelists who questioned Paul's credibility. Paul responded to this by comparing his activities and honest words to the other itinerant philosophers who sold people on their wisdom by flattery and rhetorical trickery (2:1-3:13). It does not appear at this point that Jewish leaders or other evangelists were implicated in this as we will see occurring later in Galatians. Apparently Paul was being compared to the traveling philosophers who were called "sophists" and who were well known to resort to flattery and trickery.

There were two new questions that had been raised by the congregation, 1) what is proper conduct for a Christian (4:1-12) and 2) what about those who convert but die before JESUS reappears; the so-called "second coming?" (4:13). The first question was easy. Paul merely told them to try to attain a life of blamelessness and holiness (4:1-12; 5:12-22). The other question presented a huge problem.

The Thessalonians were apparently worried about the salvation of their fellow Christians who died after Paul's visit but before JESUS returned. Everyone, including Paul, expected that event to be very soon. First, this suggests that Paul had been preaching that JESUS would again appear as he did after his resurrection and at that time, those embracing JESUS' message would ascend to Heaven with JESUS. This appears to be the very first reference in any document to the concept of anyone going to Heaven at JESUS' second coming. Second, this is the first time someone wondered about the fate of Christians who died after conversion but before the event. That is not to suggest that the ancient Hebrews never thought of what happens after death. The Hebrew Scriptures state that, upon death you went to a place called Sheol. It was described as darkness and silence, probably located underground (Ps 88:13; Job 10:21, 22). Apparently, GOD puts people there. In an early suggestion of people rising from the dead, the spirits of people in Sheol are seen to rise up to greet leaders who have died.

Paul's response became a major addition to Christian beliefs. He said that, at the coming, the Lord would "bring with him those who have died (4:13-15)." Paul envisioned an archangel sounding a trumpet and both the dead and the living rising to meet the Lord in the clouds and be with GOD forever (4:16-5:3). This idea of the dead rising to Heaven is a very Jewish concept, although a distinctly minority belief, where the *spirit* of the dead, not the body, would arise to be present at the judgment day.

SHEOL TO HELL

The Hebrew word *Sheol* means "abode of the dead," and it was the final abode for both the righteous and the sinful. It was, basically, nothing more than non-life. It appears more than 60 times in the Old Testament, mostly in Psalms and the Wisdom literature. It was translated into Greek as "Hades."

A first century book called Enoch, while never reaching canonical status, was popular among the Hebrews. It referred to Sheol as the place where good people go. It used the Greek word *Gehenna* as the place where evil people reside in eternity after death.

The New Testament books picked up on this. They continued the Greek use of "Hades" for *Sheol* but changed its meaning, using it to describe a temporary abode for the righteous who were awaiting resurrection. They used the word "Hell" for *Gehenna* as the place of eternal damnation. The word Hell comes from a word in German mythology, *halja.* The Old English translation was "hel" or "helle."

While the older translations such as the KJV tend to use the word "Hell" for everything, modern translations generally use the original Greek tradition of having two words to describe the concept of an afterlife. They do not all use the same two words, however.

Suddenly, there is an apocalyptic aspect to Christianity, but it was a very different type of apocalyptic message. In previous Jewish writings an apocalypse was predicted where the virtuous were about to be overcome by evil. GOD will then come down and destroy the evil one and save the virtuous; the bad will perish and the good will be saved. Revelation is a perfect example. That is nothing like the problem Paul was trying to solve.

Paul's solution in First Thessalonians is certainly not what most twenty-first century Christians anticipate. Christians do not believe that they have to wait until the return of JESUS to go to Heaven. They expect that to occur *eo instante* upon their death. One dies and goes to Heaven. If a relative dies, he is with GOD. All of those good Christians who died in the last 2100 years do not have to wait until the Second Coming in order to ascend to Heaven. They are already there. Under Paul's theory, on the other hand, eternal life would occur only at the end of time. The Thessalonians bought it, however, because they expected the Second Coming to be within the lifetime of most of those now living. That is what they were told.

Paul must have recognized that he had been a little hasty with this explanation because he tempered it in later writings. For example, he suggested that upon his own death he would "depart and be with Christ (Phil 1:23)." This either assumes that JESUS would come within Paul's lifetime or that one did not have to wait until the coming apocalypse to go to Heaven. This was merely his first shot at the problem; he later refined this argument.

There is one section of 1 Thessalonians that was not written by Paul. It was an obvious addition by someone writing long after Paul's death because it cryptically refers to the destruction of the temple when it refers to GOD'S wrath catching up to the Jews. This is 1 Thess. 2:14-16 where there is language that specifically states that the Jews "killed JESUS and "drove us out." Paul would never say something like that. Paul was pushing a new version of Judaism called Christianity, but he was still a Jew through and through.

Second Thessalonians, unlike First Thessalonians, was not likely written by Paul. Almost one-third of it is a word-for-word identical copy of 1 Thessalonians. The apocalyptic story in 2 Thessalonians is based on Jewish stories dated after the destruction of the Temple in 70 C.E., such as, "the Lord JESUS is revealed from Heaven with his mighty angels in flaming fire, inflicting vengeance . . . on those who do not obey the gospel of our Lord JESUS. These will suffer the punishment of eternal destruction. . . .(2 Thess 1:7-9)" This could never have been written by Paul.

Paul's Letter to the Galatians

Galatia was not the name of a city, but of a Roman province that comprised much of what is modern day Turkey in the central part of Asia Minor. Paul had apparently been preaching there for some time, or at least was well known there, before going to Philippi and Thessalonica. He addressed his epistle to several churches in the area. Unfortunately, we know nothing of when or where the letter was written as we only have a general statement on the subject in Acts. However, there seems to be a growing consensus that the letters were written from Ephesus between 52 and 54 C.E., shortly before his letters to the Corinthians.

One thing is certain, he knew the recipients of the letter very well. He ignored the flowery thanksgiving and commendation that is typical of letters at the time and also typical of the other letters Paul sent. He just jumped right into the controversy raised by the Galatians and did not have any problem leveling a blast at them right out of the gate, "You foolish Galatians, who has bewitched you (3:1)?" Paul then blasted those whom he believed misled the Galatians, even though they were absent and unable to defend their position, with the rhetoric that I referred to earlier, "Damn them, damn them. I wish those who unsettle you would castrate themselves!"

Just what was it that pushed Paul's buttons like that? Some apostles championed "another gospel" (1:6-7; 4:17) and were telling the Galatians that they would have to be circumcised. This presented a critical challenge to Paul's whole theory. Whomever the interlopers were, they had successfully challenged Paul's credentials and also convinced many of the Galatians that, if they wanted to enjoy the benefits of the Jewish god they had to both obey the Law *and* get circumcised. They rightfully believed that they would have to get circumcised if they wanted the full benefits of belonging to the Jewish community. True, but Paul said that if they got circumcised, they would have "cut [them]selves off from Christ" (5:2-4) (I'm sure Paul meant that figuratively). Neither circumcision nor uncircumcision counts for anything; the only thing that counts is faith working through love."

What so thoroughly frustrated Paul was that they were correct, but, since GOD was now a god for all of the people, it was no longer necessary to become Jewish to enjoy the benefits offered by GOD. Christians could enjoy the benefits of the god of Israel just as easily as Jews, and they did not have to suffer the pain of circumcision to do so. This was a threat to Paul's entire gospel and he had to nip it in the bud (again, figuratively).

He easily dispensed with the authority issue by arguing that the Pillars had agreed that his position on circumcision was correct and they certified him as an apostle for the gentiles. This was a pretty generous interpretation of what the Pillars decided, but who was going to argue?

As to the total concept supporting his own gospel, Paul put all of the polemic skills he gleaned as a Pharisee to work out a very convoluted application of the scriptures to support his position. Paul turned the position of the interlopers back on themselves. Since they contended that you cannot be a Jew unless you lived like the Jews, he devised a way to show that the Christians really were Jews, or at least Children of Abraham which is the same thing. As an attorney, I am rather appalled that Paul could get away with an argument as flawed as this, but he did. Here is how it went.

Abraham was the patriarch of all of Israel. In the stories of Abraham there are numerous references to a *promise* that GOD made to him that his *children* (seed) would be without number and that "all the *nations* would be *blessed* in him[*]." I have emphasized the words "promise" and "children" because the promise was made to Abraham and his children. And by "children," all the passages cited refer to Abraham's direct lineage. Children was not a metaphor to describe some other group of people. I also emphasized the words "nations" and "blessed" because it was the nations that were blessed, not something else. Paul "spun" this to hold that the *blessing* was *promised* as a result of Abraham's faith and righteousness because "Abraham believed GOD and it was reckoned to him as righteousness" (Gal 3:6-9; Gen 15:6)."

Where did Paul go with all of this? He suggested that since the promise to Abraham was made 430 years prior to the time GOD gave Moses the Law (actually, it was more like 800 years), that the Law was added to the promise (3:17). The law had to be added by GOD because of the many transgressions of the Hebrews (3:19). Paul then argues that the Law does not make anyone righteous and that those who relied upon it were merely serving as guardians "until the offspring would come to the person to whom the promise had been made" (3:10-24). You can probably see where Paul is headed. Since the promise was still there, Paul concluded that the promise GOD made to Abraham must have been meant for JESUS who, like Abraham, was "faithful" and "righteous," and because of JESUS, GOD regarded the nations (read "gentiles") as "faithful" and "righteous" as well.

There was one key fact that seemed to hold Paul's argument together. Paul, of course, used the Septuagint for his biblical authorities. In that book, the term for Abraham's "seed" was in the singular (*sperma*) (Gen. 12:17; 22:17-18). Paul said that, because it was singular, "seed" could not refer to the children of Israel, because they are many. Since it was singular, it could only refer to "one person, who is Christ (3:16)." Then the *coup de grâce*, Paul's summation to the jury, that, "If you belong to Christ, then you are Abraham's seed, heirs according to the promise" (3:19). You have to reread this several times to fully grasp the argument.

This convoluted reasoning must give headaches to strict constructionists of the Bible because Paul ignores the plain meaning of the passages from Genesis in order to build a case for his own gospel. This was only the basic foundation of the argument. Paul scoured the Torah for anything that he could find to support his position and arranged them into a mishmash of arguments making it very difficult to determine his reasoning. He even found a few quotes from the prophets. His final conclusion after all of that was that gentile Christians did not

[*] Gen. 12:1-2; 7; 15:5-7; 12:1-8; 18:17-19; and 22:17-18

have to keep the Law, a conclusion that was to haunt him later..

What is truly amazing is that nobody questioned the twisted logic until the twentieth century when a few scholars looked at Paul's arguments and said, "Whoa. How did he ever sell that?" But he did. He combined so many minute arguments that it was very difficult to trace his reasoning from beginning to end. It was only by stripping the argument down to the basics that it finally became manageable.

There was one huge problem with this argument—in writing the Christians into GOD's will and testament, Paul wrote the Jews out of it. He basically replaced the Jews as a group with one comprised of Jewish Christians and Christians who became Jews as the children of GOD. He also completely negated over 2000 years of Jewish tradition, laws, history, feasts and festivals as being superfluous and unnecessary. That was not a move that was going to bolster his dwindling popularity with the Hebrew leaders.

Once again we run into that pesky Greek preposition *en* which can mean either "in" or "by means of." In this case the phrase "all nations [meaning gentiles] will be blessed *in you*" (Gen 12:3; 18:18; Gal 3:8). Although it is not always easy to tell which meaning is proper for a given use of the phrase, in this case it should probably be translated as "by means of you" or "because of you" as the pre-Paul interpretation, and the logical interpretation, was that the *promise* went to Israel and the *blessing* was intended for "the nations." The preposition *en* is particularly difficult in the phrase *en Christo* which can mean "in Christ" or "by means of Christ." When translated as "in Christ" it implies a rather mystical meaning. The preferred translation in most cases is "by means of Christ" or "because of Christ."

As if that wasn't enough, Paul went even further. He went from Christians being the children of Abraham to being children of GOD.

> *But when the fullness of time had come, GOD sent his Son, born of a woman, born under the law, in order to redeem those who were under the law so that we might receive adoption as children. And because you are children, GOD has sent the Spirit of his Son into our hearts, crying, "Abba! Father!"So you are no longer a slave but a child, and if a child then also an heir, through GOD* (4:4-7).

That is, Christians were the children of GOD because they have the spirit of GOD's son in their hearts. This is stretching the metaphor a bit too far for most scholars.

This quotation from Galatians is interesting in another way altogether. It says that JESUS was "born of a woman, born under the law . . ." That is, there was nothing devine or mystical about his birth. There were no angels, no wandering star, no magi bearing gifts, no manger, and no virgin birth. Paul stresses both JESUS' human and Jewish birth. Born under the law means that he was born Jewish and went through the various rituals that a Jewish infant must endure by law, including circumcision on the eighth day. JESUS had a much more natural birth than we find thirty or so years later in the gospels of Matthew and Luke.

Paul's Corinthian Letters

Corinth was a very Greek city/state that guarded the crossing between Achaea and the Peloponnese. It was destroyed by the Romans in 146 B.C.E. and later rebuilt in 44 B.C.E. by Julius Caesar as a Roman colony. Rome sent the dregs of humanity there to repopulate it, ridding Rome of many of its manumitted slaves and lower class peasants. It rebounded to its old self in 27 B.C.E. when Augustus named it as the capital city of the entire Roman province of Greece. It was a very busy seaport and a commercial center. Corinth was a marvelous city, with extensive walls, numerous springs and fountains, an upper and a lower marketplace, theater, temples, fountains, monuments, baths and the like. It hosted the Isthmian Games, the second most prestigious panhellenic games. It was also renowned for its prostitutes and, being a seaport with numerous transient sailors, it was deservedly well known around the Mediterranean as the center of sex and immorality. It's people were free spirits and the city had a reputation much like San Francisco's Haight-Ashbury district did during the 60s and 70s. Paul discovered he was woefully unprepared for Corinthian society.

Paul visited Corinth twice. On his first trip he spent 18 months there starting about 50 C.E. and made a second visit within four years of the first. There are two letters from Paul to the Corinthians in the Bible, but they are actually a compilation of six different letters. First Corinthians is basically a single letter that remains pretty much intact. The letter refers to earlier letters from the people in Corinth to Paul, all of which have been lost. There was also an earlier letter from Paul to the Corinthians that has likewise been lost (1 Cor 5:9). The other five letters are combined in Second Corinthians, but portions have probably also been lost.

Corinth was Paul's first truly Greek venture. He was quite successful in his mission and repeatedly spoke to a half dozen or so small household-type groups that occasionally met together as one large church. He heard from "Chloe's people," people from one of the churches, about some conflicts or divisions within that group regarding how to handle certain conduct. Some of these conflicts are about very specific instances that must have shocked and stunned Paul, such as what should one do about a man who is living with and having sex with his father's new wife. Wait, what? "Having sex with whom? I'm not Dr. Ruth!"(1 Cor 5). Some of the questions were more philosophical and general such as eating food that was sacrificed to idols or spiritual gifts such as speaking in "tongues." The churches were also engaging in public ecstatic experiences, sexual conduct, baptisms for the dead, and mystical experiences, and Paul was devastated. These were purely pagan demonstrations.

You can imagine Paul's horror at receiving the letters from Chloe's People (1 Cor 1:11)? This had nothing to do with what Paul had been teaching them for a year and a half. Paul's message to the Corinthians had been about the meaning of the "cross of Christ" and the "law of Christ." The Corinthians had difficulty dealing with these concepts. What got their attention was the spirit of this new god-like person called JESUS and the chance of entering into the Kingdom he spoke about. They took to displaying in public what they felt was their immediate contact with the Christ spirit. Paul was having enough troubles without inviting outside scrutiny. About this time Paul was having encounters in Ephesus that eventually led to his imprisonment and a harrowing escape.

In this letter we see Paul doing his best to quell the disaster. He tempers both his previous views on the spirit and freedom and seems to contradict his previous position on other issues. This was primarily a gentile Christian congregation. Unfortunately, there are no letters or other documents written by the Corinthians, so we do not know for sure what their feeling was. There are plenty of hints in Paul's letters, though. Clearly there was a serious breach in Paul's relationship with this church.

At the time Paul left Corinth he clearly felt that the churches believed in Paul's gospel and in the Kingdom of GOD. They regularly met in groups and faithfully practiced baptism and the Eucharist ceremonies. That is a perfect description of the practices and beliefs of the Christ Cult* that Paul taught them. Paul describes for us the ways the Corinthians misinterpreted the JESUS message with dripping sarcasm. Paul flung back in their faces some phrases that apparently were used frequently by the Corinthians: "We are rich;" "We are free;" "We are kings;" "We have all we want; (4:8)" "We are strong (4:10);" "All things are lawful (6:12);" "Food is meant for the stomach, and the stomach for food (6:13);" "Food will not bring us close to God (8:8);" "No idol really exists; There is no GOD but one (8:1);" "We have spiritual gifts and power (12-14);" and "There is no resurrection of the dead (15:12)."

What the Corinthians had done was to meld Paul's gospel with their

---

* The Christ Cult at this time was a branch of Judaism that believed in the teachings of JESUS. It shared the conservative social views of the Greek Stoics and GOD was perfectly omnipotent, all knowing, and GOD actually 'divinely predestined' everything that was to take place on the earth 'before even creating the world.' Note that there was a much later, unrelated group of priests that were called the Christ cult.

own Hellenistic philosophical beliefs, particularly those of the Stoic and Cynic philosophical traditions, along with their previous pagan myths and beliefs. Future evangelists would find that this was hardly an unusual practice. Nearly every converted group kept some of their former religions in their new Christian beliefs. The Germans, for example, have a strange blend of their former mythology with their spiritual forests; and the Irish blend in some of their ancient Celtic influences. Even in the United States, we have traditions from ancient religions such as the Easter bunny blended into the Christian tradition. The stories of Parsival in Germany and Percival in England and their searches for the Holy Grail are other examples of how mythology and Christianity have merged somewhat. The Corinthians were simply the first to do so. Paul was totally flabbergasted and felt betrayed.

What is clear is that the Corinthians believed in the concept of the crucified son of GOD, that they did form small churches that met singly and occasionally together, and they believed the Kingdom of GOD was a spiritual place they could reach. Most importantly, they had no trouble with the concept that JESUS was a mortal at one time, that he died in a terrible, but very human way, and that he had then been transformed into a spiritual being of some kind. Greeks already believed that the human spirit and the divine spirit were pretty much the same, so this was an easy transition. They had combined many familiar concepts from their pagan beliefs and from their heroic "tragic death" stories with what Paul preached about Christianity. We can only speculate how the Corinthians went from this to demonstrating their ecstatic and charismatic performances in public.

What most distressed Paul was that his message, that for pagans to be able to enjoy the benefits of the Jewish god they did not have to be circumcised or to meet the strict purity standards, had been construed to mean that converted gentiles did not need to obey the rest of GOD'S laws either. Paul had praised the freedom of Christians from any need to abide by the Jewish laws. Now he had to temper that broad proclamation. Paul apparently assumed that everyone understood that they still had to lead moral and ethical lives. The particular moral and ethical considerations that were of immediate importance were sexual mores, celibacy, women prophesying without covering their heads, eating food offered to idols, class distinctions, marriage and children, and the public display of their spirituality. Paul stated that it was only the Jewish rules on circumcision and the purity laws that could be avoided, not the ethical and moral laws; that "obeying the commandments of GOD was everything (7:19)."

This was where Paul first put forth the oft-quoted metaphors regarding the "body of Christ" and that one's body was a temple. It was the human *spirit* that was getting the Corinthians in trouble, so Paul took to emphasizing the *body*. What one did was how one would be judged by

GOD. That is, all of one's acts had consequences, some good and some bad. These were functions of the body, not the spirit. He said, "[Y]our bodies are members of Christ . . . whoever is united to a prostitute becomes one body with her . . .The two shall be one flesh. . . anyone united to the Lord becomes one spirit with him. Therefore, shun fornication! Every sin that a person commits is outside the body; but the fornicator sins against the body itself. . . your body is a temple of the Holy Spirit within you, which you have from GOD. . . You were bought with a price; therefore glorify GOD in your body" (6:15-20).

Within all of this was the statement, "You (plural) are the body of Christ and individually members of it (12:27)." This was the first statement of the concept that the church is the body of Christ.

Then Paul took on the question of the raising of the dead. (Incidentally, Paul did not refer to "the dead." He used the euphemism, "those who have fallen asleep"). The Corinthians flat out said that "There is no resurrection of the dead (15:12)." They understood that the resurrection was purely of the spirit, not an actual body. That they could deal with. What was Paul to do with his body metaphor in this circumstance? He came across an idea that combined the Greek and Jewish traditions. He created the "spiritual body" (this entire argument is contained in Chpt 15).

He recited the Kerygma and emphasized the part about "he was raised on the third day . . ." Then he argued, "If there is no resurrection of the dead as the Greeks claim, then Christ has not been raised and your faith has been in vain and . . . we are found to be misrepresenting GOD, because we testified of GOD that he raised Christ. . ." Paul referred them to their own pagan tradition of baptizing people on behalf of the dead, showing that they believed that baptism was in the "cloud" and the "sea." Then came a rather strange argument from a purely logical standpoint, but it was apparently sufficient to convince the Corinthians.

He started by speaking of plants and animals. "What you sow does not come to life unless it dies. And as for what you sow, you do not sow the body that is to be, but a bare seed. . . But GOD has given it a body . . . and to each seed its own body. Not all flesh is alike, but there is one flesh for human beings, another for animals, another for birds, and another for fish. There are both heavenly bodies and earthly bodies. . . ."

Then he moved on to put human beings into the argument. "So it is with the resurrection of the dead. What is sown is perishable, what is raised is imperishable. . . It is sown a physical body, it is raised a spiritual body. If there is a physical body, there is also a spiritual body." In a final flourish, he added an apocalyptic note, "Flesh and blood cannot inherit the Kingdom of GOD, nor does the perishable inherit the imperishable. . . We will not all die, but we will all be changed, in a moment, in the twinkling of an eye, at the last trumpet. For the trumpet will sound and the dead will be raised imperishable, and we will be changed. . . ."

This contradicts JESUS' message that the Kingdom of GOD is already here, all you have to do is see it. This also means that you will not go to Heaven until the apocalypse, which is not what most Christians believe. Most people will say about a recently departed that "he is with GOD now." According to Paul's argument, which was consistent with his statement to the Galatians, the ascent into Heaven will occur only upon the return of JESUS.

After Paul wrote the letter that we know as First Corinthians, he sent his companion, Timothy, back to Corinth to check on how things were going. Timothy returned to report that Paul's churches in Corinth were visited by other apostles who had entirely different gospels than Paul. Since Paul had thrown cold water on all of their spirited celebrations of the spirit of Christ, the new apostles showed them a new way, and they were entranced. So Paul felt compelled to make another trip to Corinth. It was a terrible experience for Paul, one that he called a "painful visit." It seems that a member of the congregation greatly offended him. Paul followed up his visit with another letter, one that has been lost, that was apparently a bit of a tongue lashing which he called a "letter of tears." This letter got someone's attention, because his friend Titus reported to Paul when they met in Macedonia that the conflict had been resolved (2 Cor 7:6-7). Paul followed up with another letter that is probably, in part, what is now contained in 2 Cor. 1.1 - 2.13 and 7:5-16. But there was yet another letter, and another, and another.

Altogether, 2 Corinthians is a combination of portions of four or five letters. The various letters are pieced together and, in some cases, it is almost impossible to state for certain where one letter begins and ends. It also makes the letter very disjoined in subject matter and does not flow like most of Paul's letters. Two of the letters are requests for contributions for the poor in the Jerusalem church which seems to have been a charity that was close to Paul's heart (8-9). Finally, he had to write a very bitter letter about the messages of the new apostles (10-13) who were poisoning his people's minds.

These new apostles were Jews like Paul, but they relied heavily on the Jewish scriptures as their ultimate authority. What was very un-Jewish was that they combined charismatic displays as part of their message. This impressed the Corinthians, and they began doing it themselves, even in public. This is the very first example we have of Christians engaging in Charismatic acts and speaking in tongues.

This was very serious to Paul. He could see all of his good work going down the drain. He called these interlopers "super-apostles" (10-13), "false apostles" (11:5; 12:11), and "Satan's ministers (11:15)" and pleaded that he is not inferior to them even though he is "untrained in speech." He said that he felt a "divine jealousy" for the Corinthians because he promised them in marriage to one husband, to present them "as a chaste virgin to Christ." The super apostles, however, were teaching a different JESUS, he proclaimed. They apparently referred to Paul as "weak" and his message lacking in power. Therefore, he was put into the unenviable position of having to brag about himself; his credentials, his gospel, and his own visions.

When he compared himself to these apostles, we learn quite a bit about Paul that we did not know before. Although it is a bit disappointing in that he sounds a little like a petulant child in his plea, the Corinthians forced him into selling himself and his credentials over the other apostles. He proclaimed that like the apostles, Paul was a Hebrew, an Israelite, a child of Abraham, and a far better minister of Christ. He claimed to have had "far greater labors, far more imprisonments, with countless floggings, and often near death. Five times [he] received from the Jews the forty lashes minus one. Three times [he] was beaten with rods. Once [he] received a stoning. Three times [he] was shipwrecked; for a night and a day [he] was adrift at sea; on frequent journeys, in danger from rivers, danger from bandits, danger from [his] own people, danger from Gentiles, danger in the city, danger in the wilderness, danger at sea, danger from false brothers and sisters; in toil and hardship, through many a sleepless night, hungry and thirsty, often without food, cold and naked (11:22-27)."

Wow! I have no doubts that Paul suffered all of this. He walked thousands of miles through dangerous territory and he was certainly blunt in his statements and undoubtedly antagonized many, especially "his own people." This is also where he told the story of being threatened by the governor of Damascus so that his friends had to lower him down a wall in a basket through a window in order to escape. Paul could never be accused of cowardice or being a "quitter." However true all of this may be, it is a non-sequitur. It does not prove that Paul's message is any more correct than the gospels preached by the super-apostles.

So what was Paul to do? The Abraham connection he came up with was just not "selling" with the Corinthians. Paul got creative one more time and delved once again in the scriptures for an answer. What he came up with may or may not have worked on the Corinthians, we have no way of knowing, but it was to have an enormous impact on Christian beliefs to this day.

He found a start for this new idea in Jeremiah 31:31-34, "The days are surely coming, says the Lord, when I will make a new covenant with the house of Israel and the house of Judah." Ahah! a new covenant. "It will not be like the covenant that [GOD] made with their ancestors when [He] took them by the hand to bring them out of . . . Egypt. . . ." GOD will "write [this new covenant] on their hearts." Paul had found his answer. A new covenant with GOD, not written in mere ink on parchment or etched in stone, but on "tablets of human hearts." He not only implied that the oral covenant with the Christians was much stronger than the written covenant of the Jews, he suggested that it replaced the covenant GOD made with the Jews! This was nothing less than the theft of one of the most important concepts in the entire Hebrew religion.

Paul then made matters even worse from a Jewish point of view. Alluding to Moses putting a veil over his face at Sinai to protect himself from the brilliance of the glory of GOD, Paul stated that, to this day, "whenever Moses is read, a veil lies over their minds; but when one turns to the Lord, the veil is removed. Now the Lord is the spirit, . . .(1 Cor 3:15-16)" He not only claims that this oral covenant was better than the old one that was in writing, he said that the Christians know more than the Jews who study the words of Moses. Christians did not need to read the books of Moses because JESUS was making the true meaning of the texts known to them. Certainly this could not possibly offend the Jewish community. What could go wrong?

Paul co-opted the image of Adam to JESUS (15:45-49), and Abraham to JESUS in Galatians, now he stole Moses. Moses was anchored in written law, but JESUS offers a whole new spiritual foundation.

Paul said one more thing that was very important in the story of the evolution of Christianity. Paul said that, "[GOD], *who in [because of] Christ* always leads us in triumphal procession, . . ." [Emphasis added]. This statement shows that the Christian movement, at least the portion of the movement based upon Paul's gospel, did not yet consider JESUS to be a god. He was still but a messenger of GOD. GOD is acting through JESUS.

Paul's Letter to the Romans

All of the previous letters written by Paul were to churches that he founded or had, at least, visited. Most of the letters were written in response to questions from the congregations or to shape them up when they had strayed from Paul's message. Romans, on the other hand, was written to a church that Paul planned to visit but had not yet done so. It was also written in the twilight of both his ministry and his life. You can just feel the toll that the years on the road had wreaked on Paul. The letter appears to be a summary of Paul's views after he has had time to sort out the concepts that worked from those that did not. Many refer to this letter, especially to chapters 1-8, as Paul's "theological last will and testament."

A theme that flows throughout the letter is GOD's faithfulness despite the human faithlessness. A second, equally important theme, is the final accountability we all have before GOD. Finally, although this is clearly a letter about his gospel directed to the gentiles, Paul also tries to mend a few fences with the Jewish community. He demonstrates his familiarity with classical rules of argument as he builds his case. As a trial lawyer, I have a special appreciation for this letter. It is like an attorney's final summation to a jury.

Right out of the box Paul came up with a startling new concept. The whole problem was sin. Note that sin is written in singular form. That was a huge difference. Traditionally, the Hebrew concept of sin was plural. Transgressions and sins were specifically references to violations of particular Hebrew laws or commandments. By using the all-encompassing word "sin," Paul included not only all wrongful conduct, he also included both Jews and gentiles. The problem was not Jews failing to follow the Law or gentiles not becoming Jews, the problem was individual sin. The Law holds everyone accountable before GOD.

Paul quoted from the Hebrew Scriptures to show that no one may claim to fully satisfy GOD'S standards:

"There is no one who is righteous,
not even one;
there is no one who has
understanding,
there is no one who seeks GOD.
All have turned aside, together they
have become worthless;
there is no one who shows kindness,
there is not even one (Ps 14:1-2; 53:1-2)."

"Their throats are opened graves;
they use their tongues to deceive."
"The venom of vipers is
under their lips (Ps 5:9; 140:3)."

"Their mouths are full of cursing
and bitterness (Ps 10:7)."

"Their feet are swift to shed blood;
ruin and misery are in their paths,
and the way of peace they have
not known (Prov 1:16; Isa 59:7-8)."

"There is no fear of GOD before
their eyes (Ps 36:1)."

Paul characterized sin as being something other than a noun for a transgression; he made it into a force that determined all of human existence before the coming of JESUS. After all of these centuries, the Law was no longer the standard for judging when a sin has occurred. It was now a "natural law" that Paul proposed. There was only one GOD, and he was the GOD of both the Jews and the Gentiles. GOD's gift was that he sacrificed JESUS as an atonement sacrifice for everyone. This is, basically, an extension of the "scape goat" atonement sacrifices of Jewish tradition combined with the traditional Greek legends of heroic death. GOD did this to show his righteousness, and to show that he dealt roughly with sin. GOD exalted the one who had faith in JESUS, and that faith was the key to atonement. The key was now righteousness which was the new standard of purity and holiness.

Paul worked through his thought process in arriving at this movement from sin to righteousness in Ch 6:11-23. He said that you can be a slave to sin or a slave to obedience. The first leads to death and the latter to righteousness, that comes from faith, and salvation. He was a bit condescending when he remarked that he was using the term "slaves" as a metaphor because it is something that the Romans were familiar with and they probably would not get the idea otherwise.

The whole concept of righteousness was already familiar to the Romans because the well-known Greek philosophies of the Stoics emphasized self-control in much the same terms as Paul described righteousness. The Cynics, another group of philosophers, had similar concepts. The idea that one had to control his lusts and passions was very Greek, and Paul borrowed it for his own theories (1:24-32).

Paul also modified his previous "end of time" idea of physical bodies being raised from the dead. This included JESUS' own ascension. Instead, it was more spiritual. Paul always had seen sin as the most significant and overarching human failing. No longer. JESUS "died to sin, once for all" and people are now "dead to sin and alive to GOD in Christ JESUS (6:10-11)." How did one gain entrance to this great Kingdom of GOD? By being baptized to JESUS. That was all you had to do.

Paul further tempered his apocalyptic warnings by suggesting something much more productive by encouraging righteousness. The apocalypse would result in the bringing together of the Jews and gentiles into the same Kingdom of GOD (9:11). This was nothing like the traditional apocalyptic movements. For over 200 years those advocating the apocalyptic traditions envisioned GOD coming down to the earth and destroying the bad and saving the good. Paul's vision was not even remotely similar to that of John of Patmos in the book of Revelation which we will discuss later.

Paul attempted reconciliation with the Jewish community by no longer contending that JESUS was the "seed" of Abraham. While Paul still professed to be the apostle to the gentiles, he now included the Jews as "his people." "[To] them belong the adoption, the glory, the covenants, the giving of the law, the worship, and the promises; to them belong the patriarchs, and from them, according to the flesh, comes the Messiah,. . ." The Jews were included as long as they were righteous in their faith.

Quite a change from his early letters.

Paul's Letter to Philemon

Paul's letter to Philemon and his next letter, to the people at Philippi, are out of order for two reasons, first that there is no clear consensus on when they were written and secondly because they add nothing to our story of the growth of Christianity as Paul conceived it.

The letter to Philemon is the only letter that Paul wrote to a single person rather than a church or group of churches. Paul was in prison and he had a helper, a slave named Onesimus. We don't know where or when this took place, but most place Paul in Ephesus. The letter does not say why Onesimus was with Paul. He could have been a runaway slave from his master, Philemon, or Philemon may have sent Onesimus to serve Paul while he was in prison. In fact, it is a bit uncertain whether Paul was really in a prison or just under house arrest*. Whether Onesimus was a runaway slave or an emissary makes a difference in how this short book should be interpreted. It makes more sense that Onesimus was sent by Philemon because it is hard to imagine that a runaway slave would intentionally get himself stuck in a prison, although even that is possible. In those days it was not uncommon for a slave to seek the help of a close friend of his owner to act as an intermediary to try to gain freedom. In any event, it appears that Onesimus was converted by Paul and wanted to stay with him.

This is a very interesting letter because Paul had to decide what to do when his Christian beliefs conflict with Roman law. Paul had a problem—slavery was, and had been for centuries, the way of life in Greek, Roman, and Hebrew civilizations. As a result, Roman law had strict rules on the holding of slaves. If one was caught abetting a runaway slave, and that is precisely what Paul would be doing if he allowed Onesimus to stay, that person could be held liable for the full damages due to the owner for the loss of his slave. A slave was valuable property, and taking a slave would be like stealing a precious gem.

What was Paul to do? Not only were both Philemon and Onesimus Paul's friends, the foundation of his Christian belief was, as we learned in Galatians, that because of Christ, there was no longer slave and free, but only "brothers and sisters" in GOD'S family. That single concept of all people being equal in the eyes of GOD was what originally fired Paul's imagination and sent him on his mission. Paul showed us in this letter that sometimes one's religious beliefs must be tempered with the realities of

---

* Apparently, at about this same period of time, the church at Philippi also sent one Epaphroditus to serve Paul during his confinement. We'll get to that when we discuss Philippians.

life. They were all Roman subjects and were subject to Roman law. Their very existence depended upon not upsetting the Roman Officials. The Kingdom of GOD was the future, but the present was Rome.

Paul reluctantly sent Onesimus back to Philemon with this letter. In the letter, Paul asked Philemon to take Onesimus back, not as a slave, but as a "beloved brother." Paul also hinted that Philemon should send Onesimus back to Paul.

Paul's Letter to the Philippians

Paul apparently had a very close relationship with the people of Philippi because Paul really laid open his feelings, both of happiness and of sorrow. This was a very personal letter as opposed to the much more formal letters to the other churches. He apparently did not have any problems with this church like he did with some of the others. This gives us our first and only intimate, "up close and personal" look at Paul as a person with human needs, desires, and frailties. The letter finds Paul in big trouble. He was concerned about his upcoming trial in which he could lose his life, and he was confronting his own mortality.

Philippi was a large and important city on the main Roman road from Byzantium to Thessalonica and all of the great Greek seaports. Paul was in prison, and traditionally it was believed that this letter was written during the time that he was imprisoned in Rome where he was eventually executed. The letter actually consists of parts of three letters. Paul was imprisoned three times, but most scholars now believe that two of the letters were written during his confinement in Ephesus, the first at about the same time as the letter to Philemon. The last of the three letters seems to have been inserted in the middle of the letter at 3:2-4:9. This letter may not have been addressed to the Philippians at all as it is a sharp break in the flow of the other letters and has different subject matter.

Epaphroditus was sent as an emissary bearing gifts to Paul from his friends in Philippi. The first part of this letter was apparently carried to Philippi by Epaphroditus who had become seriously ill while looking after Paul. Paul had his friend Timothy accompany Epaphroditus on the trip. Paul thanked the Philippians for the gifts and reminisced about gifts that they had given him in the past.

The fact that Epaphroditus was sent to the prison and that, in one of the last verses of Philemon Paul refers to "Epaphras, my fellow prisoner in Christ JESUS, ..." leads many to believe that these letters were written about the same time. Epaphras and Epaphroditus are the same name. One is just the shorter version like Nick is to Nicholas. The odds against two people by the same name just happening to show up in prison with Paul are extremely high.

What is immediately apparent about this letter is the passion with which Paul refers to his Christian beliefs. My feeling, when I read this letter, is that Paul was concerned about his own mortality. He was facing trial and possibly death. There was a good bit of reminiscing. He talked about those other evangelists who disagreed with him or who tried to send other messages to his followers. He ascribed various motives for their acts (1:15-18). Paul's main goal was to reach the heavenly kingdom. "I want to know Christ and the power of his resurrection and the sharing of his sufferings by becoming like him in his death, if somehow I may attain the resurrection from the dead (3:10-11)" Paul wanted to "press on toward the goal for the prize of the heavenly call of GOD in Christ JESUS."

Letters Attributed to Paul but not Written by Paul

Many letters originally attributed to Paul were actually written posthumously by followers of Paul's gospel and who psuedepigraphically attributed the letter to Paul. Many of these are obviously not written by Paul as they discuss matters that had not occurred until long after Paul's death. In the Middle East at the time, it was common practice to write such documents in the name of someone famous or highly respected to give them more credibility. This sounds like a contradiction in terms, but it made perfect sense in the first century.

Even though the majority of scholars doubt Paul's authorship of all these books, not all share the same degree of doubt as to authorship. On a scale of one to five, with one being slightly more than 50% consensus and five being almost unanimous consensus, the books would rate about like this:

1 Timothy	5
2 Timothy	5
Titus	5
Hebrews	5
Ephesians	4
Colossians	3
2 Thessalonians	2

We will continue to examine the books in the probable order in which they were written, although there is a considerable absence of consensus on the issue of time.

There is far less literature on these pseudepigraphs than on the books that were actually written by Paul. Paul defined Christianity. Those who came later are not generally considered authority on the genesis of Christianity, although they may be very informative about later church dogma. Many consider Paul next to godliness, and his words carry a considerable power. There is far less scholarly discussion of the other letter writers. They seem to be placed in the category of other early church writers such as (St.) Augustine, or Origin.

Letter to the Colossians

Colossae was a town on the Lycus river in what was then in the Roman province of Asia, modern day Turkey. This was not a coastal city, but it was on a busy trade route. The church there was founded by a friend and follower of Paul's by the name of Epaphras. There is that name again! We had the fellow prisoner Epaphras in Philemon, the emissary from the Philippians by the name of Epaphroditus, which is a longer version the same name, and now the name pops up again. This was not a hugely common name, so the odds of this being three separate people are minuscule. Of course, the fact that the other two references to this name were in authentic Paul letters and this is not might be the difference. There is also a growing consensus that this letter was written about the same time as the two letters Paul wrote from prison in Ephesus, so it is possible, even likely, that this unknown author met and knew the Epaphras that Paul wrote about. Other scholars, noting the similarity in Colossians to many parts of Philemon, a genuine Paul letter, believe that Paul may have written both letters himself at about the same time, and that is part of the reason Colossians rates a "3" on the chart above. The letter starts out with very flattering statements about the progress of the church members and praise Epaphras. This suggests to me that Epaphras may have even been the author of this letter.

The letter talks about the supremacy of JESUS as being,

> *[T]he image of the invisible GOD, the firstborn of all creation; for in [or through] him all things in Heaven and on earth were created, things visible and invisible, whether thrones or dominions or rulers or powers—all things have been created through him and for him. He himself is before all things, and in [or by] him all things hold together. He is the head of the body, the church; he is the beginning, the firstborn from the dead, so that he might come to have first place in everything. For in [or because of] him all the fullness of GOD was pleased to dwell, and through him GOD was pleased to reconcile to himself all things, whether on earth or in the Heaven, by making peace through the blood of his cross* (1:15-20).

JESUS is certainly the lord over everything worldly as the word "lord" meant in those times, and he is certainly the favorite of GOD and GOD works through JESUS, but he is not yet considered to be devine. He is not yet described as being a god. This excerpt does emphasize the importance of the cross as do other passages in this letter The letter warns against allowing people to lead you astray with various religious practices such as matters of food and drink, festivals, new moons, or various Sabbaths. The letter is also outspoken against Jewish purity regulations (2:16-25).

There is a long section in which the penalties for violation of religious ethics are listed (3:1-11). The writer decries the sins of life such as "fornication, impurity, passion, evil desire, and greed" (collectively a term for idolatry at that time). On account of these sins, the wrath of GOD will descend on all sinners. He urges the readers to rid themselves of "anger, wrath, malice, slander, and abusive language."

Having warned about sinful conduct and what not to do, the writer next tells you what you should do: be, "holy and beloved, clothe yourselves with compassion, kindness, humility, meekness, and patience. Bear with one another and, if anyone has a complaint against another, forgive each other. . . clothe yourselves with love (3:12-4:6)." The letter also sets out proper conduct for wives, children, and fathers, how to treat your slaves, and to devote oneself to prayer.

Letter to the Ephesians

Ephesus was a very important port city on the coast of what is now Turkey, directly across the Aegean Sea from Athens. Paul spent a lot of time in Ephesus and wrote several of his letters from that city. He did not write this letter to the Ephesians, however.

The author of Ephesians borrowed the poetry of early Christian hymns and the ethics from the Jewish scriptures. It is generally broken down into two parts, Chapters one through three being writings about theological subjects and chapters four through six being about ethics.

The theological section contrasts life before JESUS with life after. You were dead because of your sinful ways but you have been saved solely by GOD's mercy and benevolence who gave you a new life through JESUS. He reminded the Ephesians that at one time they were called "the uncircumcision," a derogatory term for gentiles by those who were called "the circumcision," referring to Jewish Christians who still demanded full compliance with Jewish laws. Because of the cross, "by the blood of Christ," there was peace because He has made both groups into one.

The ethics section gives mostly "don'ts" and a few "dos." Unity and peace are made possible by JESUS, and the seven bases of unity are described, "There is one body and one Spirit, just as you were called to the one hope of your calling, one Lord, one faith, one baptism, one GOD and Father of all. . . ." Fornication and impurity of any kind; greed; obscene, silly, and vulgar talk are proscribed. The author set out rules for various relationships including wives to husbands, slaves and masters, children and fathers. These relationships are all related to Christ being the head of the church, and just as the church is subject to Christ, wives, slaves and children are subject to husbands, masters, and fathers, but they in turn must love their wives, slaves and children as CHRIST loves the church.

Finally, there is an apocalyptical ending as the author asked the readers to "put on the whole armor of GOD so that you may be able to stand against the wiles of the devil."

Hebrews

This book was originally known as "The Epistle of Paul to the Hebrews," but it is not an epistle at all. It is, in all likelihood, a sermon. Even the very early second century church leaders such as Origen, [St.] Clement, and Tertullian recognized that there was no way that Paul could have written this document. Clement thought that Luke may have had something to do with the authorship and Origen thought that a disciple of Paul must have written it. Much later other authors were suggested such as Apollos and Priscilla. Today, while there isn't a clue as to the identity of the author, nobody suggests that it was Paul. The date that it was written is just as uncertain, probably in the range of 60 - 100 C.E.

The book has the typical closing of a letter, but it lacks the usual flowery greeting. In the closing, the author refers to the document as his "word of exhortation" which was the usual way of describing a Jewish sermon in the synagogue (eg Acts13:14). Therefore, it is generally considered to be a sermon. Although the title of the book is "Hebrews," it was most likely a sermon delivered to both Jewish Christians and gentile Christians who had been badly persecuted by the Romans and, perhaps, had even renounced their faith. The writer emphasizes the importance of the Hebrew Scriptures and the laws but also argues that JESUS is superior to the Jewish traditions.

Scholars traditionally organize the book into four sections; the first discusses the word of GOD as spoken by the Son (1:1-4:13), the second transforms JESUS into the eternal high priest and contrasts him with the Hebrew priesthood (4:4-10:31), the third talks of living by faith (10:32-12:29), and the fourth part gives some practical advice (Ch 13). It appears, from the subject matter, the audience was well versed in both the Septuagint and the Jewish Tradition. The author quotes extensively from the Old Testament and assumes the readers are familiar with what is being quoted as he doesn't even bother to reference the books.

Hebrews begins with a comparison of the way GOD spoke to "our ancestors" in the past with the way he now communicates, through "a Son" who sits at the right hand of GOD and is superior even to the angels. JESUS is described as being present at the creation (as in the Gospel of John). The phrases, "[H]e sustains all things. The reflection of GOD's glory and the exact imprint of GOD's very being, . . ." refer to Hebrew wisdom writings (Prov 8:22-31; Wis 9:9). In Jewish tradition, Wisdom is a female who was present at the time of creation and came to earth to dwell and later returned to her place in the heavens. JESUS has now replaced the figure of Wisdom. Note that JESUS was not yet recognized as a god, or if he was, it was a lesser god of some kind like Wisdom. The writer quoted seven excerpts from the Hebrew Scriptures in which he claimed that GOD was speaking about or to JESUS*. After stating that JESUS ranks higher than the angels, the author then pointed out that what JESUS said is more important than what Moses said because Moses got his information second hand from the angels.

JESUS was then shown to be appointed by GOD as the new high priest. He was able to assume this position because he shares human weaknesses and he learned obedience from his suffering on the cross. The sermon mentioned GOD'S promise to Abraham and reminded the readers, as they are all Abraham's descendants, GOD'S promise applied to all Christians. There follows a number of references to a shadowy figure from the Old Testament, Melchizedek, who, although only mentioned twice in the Old Testament, plays a rather important part in the theology of Hebrews and in later church dogma.

Melchizedek is described as, "*Without father, without mother, without genealogy, having neither beginning of days nor end of life, but resembling the Son of GOD, he remains a priest forever*" (7:3). This has been interpreted very differently by different Christian denominations. Some feel that having no father or mother or genealogy, that he is either the son of GOD or something very close to it. Others contend that it is a mistranslation and that which is "without a lineage" is the priesthood and all that it means is that Melchizedek is not a descendent of Levi as required. There are other interpretations as well.

Much of the book seems to be educating people about how the old Hebrew traditions are being replaced with JESUS traditions—the old Jewish practices versus the new Christ ministry (8:1-6; 10:1-18) and the old covenant with Moses versus the new covenant propounded by Jeremiah (8:7-13). It speaks of the death of JESUS as the only sacrifice needed to atone for the sins of humanity (9:11-28). Finally, it closes with a long narrative of the power of faith and how JESUS is the supreme example of faith in GOD for which everyone should emulate.

First and Second Letters to Timothy and Letter to Titus

In the eighteenth century, these three letters began to be referred to as the "pastoral epistles" because they all shared the primary theme of how the Christian church leaders, the pastors, should govern the churches. The word *Pastor* is Latin for shepherd, but it was not used to describe a church leader until long after Paul's death. Very early on church

---

* Heb 1:5-13-(5-Ps 2:7; 2 Sam 7:14; 6-Deut 32:43; 7-Ps 104..4; 8-Ps 45.6-7; 10-12-Ps 102:25-27; 13-Ps 110:1). Note that Ps 110:1 is interpreted a little differently in Acts 2:24 and 1 Cor 15:25 where, instead of being the high priest it is suggested that JESUS will be the messiah who will lead them into battle

leaders suspected that it was highly unlikely that Paul had anything to do with these three letters. (St.) Ignatius and Origin both questioned this in the second century. Paul had a certain distinctive writing style as most people do, and there are words and phrases that he favored for use in certain situations. For example, these letters now exchange Paul's metaphor that the church is the body of Christ for an emphasis on rules and traditions. These three documents share a common writing style, but it is far different from what Paul used in those letters that scholars generally believe were written by Paul. The vocabulary is also different and none of the recurrent themes that flow through all of Paul's writings appear in any of these books.

Most importantly, they address situations that did not even occur until after Paul's death. There is a degree of church structure that was unknown during Paul's lifetime. The church became institutionalized about the second century and was no longer a series of small house churches where early Christians would get together informally from time to time. They became part of much larger units. The letters refer to "bishops" and "deacons" which were positions in the church that did not exist in the time of Paul and, in fact, were not needed for the little churches where Paul preached.

At the time the books were written, the Catholic Christians were threatened by two large groups, the Gnostic Christians and the Carpocratians, a branch of the Gnostics (see the Secret Gospel of Mark). These three epistles were written to counter some of the practices of these groups. For example, the Gnostics believed that once you reached the state of gnosis, you no longer needed assistance from the church. You were fully qualified to do everything GOD wanted yourself. This did not ingratiate them with the priesthood.

Today, some of the most often quoted verses are found in these three books. The author(s) accomplished precisely what he intended when he wrote these letters in Paul's name because they are now cited by church leaders as Paul's authority for these propositions. In fact, they sound very little like anything that Paul would say.

For example, this is what 1 Tim. has to say about women in church:

> *[W]omen should dress themselves modestly and decently in suitable clothing, not with their hair braided, or with gold, pearls, or expensive clothes, but with good works, as is proper for women who profess reverence for GOD. Let a woman learn in silence with full submission. I permit no woman to teach or to have authority over a man; she is to keep silent. For Adam was formed first, then Eve; and Adam was not deceived, but the woman was deceived and became a transgressor. Yet she will be saved through childbearing provided they continue in faith and love and holiness, with modesty* (1 Tim 2:9-15).

The Catholic Church quotes this when women ask to be accepted into the priesthood and by other men to demonstrate that GOD intended them to dominate women and that women should stay at home and bear children because it threatens conventional domestic order for them to do otherwise. This is entirely inconsistent with Paul's stated feelings. He had many women in positions of authority in his churches. For example, Paul refers to "Chloe's people" (1 Cor 1:11); Chloe was apparently a church leader or teacher of some sort, and a woman. In Romans, Paul lists 27 Christians, ten of which are women and 17 men, and he singles out five women and six men for special praise (16:1-15). There are other references as well. Further, according to Luke, JESUS had many women among his followers, some of whom helped finance his ministry. So this quote is clearly later church dogma added by men who hoped to keep the priesthood an exclusive mens' club.

Another quote that gets a lot of ink is where the author claims,

> *All scripture is inspired by GOD and is useful for teaching, for reproof, for correction, and for training in righteousness, so that everyone who belongs to GOD may be proficient, equipped for every good work* (2 Tim 1:16-17).

We discussed this passage previously, but it is often advanced to prove that the Bible was inspired by GOD and is, therefore, inerrant. Once again, this is a second century church leader talking, not Paul. Paul was unlikely to state that his own letters would someday be considered "scripture inspired by GOD," and none of the other New Testament documents had even been written.

The General Letters

In addition to the letters that were either written or purportedly written by Paul, there is another general classification of documents that are usually referred to as "general letters." These are the letters that are written in the names of James, Peter, John, and Jude, but none of which were written by those persons. Most of these documents were not even letters but are more like religious tracts; some may have even been sermons.

The Letters of James and Jude

James, the brother of JESUS, pretty much by default, became a high church leader upon JESUS' death. Often his name was attached to documents to lend them credibility, but there does not seem to be any surviving documents that were actually written by James who was probably illiterate.

This document was directed to the "twelve tribes [of Israel] in the

Dispersion (diaspora)." Some feel that the underlying message may have been based upon a sermon by James before his martyrdom in the mid-sixties, but there does not seem to be a consensus on this. The Book is an attempt to reach those Jews who found it difficult to rationalize their beliefs in Christianity with the strong Jewish traditions of the Torah. It takes issue with some of Paul's interpretations of the Scriptures.

Jude is very similar. Jude is, of course, another brother of JESUS. After the deaths of James and Jude, JESUS' teachings gradually faded as a version or sect of Judaism. Those Jews who did not follow the teachings of JESUS adopted Rabbinical Judaism, forsaking the priesthood, and the Christians became ever more a Gentile religion, no longer dwelling on its Jewish roots.

The Two Letters of Peter

First Peter is actually a real letter. It was just not written by the apostle Simon called Peter. It was originally thought to be a baptismal liturgy that was changed to a letter format. Now it is believed that it was always a letter. This was written during a time of turmoil for Christians. They were persecuted, but the persecution, up to this point was mostly verbal. This is an exhortation to "suck it up." They were reminded that Christianity was nothing more than a period in time between JESUS' death and his second coming, so hang in there for the big reward at the end.

Second Peter is much different and is a little strange. It is like a third person report of the last words of a church leader to his sons, except that it is written in the first person, as if it was Peter writing. It is almost certain, however, that neither Simon called Peter wrote this nor did the author of 1 Peter. It relates an apocalyptic vision because the world is so corrupt that its destruction is the only possible outcome. The writer appeals to the teachings of the apostles, including Paul's, and exhorts the reader to ready him or herself for the coming apocalypse.

Three Letters Written by John

Although 1 John does not have the usual greeting and closing that is common to all letters at the time, all three of these are actual letters. They were written about the start of the second century by one or more teachers who believed in, and followed, the teachings of the apostle John. Late second century writers, Eusebius and Irenaeus, believed that John himself was the author, but that position has long been abandoned.

The letters were most likely written by the same person as they are very similar in language and in the situation discussed. However, the first letter begins with a reference to "we" which seems to indicate that the author was one of several teachers of the Christian faith on the model of John's gospel. In the second letter the author refers to himself as "the elder" and the letter is directed to the "elect lady" and her children. In the language of the day, "Elect lady" is probably a reference to one or more of John's churches. The difference between "we" and "the elder" indicates to some that the authors may be different people. The third letter also purports to be written by "the elder," but the letter does not refer to the problem with the dissidents that is the subject of the first two letters, so this has led some to suggest that this is not the same "elder." Most scholars, however, believe that the same person wrote all of them.

These letters are very short and without a lot of substance, so they are not often referred to in sermons and some wonder how they ever got into the Bible. The conclusion seems to be that John's followers, who were numerous, needed something in the Bible to support John's position. These letters, written in his name, did just that.

What is unusual about these letters is that, while the Gospel of John relates a truly hostile dispute between Christian and Jewish claims to JESUS, these letters say not a word about it and, in fact, gives us two new targets: pagans and those Christians with a different viewpoint. John's gospel was very hard on Jews and suggests that JESUS' problems all stemmed from the Jewish community. The inflammatory language in the gospel of John has been used throughout history to justify persecution of the Jews. The first two letters completely ignore this position and save all of their venom for pagans and dissident Christians who are threatening those who believe in John's message. They are even referred to as the "antichrist." The first letter does continue the John position that love is from GOD and that everyone who loves is born of GOD and knows GOD; whoever does not love does not know GOD for GOD is love (4:7-12). This is a position only found in John's gospel.

The second letter goes a step further than the first letter and urges the followers to reject the dissident teachers and to deny them any hospitality, for to do otherwise would be to share in their evil work.

The Revelation to John

Finally, there is the book of Revelation. This is not a letter but apocalyptic literature that does not fit into any particular category of Biblical books. Apocalyptic books and teachings had been very popular among the Jews since the beginning of the fourth century B.C.E. Many are found in the Apocrypha such as Baruch, 2 Esdras, and Enoch. In fact, there are over 100 apocalyptic books known today. Why Revelation was chosen over all of the others to include as canon is lost to history. We do know it was far from a unanimous choice; the Apocalypse of Peter was originally the favorite.

Revelation is comprised of a series of interconnected sections that progress to the end of time. It is generally broken down as follows:

Prologue Chapter1:1-3
Salutation as in a letter. 1:4-8

Introductory vision.	1:9-20
Letters to each of the seven churches.	2:1-3:22
Vision of God on throne and JESUS as a lamb	4.1-5.14
Series of Seven visions	
Opening of seven seals	6.1-8.5
Sounding of seven trumpets	8.6-11.19
Woman, child. and dragon	12.1-17
Two beasts.	13.1-18
Victory and vindication of the faithful	14.1-20
Outpouring of bowls of devine wrath	19.1-10
Fall of Babylon	17.1-18.24
Great doxology	19.1-10
Eschatological victory	19.11-21
Defeat of Satan	20.1-10
Last Judgment	20.11-15
Vision of the new Jerusalem	21.1-22.5
Epilogue	22.6-21

Apocalyptic Literature

The primary apocalyptic story in the Old Testament is, of course, Daniel. The theme of all such stories is that GOD will someday come down and destroy all of the evil people and save the good. Revelation goes a step further and prophesies the coming end of time. The word "apocalypse" comes from the Greek *apokalupsis* which means "revelation or "disclosure." It is sometimes translated as "the lifting of the veil." It is an outgrowth of the predictions in earlier literature. Like all such books, they purport to be the writings of someone to whom GOD has imparted some special knowledge. Unlike all other known apocalyptic books, this writing has a name for the author, John.

Apocalyptic literature written just before and just after the turn of the first millennium had many things in common. Revelation is typical in most respects. For example, most apocalyptic works were predated; that is, they were purportedly written at a much earlier time than they were actually written. This allowed the writer to make "predictions" of future events that the writer already knew had occurred. That gave his actual predictions much more credibility. Daniel is a good example of this as the author "predicted" the conquests of Alexander the Great down to the reign of Antiochus and the destruction of his kingdom, all of which had already occurred. He then continued with an equally vivid description of events that had not yet taken place. The readers would look at all of the predictions and say, "Well, he was correct in all of his previous predictions about Alexander, so he must be correct about the apocalypse too." The author of Revelation used the same deception. He "predicted" the persecution by Rome and the destruction of the Temple which had occurred in 70 C.E. before Revelation was written.

The books are all dualistic in nature—it is always good (GOD in this case) against evil which takes many forms in Revelation. The hidden wisdom is always revealed in a vision or a dream (hence the revelation) and the story of the vision is always written in the first person. GOD rarely tells the recipient the hidden wisdom Himself; it is communicated by devine messengers, usually angels, who are purportedly carrying GOD'S message. The story always relates how GOD'S justice will be dispersed in the future and has a very religious purpose—if you are good GOD will save you, but if you are bad GOD will destroy you—and goes on to describe how it will be done.

The revelation is always very mysterious and the story is filled with mystical visions of beasts and other living creatures which often take on the characteristics of men or animals as well as purely imaginary, and usually grotesque and scary, creatures, often with demons and dragons. They also use beings found in the Hebrew Scriptures such as "leviathan," "serpent," and behemoth" and give them new powers and identities. The writings always contain mysterious symbolism such as "the number of the beast," and often reference the Hebrew tradition of numerology such as the number "666" in Revelation.

Not every apocalyptic story has all of these factors, of course, but many do. There is one particular factor present in every apocalyptic story—every writing predicts the eminent end of time, and they are all wrong, evidenced by the fact that I am writing this and you are reading it. None of the predictions give an actual date. They are all contained in some, usually mysterious, formula. Paul was the most straightforward. He told his followers that there were those who heard his words who would be present, a prediction that was, of course, incorrect.

People have to calculate the doomsday date based upon their own interpretations of hints suggested by the apocalyptic writer and everyone waits around for "it" to happen. . . and then it doesn't. Followers of the writer's viewpoint never conclude that the author was incorrect, though; they always decide that it was their own fault—they just did not correctly understand what the writer said so they had calculated the date incorrectly. There is usually some attempt to recalculate. The apocalyptic prediction in Daniel was recalculated by Mark and then recalculated again by Matthew. The last known calculation was by Sir Isaac Newton who predicts it will be 2060. As those of us who remember the dire predictions of Y2K can well attest, recalculations are still being made. No one ever says that the predictions are untrue, just that they had been interpreted incorrectly.

Who Wrote The Revelation to John?

Very early Christian writers, such as Justin Martyr, believed that

Revelation was actually written by the author of the gospel by that name. Not too much time passed before later scholarship challenged this view. Various items mentioned by the writer refer to events that occurred long after the death of John, son of Zebedee. What is known about the actual author is that he knew a lot about the Temple in Jerusalem and all of the Jewish rites that were associated with the Temple, and he had an encyclopedic knowledge of the Old Testament. Of the 404 verses in Revelation, approximately 275 contain or relate to passages in the Hebrew Bible, probably the Septuagint, although most people would not recognize them as such. He also wrote in the manner and style of Jewish writers from the area around Jerusalem.

The author directed his letter to "the seven churches that are in Asia," a reference to seven churches located in the west end of what is now the Turkish peninsula: Ephesus, Smyrna, Pergamum, Thyatira, Sardis, Philadelphia, and Laodicea. He then writes that "I, John, your brother who share with you in JESUS the persecution . . . . " and he exhibits a knowledge of the specific problems each of the churches is experiencing and identifies individuals from them by name. This suggests that the people in those seven churches knew him well.

From his intimate knowledge of the Temple and its rites, his knowledge of the scriptures, his writing style, and the fact that he was well known in the peninsula of Turkey, suggests to the scholars that John was probably a Palestinian Jew who was exiled by the Romans after the First Jewish War against the Romans and later adopted Christian beliefs. He was probably an apostle like Paul, but he makes it clear that he was not one of the original disciples because he refers to "the twelve" and does not include himself as one of them*. The most likely date for the book was sometime toward the end of the reign of the emperor Domitian who ruled between 81 and 96 C.E. and the date most often used is 94 C.E.

Christian life at the time John was sent to prison on the island of Patmos, where he received the visions of which he writes, was a period of incredible, widespread persecution of Christians by the Romans. The persecutions, including John's own imprisonment, were carried out against Christians "because of the word of GOD and the testimony of JESUS," and many were slaughtered. John mentions this in general terms and also refers to one particular martyr, his friend Antipas (2:13).

The mystery and symbolism is certainly a huge part of Revelation as in is in other apocalyptic literature. Jerome, whom you remember as making the first Latin translation of the Bible, commented that "it

---

* Rev 21:14 The fact that he did not include himself in the twelve also lends credence to the conclusion that this was not written by John son of Zebedee.

contains as many mysteries as it contains words." The early Christian writer Origen commented that, "Who can read the revelations granted to John without being amazed at the hidden depth of the ineffable mysteries, a depth apparent even to the person who does understand what the text says?" While Origen suggests that there are actually people who do understand what the text purportedly says, I have yet to locate such a person. In fact, even John himself needed the help of an angel to interpret one vision (17:7).

Interpretations of Revelation Mysteries

It seems every modern evangelist has a different interpretation of what Revelation means. I recall at the time of the tragic fire that consumed most of the Branch Davidian Christian sect in 1993, a national news anchor described the leader of the group, David Koresh, as, "quite the religious scholar... especially regarding his interpretations of the book of Revelation." While I dispute his description as a "scholar," he did interpret Revelation and Koresh's interpretation was that the apocalypse described in Revelation had already started. That is the reason that his followers were holed up in a farmhouse in Texas. He was wrong, of course.

There have been numerous interpretations of the symbolism in Revelation—what "666" stands for and the identity of "the beast" for example—along with almost everything else in the book. A great many of the strange references in Revelation are actually references to portions of the Old Testament writings and from other ancient Near Eastern literature including Greek and Roman. Scholars have struggled with the interpretation problem for centuries. There is virtual consensus about many things, but as to others there is no agreement whatsoever. I will attempt to share with you those interpretations that are grounded in genuine scholarship and that are generally accepted as accurate.

To help guide you in your reading, here are a few guidelines. First of all, remember what was going on at the time. Jerusalem and the Temple were destroyed by the Romans in 70 C.E. John identified this with the earlier destruction of Jerusalem and the original Temple in 587 B.C.E. by the Babylonians and therefore he often refers to Rome as "Babylon." This may have been so that he would not further rile the Romans who might then reconsider whether his vacation on a Mediterranean island was sufficient punishment for his indiscretions.

All cities at the time were feminine, the way we refer to boats today, for example, and the ancient Hebrew prophets often referred to cities variously as "brides," "wives," and even "harlots." John made the same references. Therefore, when you see "the great whore" in Revelation it simply refers to the city of Babylon and, by implication, Rome.

At this time the Roman emperor was considered the devine son of god and often that deification was thrown into the faces of the Jews and Christians and was actually competing with Judaism and Christianity for the religious beliefs of the populace. Therefore, John warns his readers against following "the beast" as he refers to the emperor. There are other meanings given to "the beast," however, such as the "beast of the sea" which refers to four beasts in the book of Daniel, and is also as a reference to the Roman Empire. The beast does *not* refer to the devil. JESUS is depicted as a "Lamb." We'll cover other cryptic references as we discuss the text itself.

But let's deal with the pesky "666 (13:18)" right now. The actual quote is, ". . . let anyone with understanding calculate the number of the beast, for it is the number of a person. Its number is six hundred sixty-six*." Numerology was a huge pastime in the ancient Hebrew culture; sort of a Hebrew Soduku. The Hebrews assigned each letter of the Hebrew alphabet a number. For example, we might do the same for our alphabet by saying that a=1, b=2, . . . Z=26. The "number of a person" means the total of the numbers in that person's name. For example, if a person was named Abba, the number of that person would be 6, the sum of 1+2+2+1. That number gives a clue as to the person's name. This is a purely human activity. People can do this calculation without any devine intervention. Of course there are hundreds of names whose letters could add up to 666 or 616, and even if you do pick the same letters that the writer had in mind, it would not necessarily be the same letters as the name of the person; in could simply be a *clue* that might lead you to that person's identity, not the actual name. Also, the letters would not be in the same order as the name.

This was a game or an exercise among the literate that was quite popular, and there were many solutions offered over the years. The most likely construction that John had in mind was "Neron Caesar," that most famous of Christian persecutors, Nero. In fact, if the number is written 616 as some of the early texts suggest, the second "n" is eliminated and it becomes "Nero Caesar." Most scholars buy this solution to the 666 reference—it refers to Nero, not Satan or any other entity as many twenty-first Century ministers assert. They seem to feel that, since 666 refers to something evil, it must be Satan. Wrong.

Certain numbers have always held a mystical significance in Hebrew religious writings, including their scriptures. The number 40, for instance, shows up repeatedly: 40 days and nights on the ark; JESUS spent 40 days in the wilderness, 40 days wandering in the Sinai desert, etc. Without

---

* Some ancient texts write the number as "six hundred sixteen." This is apparently one of those problems caused by the absence of vowel sounds in the Hebrew alphabet and 666 and 616 are written the same.

getting into the subject too deeply as it is incredibly complex, certain numbers, many of them historically important in Hebrew writings, show up over and over in Revelation. The number seven is used in numerous references. Some are merely because he is writing to seven churches; the seven letters, for example. Most are because of the importance of the number. Seven is a symmetrical number, three up, three down, with one in the middle. You rest on the seventh day, you rest and leave your fields fallow in the seventh year, you free your slaves and forgive debts in seven years, and you redistribute the wealth after the 49th (7x7) year. That 50th year is called the Jubilee Year. There are seven branches in the menorah. . . and the list goes on. In Revelation, in addition to the seven churches, there are seven sealed scrolls from GOD, seven visions, each after opening one of the seven seals, followed by the sound of seven trumpets, seven stars, seven golden lampstands (menorahs), and so on. There are many other numbers that had religious meaning to the ancient Hebrews and many of them are also used in Revelation.

What the Book Says

Revelation starts off quietly with the usual greetings and salutations in chapter 1 that begin nearly all correspondence from those times. Then, in verses 9 through 20 John relates a sort of preview of his future visions while he was "in the spirit," referring to an altered state of consciousness. The vision is of a man, presumably JESUS, who tells John to write down all that he sees and to send it to the seven churches. John begins his work in chapters 2 and 3 by sending a letter to each of the seven churches. These are basically complementary as the churches have all been doing well, but he takes shots at those with whom he disagrees or who are giving the churches a hard time.

Then it starts to get weird. John was in a Roman prison camp, and any seditious writing would be confiscated and the writer punished. So John wrote in a sort of code, referring to the scriptures that the Romans would not understand. I mentioned above that there are at least 275 references to the Hebrew Scriptures in Revelation. Most of those references are hidden, and only those who really know the old Scriptures are able to pick them out. Some of these references sound like the rambling of a lunatic if you do not realize that he is referring to something elsewhere in the Bible. For example, look at this passage:

> *And the four living creatures, each of them with six wings, are full of eyes all around and inside. Day and Night without ceasing they sing,*
> *'Holy, holy, holy,*
> *the Lord God the Almighty,*
> *who was and is to come* (6:8).

This was a reference to Isa 6:2-3. It sounds pretty bizarre until you go back and read what Isaiah said (remember, John was quoting the from memory, so they are not identical):

> *Seraphs were in attendance above him; each had six wings:*
> *with two they covered their faces, and with two they covered their feet,*
> *and with two they flew.*
> *And one called to another and said:*
> *"Holy, holy, holy*
> *is the Lord of hosts;*
> *the whole earth is full of his glory."*

Unfortunately, few of those who are publically stating their interpretations of Revelation have a sufficient knowledge of the old Scriptures to understand this, and that is one of the reasons that there are so many different interpretations. I am in that group. I have studied Isaiah, but I sure did not recall that reference. Therefore, in the following discussion of Revelation I will attempt to remove some of the mystery by showing a little of the strange symbolism that is taken from ancient texts. The references are not only to parts of the Bible. Many of the references are to other ancient works. I have omitted these references because few, if any, of the readers will have access to those books to verify them. Also, the references I make are to just the one or two verses where the actual quote occurs. In order to understand what the ancient quote is all about you might have to read several verses both before and after the cited verses. It will greatly help in understanding this analysis if you follow along in your Bible.

John apparently wrote for a very knowledgeable group of readers. The uncertainty about much of Revelation vanishes when you cross-reference Revelation to the ancient works that he quoted. Most of the quotes refer to quite ordinary and understandable phenomena. They are not all about creatures with six wings. It is only when a person unfamiliar with the other books reads about these strange beings and happenings in Revelation, especially where John only quoted a few of the key words, which presumably his readers would recognize, that the sayings become mystical. For a modern example of what I mean, in a speech, President Bush once referred to the "road to Jericho." Those familiar with the Bible knew instantly that he was referring to the story of the Good Samaritan. Those who were not familiar with the story wondered what the heck Bush was talking about. Much of Revelation is like that—it is easy to understand once you know the keys. Don't get me wrong though; there is still plenty of mystery and magic in Revelation, but understanding the Old Testament references makes it much clearer.

Chapter 4 begins with a vision of an open door which represents the "gate of Heaven" in Jacob's dream of the ladder or stairway used by GOD to do down to earth and visit (*Gen 28:17*). The voice of JESUS invites John to come up into Heaven (Ezek 8:3 and 11:1). The "first voice" refers to the voice of JESUS mentioned in Rev 1:10 et seq. He sees GOD who is personified as precious stones and is sitting on a throne. Around him are 24 elders who are believed to symbolize the 12 tribes of Israel and the 12 apostles. There are seven flaming torches* and four living creatures which are heavenly beings representing mankind and all animals**. They each have six wings and they sing a song in praise of GOD which is the ancient holy, holy, holy song from Isaiah***. In 4:11, John pens a new song for the new era of JESUS in which he refers to JESUS as our "Lord and GOD," terms commonly used to describe the Roman Emperor. He also refers to JESUS in the same terms that Isaiah used to refer to GOD suggesting JESUS' devine status. While all of this language is pretty mysterious, all it means is that John is proclaiming JESUS' status.

Chapter 5 starts with the reference to a "scroll." The scroll contains GOD'S plan of judgment and salvation (Ezek 2:9-10). The scroll had seven seals, meaning that it was not altered by anyone and that nobody else knows its contents*. Then an angel proclaims that nobody in Heaven or earth can open the scroll except the Lion of Judah (from Gen 49:9-10, "Judah is a lions whelp; . . ."), the Root of David,** both of which refer to the messiah.

---

* Zech 4:2-3. "I see a lampstand all of gold, with a bowl on the top of it; there are seven lamps on it, with seven lips on each of the lamps . . . ." The references to the seven torches and golden lampstands (menorahs) is a reference to 49 blessings (7 branches of the menorah times seven menorahs) from Zechariah's fifth vision.

** Ezek 1.5, 10. "In the middle of it was something like four living creatures. This was their appearance: they were of human form. Each had four faces, and each of them had four wings."

*** Isa 6.2-3. This is from a description of GOD'S throne room. With two wings they covered their faces (so as not to see GOD), with two they hid their feet (genitals; the Bible uses many euphemisms for human genitalia; others are thighs, hanging fruits, pomegranates, and mandrakes), and with the other two they flew.

* From Dan 12:4. "But you, Daniel, keep the words secret and the book sealed until the time of the end.

** Isa 11:1, 10. "A shoot shall come out from the stump of Jesse, . . ." Jesse was the father of David according to 1 Sam 16:1-20. There are a lot of overlapping references.

Are you getting the idea? These strange visions are not really so strange when you realize that John is referencing images from the Hebrew Scriptures which he believes, because GOD is now revealing them to him, portend the imminent apocalypse. If you or I were to pick up Revelation and read it without a really, really good background in Old Testament scriptures, we would probably think that John was ready for a "rubber room"; that he had spent too much time alone in the cave. What John is doing is laying the groundwork for the coming apocalypse by showing that all of the scriptural references that could pertain to the coming of a messiah to lead them out of eternal death and the apocalypse that GOD will wreak are here and now. GOD told him so by conveying these images.

The world after its destruction by GOD is described in Ch 21 and 22. It begins with John telling us that he saw a "new Heaven and a new earth." That refers to a portion of Isaiah that is usually referred to as Third Isaiah (Isa 65:17; 66:22) which was written quite a long time after the return from Exile. This is also a reference to Paul's discussion of the new creation (Rom 8:19-21) where the world will be renewed and freed by GOD "that the creation itself will be set free from its bondage to decay and will obtain the freedom of the glory of the children of GOD (Rom 8:21)." The "New Jerusalem" is "coming down out of the heaven" and she is prepared as a bride (Isa 61:10). This is to contrast with the way John describes Rome as the whore Babylon (17-18); that is, Jerusalem = bride and Rome = whore.

Then a loud "voice from the throne" speaks, paraphrasing Ezekiel, that GOD will live with the Israelites*. He will wipe tears from their eyes and death will be no more and pain and sorrow shall go away (Isa 25:8; 35:10). In 25:5 we are finally told that the mysterious voice from the throne was GOD.

GOD then tells John that He is done and that He is the alpha and the omega** and that He is going to give the "water of life***" as a gift. John then says, "Those who conquer will inherit these things, . . ." This refers

---

* Ezek 37:27, "My dwelling place shall be with them; and I will be their God, and they shall be my people."

** Alpha and omega are the first and last letters of the Greek alphabet so GOD is saying that he is the beginning and the end and everything in between. It would be like us saying, "I am the whole thing from A to Z."

*** Isa 55.1. The Water of Life was apparently a common expression at the time because the author of the gospel of John, who wrote after John of Patmos wrote Revelation, also speaks of the waters of life (John 4:14, 7:37).

to the endings of Johns seven letters to the seven churches in Ch 2 and 3. Each refers to "those who conquer" and describes their reward for doing so. All of those who are bad, on the other hand, will suffer the "second death" in the lake that burns with fire and sulphur (21:8).

Then he reprises the seven angels holding seven bowls full of the seven plagues that were the subject of Ch 16 to introduce the bride who is "the wife of the Lamb;" that is, Israel is the bride of GOD (Isa 54:5; Hos 2:19-20). An angel took John to a high mountain (Ezek 4:2) and showed him the city of Jerusalem coming out of Heaven[****].

Next comes a measurement of the new city of Jerusalem. Both the city and its measurements, which are all in multiples of 12, are purely symbolic, referring to the 12 tribes of Israel and the 12 disciples. It had a high wall with 12 gates, three on each of the four sides of the city, inscribed with the names of the 12 tribes, and 12 angels at the gates[*]. This is precisely how Ezekiel described it (Ezek 48:30-34). The wall has 12 foundations and on them are the names of the 12 apostles (Eph 2:20). The city is foursquare, which means that it is constructed of streets laid out on a grid that intersect at right angles. This is just the opposite of the walls of Jerusalem at that time which are curvy and irregular, following the contour of the hill, and they are that way still in the Old City. The layout of the new city forms a perfect cube, a distance of 12,000 stadia on each side and 12,000 stadia high. John lists a series of precious stones that described the stones on the high priest's breastplate (Ex 28; 17-23; Isa 54:11-12).

There was no temple in the city because the new temple is GOD (Isa 24:23; 60:1; 19) and no sun is needed because "the lamp is the Lamb"[**]. The gates will never be closed in the day and there will be no night[***] so the city will always be safe. The only people allowed into the city will be those who are written in the Book of Life, the log in which GOD keeps a list of those person who will be redeemed. (13:8; 17.8; and 20:12,15. See also, Ex 32.:32; ps 69:28. Dan 12:1, Mal 3:16; and Lk 10:20).

[****] Heb 11:10. Note that this differs from Paul's description in Gal 4:25, 26 which recalls Isa 51:2-6, 60, and 62:1-2 and Zech 2:10-12

[*] There are many things in the Old Testament that are in twelves. The Hebrews had a very strong system of numerology that they employed throughout history and carried over into New Testament works

[**] Ps 132.17, the lamp that GOD prepared for the anointed one.

[***] In ancient cities, the gates were always open during the day, except when enemies approach, and closed at night for safety. This is a statement that the city will always be safe. See Isa 60.11 and Zech 14.

Finally, the angel showed John the river of the water of life with trees of life on both sides of the river with their 12 different kinds of fruit, producing fruit each month[****]. By this time we all know the symbolism of the number 12. To see GOD'S face (Ps 10:11; 42:2) means to be fully aware of GOD'S presence, and vice versa. The phrase "on their foreheads" refers back to a statement John (7:3) which is a reference to a seal telling others that someone so marked is under GOD'S protection (Ezek 9:4-6). Finally, GOD will be the light of those who worship him and they will reign forever and ever (Dan 7:18, 27).

Beginning with Ch 22: 6, we have what is generally referred to as the epilogue. In the epilogue, John tells us that all of this will occur "soon."

[****] The "river" refers to the river flowing from Eden. Gen 2:10; Ps 46:4; Ezek 47:1; Zech 14:8.

14

The Gospels

The beginning of the good news of JESUS *Christ, the Son of God*

Mark 1.1

Gospel is from the Saxon word *godspell* for "good tidings." The original Koin Greek word is *euangelion* ("good news) and that is the way that it was originally written in the Bible. Euangelion, when used in religious writings, always refers to either the act of preaching or the content of the sermon. The same word appeared in secular writings also, usually announcing something momentous such as the birth of a child or a military victory. The Latin translation is *Evangelion,* and that is, of course, where our word "evangelist" originates, describing those who spread the good news.

The most common use of the word gospel today is the designation for written accounts of the ministry, death, and resurrection of JESUS. The Bible has four such gospels, Matthew, Mark, Luke, and John, although there are other gospels embedded within each of these works. These four are usually referred to as the canonical Gospels and usually written with a capital "G." The first of the four Gospels to be written was that of Mark, although it follows Matthew in the Bible. There were other gospels that predated Mark, however.

As JESUS' audience was predominantly comprised of peasants, few people who heard him speak could write, so people began verbally telling others the words that JESUS spoke. This oral history continued for many years. At some point, people who were literate heard the stories and began writing down the memorable words of JESUS that they heard from others. Occasionally they may have heard the words directly from people who saw and heard JESUS speak, but more often they were getting the words second or third hand, or more. These writings became little private collections of JESUS' sayings. Some of these books still exist and are generally referred to as "sayings Gospels." The Gospel Q was a sayings Gospel as was the Gospel of Thomas.

The four canonical Gospels differ from the sayings gospels in that they not only contain the sayings of JESUS, they also contain a narration of some of the things that JESUS did. These are called, for obvious reasons, "narration gospels." Unlike the sayings gospels, we presently know of no other narration gospels than the four contained in the Bible.

There were many gospels written in the first century. We have fragments from about 20 of them and know of the existence of more than 40. There were undoubtedly many more that have no remaining record. A few of the other gospels in which we have all or portions today are the Egerton Gospel, Gospel of the Ebionites, Gospel of the Hebrews, Gospel of the Nazoreans, Gospel of Thomas, Gospel Oxyrhynchus 840, Gospel Oxyrhynchus 1224, Secret James, and the recently discovered Gospel of Judas.

Most people recognize that there are many different versions of Christianity today. Some are quite different from the others. But if you were to ask the average person in the pew what Christianity was like 2000 years ago, they would likely tell you everyone was pretty unified in their beliefs—there was just "The Church." Just the opposite was true. There were numerous factions, many of which are barely recognizable today as being Christian. In fact, few of the early versions of Christianity even believed in JESUS' divinity. It was a very long time before anyone recognize him as a god. Even his disciples usually called him *Rebbe* which means, simply, "teacher."

As Paul wrote in his letter to the Corinthians, some Christians call themselves "Pauls," some are "Apollos," some "follow Cephas," and some are called "Christs (1 Cor 1:12)." That is four different sects within 20 years of JESUS' death *in just one city*. The First Letter of John refers to some JESUS followers in his town who consider themselves Christians but were, according to John, "antichrists (1 Jn 4:2)."

Basically, there were two widely different philosophies, each of which had numerous subsets. The first was the group that believed JESUS was a teacher of wisdom as we have defined wisdom in earlier chapters. Those followers believed that JESUS came to tell us how to live and how to know our true nature. We find the writings of this group in such works as the Gospel of Thomas. They are the "Gnostics." The second group are those who saw JESUS as a god, or at least a close associate of GOD, dying for our sins and who rose again so that we may all, in turn, be resurrected on the last day. This is the theology of Paul as we have seen. Ultimately, Paul's ideas won out, but that was no sure thing at the time the Gospels were written. Both groups were equally strong.

That was a problem for the writers of the Gospels. They did not want to back the wrong side. Many gospel authors did just that, and their writings are lost forever. The Gospel of Thomas was lost until the 1945 discovery of Gnostic writings at Nag Hammadi that had been buried for subsequent generations to find. The Gospel of Q was lost until scholars discovered portions of it embedded in Matthew and Luke. Neither Thomas nor Q contain a story of the death, resurrection, or appearance of JESUS, only his teachings. While Q does have some early apocalyptic language, the primary message is the wisdom teachings of JESUS.

When I refer to "wisdom teachings" of JESUS, you need to refer back to the chapter on wisdom works in the Jewish scriptures and the books of Proverbs, Lamentations, Ecclesiastes, and the others discussed in the Old Testament portion of this book. It is a much deeper concept than simply wise teachings and is very spiritual. We are talking about a Wisdom tradition handed down over centuries. The Gnostic works, including Q and Thomas, are collections of the sayings of a wise teacher, JESUS. This is his "sapiential" message as opposed to the apocalyptic message we find in much of Paul's writings.

The four canonical Gospels that contain those sapiential stories also include the teachings of Paul and his followers. So the four authors of the canonical Gospels tried to tell the "good news" by combining both concepts into a single work. Mark contains very little of the Gnostic tradition. Matthew and Luke drew quite heavily on Q, and John drew on Thomas, so those three Gospels contained considerable more sapiential messages. Although there are only five verses from Thomas that have parallels in John, his entire gospel tends to be somewhat sapiential and was highly regarded by the early Gnostic communities.

Recent research has now discovered that the stories of JESUS' birth in Matthew and Luke, along with all of the resurrection stories in all four Gospels, were added at a later time. The birth stories add nothing to JESUS' message, so it is understandable that they were an afterthought. However, the resurrection stories are very important to the fundamentals of Christianity.

Mark

In spite of the fact that the original manuscript or one of the very earliest copies of Mark was lodged in Alexandria, it is believed that the author wrote the book either in the north of Palestine, above the Galilee, in what was then southern Syria, about 40 years after the death of JESUS. There appeared to be a community in that area who followed the beliefs set forth in the book of Mark. It appears that they were a community of Gentile Christians that were persecuted or harassed by the Jews of the local synagogue, and Mark takes some pretty tough shots at the priests and pharisees.

Mark's narration is a series of escalating conflicts. The principal conflict is JESUS' problems with the high priest/rulers and their Roman overlords. The conflicts begin when his preaching irritates the priesthood and ultimately results in his death. A good portion of this, the shortest of the four Gospels, are the stories about JESUS actions and his disputes with the scribes and Pharisees.

Throughout the book, JESUS is shown preaching the Kingdom of GOD as a new phase in the Hebrew religion, but not as a new religion. Mark frequently compares JESUS to Moses and the great prophets. JESUS is portrayed as the son of GOD, not as a god himself. This is the first known writing where JESUS was portrayed as the son of GOD (but see the sidebar).

There are some very serious problems with Mark's gospel that have troubled New Testament scholars for centuries. Some aspects are so unlikely and improbable that it does not seem possible to reconcile them with what is established knowledge about the history of the time and place. For example, according to Mark:

- JESUS' trial was held at night. That was not only unlikely, it was

SON OF GOD

The word "son" in the Old Testament was not only a reference to family, it referred to any close relationship. The term "son of . . ." was a very common description. A hero, for example, might be called a "son of strength." The phrase "Son of God" must be carefully evaluated depending upon how it is used. In the Old Testament, there was a Hebrew designation occasionally used, Benei Elohim, which was sometimes translated as "sons of God." Sometimes the ancient Israelites were called "son of God" using the singular form of son. However it was generally used in reference to persons or entities that were very close to GOD such as angels and the like, and later to certain people of power such as the judges. Then it became the traditional designation for King David and the Israelite kings that followed him. (2 Sam 7:14; Ps 2:7; 89:26-28).

Then came the Romans. Julius Caesar was deified after his death, and his son, Augustus, who became emperor, assumed the divine designation of divi filius, which meant "son of the Divine One." He did not, however, use the title deus filius or die filius which means "son of God." In Greek, the designation was huios theou which can mean either. Augustus also assumed the titles of "Divine," "God," "Lord," "Redeemer," "Savior of the World," and others. All of these titles were then given to JESUS by his followers. JESUS is referred to in the New Testament as huios theou (sons of God) three times, but he is called numerous times ho huios tou theou which means "the son of God." Huios theou refers to many people and to groups of people in the New Testament, but only one person is called ho huios tou theou, and that is JESUS. However, that does not imply that the term was used to describe his filiation as GOD'S actual son.

illegal.

- The witnesses against JESUS did not agree. Under Roman law, that would require the Roman equivalent of a mistrial. While Pilate was certainly capable of executing someone without a trial, an event that was apparently all too common, he would never have done so after a trial where the witnesses could not agree. Remember, Pontius Pilate's court records were complete and exist to this day. They are detailed and clear. As to the question that you probably have right now, the answer is no, there is no entry that could have been what is described in the book of Mark about JESUS, no matter what name was used for the defendant.

- The charge of blasphemy is uncertain and ambiguous at best. It is a religious transgression and does not make much sense in Roman law.
- The Sanhedrin, the term for a meeting of Jewish leaders, at this time no longer had the power to charge someone with death, nor would they have been so audacious as to suggest it to the Roman governor.
- Mark's version of the crucifixion took place on Passover. This would have been a blasphemy that would have outraged the citizenry just at the time that Pilate was doing everything that he could to keep the pilgrimage peaceful.
- Why did Pilate convict him for being the "king of the Jews?" There was not a whit of evidence presented at JESUS' trial, as described by Mark, to suggest that he was anything remotely resembling or hoping to become the king of the Jews.
- The high priests, apparently all of them, joined the crowd in mocking JESUS, something that they would never have done even if they believed everything that was said was true. That is conduct that would have been highly uncharacteristic of the priesthood.

That is only the beginning of the questions that the scholars have raised. A twenty-first century reader, especially one who has been raised from birth to believe that every word in the Bible is true and correct, might say, "So what? So there are a few questions." However, to historians familiar with the era, these events simply could not have happened. These are not minor discrepancies, but are major problems in the text.

There are other problems with Mark. He was not nearly as familiar with the Jewish scriptures as either Matthew or Luke, and certainly not as learned as Paul. He also believed that the society of JESUS' true followers was a private, secret society which contained many secrets that must be kept from the general public. These two items, his penchant for secrecy and his lack of scriptural knowledge, caused no end of frustration to Matthew and Luke who had to "clean up" Mark's act. They did this, for the most part, by just quietly, and without comment, making the changes in the text of their own books.

One example of this is Mark's understanding of why JESUS often spoke in parables. Mark thought that the purpose was to conceal the real meaning from the rabble:

> *To you [the Disciples] has been given the secret of the Kingdom of God, but for those outside, everything comes in parables; in order that*
> *"they may indeed look, but not perceive,*
> *and may indeed listen, but not understand;*
> *so that they may not turn again and be forgiven."* (4:11-12)

In Mark's view, the disciples were something of a secret society; a privileged cult to which others should not gain access to the cult's secret information. That is not to imply that there were no secrets in the religion—there were. In fact there were complete subjects that were reserved for the priesthood and other knowledgeable insiders. However, that was never something that was part of JESUS' ministry; that was solely the work of the early church leaders.

The internal quote in Mark's statement above, ". . . they may indeed look, etc." was from JESUS, but he was quoting Isaiah (Isa 6:9-10). Matthew knew that Mark did not understand that JESUS was just quoting Isaiah (Mt 15) and that JESUS' use of parables had nothing to do with secrecy. So he had to tidy up the misconception. Matthew clears it up when he has JESUS respond to the question from his disciples about why he speaks in parables:

> *To you it has been given to know the secrets of the Kingdom of Heaven; but to [those others] it has not been granted. . . That is why I speak to them in parables; for they look without seeing and listen without hearing or understanding. For those who have, more will be given, and they will have an abundance; but from those who have nothing, even what they have will be taken away. The reason I speak to them in parables is that "seeing they do not perceive, and hearing they do not listen, nor do they understand."* (Mt 13:10-14)

What JESUS was attempting to communicate to his disciples by using the parables was, as Isaiah suggested, to *clarify* His message, not hide it. That is likely the reason that Matthew quoted the entire passage from Isaiah in the next verse, a passage that Mark apparently did not know. JESUS wanted to make sure that those who are not granted the power of understanding may yet understand.

This story also illustrates another point—Mark was a tad weak in his grasp of the Hebrew Scriptures. Matthew and Luke frequently had to correct him, but neither ever mentions the corrections. Scholars are almost certain that both Matthew and Luke intended their gospels to replace Mark's, so they did not expect Mark's gospel to be around for others to compare, so there was no reason to make Mark look foolish.

When the Pharisees complained that JESUS' disciples were picking grain on the Sabbath, Mark has JESUS say,

> *Have you not read what David did when he and his men were hungry and had nothing to eat? He went into the House of God, in the time of Abiathar the High Priest, and ate the sacred bread* (2:25-26).

The problem here is a minor scriptural defect. Abiathar was not the High Priest at the time. It was actually his father, Ahimelech (Sam 21:1-6). Matthew just quietly made the correction. Of course, we do not know what JESUS actually said, but Matthew has JESUS use the name of the actual High Priest at the time.

In another example, Mark has JESUS misquoting the Ten Commandments by adding in a wholly new commandment. Mark also has JESUS deny that he is "good." Both of these items apparently offended Matthew. In Mark's version,

> *Why do you call me good? No one is good except GOD alone. You know the commandments: "Do not murder; Do not commit adultery; do not steal; do not give false evidence;* do not defraud; *honor your father and mother* (10:17-19).

In Matthew's version (19:16-19), both the statement that JESUS is not good and the new commandment not to defraud are merely dropped from the quotation. To Matthew, JESUS was the very definition of good. As to the commandment not to defraud, he knew that there was no such commandment and simply left it out.

Matthew

Matthew was writing for an entirely different audience than Mark. Matthew's group was Jewish Christians where Mark was writing for gentiles. Jewish Christians were already familiar with the Hebrew Scriptures and the Law and did not need to be reminded of what they said. Also, where Mark was straight-foreword and factual in his account, Matthew was flamboyant. He added to and embellished almost every verse of Mark and added mystery and magic. It is really interesting to compare verse by verse the words of Mark and the later words of Matthew. He embellished Mark and added much of the magic, mysticism, and mystery found in the New Testament.

Matthew had an overwhelming fascination with Hell, gnashing of teeth, weeping and wailing, burning pits, and eternal punishment. If you were to delete Matthew from the Bible, a huge portion of the Hell and damnation language would cease to exist. As Bishop Spong noted, Matthew did not invent Hell, but he sure brought it to our attention.

Some examples of the way Matthew changed Mark are, where Mark told us only that "*the veil of the temple was torn in two, from top to bottom*" (15:38), Matthew added,

> *The earth shook, and the rocks were split; the tombs also were opened, and many bodies of the saints who had fallen asleep [died] were raised, and coming out of the tombs after his resurrection they went into the holy city and appeared to many* (27:51)."

You can't get much more graphic than that unless he were to describe the physical appearance of those resurrected bodies.

Another example of his penchant for embellishing Mark and adding supernatural forces is in the story of the resurrection. Matthew added an earthquake and a descending "angel of the Lord" to explain how the tomb was opened (28:2). The supernatural aspects of the angel were enhanced by such words as "*his appearance was like lightning and his raiment white as snow.*" In almost every verse, Matthew embellished Mark and, whenever possible, added some supernatural force into the equation.

Throughout the book, Matthew emphasizes JESUS' Jewish origin and that of his followers as well. JESUS is portrayed as a new Moses, and the author inserts many parallels between JESUS and Moses. This would mean nothing to Mark's audience of gentiles, but Matthew's Jewish Christians would instantly identify with it. Matthew often differs from Mark in basic underlying philosophy. Their views on divorce are a typical example. Mark says,

> *Whoever divorces his wife and marries another commits adultery against her and if she divorces her husband and marries another, she commits adultery.* (10:11-12)

Matthew has a different view; When the Pharisees ask JESUS to comment on why Moses commanded a man to give a certificate of dismissal and to divorce his wife. Matthew's JESUS responded,

> *It was because you were so hard-hearted that Moses allowed you to divorce your wives, but from the beginning it was not so. And I say to you, whoever divorces his wife, except for unchastity, and marries another commits adultery.* (19:9)

Matthew has JESUS granting an exception not allowed by Mark, unchastity. However, this is not the first time Matthew discusses divorce. These comments also differ greatly from Mark's version:

> *It was also said, "whoever divorces his wife, let him give her a certificate of divorce," But I say to you that anyone who divorces his wife, except on the ground of unchastity, causes her to commit adultery; and whoever marries a divorced woman commits adultery.* (5:31-32).

According to Matthew, then, if a man divorces a woman it is the woman who commits adultery. Further, a man cannot marry a woman who was previously divorced because that is adultery. Note that the Greek word for "unchastity" refers to both adultery and marriages between close kin.

While we are at it, let's see what Luke has JESUS say about this:

> *Anyone who divorces his wife and marries another commits adultery, and whoever marries a woman divorced from her husband commits adultery.*

Luke sort of combines portions of Matthew and Mark. It should be noted, however, that many scholars who study early New Testament society believe that both Mark and Luke were only describing a situation when a man, or in the case of Luke, a woman as well, divorces his or her spouse in order to marry another. That is, if a man or woman divorce, it is permissible to later remarry someone else as long as the reason for the divorce was not to get rid of the spouse in order to marry another.

Matthew was written at a time of extreme turmoil in Judea. There had been a tragic famine in the 40s. The Romans destroyed the temple in 70 C.E., after the Jewish revolt, and there was systematic destruction of both the Jews and Jewish society. Further, there were huge divisions within the Jewish community itself. Traditional Judaism with the priesthood was being replaced by rabbinic Judaism. Some Jews formed cult-like communities and lived like monks such as the Essene at Qumran. There were also the Zealots and the Sicarri who were activists against Rome—forerunners of today's terrorists. Further, more and more gentiles (pagans) were becoming followers of JESUS. Matthew wrote on how to handle these internal conflicts with opposing groups (17:15-21; 23:1-3) and he set forth rules of ethics to follow (Ch 5-7). This was definitely a book written for an audience of Jewish Christians.

Matthew's book was also modified from the original. One of the most beautiful and poignant passages in the Bible is that portion of the Sermon on the Mount about the Lilies of the Field (6:28). Let me quote the familiar King James Version to show you what I mean.

Consider the lilies of the field, how they grow;
they toil not, neither do they spin.
And yet I say onto you, that even Solomon in all his glory is not
arrayed like one of these.

I can picture JESUS, having just finished his sermon on the mount, sitting in a field of wild flowers, holding one of them up, and telling that story to his followers. What a graphic picture he presents! What a powerful statement he makes in so few words! What a beautiful message, that even the most inconsequential of GOD's creations, this simple wildflower, has more beauty than what man can create with all of his power and riches.

But Matthew did not write those words. They appear on all of the surviving Greek texts from which this passage was translated. But they do not correctly translate the original. The two oldest Bibles in existence, which date from the fourth century, are the Codex Vaticanus which is the property of the Vatican and the Codex Sinaiticus. In 1938 the British Museum made the purchase of a lifetime. It bought the Codex Sinaiticus which was the property of Russia; Stalin was glad to get rid of what he considered to be junk and to turn a tidy profit while he was at it.

The British scholar T. C. Skeat was examining the text under an ultra-violet light when he noticed something remarkable. He discovered that the opening clause of the "Lilies" verse had been erased from the manuscript and replaced with the Greek version of the verse I quoted above. The original said, "*Consider the lilies of the field: they neither card nor spin.*" The rest was the same. The author of Matthew said nothing about "growing" or "toiling." (Actually, the word for "lilies" really referred to a flower called Sternbergia and is not a lily at all). The verse just does not flow in the original version. Clearly the original version was not nearly as poetic as its Greek replacement.

So the text was edited. So what? The edited version really is much better. We have no way of knowing which version, if either, truly reflects the actual words of JESUS, or even whether he spoke about this subject at all. Both are certainly consistent with the message that JESUS was trying to get across, so either version is something that he could well have said.

It doesn't really matter. What is important is that it is a faithful recollection of what his followers believed that JESUS said. Is it any less valid because it might not be His precise words? I think not. It remains the recollection of JESUS' message by those very early Christians who lived within one or two generations. This was an important part of his philosophy and made such an impression on them that they wrote it down for posterity. Personally, I find the poetic version much more consistent with JESUS' mastery of language.

Luke

The author of Luke did not add the flamboyant language and the magic and mystery to Mark's text like Matthew did, but his Greek was magnificent. In fact, he was Greek and it was his first language. He very often "tidied up" Mark's grammar. I do not read Greek, let alone ancient Greek, but those scholars who do remark on the beauty of Luke's use of the language. It also translates very well into English. Luke is a very "good read." It does not have the beauty of John's prose, but it is written in such a way that one wants to read further.

Examples of Luke's changes to the Mark version are where Mark wrote, "*everything she had her whole living* (12:44)." Luke, with his classical Greek education had to have been appalled. He rewrote this passage in his Gospel to read, "*all the living that she had.*" Mark wrote, "*and a great multitude from Galilee followed; also from Judea and Jerusalem and Idumea and from beyond the Jordan and from about Tyre and Sidon* (3:7-8)." This awkward phrase apparently "got to" Luke and he was compelled to change it to read, "*[A]nd a great multitude of people from all Judea and Jerusalem and the seacoast of Tyre and Sidon who came to hear him* (6:17)." These horrible sentences by Mark are typical of translations by someone who does not have a really good grasp of one of the languages. There are major structural differences between Aramaic, in which JESUS spoke and Mark wrote, and the Greek into which he translated his Aramaic.

I have already referred to the opening lines of Luke, but it is time to look at them more closely. Here are the first four verses:

> *Since many have undertaken to set down an orderly account of the events that have been fulfilled among us, just as they were handed on to us by those who from the beginning were eyewitnesses and servants of the word, I too decided, after investigating everything carefully from the very first, to write an orderly account for you, most excellent Theophilus, so that you may know the truth concerning the things about which you have been instructed.*

This book, as was the sequel, *The Acts of the Apostles*, was directed to "Theophilus," who may have been either be a real person, suggested by the address "most excellent" which generally indicted someone of high status, or the name more likely may have referred to a group of Christians as *Theophilus* is a Greek word meaning "friends of GOD." It would be like a newsletter sent to the L.A. Philharmonic (*Phil* "lovers" and *harmonic* "music"), for example. It is the rest of the statement, however, that is so striking.

Luke says that "many" have written similar stories "of the events" he is passing on. To date, only the four Canonical gospels meet the description of recording "events," and one of them, John, was written after Luke's gospel and scholars agree that Luke never saw Matthew's gospel. All of the other gospels known today, and there are about 40 of them, are sayings gospels which record only what JESUS purportedly *said*, not what he *did*. That means that there were once many other narrative gospels, that were accounts of what JESUS did, that may well differ from the four in the Bible. Luke wrote that these other gospels recorded what was orally told to those writers—that is, none were first-hand accounts. They were what we call hearsay. In addition to the oral information he received, Luke apparently scoured these unknown writings as well as Mark's gospel in writing Luke and Acts. What we have in the Gospels, then, is hearsay based on other hearsay.

Luke tells us the purpose of this writing was so that Theophilus would know the truth concerning the "matters on which he had been instructed." Theophilus, whoever or whatever he was, apparently had been schooled in the story of JESUS and that Luke's gospel would be a written version of what Theophilus learned. Luke indicates that only those that were written ("set down") were narrative gospels and that all of their prior knowledge was oral. Luke was incorrect that they were passed on by eyewitnesses, though. We know for a fact that neither Mark nor Q were eye witnesses and that is where nearly all of Luke's narrative works came from except for the resurrection and appearance stories. In other words, everything Luke tells us was pure hearsay. In the United States legal system hearsay testimony is not allowed because it is deemed to be inherently unreliable. Further, Luke indicates that he is *interpreting* numerous documents and oral transmissions and stitching them together so that Theophilus can "know the truth." In short, Luke was interpreting what people told him and what others wrote and stitching everything into a story. If you ever entertained the idea that the four Gospels are actual history, you now know for sure, by Luke's own words, that they are not.

For someone interested in writing, Luke is the most fun to read of all the books in the Bible. Whatever else he (or she) might be, Luke is nothing less than a master story teller. Many later events grow out of earlier portions of the story. That is, he provides "teasers" of things to come later. Like Matthew, Luke gives us a birth story, but he uses it as an introduction to John the Baptist who becomes part of the story and whose presence in turn leads to yet another later story. Everything is tied together like a good novel. Those scholars who read Greek, which is nearly all of them, report that Luke also flows freely between different writing styles depending upon the subject matter and the audience that Luke has JESUS trying to reach.

The birth and birthplace of JESUS was important to many of his followers. Much of the messianic literature predicted that the new messiah would be a descendent of David and, like David, would destroy their enemies and lead them to new heights of glory. David's birthplace was, of course, Bethlehem. One of those early prophets was Micah of the Old Testament (Ch 5:2) who stated that the Messiah would come from Bethlehem. Therefore, both Matthew and Luke had to find a way to have JESUS born in Bethlehem in order to fulfill the prophecy.

Most of our knowledge of JESUS' birth comes to us in Luke's Gospel. Matthew's version is much shorter and has often been combined with Luke's version. Every Nativity scene that I have ever seen has the three wise men from Matthew's version standing next to Luke's shepherds at the manger. However, only Luke has shepherds and a manger and only Matthew has the three magi. The birth story written by Matthew is irreconcilable with that of Luke. Matthew has JESUS born in a house where Mary and Joseph already reside. Only Matthew has a wandering star that leads the magi to JESUS. Only Matthew has King Herod ordering the death of all of the Jewish infants requiring Joseph and Mary to take their newborn baby to Egypt to await Herod's death, reminiscent of the story of Moses. Only after Herod dies does the family move to Nazareth.

Luke, on the other hand, has Mary and Joseph traveling from their home in Nazareth to Bethlehem because of a tax registration, an event which did not exist in Roman history. Only Luke has the manger and the shepherds with angels telling them to go to Bethlehem to find the messiah. After the birth according to Luke, everything is normal for a Jewish baby*. He is taken to the *mohel* on the eighth day, as prescribed in Jewish Law, where he is circumcised. There is no rush. Eventually they get back to Nazareth, but we are not told when. Both Matthew and Luke give us a genealogy of JESUS in order to connect him to David, but the two genealogies very different (Mt 1:1-17; Lk 3:23-38). In fact, there are very few common ancestors listed.

John did not even try to place JESUS' birth in Bethlehem. He plainly admits that the prophesy was incorrect when he has the people question JESUS' bonafides,

> *Surely the Messiah does not come from Galilee, does he? Has not the scripture said that the Messiah is descended from David*

---

* Luke 2:3-4. The story does not make a lot of sense. Each person was to go to their own towns to be registered, but Joseph and Mary had to go to Bethlehem because he was descended from David. Having to travel to the birthplace of an ancestor who had been dead for 1000 years to register when everyone else merely registered in their own town is nonsense. Both Matthew and Luke created genealogies showing how JESUS descended from David and both found a way to have JESUS born in David's birthplace, Matthew by having Joseph and Mary living there and Luke having them travel there for a tax registration.

> *and comes from Bethlehem, the village where David lived?* (7:41-42).

Paul, writing many years before either Matthew or Luke, says nothing about JESUS' birthplace but he makes it very clear that it was a normal birth. JESUS was "*born of a woman, born under the law, . . .*" (Gal 4:4-5). These were the first written words preserved describing the birth of JESUS. They were written by Paul between 49 and 55 C.E., about 19 to 25 years after JESUS died. This was half a century before the Gospel of Matthew was written. Using the general rule that writings closest in time to the occurrence are likely the most reliable source, it follows that there was no virgin birth or supernatural parenting. According to Paul, JESUS was born of a woman, completely normal and completely human.

Paul made one other reference to JESUS' birth (Rom 1:3-4):

> *[T]he gospel concerning his Son who was descended from David according to the flesh and designated son of GOD in power according to the Spirit of holiness by his resurrection from the dead.*

There is nothing unusual about his birth according to Paul. He descended from David *according to the flesh*, and was designated son of GOD which was the common designation of a Hebrew king, not a human issue from GOD. The phrase "in power" also suggests that Paul was describing a king-like person. Nothing supernatural at all.

Matthew mistakenly gave us a virgin birth. It was an easy mistake for Matthew to make. In nearly every other Middle Eastern religion a leading god was born of a virgin and many secular heros such as Hercules were the sons of Gods. Even the flesh and blood Alexander the Great was considered to be the son of god but born of a woman.

Christians look at the Egyptian God Horus who was born of the virgin Isis and have no problem saying that her virgin birth is a myth. They have no problem labeling the virgin births of Mithra, Zoroaster (Zarathustra), Krishna, Adonis (son of Ishtar), Atthis, and Buddha, as myths. But they cannot bring themselves to believe that the virgin birth described in the Bible did not occur.

It really does not matter. What is important is what JESUS said and did. What is important is what happened on that first Easter when he communicated with his followers. His birth was simply not very important to the early Christians. In all of the writings of Paul there are only those two very short references to his birth. Paul did not care about JESUS' origins and neither, apparently, did the other early Christians.

It was like the old Lone Ranger radio shows that I listened to as a youth. The Lone Ranger drifted into town, wearing a mask, yet, fought the "bad guys," and saved the town and no one cared who he was. It was only at the end of every show, after he and his Indian companion Tonto rode off into the sunset, that someone finally asked, "Who was that masked man anyway?" It was the same with the early Christians. It was only later, long after JESUS' death, that people started asking, "Who was this man, this son of GOD. Where did he come from?" That was when they tried to reconstruct his origins.

We did the same thing with our myths about George Washington chopping down the cherry tree and throwing the silver dollar across the Potomac. When I was in elementary school, we were told that those events actually happened. It was only recently that they have been revealed as myth.

I mentioned above that Luke, with his beautiful classical Greek and his far superior knowledge of the Hebrew Scriptures, "cleaned up" Mark's account of JESUS' gospel. He wasted no time writing a birth story starting with JESUS' baptism in Chapter 1. Mark described a disembodied voice coming "*from the heavens, 'You are my Son, the Beloved*; . . ." and a few more lines of rather convoluted text which is a combination of Old Testament sayings, primarily from Isaiah 40:3, but including some of Malachi 3:1 and Exodus 23:20 mixed in. It was as if Mark knew parts of the scriptures and just linked phrases that seemed to go together. Luke changed this so that the voice shouting from the heavens was no longer from something unknown but was the angel Gabriel speaking and Luke skipped the strange Malachi and Exodus references and merely quoted the correct verse from Isaiah 40:3 (Lk 2:26).

Another example of Luke changing Mark is when Mark seemed to miss the point that JESUS was trying to make. According to Mark JESUS told this story about a lamp:

> *Is a lamp brought in to be put under the bushel basket, or under the bed, and not on the lampstand? For there is nothing hidden, except to be disclosed; nor is anything secret, except to come to light.* (4:21)

This did not make sense to Luke (nor to me for that matter), so JESUS said this in Luke's version:

> *No one after lighting a lamp hides it under a jar, or puts it under a bed, but puts it on a Lampstand, so that those who enter may see the light. For nothing is hidden that will not be disclosed, nor is anything secret that will not become known and come to light.* (8:16). Luke later repeats the story to make another point. (11:53)

Instead of JESUS posing a question that he does not really answer, and forgetting that the lamp had to be lit for this parable to make any sense, Luke makes the whole story clear and, in the process, is more grammatically correct.

Luke did a lot more than spruce up Mark. He also added some entirely new material to the Gospel of JESUS that neither of his predecessors included. Remember in Chapter 12 when we discussed Matthew adding materials from an unknown author referred to as M and Luke by an author referred to as L? I am referring here to the materials Luke added from L. Incidentally, scholars suspect that L may very well be more than one person, but so far nobody has been able to convincingly identify more than one writer. Here are some of the great contributions from L: (parables)The Good Samaritan (10:30), Prodigal Son (15:11-32), Shrewd Manager (16:1-8), Lost Coin (15:8-9); Corrupt Judge (18:2-5); (proverbs and other sayings) Aged Wine (5:39), Friend at Midnight (11:5-8), Satan's Fall (10:18), and Barren Tree (13:6-9). And don't forget this marvelous story of the Pharisee & the Toll Collector (18:10-14):

> *Two men went up to the temple to pray, one a Pharisee and the other a tax collector. The Pharisee, standing by himself, was praying thus, "GOD, I thank you that I am not like other people: thieves, rogues, adulterers, or even like this tax collector. I fast twice a week; I give a tenth of all my income." But the tax collector, standing far off, would not even look up to Heaven, but was beating his breast and saying, "GOD, be merciful to me, a sinner!"*

At this point, JESUS' audience probably admired the Pharisee who devoted himself to learning and teaching the scriptures, and who followed all of GOD'S laws, did everything right and was entitled to GOD'S favor. Tax collectors were notorious for their corruption because they always extracted more in payments than Rome demanded and kept the overpayments for themselves. He even admitted that he was a sinner. But JESUS, as was his wont, then gave his audience the "kicker," when it was the tax collector who was blessed:

> *I tell you, this man went down to his home justified rather than the other;*
>
> *for all who exalt themselves will be humbled,*
> *but all who humble themselves will be exalted.*

This is so typical of the genius of JESUS teachings. Who could not remember this lesson with its unexpected punch line written in a rememberable couplet. Everyone was behind the Pharisee who seemed to be doing everything right, but he did so in order to impress GOD and receive His favors. The toll collector, on the other hand, recognized his shortcomings and honestly humbled himself before GOD asking for forgiveness and it was he who found GOD's favor. Again, JESUS set his audience up like a fisherman with a lure, and then set the hook with the surprise ending. That is how a great teacher, such as JESUS, teaches and how a great writer, such as Luke, writes.

Luke also looked to the Hebrew Scriptures for a great deal of his material, but he did not use the original Hebrew, he used the Septuagint. Luke, even more than Matthew, seemed to be driven to show that prophecies in the Old Testament were fulfilled by JESUS. Luke repeatedly uses the phrase "the fulfillment of all that is written." The wording changes with the translations, sometimes it is worded, "having been fulfilled." Whatever the actual wording, it is always a past tense, passive voice indicating that some prophecy in the Hebrew Scriptures has been fulfilled. The scholars have coined the phrase "divine passive" to describe this phrase. The Greek word for the phrase, as used in the Septuagint, is the impossible to pronounce *peplērophorēmenōn* which literally means "having been fulfilled."

It was very important to Luke, both in this book and its sequel, Acts, that the ancient prophecies be fulfilled by JESUS. In chapter 24 there is the incident in the village of Emmaus in which JESUS tells the people that he fulfilled the prophecies of everyone from "Moses to all of the prophets." Moses was then thought to be the author of the Torah and, together with the books contained in The Prophets, constituted much of the rest of the Hebrew Canon. To Luke, JESUS was the fulfilment of all of the prophecies from the Exodus to the present which was the end of the first century.

The Synoptic Gospels

Before I get to the gospel of John, I need to say a few words about the previous three Gospels. They are collectively called the "synoptic" gospels. *Synoptic* is a Greek word that means "same eye," or "one eye, (*syn-optic*). That is because all three of these gospels are basically the same. The gospel of John, on the other hand, is hugely different.

Why are three of the gospels called synoptic and the fourth something else? Because, as we have seen, the authors of Matthew and Luke "cribbed" Mark. Matthew used nearly all of Mark and Luke used well over half. They changed Mark, cleaned up his clumsy lower class, conversational Koine Greek, and added their own ideas, but they both used his gospel as the starting point for their own works. This is not apparent when you read the Gospels the way they are assembled in the Bible, one after the other, but if you put the common or parallel verses side by side it is obvious. For example, compare the famous mustard seed statements in the three Gospels where JESUS is trying to explain the

Kingdom of GOD to his disciples by comparing the kingdom to a mustard seed:

Mark 4:30 - 32:
He also said, "*With what can we compare the Kingdom of God, or what parable will we use for it? It is like a mustard seed, which, when sown upon the ground, is the smallest of all the seeds on earth; yet when it is sown it grows up and becomes the greatest of all shrubs, and puts forth large branches, so that the birds of the air can make nests in its shade.*"

Matthew 13:31-32:
He put before them another parable: "*The Kingdom of Heaven is like a mustard seed that someone took and sowed in his field; it is the smallest of all the seeds, but when it has grown it is the greatest of shrubs and becomes a tree, so that the birds of the air come and make nests in its branches.*"

Luke 13:18-19:
He said therefore, "*What is the Kingdom of God like" and to what should I compare it? It is like a mustard seed that someone took and sowed in the garden; it grew and became a tree, and the birds of the air made nests in its branches.*"

The quotation marks are shown in the Bible. These gospels all purport to be quoting JESUS word for word, but there are substantial variances between the three versions as you can see. This is not an example of three people hearing the same story differently. Both Matthew and Luke were copying Mark here, so the variations from Mark's original were intentional.

Even though the synoptic gospels have similarities, as in the mustard seed parable, they are often at odds with each other, so much so that it is impossible to reconcile them. Why do they all tell different versions of very important matters? Everyone knows that the fourth Gospel is at odds with the other three. But the first three purportedly view what happened with one eye. They should all agree in those instances where Matthew and Luke copied Mark and Matthew and Luke should agree where they both copied Q, but they don't.

There are also instances where they are not copying anyone else and in those cases they differ drastically. Consider the birth stories that we discussed earlier. The actions of Mary and Joseph after the birth are also different. Matthew has JESUS escaping to Egypt because King Herod ordered the death of all babies in a reprise of the story of Moses in Egypt, and then the family sneaking back into the country after the death of Herod the Great and settling in Nazarath. That way he had JESUS born in Bethlehem but Nazareth could still his home. In Luke JESUS' parents are already living in Nazareth but have to travel to Bethlehem for the birth. They take their time after the birth and casually follow the Jewish birth traditions—after 8 days they have him circumcised, and after forty days present him to the priest in Jerusalem. This is a pretty tough trick if you have already escaped and are hiding in Egypt. Matthew and Luke cannot both be right. The stories are fundamentally different..

JESUS' last words were, according to the authors of Mark (in Aramaic, "Eli, Eli, lama sabachthani?") and Matthew, (in Hebrew, "Eloi, Eloi, lama sabachthani?") both translate as "My GOD, my GOD, why have you forsaken me?" (Quoting Psalms 22:1 written during the time of the Diaspora). Luke, on the other hand, says that his last words were, "Father, into your hands I commend my spirit." (From another Psalm, 31:6). John disagrees with them all. He said that JESUS said, simply, "It is finished."

There are also statements about the anticipated apocalypse in all four Gospels. Let's examine them in a similar side-by-side comparison of Mark, Matthew, and Luke side by side in a chart. John, which is entirely different, will be discussed separately. However, before we get to the chart, let's look at Mark's statement of the predicted apocalypse.

Mark introduces his apocalyptic message in Chapter 9 when he has JESUS tell his disciples,

> *Truly I tell you, there are some standing here who will not taste death until they see that the Kingdom of GOD has come with power.*

In Mark 13, JESUS gets very specific. One of his disciples points to the Temple and comments about the size of the structure and the huge stones. JESUS then tells the disciples, "*Do you see these great buildings? Not one stone will be left here upon another; all will be thrown down* (13:2)." It is important to understand that Mark wrote this *after* the destruction of the Temple in 70 C.E. but made it appear that JESUS was speaking of the future. Mark's readers knew that the Temple had been destroyed but believed that JESUS was making a prediction of a future event. Remember the section on apocalyptic literature in the last chapter? Apocalyptic predictions were nearly always preceded by simulated predictions to give credibility to the predictor's ability to foresee future events. JESUS' apparent prediction about the destruction of the temple adds credibility to the next prediction which is a real prediction of the future:

> *But in those days, after that suffering,*
> *The sun will be darkened,*
> *and the moon will not give its light*
> *and the stars will be falling from Heaven,*
> *and the powers in the heavens will be shaken,*

> *Then they will see "the Son of Man coming in the clouds" with great power and glory. Then he will send out the angels and gather his elect from the four winds, from the ends of the earth to the ends of Heaven.*
>
> * * *
>
> *So also, when you see these things taking place, you know that he is near, at the very gates. Truly I tell you, this generation will not pass away until all these things have taken place* (Mk 13:34-30).

At the time that Mark wrote his gospel, some of the people who had heard JESUS actually speak were probably still living, although they would be somewhere in their 70s. So it stood to reason that the Second Coming was near.

Mark relies heavily on Daniel in making this prediction. In particular, Mark refers to "the desolating sacrilege" or, depending on the translation, the "abomination of desolation" (KJV) (13:14). This peculiar phrase appeared only in the Book of Daniel (12:6-11):

> *"How long will it be until the end of these wonders?" . . . it will be for a time, two times, and half a time," and that when the shattering of the power of the holy people comes to an end, all these things would be accomplished. I heard but could not understand; so I said, "My lord, what shall be the outcome of these things?" He said, "Go your way, Daniel, for the words are to remain secret and sealed until the time of the end. . . . From the time that the regular burnt offering is taken away and the* abomination that desolates *is set up, there shall be one thousand two hundred ninety days."* [Emphasis added].

The "time, two times, and half a time" that Daniel refers to, in the language of the time, meant three and a half years or 1,290 days and is apparently to be measured from the "abomination that desolates." Mark apparently figured that Daniel must have been referring to the second destruction of the Temple which was in 70 C.E. That was the cataclysmic event for all Jews that could only be the "abomination that desolates." That would make the date for the Second Coming of Christ 3½ years later or some time in 74 C.E. This prediction that the apocalypse would occur shortly after the destruction of the Temple was not limited to Mark. It was a pretty universal belief at that time among apocalyptic speakers, but to my knowledge it is the first time, but certainly not the last, that anyone calculated the time based upon the prediction in Daniel.

As we all know, the apocalypse did not occur as Mark predicted. This presented a problem to Matthew and Luke because they were trying to update and "clean up" Mark's gospel. They both independently decided that the logical reason that the apocalypse did not occur as predicted was that Mark had simply calculated the date incorrectly. In fact, the failure of the apocalypse to appear as predicted was likely one of the main reasons that Matthew and Luke felt compelled to rewrite Mark.

Let's now compare the three versions in a chart (note that all three versions purport to quote JESUS word for word, that Matthew and Luke were copying Mark, yet in many respects they differ. Just because the words of JESUS are written in red does not mean that he spoke them):

The Gospels and the Apocalypse

Mark	**Matthew**	**Luke**
As he came out of the temple, one of his disciples said to him, "Look, Teacher, what large stones and what large buildings!" Then JESUS asked him, "*Do you see these great buildings? Not one stone will be left there upon another; all will be thrown down.*" (13:1-2)	As JESUS came out of the temple and was going away, his disciples came to point out to him the buildings of the temple. Then he asked them, "*You see all these, do you not? Truly I tell you, not one stone will be left there upon another; all will be thrown down.*"(24:1-2)	When some were speaking about the temple, how it was adorned with beautiful stones and gifts dedicated to God, he said, "*As for these things that you see, the days will come when not one stone will be left upon another; all will be thrown down.*" (21:5-6)
When he was sitting on the Mount of Olives opposite the temple, Peter, James, John, and Andrew asked him privately, "Tell us, when will this be, and what will be accomplished?" "*[W]hen you hear of the wars and rumors of wars, do not be alarmed; this must take place, but the end is still to come. For nation will rise against nation, and kingdom against kingdom; there will be earthquakes in various places; there will be famines. This is but the beginning of the birth pangs.*" (13:3-8)	When he was sitting on the Mount of Olives, the disciples came to him privately, saying, "Tell us, when will this be, and what will be the sign of your coming and of the end of the age?" "*[Y]ou will hear of wars and rumors of wars; see that you are not alarmed; for this must take place, but the end is not yet. For nation will rise against nation, and kingdom against kingdom, and there will be famines and earthquakes in various places: all of this is but the beginning of the birth pangs.*" (24:3-8)	They asked him, "Teacher, when will this be, and what will be the sign that this is about to take place?" "*[W]hen you hear of wars and insurrections, do not be terrified; for these things must take place first, but the end will not follow immediately.*" (21:7-9)
"*For in those days there will be suffering, such as has not*	"*For at that time there will be great suffering, such as*	

been from the beginning of the creation that God created until now, no, and never will be. And if the Lord had not cut short those days, no one would be saved; but for the sake of the elect, whom he chose, he has cut short those days." (13:19-20)

has not been from the beginning of the world until now, no, and never will be. And if those days had not been cut short, no one would be saved; but for the sake of the elect those days will be cut short." (24:21-22)

"But in those days, after that suffering,
the sun will be darkened,
and the moon will not give its light,
and the stars will be falling from Heaven,
and the powers in the heavens will be taken.
Then they will see 'the Son of Man coming in clouds' with great power and glory. Then he will send out the angels, and gather his elect from the four winds, from the ends of the earth to the ends of Heaven.(13:24:27)

"Immediately after the suffering of those days
the sun will be darkened,
and the moon will not give its light;
the stars will fall from Heaven,
and the powers of Heaven will be shaken.
Then the sign of the Son of Man will appear in Heaven, and then all the tribes of the earth will mourn, and they will see 'the Son of Man coming on the clouds of Heaven' with power and great glory. And he will send out his angels with a loud trumpet call, and they will gather his elect from the four winds, from one end of Heaven to the other" (24:29-31)

"There will be signs in the sun, the moon, and the stars, and on the earth distress among nations confused by the roaring of the sea and the waves. People will faint from fear and foreboding of what is coming upon the world, for the powers of the heavens will be shaken. They then will see 'the Son of Man coming in a cloud' with power and great glory. Now when these things begin to take place, stand up and raise your heads, because your redemption is drawing near." (21:25-28)

"From the fig tree learn its lesson: as soon as its branch becomes tender and puts forth its leaves, you know that summer is near. So also, when you see these things taking place, you know that he is near, at the very gates. Truly I tell you, this generation will not pass

"From the fig tree learn its lesson: as soon as its branch becomes tender and puts forth its leaves, you know that summer is near. So also, when you see all these things, you know that he is near, at the very gates. Truly I tell you, this generation will not pass

Then he told them a parable: "*Look at the fig tree and all the trees; as soon as they sprout leaves you can see for yourselves and know that summer is already near. So also, when you see these things taking place, you know that the kingdom of God is near.*

away until all these things have taken place." (13:28-31	*away until all these things have taken place."* (24:32-34)	*Truly I tell you, this generation will not pass away until all things have taken place."* (21:29-33)

First a few observations about the statements in general. When the Romans destroyed the Temple they proved that they were as good at tearing something down as they were in building it. By the time they were finished, the temple was nothing more than a pile of rubble and the rubble naturally became a quarry. Most of the stones were reused in other structures that were being built. The only thing remaining then, as now, was the west wall, known as the "wailing wall." Secondly, all of the gospel writers wanted to make sure that the listeners understood that the Jewish war itself was not the beginning of the apocalypse. While it was truly devastating and certainly qualified as an *abomination that desolates,* it was not *the* abomination that Daniel was talking about. It was merely a *sign* pointing toward the abomination that desolates. Mark, remember, said that it would occur in three and a half years.

The "son of man coming in a cloud" is also a clear reference to Daniel. The phrase "nation rising against nation" is not the same as what we understand the term to be today. In Hebrew, the word is *goyim.* It can be translated as either "nation" or "people," meaning a large, identifiable body of people. The Greek Septuagint translators chose the word "nation" over "people," but the concept of a nation as a political body, an independent state, had not yet developed. A more accurate first century translation of the phrase would be "people rising up against people."

Matthew and Luke knew that Mark had the date wrong. They knew because they were writing their own gospel long after the year 74 when Mark predicted the apocalypse. They independently figured that Mark just did not understand Daniel and that Mark incorrectly calculated the date. Matthew and Luke knew that the destruction of the Temple was not the beginning of the end. They figured that it was just another sign that the end was coming, so they added a phrase to Mark's statement. When the disciples asked JESUS, "Tell us, when will this be," Matthew and Luke had them add the phrase, "*and what will be the sign of your coming and of the end of the age*?" The destruction of the Temple then became just another sign of the Second Coming, not the beginning.

Mark said that just after the Jewish War, "*He has cut short those days* (13:20)." Matthew, writing about 20 years after the destruction of the Temple, modifies this statement to, "*those days* will *be cut short.*" That is, instead of GOD already having cut short the time, He will do so in the future. Luke also moved the day into the future, "*but the end will not follow immediately.*"

Matthew then adds three lesser known parables to explain the long delay of the Second Coming: in the first, some bridesmaids took lamps to meet the bridegroom but failed to take extra oil so their lights burned out and they missed out on seeing him when the bridegroom was late (25:25); second, the parable of the man going on a long journey and leaving money to his three servants to invest (note the classic use of three) and then came back to settle accounts (25:14-19) to find that some had invested wisely and one who did not; and finally, the parable of the "Bad Servant" who, upon discovering that his master would be late, beat the other servants and displayed other bad conduct (25:48). These parables are all designed to explain the delay in the Second Coming and to caution on being prepared, doing good deeds, and being ever vigilant while waiting because the day of reckoning will eventually come when you least expect it.

There is considerable doubt as to the authenticity of those parables. They are very unJESUS-like. The bridegroom parable, for example, merely tells about six bridesmaids taking lamps so that they can meet the groom when he arrives at night. Half of them forget to bring oil for the lamps, so they don't have any light. Therefore the three fall asleep and miss seeing the bridegroom. This tells Matthew's message, but it is very unlike the parables for which JESUS is so well known. There is neither a surprise ending nor any huge hidden message. They forgot the oil so they had no light and fell asleep. That is just what you would expect to happen. It doesn't require any exercise of the gray matter to figure out. The message from Matthew is be prepared at all times because JESUS may return at an unexpected time. It's kind of a "no duh!" As a result, many scholars do not believe that these parables were actually spoken by JESUS. They believe that Matthew made them up himself to explain to his group of Christians why the apocalypse that they had been waiting for was so late in coming.

Trying to calculate the date for the end of time from the formula in the book of Daniel has long been a serious pastime for many. The last person that I know to try his hand was, arguably, the greatest genius in history, Sir Isaac Newton. He analyzed Daniel's prediction in 1704 which he set out in a letter. The letter exists, but it does not include his calculations. He predicted that the Apocalypse would come in 2060—exactly 1,260 years after the foundation of the Holy Roman Empire, adding, "It may end later, but I see no reason for its ending sooner." No one knows how he made the 1,260 year calculation instead of 1,290 days or where it came from, but the Holy Roman Empire was officially founded in 800 C.E. by Charlemagne, so the arithmetic works.

How did John handle the apocalypse in his gospel? Very differently, as you might expect. John believed the apocalypse had already occurred! He wrote that those who believed that someday JESUS would return and complete his task simply did not grasp JESUS' message. The first coming of JESUS was the key event and no further "coming" is going to happen. That is, the Son of Man has already come and gone. JESUS himself was the apocalyptic event.

> *Very truly, I tell you, anyone who hears my word and believes him who sent me has eternal life, and does not come under judgment, but has passed from death to life* (5:24).

John also has JESUS tell us after the resurrection of Lazarus, when Martha expects her brother to "rise again in the resurrection on the last day," that Martha has it all wrong because,

> *I am the resurrection and the life. Those who believe in me, even though they die, will live, and everyone who lives and believes in me will never die* (11:25-26).

JESUS is "the resurrection and the life." He gives eternal life now, not at some later date. To John, death has taken on an entirely new meaning. It is no longer the end of life. It has become a metaphor because "everyone who lives and believes" will have eternal life. Death is nothing more than the process of moving on from our transient life on earth to eternal life with GOD.

Even at the very end of his life, instead of crying out a phrase from Psalms, as he does in the other three gospels, JESUS says only, "It is finished" (or "it is accomplished" or "everything GOD sent me to do has been accomplished" depending on the translation). According to John, JESUS' work is over. If you are expecting a Second Coming, you will have a very long wait indeed.

So there are some huge differences between the Gospels that simply cannot be reconciled. "Each of the writers shaped the narrative to emphasize particular features of JESUS and his teaching." However, in all fairness, in many respects they are very consistent, varying only in certain philosophical aspects. Let's check a few.

First, let's look at a comparison where there are very different statements.

Comparison of the Gospels' Accounts of the Trial of JESUS

MATTHEW	LUKE	JOHN
JESUS entry on Palm Sunday draws a crowd, but is not followed by explicit opposition from the Temple authorities. It is JESUS' later action in the Temple which	The Temple incident is the cause of the problems with the priests. No mention of Lazarus.	The high priest and Pharisees outlaw JESUS after his teaching at the Feast of Tabernacles, but they are afraid to arrest him when he comes into town with

brings the Jewish leaders' fears to a head; they are reputedly also afraid of the crowds who are gathering for Passover, but the Gospelers cannot possibly know what they were thinking. There is no mention of Lasarus.		thousands of followers. They intensify the complaint after the raising of Lasarus. The incident at the Temple is at the beginning of JESUS' ministry in John, not at the end.
The Last Supper took place on the day of Passover	The Last Supper took place on the day of Passover	The Last Supper took place on the day *before* Passover
JESUS was arrested by a group of unspecified status which was organized by the high priest	JESUS was arrested by the Temple police	JESUS was arrested by Roman soldiers
He is brought to the high priest and accused by witnesses before the "Chief priests and all the council" (a Sanhedrin) at night.	He is taken to the high priest's house	He is taken to the high priest's house
JESUS tells the high priest that he is the Messiah and that the Son of Man (from Daniel) will soon be seen coming in clouds of glory. The high priest exclaims that this is blasphemy and the meeting adjudges him fit to die.	No meeting is held	No meeting. JESUS is taken directly to Pilate
A second meeting in the morning holds a consultation and concludes by handing him over to Pilate	The next morning the council meets and asks him questions; first is he Christ; second, is he the son of God? No witnesses testified	
JESUS was not bound until after the hearing with Pilate.	JESUS was not bound until after the hearing.	JESUS was bound as soon as he was arrested by the soldiers.

Pilate asks him without prompting (presumably because the Jewish council has given him a formal statement of the charges), "Are you the King of the Jews?" JESUS does not answer and the priests accuse him "instantly," but still JESUS remains silent.	The priests charge JESUS openly, presumably because they did not hold a formal council (a Sanhedrin) and thus had no formal charge. There are no witnesses called. Pilate does not question him. Can find no fault and sends him to Herod Antipas (the ruler of Galilee) who also finds him innocent. (No other Gospel mentions this).	Jews wait outside as it is Passover and they would become unclean if they enter. Pilate asks JESUS if he is the King of the Jews. Pilate goes on to tell the Jews that he can find no guilt. Pilate goes back and forth between JESUS and the Jews.
Pilate has a custom of releasing a prisoner at Passover and the crowd presses him on it. He offers JESUS and they ask for Barabbas.	Pilate decides to flog JESUS and send him on his way, but the Jews shout at him to crucify JESUS and release Barabbas. He gives in, but there is no mention of the Passover custom of releasing a prisoner.	The crowd call for Barabbas, but there is no mention of the Passover custom. JESUS is scourged, crowned, and mocked , and then brought out, being declared innocent. Jews claim that JESUS is the son of God; Pilate becomes afraid and goes back in to question JESUS. He returns, and the Jews threatened that he will not be "Caesar's friend" unless he does as they ask.
There is no formal judgment and no reported sentence. Pilate's formal seat of judgment is described in Matthew but not in Mark.	There is no formal judgment and no reported sentence. The seat of judgment is not mentioned.	Pilate then goes to his official seat of judgment and officially sentences JESUS.
The charge against JESUS is a simple political charge that he claims to be the King of the Jews. The crowd then asks for JESUS' death. He gives in to them and has JESUS		The charge against JESUS is secular (although brought by the priests) outlawing JESUS. No Jewish Sanhedrin, no preliminary hearing, accusation, or judgment

scourged.		
Place, day, and hour not specified.	Place, day, and hour not specified.	The exact place, day, and hour is specific.
JESUS' last words were, "My God, my God, why have you forsaken me?" (Quoting one of the Psalms written during the time of the Diaspora, Psalm 22).	JESUS' last words were, "Father, into your hands I commend my spirit." (Quoting Psalm 31)	JESUS' last words were, "It is finished."

Here I have only compared three of the Gospels. In the arrest and trial of JESUS, Matthew is basically the same as Mark, so I omitted the Mark version in this analysis. That is not to say that Matthew did not add to Mark's original story. He added, for example, the suicide of Judas, the high priest's questions, Pilate's wife knowing that JESUS was innocent, having realized it in a dream, and Pilate washing his hands of the whole affair. But for the arrest and trial portion of the Gospels, Mark and Matthew are much the same.

When you read the Gospels one at a time, they all appear to tell the same story. When you take the same passages from each and lay them out side by side, however, you see that they are often very different. If you are interested in seeing all of the words of JESUS set out with the parallel verses from all of the gospels plus that of the Gospel of Thomas, I highly recommend *The Four Gospels* edited by Funk.

Selected Comparisons of the Gospels

The differences between the Gospels is not always as clear as it is in the above analysis, although many are. On the other hand, may differ only in the details. When Matthew and Luke rely upon Mark, for example, the general gist of the message is the same, but there are usually discrepancies in the details. Sometimes those differences can be meaningful. I have included two of them for illustration:

1. What should the disciples take with them

JESUS was very much into the counterculture life style (but not the philosophy) of the cynics—radical, itinerant philosophers of the time. Cynics roamed the country sides, gathering listeners, and discussing their philosophy, usually interacting with the audience in a question and answer discussion. It was all very much the way JESUS taught. He also traveled from, place to place, gathering people around who wanted to learn. He spoke and when they asked questions, he would answer by making them come up with the answers themselves, a technique known today as the "Socratic method." The Greco-Roman Cynicism was studied by Leif

Vaage, and this is what he had to say about the dress of the Cynics:

> *The standard uniform of the Cynics was a cloak, a wallet, a staff. Typically their life included barefooted itinerancy viz. indigence, sleeping on the ground or in the baths and other public buildings, a diet of water and vegetables.*

They also had shaggy, unkempt hair and beards. Compare Vaage's description of the Cynics with the New Testament statements about JESUS. and the similarities are striking.

JESUS sent his disciples out to preach his message, and he gave them explicit instructions on several things, including what to wear and take with them and what not to take. Here is how the synoptic gospels handled JESUS' instructions (again, note the similarity to the Cynics):

> Mark 6:8 "*He ordered them to take nothing for their journey except a staff; no bread, no bag, no money in their belts; but to wear sandals and not to put on two tunics.*" (Note, in Mark, JESUS sends out "the twelve" disciples, two at a time together).
>
> Matthew 10:9,10 "*Take no gold, or silver, or copper in your belts, no bag for your journey, or two tunics, or sandals, or a staff; . . .*" (Matthew also has JESUS sending out only 12 disciples, two at a time together, whom he names).
>
> Luke 10:4 "*Carry no purse**, *no bag, no sandals; and greet no one on the road.*" (Luke has JESUS sending out 70 disciples, also two by two).

To summarize:

Mark prohibited:	**Matthew** prohibited:	**Luke** prohibited:
money, bag, two tunics, and bread; allowed a staff and sandals.	money, bag, and two tunics; also a staff and sandals which mark allowed.	purse, bag and sandals; also forbid greeting people on the road.

2. Feeding the multitudes bread and fish

If you only make a quick browse through the four versions of this

* A "purse" is nothing like a modern purse. It was just a bag to carry personal items, often having a shoulder strap. Today the word suggests that there is money in it. That was not necessarily true in the first century.

story below it will seem, at first blush, that they are all entirely consistent. If you take a little time and compare them, however, you will see that they disagree on some very important details. I'll let you discover the differences on your own this time.

This story, of course, parallels Moses' feeding of the multitudes. I have included the John version as well. This is one of the rare instances where John also had the same story. Since John does not appear to have ever read the other three gospels, he must have heard the story from another source, indicating that it may have been widely told. In all four versions, JESUS takes his disciples off to a quiet place to be by themselves, but they are recognized and are followed.

> Mark 6:35 - 44 "*When it grew late, his disciples came to him and said, 'This is a deserted place, and the hour is now very late; send them away so that they may go into the surrounding country and villages and buy something for themselves to eat.' But he answered them, 'You give them something to eat.' They said to him, 'Are we to go and buy two hundred denarii worth of bread, and give it to them to eat?' And he said to them, 'How many loaves have you? Go and see.' When they had found out, they said, 'Five, and two fish.' Then he ordered them to get all the people to sit down in groups on the green grass. So they sat down in groups of hundreds and of fifties. Taking the five loaves and the two fish, he looked up to Heaven, and blessed and broke the loaves, and gave them to his disciples to set before the people; and he divided the two fish among them all. And all ate and were filled; and they took up twelve baskets full of broken pieces and of the fish. Those who had eaten the loaves numbered five thousand men.*" (Note, this story occurs right after the story of the death of John the Baptist, but JESUS merely asks the disciples to go with him to rest. It is apparently unrelated to John's death).

> Matthew 13:15 - 21 ". . . '*this is a deserted place, and the hour is now late; send the crowds away so that they may go into the villages and buy food for themselves.' JESUS said to them, 'they need not go away; you give them something to eat.' They replied, 'We have nothing here but five loaves and two fish.' And he said, 'Bring them here to me.' Then he ordered the crowds to sit down on the grass. Taking the five loaves and the two fish, he looked up to Heaven, and blessed and broke the loaves, and gave them to the disciples, and the disciples gave them to the crowds. And all ate and were filled; and they took up what was left over of the broken pieces, twelve baskets full. And those who ate were about five thousand men, besides women and children.*"(This story also follows the death of John, but the reason for retiring to a quiet place was for JESUS to be by himself. He was apparently bothered by the report of John's death).

Luke 9:12 - 17 "*The day was drawing to a close, and the twelve came to him and said, "Send the crowd away, so that they may go into the surrounding villages and countryside, to lodge and get provisions; for we are here in a deserted place.' But he said to them, 'You give them something to eat.' They said, 'We have no more than five loaves and two fish—unless we are to go and buy food for all these people.' For there were about five thousand men. And he said to his disciples, 'Make them sit down in groups of about fifty each.' They did so and made them all sit down. And taking the five loaves and the two fish, he looked up to Heaven, and blessed and broke them, and gave them to the disciples to set before the crowd. And all ate and were filled. What was left over was gathered up, twelve baskets of broken pieces."* (This also follows John's death, but is unrelated to it. They retire to a city called Bethsaida with the Disciples. Since they were in a city, the suggestion that the people be allowed to go into the surrounding villages and countryside does not seem to make much sense).

John 6:5 - 13 "*When he looked up and saw a large crowd coming toward him, JESUS said to Philip, 'Where are we to buy bread for these people to eat?' He said this to test him, for he himself knew what he was going to do. Philip answered him, 'six months' wages would not buy enough bread for each of them to get a little.' One of this disciples, Andrew, Simon Peter's brother, said to him, 'There is a boy here who has five barley loaves and two fish. But what are they among so many people?' JESUS said, 'Make the people sit down.' Now there was a great deal of grass in the place; so they sat down, about five thousand in all. Then JESUS took the loaves, and when he had given thanks, he distributed them to those who were seated; so also the fish, as much as they wanted. When they were satisfied, he told his disciples, 'Gather up the fragments left over, so that nothing may be lost.' So they gathered them up, and from the fragments of the five barley loaves, left by those who had eaten, they filled twelve baskets.* (The John version does not follow a story of the death of John the Baptist. The reason for the need to feed the people is explained by noting that it was now Passover, the Jewish festival)

These are just two examples out of dozens that I could have used, but they show how the authors interpreted the same words and acts of JESUS in different ways. The fact that they are separated from each other in the Bible makes it easy to see how the differences might go unnoticed. But, in many cases, when placed side by side, the differences are so obvious that they just can't be reconciled. Remember, the changes Matthew and Luke made in Mark were intentional.

John

John is much different than the other gospels, including his chronology. According to John, JESUS visited Jerusalem several times; the synoptic gospels say it was only one trip, at the end of his life. John says that JESUS' ministry lasted three years; the others limit it to a single year. John goes to great lengths to show that JESUS was a human being and had a part in society just like every other human being, but John starts his gospel with a restatement of the Creation, "In the Beginning . . ." but he has JESUS sitting with GOD at the very beginning of creation and as a participant in it. John's version of the gospel reveals that he fell within the group who believed that JESUS was always a god, even before his human birth. But notably, John stresses that JESUS was also a human being burdened with the same human frailties as the rest of us.

This is a difficult concept for twenty-first century Christians to grasp, but first century Christians were used to pagan gods coming to earth as humans. The JESUS John wrote about wasn't simply a healer and a charismatic Jewish teacher—there was no shortage of people like that wandering around at that time. The JESUS that John wrote about was also a god in his own right.

Nevertheless, the prologue to this Gospel stresses that JESUS was a mortal. "The Word became flesh and lived among us (1:14)." So while it depicts JESUS as the word of GOD incarnate, it is equally a part of the story that JESUS was a person of the flesh. John is a much more spiritual book than the synoptic Gospels. It is written in beautiful, graphic prose; but if you want to understand what John is all about, you must keep in mind that, while John believed that JESUS was with GOD at the creation, he also believed, more importantly, that he was also a flesh and blood person, not just a god in disguise.

The Gospel is generally divided into four parts, the Prologue (1:1-18), the "Signs" stories that were by a different author (1:19-12:50), the Crucifixion, Resurrection, and Ascension (13:1-20:31), and the Epilogue which includes JESUS' appearances after his death (21:1-25).

Judaism was going through a major structural change at this time that affected all of the various Jewish sects. The traditional temple-centric religion was fading. The Rabbinic movement began taking shape perhaps 150 years before Christianity, and it was just as revolutionary to traditional Judaism as Christianity was. In other words, if Moses were to suddenly appear on the earth at the end of the first century, it is unclear that he would recognize either Rabbinic Judaism or Christianity as part of the Hebrew faith that he knew. The old Temple priesthood still had muscle, but the priesthood had become little more than a tool of control for the Romans.

It appears that John was written, in part, to emphasize the differences between Christianity and the old ways. Remember, John was not written until early in the second century. The Temple that had been destroyed in 70 C.E. had been under reconstruction for 64 years. Christianity was no longer a sect of Judaism, yet it was not quite a full-fledged religion of its own, although it was getting close. The problem was that there were different views of what that religion should be like.

John presents JESUS as the Word incarnate. "The Word was GOD." JESUS is the Messiah, the King of Israel, the only begotten Son, the Holy One of GOD, and totally in control of his life and death. John has JESUS referring to himself in the same way that GOD refers to his own self in the Old Testament (Ex 3:14; Isa 41:4; 43:10; 46:4) as "I am," or as it is written in the original Greek, "*ego eimi*." This is a very important clue as to John's message. Remember back in Chapter 5 when Moses asked what he should tell the people GOD'S name was? The answer from the burning bush was *Ehyeh* which means "I am" in Hebrew. John uses the Greek version of the same name, *ego eimi* to portray JESUS as replacing many aspects of traditional Judaism. John also replaces many natural elements of the world with other names for JESUS: he is "the light (8:12)," or even life itself (11:25), and replacing both the Temple and Passover (6:1-4).

The biggest problem with John is his blistering attack on the Jews, apparently laying the blame for JESUS' death at the feet of all Jews everywhere. This anti-Semitic message has been a justification for the persecution of Jews ever since. And what an indictment it is!

> *You [Jews] are from your father the devil, and you choose to do your father's desires. He was a murderer from the beginning and does not stand in the truth because there is no truth in him. When he lies, he speaks according to his own nature, for he is a liar and the father of lies. But because I tell the truth, you do not believe me. Which of you convicts me of sin? If I tell the truth, why do you not believe me. Whoever is from GOD hears the words of GOD. The reason you do not hear them is that you are not from GOD.* (8:44-47).

This is just one of John's incredible attacks on the Jews. Church leaders suggest that John was not referring to the Jews as a social unit, but only to the priesthood, those who were personally involved in the persecution of JESUS. Well, it is an argument. The fact is, though, that the words of the Gospel of John have been used to persecute Jews for two thousand years, and unfortunately, nothing seems to suggest that this will change any time over the next two thousand.

John was also edited. At Jn 8:1-11 someone added another story to the original text. This is the story of JESUS' defense of the adulterous woman who was about to be stoned for her sins. He states the often quoted lines, "*He that is without sin among you, let him first cast a stone at her.*"

And, "*Neither do I condemn thee: go, and sin no more.*"

This entire episode is missing from the early Bibles and it cannot be found in any other early writing, although the general subject matter was often discussed. Scholars agree that the style of this text is different from the rest of John and it interrupts the flow of the text where it is inserted. The first suggestion that it might be a later insertion was by [St] Jerome about 400 C.E. when he questions its credentials. It is now certain that it is a late second century or early third century addition to the Gospel.

One final word about the Gospel of John. Most Biblical scholars are hard-pressed to find a single word in the entire book of John that they believe JESUS uttered or a single act that he actually performed. The author of John is so far removed from the historical JESUS and so concerned with propagating the particular message that this sect followed, that it is considered to be highly unreliable in any historical sense.

This is unfortunate, because it is the most beautifully written of the four Gospels. It is magnificent prose, and many of the most quoted passages in the Bible are from John. Nearly every Christian can recite passages of John from memory even when they cannot quote from any of the other Gospels. Some of these oft-quoted chapters and verses guide people in their daily lives and provide solace and comfort in times of sorrow; but John is neither history nor a biography. Sorry. But that does not mean that John is not faithful to JESUS' message, just not to His words. Those beloved passages may very well be true expressions of JESUS' message.

What are the Gnostic Gospels?

We briefly discussed Gnosticism earlier. Briefly recapping, Gnostic comes from the Greek word, *gnosis*, which means "knowledge." But Gnosticism is much more. It is an outgrowth of the Greek mysteries which used a lot of allegories and symbols of a "deeper truth." It is also an outgrowth of the Hebrew wisdom literature. It refers to the possession of secret knowledge about the nature of human life and its relation to the world, the formation of that world and explanation of its evil, and how such knowledge can be used to achieve salvation.

Many of the early Christians were converted pagans, and many brought the Greek Mystery traditions with them. Many Christian Jews had their own Jewish Mysteries that often paralleled those of the pagans. But the Jewish monotheism did not allow for a savior god. There were no subordinate gods in the Jewish pantheon any more. So Jewish Christians adopted the Messiah concept and looked upon JESUS as the Devine son of GOD and a savior.

Christian Gnosticism, on the other hand, followed the pagan model, especially as to the savior gods and the concept of achieving knowledge of the self. This movement became a very powerful part of early

Christianity. In fact, it may have been the largest segment of the early church. JESUS' was a sapiential[1] preacher, and his primary teaching dovetailed perfectly with the ancient gnostic traditions.

In order to understand where this Gnostic tradition fits into the overall picture, it is necessary to understand what was going on in the Middle East at the time. The Romans so oppressed the Jewish peasantry that they were often in open rebellions which were brutally repressed. Any hint of sedition was met with death. The peasants found four ways of dealing with the problem: 1) revolution, 2) non-violent movements, 3) apocalyptic movements, and 4) messianic movements.

1. Revolution

Many people believed that the only solution was to overthrow the Romans. This resulted in a series of revolutions that morphed into the two Jewish Wars. There were quite a number of these revolutionary groups. Of them, the Zealots are probably the most well known. The Zealots I am referring to was an organized political entity determined to overthrow their Roman governors, not to individual zealots as that term is usually used today. The Zealots elected a peasant as the high priest and regularly executed Herodian nobles.

There were groups like the Sicarii who got their name from the sicarii daggers they carried hidden in their clothing and used to kill people in crowded markets and at rallies. They generally escaped detection by yelling in outrage at the killings and then immediately melding into the crowd.

There were also some Jewish Robin Hood-types, living in the hills. They robbed from the rich and gave to the peasantry. Some of these became messianic figures with huge followings.

Together, these groups, and others like them, were generically referred to as "bandits." When you read in the Gospels that JESUS was crucified along with two bandits, this are what they refer to, not simple thieves as we understand the word today. A more descriptive word today would be "insurrectionists." The usual penalty for insurrection was crucifixion. Mere thieves were never crucified.

There were also prophets who wandered the countryside preaching that the time will come to rise up and throw out the oppressors. Herod Antipas' mistaken concern that John the Baptist was such a prophet undoubtedly led to John's demise, although he was beheaded rather than crucified.

2. Non-violent Movements

There were some, such as the Essene, who simply dropped out of society and retired to their own town and lived a monastic existence, waiting for a better life the next time around. The city of Qumran was one such town. The Dead Sea Scrolls were found in the caves around this town, apparently hidden from the Romans by the inhabitants. According to some of the civil documents found among the religious scrolls, the Essene required strict adherence to "The Law," and the slightest misfeasance or malfeasance meant banishment or other severe punishments. It did not have to be much of an indiscretion either. They worried that the sins of one would pollute the entire city so they guarded against even minor infractions.

3. Apocalyptic (Eschatological) Movements

These were very popular beliefs. There were hundreds of books, similar to Revelation, that counseled that GOD was going to cleanse the earth of evil and leave only the righteous to rule. John the Baptist was an apocalyptic preacher. John apparently had a charisma to rival that of JESUS, but his message was quite different. John believed that you cleanse your souls and wait for GOD to cleanse the land of the oppressors. Baptism at the time of John was not what Christians practice today. It was a Jewish tradition, far different from Christian baptisms. As Josephus, who was trained in the Jewish priesthood, wrote in *Jewish Antiquities*:

> *[H]e had exhorted the Jews to lead righteous lives, to practice justice towards their fellows and piety towards GOD, and so doing to join in baptism....* They must not employ it to gain pardon for whatever sins they committed, *but as a consecration of the body implying that the soul was already thoroughly cleansed by right behavior [emphasis added].*

The baptism itself was very symbolic. The candidates. both literally and figuratively, passed through the river Jordan from the desert in the east to the Promised Land in the west just as the followers of Moses did centuries before. This was more than a simple emersion in the river. Afterward they were then to go home and await the imminent apocalypse.

There were a lot of eschatological preachers like John; he just happened to be the most famous. And the great majority of Biblical scholars believe that John did, in historic fact, baptize JESUS. The later apocalyptic preachers, like Paul, believed that the Kingdom of GOD was in the future, after GOD cleansed the earth.

4. Messianic Movements

The final group of protesters were those who expected a messiah to arrive and lead them to victory. Where most conquered people lose their old national identity after a couple of generations, the Hebrews, because they always had their Scriptures to remind them of their previous culture, never lost their identity. Hebrew scriptures written after the Exile are replete with stories of a messiah leading the Jews to their former preeminent position. There were basically two different messianic movements; the nonviolent and those that believed in change by force. The nonviolent movements were led by peasant prophets and were based upon the Moses and Joshua stories. The violent and militaristic messianic movements were usually lead by peasant messiahs and were grounded in the Saul and David stories. Where Moses and Joshua led by the force of their personalities and charisma, Saul and David were elected as the first and second kings of Judah because of their power as war leaders. Their job was simple, kill the Philistines that threatened the Israelites with their new iron age weapons.

The most common Old Testament prophecies repeatedly stated that the new messiah that would lead them from oppression would be from the house of David. That is, he would be a descendent of King David. Both Matthew and Luke went to great pains to show a genealogy of JESUS that connected with David. Unfortunately, they were not consistent with each other and reflected only a few common ancestors, but that was the intent of each. Both believed that the long awaited messiah had come and that he was JESUS.

Back to the Gnostics. When you cut through all of the chaff, JESUS was a sapiential preacher. If you read all of the words scholars almost unanimously attribute to JESUS in the Bible, his message was clear. The Kingdom of GOD is already here. All you have to do is open your eyes and you will find it. When a wealthy man asked him what he had to do to find the Kingdom of GOD, JESUS told him to get rid of all of his wealth and he would be able to find the Kingdom, for it is the poor, the peasantry, who will inherit the earth. When you read the Gospels and other New Testament books, however, you will find many references to the coming apocalypse. Why do you think that is?

Well, scholars believe one of the reasons is that, after his martyrdom, John's disciples searched for a new leader and a great many were drawn to JESUS' message and personality. Those early apostles and other church leaders, welcoming John's disciples into the fold, needed an apocalyptic message from JESUS to make sure they stayed, so they provided one.

Paul himself, as we will see in the next chapter, held apocalyptic views, contrary to some of the other early church leaders like Peter and James. Paul was outspoken about his opposition to those who believed in wisdom instead of spirituality. For example, in his first letter to the Church in Corinth he blasted the Gnostics who placed their lives in the hands of wisdom. The Gnostics believed that once you obtained wisdom, you no longer needed the help of anyone—not JESUS, not the priesthood. You already had all you needed for entry into the Kingdom of GOD. Needless to say, that was not a position that ingratiated them with the newly forming Christian priesthood and was eventually responsible for their downfall when emperor Constantine outlawed the sect.

Paul's views finally won out, but it was not settled until long after his death. Paul became the predominant apostle of JESUS ahead even of JESUS' brother James and the popular Simon whom JESUS called Peter. When it came time to decide which books would comprise the New Testament at the end of the fourth century, the Gnostic movement that had once threatened to overpower Catholic (universal) Christianity had already been deemed heresy and was pretty much reduced to a footnote in history. After the famous council at Nicea, anyone caught with gnostic literature was put to death. As you might suspect, gnostic books were then either hidden or destroyed. A few of those hidden texts have shown up so that we now know a lot more about these people and their beliefs. A real treasure trove of Gnostic literature was discovered in 1945 at Nag Hammadi. The destruction of the gnostic scriptures meant that Paul's views were paramount, and none of the Gnostic gospels made it into the Bible. They added the apocalyptic book of Revelation to official Canon to make sure once and for all that the Gnostic message was nothing but an historical footnote. A brilliant analysis of the Gnostic scriptures is the highly regarded, award winning book, *The Gnostic Gospels* by Elaine Pagel, now a professor at Princeton.

Acts

Acts is the story of the first 30 years of Christianity. It introduces us to the reigning superstar, Paul. Unlike JESUS, we do have a brief description of Paul, "meeting eyebrows and a rather large nose, bald-headed, bow-legged, strongly built, full of grace." He has been described as arrogant and short tempered, and the evidence from his own letters would seem to support that evaluation. More than one scholar has described him as "troubled" and having many personal "demons." There is solid evidence that he developed very strong friendships and his associates had an almost messianic devotion to him. In spite of his acerbic personality, he must have been enormously charismatic.

Whatever else he may have been, Paul was a man of incredible physical endurance and stamina. It is difficult to determine just how many miles he traveled during his lifetime, but the most popular estimate is 20,000 kilometers (about 12,427 miles) more than the average driver in the U.S. puts on a car in a year of driving. All such estimates that I have seen are highly speculative, however. He occasionally traveled by sea and those making the estimates do not always subtract his three sea voyages from his travels on foot and most are strongly grounded in comments from the book of Acts which, as I have already mentioned, is not considered by scholars to be a very accurate history of Paul's activities. In any event, whatever the actual mileage, he spent a good portion of his life traveling on foot over very dangerous land; through deserts, swamps, and mountains. I would personally add to his other attributes, enormous bravery.

Paul was vigorous in both his travels and his evangelism. His voyage to Rome, his last trip, although it was over the sea rather than by land, was not a restful cruise in the Mediterranean because he was in Roman custody. Custody or not, sea travel in the first century was arduous and far more dangerous than land travel because of pirates and the unpredictable weather. Even though the Romans claimed Pompey defeated the pirates in the eastern Mediterranean, there were a lot of pirates back in business. Paul also claimed to have been involved in three shipwrecks (2 Cor 11:25). Further, to add to the already treacherous conditions, this trip to Rome occurred when Paul was in his mid-fifties.* This was a very advanced age considering Jewish peasants at that time had an average life expectancy of only 28 years and even the most pampered of the Roman aristocracy rarely reached their sixties.

This was a terrible time to be preaching unpopular or seditious ideas. The Roman Emperors during Paul's ministry were none other than Caligula, Claudius, and Nero, insane, brutal rulers who were legendary for their persecution of Christians. They frequently used Christians as lion bait in the "games," and even that ghastly treatment was trumped by Nero who had Christians impaled on poles while still alive, then smeared with pitch, and burned to provide light for his gardens at night. So it is no wonder that all four of the Gospel authors went out of their way to show Pontius Pilate and the other Romans as being basically innocent in the execution of JESUS and goaded into the crucifixion by the Jews. The authors obviously did not want to do anything to call their attention to the Roman rulers lest they become light for the garden. It was safer to make the Jews the villains, especially since they had all been either killed or exiled from the country by the time the last three of the Gospels were written.

Acts also has another hero besides Paul, Simon whom JESUS nicknamed "the rock" because he was to be the foundation upon which the church was built. Rock is *Cephas* in Aramaic and *Petra* in Greek. In English the Greek Petra is modified to"Peter" rather than being translated into "Rocky," so he is usually referred to in English Bibles as Simon called Peter or simply as Peter. Paul almost always called him "Cephas." The first part of Acts is about Peter, but once Paul enters the picture, he takes center stage. The full name of the book we call "Acts" is "The Acts of the Apostles," but we are really talking about just two apostles, Peter and Paul, but Luke does not even identify Paul as an apostle. So I guess a more accurate title for the book would be "The Acts of an Apostle and That

---

* Paul's date of birth is uncertain. Some say that he was born in 10 C.E. which would have made him about 25 years old when he began his ministry in 35 C.E. That seems a little young to gain so strong a following, but I am using that date to compute his age at death

Other Guy."

The initial chapters of Acts are about Peter's ministry and about the times he spent imprisoned. It details the selection of Matthias to become the 12th disciple, replacing Judas who had just come to a nasty end. It also relates the first Christian Pentecost (2:1-41). The Pentecost, also called the "Feast of Weeks," was a Jewish tradition. Pentecost means "fiftieth," and it was the traditional day of the barley harvest that was 50 days after Passover. But Christians coopted this celebration to be the first birthday of Christianity because of the story in Acts, so in the New Testament the day of the feast is the fiftieth day after Easter, not Passover.

The apostles and a lot of other people, mostly Jews, from many countries around the Middle East, were sitting around on the ground about 9:00 on the morning of the Pentecost when there came a sound like a violent wind from the heavens. Suddenly, the people present all began speaking in their native tongues. It was a sort of Tower of Babel story only in reverse. Peter used this opportunity to preach The Way and he is said to have converted three thousand people in that single day. The reason given for the people speaking in their own tongues was so that they could go forth to their own countries and teach their countrymen The Way. This was definitely not a reference to the speaking in tongues that Paul described in 1 Cor 14:1-33.and is part of certain evangelical and ecstatic worship. This referred to speaking in their naive tongues.

Peter is shown primarily as preaching to his fellow Jews, although he was the first to include gentiles in his ministry. Peter believed that anyone who wanted to become one of "The Way," as the term "Christian" had not yet been fashioned, had to first convert to Judaism. And you know what that meant. . .The Knife. You can probably imagine that once they realized that the prelude to conversion was circumcision, the adult males often had second thoughts about this whole conversion idea. For this reason, Peter's audiences were primarily of Jews who had already met the *mohel* as infants and had nothing to lose, no pun intended.

Paul, on the other hand, was off doing some converting of his own, only his method didn't require gentiles to first convert to Judaism. Unlike Peter, Paul viewed circumcision as an unnecessary step. The early church leaders were divided on this point—some agreed with Paul and some agreed with Peter. This deeply divided the followers of JESUS, and according to Acts, in 49 C.E. they held a council of apostles in Jerusalem. James, JESUS' brother, was growing in power among the apostles, and he proposed a compromise which everyone accepted (15:5-20). Under the compromise, gentiles did not have to comply with some of the strict Jewish laws, including most dietary laws and circumcision but would have to comply with most other Hebrew laws.

It is in these areas that Luke showed just how little he actually knew about either Peter or Paul other than legend. For example, in an interchange regarding table fellowship, Luke had Peter speaking about The Law as being "a yoke that neither our ancestors nor we have been able to bear" (15:10). That was not true according to Paul who says he told Peter that he was being a hypocrite. While, at that time, the practice of eating with gentiles was no longer forbidden in the more liberal interpretations of The Law, not eating gentile food was still a sign of loyal devotion to GOD (Dan 1:8-16; Tob 1:10; Jdt 10:5). James had sent messengers from Jerusalem insisting on that stricter interpretation. That is when Paul upbraided Cephus, because, while Peter used to eat with the Gentiles, he no longer did so out of fear of the"circumcision faction" and that basically relegated the gentiles who did not submit to circumcision to being second class Jews (Gal 2:12-14). Clearly Luke had no knowledge of this exchange.

Another example where Luke exhibits a lack of knowledge about Peter is in the same chapter where Peter states, "My brothers, you know that in the early days GOD made a choice among you, that I should be the one through whom the gentiles would hear the message of the good news and become believers (Acts 15:7)." Paul, who was there at the time, told us that it was Paul who "had been entrusted with the gospel for the uncircumcised, just as Peter had been entrusted with the gospel for the circumcised (Gal 2:7)." Luke's statement is the exact opposite of Paul's' recollection. Since Paul was there, his recollection is more credible.

Earlier, we noted Luke's obsession to characterize JESUS as fulfilling every Old Testament prophecy that he could find. One scholar noticed a similar process with relation to Peter fulfilling the prophecies of Ezekiel. Using the Septuagint translation, Ezekiel had a series of visions and Peter had the same visions. Ezekiel sees Heaven opened (Ez 1:1) and Peter also has a vision of "the Heaven opened" (Acts 10:13). Then Ezekiel is told to eat (Ez 2:9) and Peter is told to eat (Acts 10:13). Ezekiel is told to eat unclean food, bread baked on human dung, but Ezekiel declines (Ez 4:14) as does Peter when he is told to eat unclean food (Acts 10:14)." Ezekiel tells GOD that he has never eaten anything unclean (Ez 4:14) and Peter tells GOD that he has never eaten anything unclean (Acts 10:14).

Luke is also incorrect with regard to Paul's acts in most cases. For example, according to Luke, immediately after Paul's conversion on the road to Damascus, he went to Jerusalem where Barnabas introduced him to "the apostles (9:27)" which suggests that Paul was introduced to all of The Pillars. However, we know from Paul's own words that he actually waited three years after his conversion before going to Jerusalem and, upon arriving, he only met James, John, and Cephus (Gal 1:18-19). Paul was having trouble dealing with the circumcision issue and went to Jerusalem to ask for guidance from The Pillars.

As you read Acts, it is important to keep in mind that the Apostles had already added Matthias as the new 12th member to replace Judas who had a rather ghastly accident (he fell and his stomach burst open and his bowels fell out[*]). So when Acts refers to "The Twelve," it does not include Paul. It is easy to assume that Paul is included in The Twelve the way it was written, but he wasn't.

Luke was a Gentile Christian who believed strongly in Paul's message. However, it is apparent that Luke did not have access to Paul's letters; at the time Acts was being written Paul's letters had not yet been collected. Luke was probably writing from his recollection of what he had read in the past or what people had told him. As a result, Acts has considerable discrepancies in both the message of Paul and the biographical information contained in Paul's letters. In one example (Ch 9) Luke describes the famous incident on the road to Damascus when a light in the sky strikes Saul blind and JESUS demands to know why Saul is persecuting him. At this point, Saul recognizes the error of his ways and converts to The Way. This is the story about Paul's conversion that you always hear in church. However, there are other stories in the Bible about Paul's conversion that are rarely heard, including Paul's own personal recollection. Acts has other versions too. The story is repeated two more times (22:4-16; 26:9-18) and, while with a casual reading they seem to be the same, there are important differences between the three stories. All three are far different from what Paul himself wrote (Gal 1:13-24). It is incomprehensible that Paul would have suffered the remarkable experience related in Acts and not include it in his own two descriptions of his conversion which were quite uneventful (1 Cor 15:4-8; Gal 1:13-24).

Some feel the version(s) we see in Acts is actually patterned after the conversion of Heliodorus in 2 Macc 3. There are certainly many parallels between the two stories, especially in verses 24 and 26. Heliodorus first went to the High Priest in his story. Paul also went to the High Priest but for letters to the synagogues at Damascus so that he could arrest anyone he found following The Way and bring them to Jerusalem. Scholars agree that the High Priest had no authority to authorize such arrests at that time. The priesthood was under the control of the Romans and only the Romans had that authority, so the validity of that story is questionable.

We are first introduced to Paul during the execution of Stephen, the first Christian Martyr. He was convicted of blasphemy by a Sanhedrin, the formal Jewish council. The penalty was stoning to death. The witnesses of the blasphemy, who were required to cast the first stones, laid their coats at the feet of a young Jew named Saul (Acts 7:58). Saul was said to have approved of the killing. It is after this Paul is said to have approached the High Priest for authority to arrest those who followed The Way.

The conversion of Cornelius (10:1-48) is a very important part of Acts

---

[*] Acts 1:18, but compare with Mt 17:5 where Judas purportedly hanged himself.

because it raises the whole issue of the conversion of gentiles. The Way is still a purely Jewish sect, but Peter is allowing gentiles to be converted on the condition that they become circumcised and agree to follow Hebrew laws. The whole story is basically repeated in 11:1-18. Luke gives Peter the credit for converting the first gentile, but this seems to contradict the stories of Philip converting the Ethiopian eunuch (8:26-39) and Stephen converting a group in Antioch (11:19-21).

Acts refers to Paul as Saul in the beginning and in 13:9 Luke switches to Paul and refers to him as Paul for the rest of the book. I was always taught in church that Paul changed his name to show that he had become a Christian. That is not what happened. There was no Christian religion at that time and the term "Christian" had not even been invented. He was always known both as Saul and Paul; Saul was his name in Hebrew and Paul was the same name in Latin. Luke likely used Saul in the first chapters because Saul had a very Jewish presence up to the time in Antioch. After that Luke began calling him Paul, probably to show that Paul was now preaching a very different message—JESUS' version of the Jewish message. It is unlikely there was anything spiritual in the name change.

In Acts, Paul, upon arriving in a new town, always goes to the town synagogue and begins his ministry there. He begins to preach the gospel of JESUS to Jews and then to gentiles later. However, there is a third group that he spoke to, the large body of pagans that were greatly attracted to Judaism. They had never fully converted primarily because of, as one writer put it, "the Jewish preoccupation with male body parts." It took a very devout person to submit to that painful, and risky procedure. Then Paul came along and said that, if you want to follow The Way, you can have the benefits of Judaism without the pain. A huge number of these people, who were already contemplating Judaism, became followers of Paul. It is no wonder that he was always in trouble with the Jews and getting banned from synagogues. He was poaching on future members of the more traditional Jewish communities.

The very foundation of the book of Acts lies in that first Easter, the resurrection (3:15; 4:10; 10:40; and in particular, 13:20-27). GOD raised JESUS from the dead. It is that event that changed Christianity from a version of Judaism to a religion in its own right.

In 14:23 Luke refers to elders being appointed in each church. This is clearly something that Luke witnessed at the time he wrote his gospels, but elders were unknown at the time of Paul. We discussed this when we discussed the pastoral gospels of Timothy and Titus. When you have small home churches, like Paul had, you do not need bishops, deacons, and elders, and Paul never mentioned them in any of his letters.

Luke again proves to be a marvelous story teller. Acts is the tale of a great man who went from struggle to struggle, all beautifully told, but historically inaccurate.

15

The Origin of Satan

The Devil made me do it!

Flip Wilson

While many of the more traditional branches of the Christian religion place little significance in angels and devils, Satan has become a huge part of the rapidly growing Christian fundamentalist message today. The devil is often described as being "very, clever." This is a phrase that I hear with increasing frequency, but I have been unable to trace its origin.

Sometime back, a noted televangelist, Jimmy Swaggart, tearfully asked for forgiveness from his fall from grace, when he was caught regularly soliciting the services of prostitutes. Mr. Swaggart claimed it was the work of Satan because he had saved so many souls for JESUS that the Devil set out traps to discredit him. Satan is very clever, Swaggart said, and he was so tempted that he just did not see what was happening. Yeah. Ri-i-i-ght! I admit the Swaggart episode caused me to lose the objectivity I have tried so hard to cultivate, but it seems to be extremely presumptuous for someone to claim they know what Satan says or does. GOD left us 613 Laws, so we have a pretty good idea what GOD wants. Jesus made it clear what appropriate conduct was—doing onto others as you would want them to do onto you. However, there is nothing comparable in the Bible that tells us what Satan expects. At best, claiming, as Swaggart did, to know what Satan did to him, or what Satan wants, or what makes Satan happy is pure speculation. The concept of having someone else to blame for inappropriate conduct launched me into tracing the fascinating origin of Satan.

This turned out to be a marvelously invigorating investigation. I found that, at one time or another, Satan has been blamed for almost everything that anyone finds offensive. We have seen it often recently. I heard a minister say, "Satan loves it when we . . . ." How sis he know what Satan loves? America has been branded the "Great Satan" by some militant Islamic groups. President Bush has referred to countries as "the axis of evil." Even Martin Luther got into the act and called all Catholic Christians, all Jews, all who participated in the Peasants' War against the landowning aristocrats, and all non-Lutheran Protestants as "agents of Satan." Who is this guy Satan anyway (he is always represented as a man)?

Satan has been a problem for theologians dating from the first century. He was too much like a god—he was so powerful that even GOD seemed to have trouble with him. That seemed inconsistent with the concept of monotheism and an omnipotent god. (Later, the concept of an anti-Christ in the book of Revelation caused much of the same alarm—yet another god-like creature that is almost as powerful as JESUS). We shall see there was never this dualism in the Old Testament. The Hebrews never blamed Satan if something went wrong; they looked inward and said, "What have I done to offend Yaweh? There is a great section of Deuteronomy (28:1-68) where this is defined. There are a series of blessings for doing what is good and for punishing people for doing what is bad. GOD was the source of both good and evil. There was no anti-god to handle the evil part.

If Satan was such a nuisance, why didn't this omnipotent GOD simply get rid of him? Or why did He create Satan in the first place? GOD finished his creations including both angels and other incorporeal beings, such as cherubs and cherubim, and corporeal beings such as humans and animals. Then he paused and contemplated his works and "GOD saw *all he had made* and it was *good* (Gen 1:31)." Did GOD create this evil angel along with other angels that felt appropriate to be in His court? How could GOD have made such a mistake that he initially felt that *everything* he created was good?

You can imagine why scholars have been bothered by this concept of Satan for so long. Let's look at the whole story. First of all, we need to define some terms, because, once again, they are terms that have very different meanings today than they did in Biblical times. We have discussed the problem of the changes that occur in word meanings over the years to where they often take on a secondary meaning that has little, if anything, to do with the literal definition of the word. That is one of the problems in translating the Bible and we have discussed it often.

The following are terms that are often used interchangeably with the word "Satan" today, but if you looked them up in a first century dictionary, had there been such a book, they would have an entirely different meaning. These definitions are what a first century Middle Eastern resident would have understood the words to mean.

aka Satan

Satan is from the ancient Hebrew word that was written *stn* or, later, *Ha-satan* which means "one who opposes, obstructs, or acts as adversary." In the Old Testament it does not represent a beast or monster, or anything else that is evil but is actually one or more of GOD'S angels and is usually shown as being in GOD's heavenly court. Satan describes a role given or adopted by certain angels, the role of adversary, not a particular character. Satan was never a proper name.

In Job, for example, we have seen that satan, far from being thrown out of Heaven, was sitting with GOD in Heaven and chatting. He and GOD are making a bet on what this mortal Job will do. Satan does not represent a beast or monster and possesses no demonic qualities in Old Testament writings. Far from disobeying or fighting against GOD, in Job he never acts beyond the parameters set by GOD. In fact, it actually describes one of GOD's angels. The satan we see in Job is very consistent with all of the other Old Testament references to satan, where GOD is responsible for both praise and punishment and satan is merely GOD's heavenly adversary.

Angel is the English translation of the Greek word *angelos* which means "messenger" or "one sent" or "one going." The Hebrew word is *malak*. *Malak* means "messenger." In both Hebrew and Greek the term was used interchangeably for either devine or human messengers. In the Septuagint the word used is *aggelos* which also can be used for either a human messenger or a spirit messenger. When the early translators translated Septuagint into Latin, however, they had a problem. Latin has one word for a devine messenger, *angelus*, and different words for human messengers, either *legatus* or *nuntius,* so the translator had to guess which word should be used. Unfortunately, these words were sometimes improperly attributed to a devine messenger when they should have been to a human messenger and vice versa.

Angels are common in the ancient Semitic religions. The earliest mention of them is in Sumarian tablets which predate the Bible by a couple of centuries. The Arab concepts of Genii and Djinns originated with the Sumerian angels. These were all spiritual beings without corporeal substance. Recent archaeological finds support certain references in the Bible to places where angels of GOD lurk (Gen 32:1-2) which are reminiscent of the Genii who were believed to haunt particular areas.

There are so many different and often confusing references to angels in the Bible that they could easily have their own chapter. Sometimes they are described as being enormous in number, even comprising armies (Dan 7:10; Ps 67:18; Mt 26:53; Rev 5:11), and, at other times, they seem to number very few. In Hebrew, angels were usually called "sons of GOD," (*ben e Elohim*) and were like GOD's royal court and at other times a Divine army. There are suggestions in both the Old and New Testaments that angels are made by GOD just as man was created by GOD; they are said to be less than a god but higher than humans (Ps 8:6; 148:2. See also Paul's comments in Col 1:16-17). The Fourth Lateran Council of the Church in 1215 C.E. held that GOD created, at the same time, two creatures, one spiritual and the other corporeal. The spiritual creations were the angels and the corporeal creations were the animals. Mankind, which has both spiritual and corporeal aspects, was created later. In the Hebrew Bible angels are nearly always messengers; determining their actual numbers with any degree of accuracy is impossible.

While angels make frequent appearances only early on in the Old Testament, they are found throughout the New Testament. We find them at the very beginning telling Mary and Zachary about the coming birth of the Messiah; we see them telling the shepherds how they witnessed the miraculous birth. Jesus told his followers that when they die they will be like angels in heaven (Mt 22:30; Lk 20:36). At the approach of the very end of time, angels again show up as JESUS says that he "sent my angel to testify to you these things in the churches (Rev 22:16)."

While Satan is described as being a "fallen angel," every reference I have seen to angels shows that they are good.

Devil is the English version of the Greek word *diavolo* and the Latin *diabolus* which translates literally as "one who throws something across one's path." The name is derived from the Greek word *diaballein* which literally means "to defame" and was often used to describe a slanderer or accuser. Since satan is similarly defined as "one who opposes, obstructs, or acts as adversary," eventually the word devil became interchangeable with satan. The Fourth Lateran Council in 1215 C.E. also settled the issue on the devil and demons holding that they "were created by GOD good in their nature but they by themselves have made themselves evil." That is, they were in the spiritual group, like the angels, full of good and innocence but they became evil on their own. That declaration removes any blame that might otherwise be placed on GOD for a faulty creation. Also like the angels, they were purely spiritual beings without earthly bodies. None of this was from the Bible, of course; it is much later thirteenth century church dogma.

The concept that the devil and his rebellious angels committed some sin that got them banished from GOD's Holy Kingdom came from Ez 28:12-16 and became church Dogma at the Fourth Lateran Council. This has caused enormous difficulty for theologians: angels seem to have great powers and knowledge. What sin could they have possibly committed? Sin had always been considered the wickedness that resulted from the weaknesses of the flesh; the ignorance or neglect of man, or the ability of something with angelic powers strong enough to lure man into indiscretions. Angels, however, had no flesh or earthy existence so how could they be guilty of carnal sin? This issue has been debated for centuries by such early theologians as Thomas Aquinas, Anselm, and Scotus, but never with a satisfactory resolution.

Demon is the English version of the Greek word *daemon* and the Latin *daimones*, both of which mean "spirit energies." When early Christian writers such as Justin Martyr wrote in the second century that "the *daimones* are responsible," they were referring to those mythical spirit energies which can be good spirits or bad spirits. Later writers interpreted these spirit energies to be all evil spirits and over time they "morfed" into Satan. After the Fourth Lateran Council referred to "the devil and the other demons" and determined that "the chief of the demons is called the devil," the word *demon* came to be used as a synonym for "devil." Again, it should be noted that this is an early church conclusion, not something stated in the Bible.

Beelzebub, or Baalzebul, was a reference to the Canaanite god Baal. It meant "Baal the exalted." Later Christian tradition associated this pagan god with Satan based upon statements by Matthew and Mark (Mt 11:24; Mk 3:22).

Lucifer means "Son of Morning Star." This is an adaptation by the Hebrews of a Canaanite myth of the gods *Helel* (Morning Star) and *Shahar* (Dawn) who are thrown out of Heaven as a result of rebellion. The Christian adaptation of this Canaanite myth is the fall of Lucifer and his attendant angels when they are all thrown out of Heaven and sent to Sheol, where the dead reside according to Hebrew tradition (Isa 14:12-15). The New Testament writers adopted this story as the origin of Satan:

How you are fallen from Heaven,
O Day Star, son of Dawn!
How you are cut down to the ground,
you who laid the nations low!
You said in you heart,
"I will ascend to Heaven;
I will raise my throne
above the stars of GOD;
I will sit on the mount of assembly
on the heights of Zaphon;
I will ascend to the tops of the clouds,
I will make myself like the Most High."
But you are brought down to Sheol,
to the depths of the Pit (Lk 10:18).

The reference by Luke to "Day Star (*Helel*), son of Dawn (*Shahar*)," is a direct reference to the Canaanite myth. The son of Helel is Lucifer. This Old Testament statement is the story of the fallen angel that is generally considered by Christians to be the evil Satan or the Devil or Lucifer. It is often merged with the passage from Ezekiel referred to above (28:12-19) which states:

You were the signet of perfection,
full of wisdom and perfect in beauty,
13 *You were in Eden, the garden of GOD;*
every precious stone was your covering,
carnelian, chrysolite, and moonstone,
beryl, onyx, and jasper,
sapphire, turquoise, and emerald;
and worked in gold were your settings
and your engravings.

On the day that you were created
they were prepared.
14 *With an anointed cherub as guardian I placed you;*
you were on the holy mountain of God;
you walked among the stones of fire.
15 *You were blameless in your ways from the day that you were created,*
until iniquity was found in you.
16 *In the abundance of your trade*
you were filled with violence, and you sinned;
so I cast you as a profane thing from the mountain of God,
and the guardian cherub drove you out
from among the stones of fire.
17 *Your heart was proud because of your beauty;*
you corrupted your wisdom for the sake of your splendor.
I cast you to the ground;
I exposed you before kings,
to feast their eyes on you.
18 *By the multitude of your iniquities,*
in the unrighteousness of your trade,
you profaned your sanctuaries.
So I brought out fire from within you;
it consumed you,
and I turned you to ashes on the earth
in the sight of all who saw you;
19 *you have come to a dreadful end*
and shall be no more forever.

The problem is that GOD was not talking about Satan, the evil fallen angel, at all. This entire section of Ezekial (Ch 26-28) is a message about the king of Tyre, based upon a mythical Ugaritic figure that appeared in the ancient Middle East as either a human or an incorporeal being**. The covering of precious stones is similar to the stones of the high priest's breastplate (Ex 28:17-20) which was also of mystical significance. Verse 14. which refers to the cherub is most likely a reference to the king himself being a cherub. Verse 16 is translated here as "and the guardian cherub drove you out . . ." but the original Hebrew says, "I drove you out, O guardian cherub." This supports the position that the king was not a human being. One thing is certain, however, this passage is not a reference to that evil being we know as Satan.

** This analysis, not done by me, of course, but by Old Testament scholars, is rather complex based upon passages in several books including Prov 16:5; Isa 14:13-14; Dan 14:14, 30:10-11; and many more

The Old Testament Satan

I was stunned to discover that Satan as an evil force is basically a New Testament creation that didn't begin to take form until the intertestamentary period. "What?" you say. What about the story of Job and the number that Satan did on him? Well, let's talk about that. As near as I can tell, there are only six places in the Old Testament where Satan is mentioned—the story of Balaam and his donkey, Job, David when he introduced a new tax, a brief mention of Satan and Soloman, and when Satan speaks for the people in Judah that are being displaced in Zechariah. Let's take them one at a time.

The Strange Story of Balaam

Balaam was, apparently, a well known character in the Middle East at the time this story was written. He also shows up in the surviving literature of other countries, although this story is unique to the Bible. The part of the story in which we are interested[***] seems out of place when read with the entire Balaam episode which actually starts in Numbers 22:1. It is part of several stories about this character that are woven together, so they are a little confusing. Balaam, after receiving permission from GOD to travel, angered GOD in some indeterminate way who then sent out an "angel of the Lord" to stop Balaam. The words that are translated into English as "angel of the Lord" are, in Hebrew, *le-satan-lo* which actually means adversary or messenger.

In this story, Balaam does not see the angel but the donkey does and gets out of the way in accordance with the angel's orders. Balaam thereupon beats the donkey three times, who then turns and speaks to Balaam, wanting to know why Balaam is beating him.

In this story, Satan was not the evil force that we associate with that name. Satan here is actually a messenger of GOD, a member of GOD's court. In fact, all of the modern translations that I have seen of the Balaam story faithfully translate Satan into "angel of the Lord."

There is a similar reference where an enemy of Solomon is described as, "Then the Lord raised up against Solomon an *adversary*." In the original Hebrew the word used was "satan." Again, this is neither a fallen angel or an evil being of any kind.

God Betting with Satan on Job

We discussed the story of Job in Chapter 8. What is important here is that, in the story of Job, Satan was part of GOD's own Court. This was not a discredited angel that had been banned to live forever in the fires of Hell. It would not make sense if it were. If Satan had been banned from

---

[***] Num 22:23-33. However, Balaam was also portrayed in other passages such as Num 31:8, 16, Deut 23:5, Josh 13:22; 24:10, and Neh 13:2. Most of the time he is presented as a rather seedy character

Heaven to spend the rest of his life in Hell, what would he be doing in Heaven again and what would GOD be doing having a friendly bet with him?

The word used in the Hebrew Bible was "*Stn*" which means "adversary" or "one who opposes." Today he would have been called the "Devil's Advocate" which is a term used by the Vatican. When they are choosing a new Pope, one Cardinal is assigned to each of the potential candidates. His job is to research everything bad about that candidate that he can find and to pass this on to the College of Cardinals when that candidate is being discussed and to argue vociferously against his candidacy. That person is called the Devil's Advocate and is like a prosecuting attorney. But in Old Testament times the satan was merely an adversary or one who opposes or accuses. He was a member of GOD's court and one of his basic duties was to accuse human beings before GOD, which is precisely what he did in the story of Job.

King David's Conflict with Satan

Chronicles has a peculiar reference to Satan. The Chronicler retells a story originally written in 2 Samuel 24, "Satan stood up against Israel, and incited David to count the people of Israel (21:1)." The correct translation is universally agreed today to be "an adversary" rather than Satan. The original version in 2 Sam 24.1 uses the phrase, "the angel of the Lord." This is not the evil demon, the fallen angel. It is a person from the Lord's court expressing GOD's anger.

Joshua's Assault by Satan

Zechariah describes a vision of Joshua, a high priest in Jerusalem. In this vision, he sees, "Joshua standing before the angel of the Lord, and the satan standing at his right hand to accuse him." Again, if you read this entire episode, it is very clear that the satan is not that evil entity, that fallen angel, that we automatically visualize when we hear that name. He is the angel in GOD's court who is the adversary. He is a member of the court, not an outcast living in Hell. The Hebrew word used in each reference was the equivalent of "the accuser."

What about the Leviathan?

Isaiah talks about the day that "the Lord with his great hand will punish the *Leviathan*, the twisting *serpent*, and will slay the *dragon* that is in the sea. (27:1) These are creatures from Canaanite mythology and the story merely shows GOD's dominance over these false gods. They are referred to in later Christian literature, especially in Revelation, as being synonymous with Satan. The Old Testament makes no such reference. It is also from Revelation that the serpent in the Creation story is often thought of as being Satan.

The Intertestamental Period

When the Babylonians conquered Judah in 586 B.C.E. the Hebrews were exposed to many new religious ideas including the monotheistic Mithras religion. This fit very well with their tradition of Yahweh being the all powerful chief god in their pantheon. The Babylonians destroyed the Temple which, in and of itself, required major modifications to the practice of Judaism. If you recall the story in Exodus of GOD instructing the Israelites in precise detail how to make a portable temple so that GOD could travel with the Israelites. After they reached the Promised Land they were to build a permanent temple for GOD's earthly home and where they were to worship GOD. With the destruction of the temple, GOD and his worshipers were now free to meet at places outside of the temple and it did not even have to be in Judah, let alone Jerusalem.

When the Jews began to move back home 50 years later they had to change many more aspects of their religious observances. For example, King Darius granted them their freedom, but since Judah would still be a Persian state it would have been unseemly to elect their own king. Therefore, the priests were quietly granted the duties of the former kings in addition to their priestly duties. That required the priests to assume some very unclean duties such as retaining police and executing prisoners. Later the Hebrews were conquered by the Greeks and others bringing even more modifications to their worship traditions.

In the 400 years following the Exile, there were a lot of Hebrew writings, some appear in the Old Testament and some in the Apocrypha, but many don't appear in either. It is in these books, beginning with Daniel, which was written at about 250 B.C.E., that the seeds of Satan as a purveyor of evil were first sown.

For a time after the Maccabees defeated the Selucid rulers everything was peachy in Palestine. Eventually, the Maccabean rulers went too far and lost the support of the Jewish populace. Most of the Jews, including the Pharisees, still backed the country as they looked upon the country as "Israel against 'the nations' *(ha goyim).*" However, there were several groups of extremists, including the Essenes, who felt differently. They were opposed to the other Jews, not the rest of the world. It was these dissident groups that began to use the term "satan" to characterize the Jews that still backed the Maccabees. Little by little they began to turn the word satan from a job description into an evil entity or even a person. Satan became, as Pagels notes, "GOD's antagonist, his enemy, even his rival. . . [denouncing] their opponents as apostate and [accusing] them of having been seduced by the power of evil, whom they call by many names—Satan, Beelzebub, Semihazah, Azazal, Belial, Prince of Darkness."

After this, beginning about 160 B.C.E., books describing Satan as being something evil were showing up everywhere. The terms moved from being applied to other Jews to angels. One set of stories, a portion of which ended up in the apocryphal book of 1 Enoch, describes how angels that GOD sent to watch over the universe fell out of favor and were banned from Heaven. The strange story in Genesis 6:1-4 where a group of angels apparently were smitten by the beauty of human women and married some of them was resurrected. The offspring of these misogynous marriages became the "fallen ones" (*nephilim*).

We know from the Dead Sea Scrolls that the Essene greatly enlarged the new evil being stories. They considered themselves to be the "sons of light" and were opposed by a group they called "sons of darkness." They actually restated the entire story of Israel and casting the Evil One as the cause of all of Israel's problems. They even developed a sacred text to identify supernatural good and evil forces so they could understand how they relate to each other.

That is it for the Old Testament and the Apocraphya. Although the Essene created The Evil One, he was never a player in the Hebrew Scriptures. It was always GOD himself who punished his people when they did wrong.

The New Testament Satan

In the decades immediately following JESUS' death most Jewish Christians maintained their Jewish traditions and followed the Law. In fact, as you might recall, the Pillars of Jerusalem strictly maintained their observance of the Law. James, JESUS' brother, even had the nickname "James the Just." Others, such as those who followed Peter, began to modify their observance of dietary and sexual laws.

Between 70 and 100 C.E. many Christian Jews were being pushed out of traditional Jewish society. They were generally rejected by Jewish leaders and often thrown out of their home synagogues. They found that they were forced to meet in homes with gentile Christians. The result was that they began to drop their historic Jewish traditions and customs. Not surprisingly, the first practice to go was circumcision followed closely by dietary laws and Sabbath laws.

By 75 C.E., most of the Jews had been expelled from Palestine by the Romans, and most Christian churches in that area were predominantly gentile and there was a strong gentile influence in the others. They still insisted, however, that they were the true and authentic Judaism rather than the Rabbinical Judaism that was gaining popularity. The degree that Jewish Christians were being squeezed out of the synagogues varied from town to town.

Matthew, Mark, and probably John were all of Jewish ancestry and the groups that followed their versions of the new religion began to drift more and more away from traditional Judaism. Luke, the only gentile author, wrote that his group had taken over and had inherited Israel's place as GOD's chosen people. John became very angry at the Jewish hierarchy as you have seen.

The concept of Satan as this evil, vicious, deceitful demon did not exist in two thousand years of Hebrew religion. It remained for the New Testament writers to introduce us to this anti-god. It took awhile, though. Paul had almost nothing to say on the issue except in passing in one letter. It was after Timothy returned from his trip to Corinth and told Paul about the other apostles that had recently come to that city and were undermining Paul's work. That's what triggered Paul to fire off one of the letters contained in Second Corinthians. Paul raged on about the "false apostles, deceitful workers, disguising themselves as apostles of Christ. And no wonder! Even Satan disguises himself as an angel of light*." The phrase "angel of light" is right out of Essene literature, and .that is pretty much all Paul has to say about Satan.

The author of Ephesians, writing in Paul's name in the late first century, exhorts his readers to:

> *Put on the whole armor of GOD, so that you may be able to stand against the wiles of the devil. For our struggle is not against enemies of blood and flesh, but against . . . the cosmic powers of this present darkness, against the spiritual forces of evil in the heavenly places.*

This was written long after Paul's death and after three of the four gospels. By that time, "devil" had become a synonym for Satan who had been defined as the spiritual force of evil.

While Paul had little to say about Satan, we don't have to read far to find references to the Evil One in the New Testament. Mark, the first book in the New Testament starts us off. We meet JESUS in the first chapter as John baptizes him in the Jordan River. JESUS then goes into the wilderness where he spent forty days and nights being tempted by Satan and the battle between JESUS and Satan begins. The forty days of wilderness testing was an Old Testament tradition. Matthew, as was his wont, throws in a couple of extra tests for good measure and gives us a couple of new names for Satan, "the tempter" and "the devil (4:1-11)." Luke's later version also uses the word "devil."

There is little dispute among scholars that all three of the gospel writers were referring to the same Evil One even though they identified him by different names. In the first century, a person who was ill was often deemed to be possessed by demons. They knew nothing about germs, so people were healed when someone could "cast out" the demons. As a healer, JESUS was frequently asked to cast out demons that were causing someone to suffer. He was apparently a pretty good healer. Unfortunately,

---

* 2 Cor 11:13-14; See also 2:11; 12:7. Satan is also referred to as "the god of this world" in 4:4 and "Belial," in 6:15. Paul really, really did not like these apostles

good healers were often accused of being tools of the demons themselves. This even happened to JESUS. The temple scribes accused him of being in league with Beelzebul. JESUS countered this accusation with his famous "house divided" story saying that Satan could not rise up against himself, thereby equating Satan with Beelzebul (Mk 3:22-27; Mt 12:14-29; Lk 11:14-23):

> *[The scribes shout that] 'He casts out demons by Beelzebul, the prince of demons'; But he said to them, 'Every kingdom divided against itself is laid waste, and a divided household falls. And if Satan also is divided against himself, how will his kingdom stand: For you say that I cast out demons by Beelzebul.'*

This is basically a series of couplets:

> *If a government is divided against itself*
> *that government will perish;*
> *If a house is divided against itself*
> *that house will perish;*

Therefore, it logically follows that:

> *If Satan is divided against himself*
> *Satan will perish.*

This brilliant argument is very typical of JESUS. What he is basically saying is that it is logically inconsistent to charge that he could be in league with Satan if he is also casting out Satan's demons. If he is casting out demons He must be on the side of good, not evil. This is not only the first time that JESUS used the word "Satan," it is the only time that he used the word in any phrase that is considered by scholars to be words that were actually spoken by JESUS. Matthew's version of this story also refers to Satan but Luke, placing this story much later in his narrative, refers only to "demons by Beelzebul." By the time of the gospels, "demons," "beelzebul," and "Satan" had apparently taken on secondary, or perhaps even principal, meanings associated with the Evil One. Scholars believe that the fact that "Beelzebul" is mentioned first indicates it retains the original meaning at the time JESUS spoke the words (the Canaanite god *Baal-ze-bul*, "Baal the Prince") and that the use of "Satan" in the last part reflects the later association with Satan.

In another parable reported by Matthew, the parable of the seeds and weeds (13:36-43), Matthew gives the parable a very apocalyptic interpretation. Matthew describes the story as a contest between the "children of the Kingdom" and the "children of the evil one" and the enemy who sowed them as the "devil." This same parable appears in other documents, but the earliest versions, such as we find in the *Gospel of Thomas* written some 35 years before Matthew, contain no such apocalyptic message. There is no contest between good and evil and there is no devil. For many reasons scholars believe that the early versions are the most accurate. The Matthew version is not at all like the usual JESUS parable. There is nothing to make each individual think about the message JESUS is trying to get across. It is all pretty well laid out. Also, there is no surprise ending. When the apocalyptic portions are removed it begins to sound like JESUS.

What the parable does illustrate, however, is that by the time Matthew wrote his gospel about 85 C.E., Christians were hearing an apocalyptic message. Matthew's story continues a few verses later with JESUS saying that the angels will come and separate the evil from the righteous and throw them into the furnace of fire along with Matthew's usual "weeping and gnashing of teeth."

All of this anger that Matthew gives JESUS is directed at the pharisees. He even calls them "children of hell (23:15)." Matthew's anger builds until it reaches its climax in chapter 23. Matthew must have had a huge grudge against the pharisees. It was common among philosophers at that time to attack their opponents with strong language. You might remember some of the examples of Paul's vilification of the "false apostles" for instance. But to accuse your opponents of being in league with the devil and calling down the wrath of GOD upon them was unheard of except from some of the fanatical Essene at a much earlier time.

Luke has JESUS making a rather strange statement about Satan. JESUS has just sent out 70 (72 in some translations) of his apostles that he has endowed with the ability to cast out demons in his name. They return and excitedly tell JESUS that in his name even the demons flee. Then JESUS says, "I watched Satan fall from Heaven like a flash of lightning" (Lk 10:18). Does this statement mean that Satan was in Heaven just a few days prior or was it merely intended as a metaphor? Is it the fallen angel Ezekiel spoke of centuries earlier? In any event, it is clear that reference to "demons" means soldiers of Satan rather than the traditional meaning of demons.

Luke also note's JESUS' struggles with the pharisees, but strangely it is a group of pharisees that warns JESUS that Herod wants to kill him (12:31-32). JESUS goes on to say that he is going to stay and cast out demons and cure people for the next three days, Herod or no Herod. JESUS is obviously speaking about bad demons, Satan. By this time demons has assumed a secondary meaning referring to emissaries of Satan. While few scholars believe that the words of JESUS in the above two situations were actually spoken by him, clearly both Matthew and Luke understood Satan is the Evil One and demons were his workers.

Now let's take a look at what John has to say. At the outset, let me remind you that few scholars believe that any of the JESUS quotations in John were actually spoken by JESUS, and in the few that they do feel have some authenticity, it is only the subject matter referred to that is authentic. This being said, John saw nothing but evil in the Jews. Using the words of John the Baptist, John has JESUS identify the Jews as the spawn of Satan.

> *You are from your father the devil, and you choose to do your father's desires. He was a murderer from the beginning and does not stand in the truth, because there is no truth in him."* (8:44)

While he was speaking primarily of the pharisees, his words are pretty all-inclusive of Jews in general and that is the way the words were interpreted throughout history. Even though John and his followers were Jews and considered themselves merely to be Jews who believed in the message of JESUS, the other Jews had been banning them from meeting in the synagogues and were treating them badly. That probably explains the invective language.

John also was the first to identify Judas Iscariot as "a devil (6:70-71)." John was speaking of a servant of the Evil One in that he referred to "a devil" rather than "the Devil." This distinction is important because it was the first hint of the contest between JESUS (good) and Satan (evil) that is the theme for the rest of John's book. When JESUS and his disciples were in Gethsemane, Matthew simply has JESUS announce the coming of Judas with, "Get up, let us be going. See, my betrayer is at hand (26:46)."John, on the other hand, has JESUS say,

> *[T]he ruler of this world is coming. He has no power over me, but I do as the Father has commanded me, so that the world may know that I love the Father. Rise, let us be on our way.* (14:33)

The "ruler of this world," as we noted earlier, is the Evil One and JESUS will submit to him so that his power will be broken by JESUS' death and resurrection.

Early Christian Writers

That is pretty much all the Bible has to say about Satan. At the end of the first century and into the second, there were a group of very influential Biblical writers. Some were called the "Apostalic Fathers," because,at the time, they were believed to have known Paul and Peter. These were Clement of Rome, Ignatius of Antioch, and Polycarp of Smyrna. They were all very prolific writers of early Christian literature. We know now that these people all lived long after the deaths of Peter and Paul, but they were, and still are, very influential writers and all set out strict moral codes. Others who also had strong moral codes, were later included in the group, including the author of the *Didache* and the author of the *Epistle of Barnabas* which references Satan. You may recall that Barnabas was a companion of Paul, but this "Epistle" was written by someone else, long after the death of Barnabas.

The moral code devised in *Barnabas* was different from the others in that he described the forbidden conduct as "the spirit of GOD" contending against "the Prince of Evil." This is much like the quote in the epigram, "The Devil made me buy this hat." You had to fight to keep Satan from misleading you. His list of prohibited conduct was long and exhaustive. He listed such things as "fornication*," the** intercourse with boys, "the arrogance of power," and standing up for the rich while denying the poor the same benefits. You have to stand up against all of this because it is the work of Satan. "The days are evil and the evildoer is still in power." He actually wrote that you must make sure you are not like the Jews (meaning Israel) who "transgressed because an evil angel was leading them into error." "They have counseled evil against themselves saying, 'Let us bind the righteous one, for he is unprofitable for us'." *Barnabas* became the most influential moral code in Christianity for hundreds of years, and even today for some Christians.

Another writer in this group was Ireneaus who was the Bishop of Lyons. In about 180 C.E. he wrote five volumes about certain Christians whom he referred to as "heretics" and whom he claimed were agents of the Devil. Those he referred to as "heretics" were Christians who held beliefs contrary to his own; that is, if you understand JESUS' message differently than I, you must be an agent of Satan. There were many such groups, and the one most familiar to us today are the Gnostics. The advocates of these other versions, Iraneaus railed, were inspired by Satan; they only pretend to be Christians in order to preach an "abyss of madness and blasphemy against Christ." His version of Christianity was the version we know today as Catholic (universal), and all of the writings of the "heretics" were destroyed. Or so he thought. Little did he know that in 1945, in the desert town of Nag Hammadi, the works of some of these "heretics" would be rediscovered. Until that discovery the first volume of the work of Ireneaus, called *Against Heresies,* was the authority on the subject.

About the same time, another influential writer, Tertullian of Carthage, lent support to Iraneaus' positions regarding Satan. Tertullian pointed out that the word "heresy" (*hairesis* in Greek) means "choice,"and he claimed that making choices was evil because it separated Christians into groups. He insisted that the populace not be allowed to ask the church leaders questions because questions are what make people heretics. Tertullian believed that JESUS was wrong to say "Ask, and you will receive; seek, and

---

* This Greek word is translated broadly and probably includes any extramarital sexual activity

** The word "the" is in the masculine form

you shall find; and knock, and it shall be opened to you (Mt 7:7)." Tertullian's response was, "Let us remember at what time the Lord said this. I think it was at the very outset of his teaching, when there was still a doubt felt by all whether he were the Christ." Now we know the answers to all of those questions so there is no need to ask them. He rails against the Jews about their responses to ask, seek, and knock. He further says that, if someone does ask, the church leaders "have a moral responsibility" not to answer. They, the "straight thinking" people (what "orthodox" actually means) must claim the Scriptures for themselves. The heretics will try to lay claim to them, but that is Satan working through them.

Mediaeval Authors and Artists

The Satan of the Gospels was seen primarily as luring people away from GOD. The Early Christian writers began to envision Satan as also having a part in wrong-doing—leading people into sin. Then along came two very influential authors in the middle ages who wrote enormously popular books about Satan and hell, Dante Alighieri's *Inferno*, part of *Devine Comedy*, written in 1321, and John Milton's *Paradise Lost*, written in the early days of the Renaissance, 1667.

Dante travels through the nine circles of Hell in the morose poetry of Devine Comedy. The circles are concentric, like a target, with each circle representing an increase in sinful behavior, and culminating at the center of the circles and the center of the earth where Satan resides in bondage. Mythical creatures and strange descriptions abound. The poetry of Dante was very graphic and became the subject of hundreds of paintings. The images in those paintings are how many people today view Hell and Satan.

In another poetic work, the epic 10 volume (later rearranged into 12 volumes) *Paradise Lost* by Milton showed us Satan (Lucifer) as a fallen angel. Satan is shown as an ambitious angel who defies GOD, his creator, and who declares war on GOD and the angels. He is defeated and he and his fellow rebel angels are cast into Hell. Milton blended paganism and Christianity as where Satan is introduced to death and sin in a rather bizarre, incestuous manner. The book, was very popular and influential and gave another boost to the character of Satan. The book was beautifully illustrated and those illustrations also affect how people today envision Satan and hell.

Many people, when they are describing Satan, do so in terms of the way he is depicted in *Inferno* or *Paradise Lost* rather than in any Biblical characterization. However, even today people are ascribing more and more identities to Satan. Many assign Satan to characters noted in he book of Revelation, for example. The book refers to the number 666, and people assume that it must refer to Satan. It doesn't. Every creature identified in Revelation is ascribed to Satan, including serpents and leviathan. The Bible doesn't say that, it is Christians interpreting the Bible (incorrectly).

16

The Fat Lady Sings

The opera is not over until the Fat Lady Sings.
Annon

This concludes are journey into the history of the Bible and brings us to the end of our story. I hope you have enjoyed the journey as much as I have. No matter how interesting history may be, it is of little value unless we learn something from it that is relevant to our lives today. There are many current issues that are grounded in religious controversy. Let's look at some of these using our new-found knowledge to guide us?

How Do We Handle Inerrancy?

By now it should be apparent that the Bible is not inerrant. Bishop John Shelby Spong, one of my favorite Biblical authors, once wrote, "When someone tells me that they believe the Bible is the 'literal and inerrant word of God,' I always ask, 'Have you ever read it'?" Inerrancy is one of the basic tenets of the Evangelical, Pentecostal, and the various Charismatic groups. In the end, though, does it really matter that parts of the Bible are not literally accurate? Bishop Spong has not lost even a smidgen of his strong religious beliefs merely because he discovered that the Bible is not inerrant. GOD is still GOD, and JESUS is still JESUS.

Even if GOD did inspire the people who wrote the Bible, we know from previous chapters that not one of those "inspired" documents still exists! Not even a tiny fragment. They haven't existed for centuries. Should that bother us? It certainly didn't bother JESUS or Paul that the only Old Testament documents they had to look at were imperfect copies. After decades of study and discussion, the Masoretes, between the seventh and the tenth centuries C.E. decided which of the many versions of the Hebrew Scriptures were the closest to the originals. Since then there have been many new discoveries of far older versions of the ancient manuscripts than any used by the Masoretes like, for example, the Dead Sea Scrolls. Even so, the Masoretic texts are far different from, and more accurate than, the faulty Septuagint used by Paul and JESUS. It didn't bother them that they were working from faulty texts.

It is estimated even today that as many as 25% of the words in the

Hebrew Scriptures are still incorrect because the original texts (those inspired by GOD?) and the copies that they made did not have any vowels. As late as the early tenth century C.E., the Hebrew scholars were still debating the correct vowel sounds until they finally decided to adopt an official Masoretic Text with vowel sounds (those little marks below the letters are the "vowel points"). This decision was far from unanimous; there were two factions with very different ideas on vowel sounds. All of the Old Testament works in English language Bibles in use today are from these Masoretic texts.

The New Testament is in the same shape. Even the oldest Greek texts in existence are many generations removed from the originals, and they are loaded with errors and discrepancies, some going to the very root of Christian belief. Assuming that the original documents were written through Divine inspiration, is it still relevant now since none of them exist? It cannot be claimed that the people who copied the documents were also divinely inspired because the copies are filled with errors that we know about. How many other parts contain errors that are not presently suspect? If GOD had inspired all of the scribes that did the copy work, would there be errors? Also, we have seen how scribes often changed the text. Entire sections have been intentionally added and deleted.

We don't have the original words, whether they were dictated by GOD, inspired by GOD, or simply written by humans to describe their religion. The inerrant texts, if there ever were such documents, do not and have not existed for centuries. They are, therefore, irrelevant. In the beginning of Chapter 2, I suggested there were five possible answers to who wrote the Bible. In truth, it doesn't matter, because all we are left with are faulty copies. Had it been important to GOD that the original texts be preserved, wouldn't He have made sure that it happened. Would He have allowed faulty copies and translations? The answer is: No." He would have preserved the inerrant documents forever. An omnipotent god is certainly capable of doing so. Therefore, the logical conclusion is that it was not important to GOD that we have the originals.

Fact or Myth

Before I completely wind it up, I feel that I would be remiss if I did not briefly cover one additional topic. There has always been controversy surrounding the Bible. Huge portions of the Bible are unsupported by any other authority. Abraham, for example, appears in no other work than the Bible. There are some highly credentialed Biblical scholars who propose that portions of the Bible have little or no historical significance and that the stories are simply tribal legends. I do not want to dwell on this subject, but much of it includes Biblical history. Cities are named in the Bible and a great many of them have been excavated. Do recent archaeological explorations of the ruins of those cities support, dispute, or are neutral to the stories in the Bible? What do contemporary texts from other civilizations say about the events depicted in the Bible?

In some cases the only reason given for doubting a Biblical story is that there is no evidence, outside of the Bible itself, of the event or person who is the subject of the story where one would expect there to be such evidence. Ordinarily the mere absence of evidence concerning an event is not necessarily evidence of the absence of the event. However, if there is absence of evidence where one would expect to find such evidence, one might infer that the event never occurred. Confused? Let's look at a couple of examples.

The court records of Pontius Pilate still exist today and are amazingly complete. There is not one single entry in those records that could possibly be a reference to the trial and/or death of JESUS. Does that mean that JESUS' trial and execution never happened? In other words, does the absence of evidence of the trial and execution constitute evidence that it never happened? Not at all. I think that it is fair to say that nearly all New Testament Scholars are convinced that JESUS was a living, breathing person who was arrested and executed by crucifixion during the time of Pontius Pilate, although they may not necessarily believe that any of the four Biblical versions of those events is an accurate record of the details of those events. There may be no court records of the execution, but there is a wealth of secondary evidence that the events did occur. It may have been a very summary proceeding where Pilate did not even get involved and no record made. JESUS made the authorities angry, they arrested him and summarily executed him. It happened all the time under Pilate's rule.

The Exodus Redux

On the other hand, what about the Exodus? Archaeologists have been unable to find any evidence whatsoever of the Exodus. I mean zilch. Nada. If there was an army of hundreds of thousands of people marching across the land fir 40 years, you would expect to find some evidence that they existed. However, if the Exodus happened, it was about 3500 years ago. Nobody is even sure what route the Israelites took. They were nomadic, never settling in one spot for any extended period. They never built any cities and the desert is an unforgiving environment that is constantly changing. All things considered, it is not at all surprising that there is no archaeological record of the travels of the Israelites. So the fact that there is an absence of evidence of the Exodus, at least in this incidence, is not evidence that there was no such event.

If the story ended there I doubt that there would be any controversy. But, of course, nothing about the Bible is that simple and straightforward. There are places where the Bible tells us something happened during the

Exodus story which has proved to be unlikely. A good example of this is the excavation of the town of Jericho where "the walls came tumbling down." When Jericho was first excavated, the archaeologists discovered the walls and they had indeed been torn down and destroyed. This was announced to the world as proof of the Bible story. Unfortunately, they were wrong.

Archaeologists have since unearthed the remains of over 20 successive settlements on the Jericho site dating back to 11,000 years ago, making it one of the oldest continuously occupied cities in the world. However, no matter which of the two dates most commonly used for the Exodus is correct, neither of them work. The walls were destroyed long before the Israelites arrived. Therefore, the walls did not come tumbling down when Joshua had his men circling the town and blowing trumpets (Jos 6:1-25). For that and other reasons, the story of Joshua and Jericho is probably legend, not fact.

There are also archaeological finds that definitely harm the story of the Exodus. The city of Arad was not conquered by Joshua either (Jos 12:7-8; 14) because we now know it did not even exist at that time.

What else do we know that might shed some light on the issue? What about the records of other countries that were contemporaneous? For example, the records of the court of Egypt during the reign of Ramses the Great, who is generally considered to be "Pharaoh" in the Exodus story, maintained a detailed account of the history of the empire. You would expect to find some reference to the plagues that GOD brought down on the land if they actually happened wouldn't you? One would certainly expect that the deaths of all of the Egyptian children during the Passover event would be worthy of some note. And it is inconceivable that there would be no entry in the records of an entire army drowning in the Red Sea or of all of the gold and jewels purportedly stolen by the slaves when they left. This is a case where the absence of evidence in fact may be evidence of absence of fact. There is a minority view that Pharoah was Thutmose III (1490-1430), but the records of his reign also make no mention of anything regarding the Exodus. There are records of Ramses II, however, that lead to a completely different story.

This story begins when the 18th Egyptian Dynasty, started by Ahmose (sometimes Aahmes or Ahmes), conquered the land east of the Nile, all of Canaan, all of the Sinai, and the west bank of the Jordan all the way to Mesopotamia up to what is now the southernmost part of Turkey, the land of the Hittites. The conquest was complete about 1546 B.C.E. The border with the Hittites crept south until Seti I (1306-1290) pushed them back and regained all of the territory through Syria. Later, the Hittites took back some of the land and Seti's son, who was none other than Ramses the Great (1290-1224), had to beat them back again. He fought one of the most famous battles in all history near the Syrian town of Kadesh. He walked into a trap that could have easily wiped out his entire army, but he managed to fight to a stand-off. Fortunately, at that time Assyria was also threatening the Hittites. They knew they could not fight both the Egyptians and the Assyrians, so they negotiated a peace treaty with Rameses, the first such treaty in history. That occupation is recorded independently in the records of both Egypt and Assyria. That treaty was in effect for many years and Egypt held all of the land from Egypt to Syria and east to Mesopotamia and all of the Sinai.

Rameses son Merenptah was his successor and he kept the peace until he ran into a fierce group known as the "Sea People" who were living in what is now the Gaza Strip. These are the people who were later called the Philistines. Merenptah tangled with them and sort of won the battle. At least he claimed victory and took many Sea People back to Egypt as slaves, but he actually won only a small part of the territory.

This whole mini history lesson is to demonstrate that, at the time of the Exodus, the Israelites would have had to travel their entire journey through Egyptian territory for the entire 40 years they wandered in the wilderness. They would not have been attacking scattered independent cities; they would have been attacking cities under Egyptian rule. It is hard to imagine the Egyptians would not send an army to put down the Israelites who were systematically destroying their cities the way they did when threatened by the Hittites and the Philistines.

Scholars also note the similarities of the Exodus to the religious stories of other contemporaneous cultures. For example, Sargon, the Akkadian who conquered Sumer and became the first Semitic king of the vast empire in Mesopotamia in about 2350 B.C.E. was, as an infant, placed in a reed boat and sent down the Nile to safety like the Bible describes happening to Moses a thousand years later (and even later to JESUS per Matthew). Is it possible that the Israelites "borrowed" that story from Sargon?

In addition, Mesopotamian legend has it that their people escaped from slavery when they were led from captivity by a hero, Mises (sound familiar), a few hundred years earlier than the Exodus story. They also wandered in the desert for a long time before they settled in their own Promised Land. Mises did many of the very things attributed later to Moses: each carried a staff from which they worked miracles such as parting the Red Sea, getting water from a stone, feeding the masses, and so forth. Was the story of Moses merely an adaptation of the Sargon/Mises stories? There are many Hebrew scholars who believe just that.

Mises also received laws from a god on a mountain and wrote them on two stone tablets, just like Moses. This was a common legend in the Middle East. The Greek lawgiver, Dionysus, is depicted holding up two tables of stone on which the law was written. The Persian god, Zarathustra, also known by his Greek name, Zoroaster, received the Book of Law from god on top of a mountain. Minos, the King of the Minoan civilization on Crete, received the law from god on top of a mountain. It is not unreasonable to conclude that the story of Moses receiving the law from GOD on two tablets on a mountain was a composite of Middle Eastern legends, and that is precisely what most Biblical scholars believe today.

The most famous body of ancient laws of all is the Hammurabi Code which was written on clay tablets and can still be seen and read today. It predates Moses by about 1200 years. This body of law was purportedly given to Hammurabi of Babylon by the Sun God, Shamash. What is particularly interesting about Hammurabi's Code is how closely it matches Moses' laws. Although Hammurabi's body of law is much larger and covers many more situations, in those places where they do overlap in terms of subject matter, they are almost identical. The Hammurabi Code also has the first known building code which, as a former architect, always sends shivers up my spine when I think about it. It basically says that if you design a building and that building falls down and kills someone, so shall you be put to death.

The Assyrians living in Mesopotamia at the time of the Exodus had a sophisticated written language and kept very detailed records of what went on in the world around them. There is not a whisper in any of those records that lends any support to the credibility of the Biblical story of the Exodus. Surely, if there was a tribe wandering around in the area destroying city after city, they would be a major concern to the Assyrians and would merit some mention in their extensive records. The absence of evidence of the Exodus, all things considered, is definitely an instance where it is evidence that the stories never happened.

All of this has led many Old Testament scholars to conclude that the Exodus, as described in the Bible, did not actually occur in history but is, instead, a legend in which the religious stories of other cultures were borrowed and adapted to the Israelites beliefs. There is also a theory that is gaining a large following that adopts a little of both concepts. It holds that the Exodus occurred, only on a much smaller scale. Under this theory, most of the Israelites are believed to have been living in Canaan the whole time and joined with their fellow Hebrews when they arrived from Egypt.

This theory is supported by findings in the records of Ramses II and by many recent archaeological discoveries. It suggests that the Israelites were actually Canaanites. The Canaanites had occupied Palestine for centuries. They were not, generally, a cohesive unit, but rather a series of independent city/states, each with its own ruler. These early Israelites were a group of lower class citizens who were badly treated. There was very likely a group of these people living in Egypt who would have been the captives enslaved during the wars of Ramses II and his father as discussed above. A few hundred of them probably did escape and worked their way across the Sinai and back to Canaan. These people passed through the town of Moab, just as stated in the Exodus story, but, unlike the Exodus story, they stayed for awhile. According to Genesis, the Moabites were ancient relatives of the Israelites. The theory further proposes that they became intrigued by the Moabite concept of monotheism and their god, YHW. Sound somewhat familiar? They purportedly took the concept of YHW (they think it was pronounced Yah-HOO, belive it or not) with them back to Palestine and he eventually became the Israelite god YHWH.

When they returned to Palestine, they were again in the lower class, but, years later, when the ruling class weakened, they led a rebellion and were able to overthrow them. This happened city by city and this is likely where King David extended the holdings of the rebels into a new empire.

This theory, if true, would explain why the Israelite God made all of those laws against the old Canaanite religious practices. The Israelites were actually Canaanites and had worshiped those gods for centuries. Old habits die hard. That would also explain the laws against gay sex, bestiality, cross-dressing, and much more. This theory fills in most of the disputed facts surrounding the Exodus narrative in the Torah and is becoming well accepted.

Archaeological Evidence Supporting the Bible Stories

One of the problems I have found in researching this book is that far too often people first adopt a theory and then "mine" the Bible to find passages that seem to support the position. Matthew and Luke certainly did that. They pored over the Hebrew Scriptures looking for any quote they could use and construe it into a prophecy of JESUS and worked it into their Gospel. Up until very recently archaeology used the same sort of methods, only in reverse. When looking at archaeological evidence, one must use great care. Much of early Biblical archaeology is criticized by scholars for using the Bible to interpret the newly discovered evidence rather than letting the results of the excavations and scientific investigation offer the conclusions. Far too many set out on a "dig" for the sole purpose of seeking evidence to support the stories in the Bible rather than trying to find out what the evidence excavated actually says and only then checking to see if it supports the Bible, thus tainting their conclusions. The original conclusion regarding the wall in Jericho is a perfect example of this.

Another can be found in the search for Solomon's gates. First Kings 9:15 speaks of King Solomon construction projects:

> *Now this is the way King Solomon conscripted the Labor Corps to build the house of the Lord, his house, the Millo, the walls of Jerusalem, Hazor, Megiddo, and Gezer.*

All four of these cities were real cities at one time and Jerusalem still is.

Their locations are well known. This seemed to some to be a good place to prove the truthfulness of the Bible. All one had to do is excavate the walls of the cities of Hazor, Megiddo, and Gezer and find the city gates. Ancient cities were fortresses. The city gates were the weak points of the walls, so they were closed at dusk and were specially designed to prevent them from being breached. At that time there were usually a series of three gates which together made up the city gate complex. The first gate was often placed at a 90° angle to the main wall. Since soldiers almost universally carried their shields on their left hands, their right side was exposed to projectiles from the walls. Therefore walls at that time were designed so that the first gate had to be entered by a road that had the city wall on the right side. If these city gates were found, they would lend support to the Bible stories.

Well, in 1936-37, archaeologists discovered the city gate attached to an ancient wall around Megiddo. They immediately concluded that this was the gate to the wall built by Solomon, thereby authenticating the story in the Bible. In 1958 similar gates were uncovered at Hazor and Gezer. The Hazor gate was almost identical to the Megiddo gate in both its plan (the view looking down from above) and measurement, so everyone assumed that it was part of Solomon's wall construction described in 1 Kings 9:15. The archaeologists promptly announced that the Hazor gate authenticated the Bible story of Solomon. When they then found the third gate, the Gezer gate, it was announced everywhere that archaeology had again verified the truth of the Bible.

The reason they identified the Megiddo wall as Solomonic was because there was another archaeology discovery, this time in Jerusalem. Under the old city they uncovered hundreds of small cubicles they decided must have been Solomon's stables for his thousand horses described in the Bible. The construction of the cubical walls was of ashlar masonry design. Ashlar masonry construction has varied over the years. It was invented by the Phoenicians and Bronze Age examples exist all over the Mediterranean. Generally, Bronze Age ashlar walls* were made of small square cut stones, 18" to 24" long, smoothly dressed and laid with very tight joints. This gives the walls an illusion of great strength, and indeed, the walls were generally very strong. The walls in all three of the cities were of ashlar masonry construction, so the archaeologist assumed that, like the "stable walls," they were gates to the walls referred to in the scriptures.

There are still stories and television shows that identify these gates as part of Solomon's construction projects and being proof of the veracity of

---

*Ashlar walls appear all over Europe and from all eras, but not all ashlar walls are constructed the same. Bronze age ashlar was distinctive.

the Bible. That conclusion was far from unanimous, however. The entire story was built upon information received from the Bible. They were using statements from the Bible to prove its own authenticity. The Bible stated that Solomon built walls around the three cities, that Solomon had horse stables; that the walls of the "stables" were of ashlar construction as were the three city walls. Ergo, the three gates must have been built by Solomon. Can you see the potential for error using this method? They were doing the excavations, not to find out the truth of these discoveries, but to prove that the Bible is true. The excavations became a self-fulfilling prophecy.

Others dated the walls differently. Someone discovered that the "stables" of Solomon's horses that had been found were not stables at all—they were storage rooms. All walled cities at that time had huge storage facilities for grain and other food as well as water cisterns in case of a siege of the city. Further, they were scientifically proven by carbon 14 tests to be from a different era than when Solomon was alive**. While it is true that they were of ashlar construction, it was a style of ashlar that dates to a different time. Remember, 1 Kings was written about the sixth century and Solomon lived in the late tenth century. A lot of memories can fade over 400 years. It is very important to make sure that archaeological discoveries are first dated in accordance with scientific methods *before* they are ascribed to specific items in the Bible.

Nevertheless, many recent discoveries have unearthed locations identified in the Bible or produced tablets, pottery, and other artifacts that identify Biblical places. Many of these finds are still going through the peer review process, but some definitely appear to support the truth of many Bible stories. Here are just a few:

- Herod's Temple—this is the famous Western/Wailing wall that is all that remains of the Temple constructed by Herod the Great. There is little dispute about this. Every day pious Jews go to the wall to pray.
- Second Temple Walls (before Herod)—The impression of the old walls of the square platform on the Temple Mount that were built before Herod expanded the temple are clearly visible on top of the present mound. These were either part of the reconstruction under Ezra and Nehemiah after the Exile or, possibly, it is a remnant of the original Temple built by Solomon. In any event, they are the remains of the temple mount before Herod. There has been a Hebrew temple on that site for centuries. Now, of course, it is the site of the Muslim mosque called "The Dome of

** Those rooms were later used as quarters by the Knights Templar during the crusades in the Middle.Ages.

the Rock."

- Hezekiah's Tunnel—After the fall of Israel to the Assyrians, the Assyrians set their sites on Judah. Hezekiah's father prevented conquest of Judah by paying tribute to the Assyrians as you may recall. Hezekiah grew tired of making the payments which were leaving the city impoverished. He stopped paying the tribute, knowing the refusal would lead to an invasion by Assyria. Jerusalem was on an easily defendable hilltop, but it had an Achilles heel—its water supply came from the Spring of Gihon in the hills above which could easily be captured and the city's water supply shut off (2 Chr 32:2-4). Hezekiah's solution was to build a wall around the spring and a 600 yard tunnel from the spring to the city cisterns (2 Kings 20:20, 2 Chr 32:30). Part of the wall around the spring can be seen in the Old City Jewish Quarter to this day. The story of the siege of Jerusalem is found both in the Bible (Isa 33:1; 36; 2 Kings 18:17; 2 Chron 32:9) and on the Assyrian King Sennacherib's victory pillar, "The Prism of Sennacherib*." Both sides claim to have won the battle, but Judah did pay a huge ransom to get the Assyrians to leave. The tunnel, often called the Siloam Tunnel, is a tunnel that was dug about 701 B.C.E. and was probably merely the widening of a pre-existing cave, although there are other possibilities. There is also a story of two teams of workers digging the tunnel simultaneously from each end, hoping to meet up in the middle. The story says that they had problems. The existing tunnel does look like an existing natural channel that was widened, however.
- Town of Lachish—was the second most powerful city outside of Jerusalem when Sennacherib went after Jerusalem. During a revolt, he captured Lachish. There are numerous Biblical references to the town**. Excavations have revealed a treasure trove of archaeological relics, many clearly identifying the town. There are some very early examples of ancient Hebrew writings and pottery, all of which covers centuries of the city's rich history. The remains of the siege ramp used by Sennacherib and mentioned in the Bible can also still be seen.
- Barrows—these are burial mounds of earth and rock over graves and are found all over the world. Nineteen of them have been

---

* This is one of the few examples of a third authority, after the Bible and the evidence of the archaeological excavation, validating a story in the Bible.

** Josh 10:3, 5, 23, 31-35; 12:11; 15:39; 2 Kings 14:19; 18:14, 17; 19:8; 2 Chron 11:19; 25:27; 32:9; Neh 11:30; Isa 36:2; 37:8; Jer 34:7; Mic 1:13.

found west of Jerusalem. They definitely date to the era of the kings, but so far none have been identified as the burial site of a particular person. The barrows as a group, however, may very well be the site of memorial ceremonies mentioned in the Bible (2 Chr 16:14; 21:19; 32:33; Jer 34:5).

- The Pool of Siloam—was fed by the Spring of Gihon. It was carved out of stone and is located in what is believed to be the original location of Jerusalem. It is mentioned in Is 8:6 and is where JESUS sent a blind man to be healed (Jn 9).
- Wall from 599 B.C.E.—very recently, part of a wall from the time of Nehemiah has been uncovered in an archeological excavation in Jerusalem. It is located just outside the old "Dung Gate" (Neh 2:13). The Bible also says that the wall was completed in only 52 days (Neh 6:16). It is loaded with pottery, bullae, arrowheads, and seals from that period. It is believed that a tower that joins the wall may be part of David's palace, but the jury is still out on that.
- Artifacts by the thousands identifying places and events. There is a wealth of less dramatic discoveries that support the stories in the Bible.

Some recent best selling books, such as those by Christopher Hitchens and Richard Dawkins, have admittedly been written to dissuade people from religion completely as if it were something inherently evil. This book was never intended to discourage religious beliefs. However, it is hoped that, after reading this book, people will, at the very least, approach their religion intelligently—that they will question and evaluate based on facts and not simply assume the speaker is correct, even if he or she is ordained and wears a black scholarly robe.. It is also hoped that they will now be able to differentiate between what comes from the Bible and what was a later invention by man and between what the Bible actually says not just what someone else interprets it to mean.

Unfortunately, some things in this book go to the very foundations of the beliefs of some. For example, it is a critical part of the beliefs of Evangelical, Pentecostal, and some Charismatic Christians that the Bible is inerrant in all respects. That is not true, and if you have read this far you should have discovered that it is not the case. But the general principles set forth in the Bible represent, at least in part, the foundations of three religions. That still holds true.

The existence of Satan is also a key part of many religious beliefs. Satan is mentioned in the Bible, particularly in the New Testament, but most of what the vast majority of Christians have been taught about Satan was invented by men living long after the Bible was written, as was the concept of the Trinity and much more.

The Rapture was not invented until the early 19th century and has never been accepted by "mainstream" Christianity precisely because it was not mentioned in the Bible or even by the "Early Fathers." Although believers claim there are references to a rapture by some of the early church leaders in Alexandria, such as Augustine and Origin, and others, it really began as a dream by a young Scottish girl. In 1830, at fifteen years of age, she claimed to be a prophet and began going into trances and making statements about the end of the world that she obtained in these trances. She belonged to a church in Glasgow and related her visions to her minister, Edward Irving. He then went to a prophecy convention that year (yes, there were such things then) and related her visions to the group.

Among those present at the conventions was John Nelson Darby, a former Anglican Priest who later formed a new religious denomination with others. He lectured on this girl's visions and became known as one of the foremost interpreters of the Bible. He visited America five times between 1862 and 1877 and spread his ideas about "dispensationalism" as it was called then. He and his followers pored over the Scriptures to find statements to support the theory. This is an example of what I referred to earlier in this chapter about people coming up with an idea and then mining the Bible for support.

My big hope is that people will begin to examine statements about their religion and about their GOD and to see if there is any support for the statements in the Bible. Every time I hear someone say, "GOD says that we should . . ." or "GOD wants . . ." or "Satan loves it when . . ." I see red flags waving. I always want to know how they happen to know what GOD'S wishes are; is it from the Bible or is it something that they decided on their own; or did GOD somehow tell them in a dream or a vision.

I find excerpts and quotes from the Bible everywhere: in song lyrics, in literature, and even in political speeches. Former President Bush often referred to Biblical concepts. He once stated, regarding U.S. relations with Middle Eastern countries, that we "would show them the way (pause) toward peace in the Middle East." We know now that "The Way" was the early name given to the message of JESUS. The President's base of Evangelical Christians, who are very well versed on references to the Bible, undoubtedly understood the hidden meaning in this statement very well, that Christianity is the key to peace. After reading this book, you also see the hidden reference.

Now that you have become more Biblically fluent, you will recognize these references to the Bible in your every day life: in literature, music, and art. You'll find that being in on the "secrets" makes everything a lot more exciting and interesting.

Suggested Reading

I began reading the brilliant works of Biblical scholars about 25 years ago. I constantly browsed the bookstores for new titles. Unfortunately, you cannot tell the scholarly books from the junk by their titles. You might say that I kissed a lot of frogs before I found the princess. Once I found a good book I made note of the authors who were listed in the bibliography. As I compiled my list, I noticed that a handful of authors were referenced in almost every book. After that, I no longer had to worry about kissing any frogs. I started following the trail of these scholars.

I always took notes of what I read, but my early notes did not usually include the titles of the books or the authors. They were just notes for my own benefit. Later, when I began to think about writing this book, I realized that the names of the books and authors were important information. Unfortunately, many of the earlier books I read and the names of their authors are not included on this list. I apologize to those scholars because they are the very people who first piqued my interest and got me started on this incredible journey which has spanned a quarter of a century.

This list of authors and their books is not merely a list of scholarly works. They are really "good reads." Most of these authors are also very talented writers.

Brown, Raymond E., S.S. A Roman Catholic priest, and an expert on the entire New Testament with extensive expertise on the Gospel of John. He was one of the first of the new scholars. Criticized by conservatives in the church for his work, and occasionally criticized by other scholars for not going far enough, he is recognized as a middle of the road scholar by all. His two-volume set *The Gospel According to John.* (Anchor Bible, 1966 and 1970); *the Death of the Messiah: from Gethsemane to the Grave: a Commentary on the Passion Narratives in the Four Gospels.* (New York: Doubleday, 1998) is excellent.

Crossan, John Dominic. A brilliant New Testament scholar and a very readable, and very prolific, author, having written some 20 books. He began his career as a Servite monk and later on as a distinguished professor, now emeritus. He is interviewed on television shows about the Bible. Everything he publishes is researched in minute detail. As he once said of himself, he doesn't just write a footnote, he writes another book instead. I have read many of his books, among them: *The Historical JESUS: The Life of a Mediterranean Jewish Peasant.* (HarperSanFrancisco, 1991); *The Birth of Christianity: Discovering What Happened in the Years Immediately After the Execution of JESUS.* (HarperSanFrancisco, 1998); *In Search of Paul: How JESUS's Apostle Opposed Rome's Empire with God's Kingdom.* (HarperSanFrancisco, 2004);

JESUS: A Revolutionary Biography. (HarperSanFrancisco,1994).

Cross, Frank Moore, *Canaanite Myth and Hebrew Epic: Essays in the History of the Religion of Israel.* (Harvard University Press, 1997)

Ehrman, Bart D., is an expert in the very difficult field of "textual criticism," the art of restoring the an ancient text that has been altered, either accidentally or purposefully, to its original wording. If this sounds boring, you have obviously never read any of Ehrman's many books. He is an outstanding writer with a knack for simplifying the subject and making it easy and exciting to understand. *Misquoting JESUS: The Story Behind Who Changed the Bible and Why.* (New York: Harper Collins, 2005); *Peter, Paul and Mary Magdalene: The Followers of JESUS in History and Legend.* (Oxford University Press, 2006)

Fox, Robin Lane. Fox is not technically a Biblical scholar but, rather an historian which gives us a little different viewpoint. *The Unauthorized Version: Truth and Fiction in the Bible.* (Random House, 1992).

Fredriksen, Paula. *From JESUS to Christ: The Origins of the New Testament Images of JESUS* (Yale University Press, 1988).

Friedman, Richard Elliott. Friedman is an Old Testament scholar. He wrote a very readable book which is primarily about the authorship of the first five books of the Bible but touches on others. It is a great book to start your quest. *Who Wrote the Bible.* (Simon & Schuster, Inc., 1987).

Funk, Robert W. The author of at least a dozen books and the founder of the JESUS Seminar; all of his books are great reads. The books he edited on the findings of the JESUS Seminar are truly remarkable, *The Five Gospels: The Search for the Authentic Words of JESUS*, which he edited with Roy W. Hoover (Polebridge Press, Macmillan, 1993) and *The Acts of JESUS: the Search for the Authentic Deeds of JESUS* [edited by] (HarperSanFrancisco, 1998). This is the companion book to *The Five Gospels*, and covers what JESUS did as opposed to what he said. He also authored many books on his own, one of my favorites being *Honest to JESUS: JESUS for a New Millennium.* (HarperSanFrancisco, 1996). His recent death is a great loss to Biblical research.

Helms, Randel, *Who wrote the Gospels*? (Millenium Press, 1996)

Horsley, Richard A., *Bandits, Prophets, and Messiahs: Popular Movements in the Time of JESUS.* (with John S. Hanson). (Trinity Press International, 1999). *Paul and Empire: Religion and Power in Roman Imperial Society.* (Trinity Press International, 1997.)

Koester, Helmut, *Ancient Christian Gospels: Their History and Development.* (Trinity Press , 1990); he also wrote some very good articles on women in the clergy and some of the other current national issues.

Lenski, Gerhard E. As a sociologist who specialized in the sociology of religion for many years, h is work, *The Religious Factor: A Sociological*

Study of Religion's Impact on Politics, Economics, and Family Life. (Doubleday, 1961), although quickly outdated, was of enormous importance in the early days of the renaissance of religious scholarship. His model for the sociological strata for the Roman agrarian society, from his book, *Power and Privilege: A Theory of Social Stratification,* (McGraw Hill, 1966), is the model used by almost all New Testament scholars in understanding first century Roman society.

Mack, Burton L., A New Testament scholar whose excellent books convincingly approached the gospels as fictional mythologies rather than history. *Who Wrote the New Testament? The Making of the Christian Myth.* San Francisco: HarperSanFrancisco, 1995; *The Lost Gospel: The Book of Q & Christian Origins.* San Francisco: HarperSanFrancisco, 1995.

Pagels, Elaine, Her marvelous work on the gospels discovered at Nag Hammadi established her as a leading Biblical scholar. *The Gnostic Gospels.* (Random House, 1989). *The Origin of Satan* (Random House, 1995). *Adam, Eve, and the Serpent.* (Random House, 1989).

Smith, Mark S., *The Origins of Biblical Monotheism: Israel's Polytheistic Background and the Ugaritic Texts.* Oxford University Press, 2001.

Spong, John Shelby, An Episcopal bishop with a religiously liberal message and a marvelous writer to boot. Not technically a "scholar," but a very learned man who researches his books very well. For someone looking to see an overview of Biblical scholarship on particular subjects, there is no better place to start than Spong's books. Pick one at random and lean back and enjoy. *Rescuing the Bible from Fundamentalism: a Bishop Rethinks the Meaning of Scripture,* (HarperSanFrancisco, 1991); *Born of a Woman: a Bishop Rethinks the Birth of JESUS,* (HarperSanFrancisco, 1992); *Living in Sin: a Bishop Rethinks Human Sexuality,* HarperSanFrancisco, 1990); *Resurrection: Myth or Reality?: a Bishop's Search for the Origins of Christianity,* (HarperSanFrancisco, 1994) and more.

Vermes, Geza, *The Dead Sea Scrolls in English,* 3rd Rev, London: Penguin Books, 1987

There were many others, and I just do not have records to reflect what I read. I remember George Nickelsburg with good feelings, but I haven't a clue of which of his several books I read. The same is true of Morton Smith, John Kloppenborg, and many others. To them I apologize.